LaPonne

Troublesome
THE Untold Story
OVERCOMING THE STORM's

Published by MindStir Media, LLC
45 Lafayette Rd | Suite 181| North Hampton, NH 03862 | USA
1.800.767.0531 | www.mindstirmedia.com

Printed in the United States of America.
ISBN-13: 978-1-962987-15-8

Dedications

To the souls that were not loved and protected in their innocent formidable stages. To my wife who continues to show me that love is a marathon and even though you may strain a growing, pull a hamstring or get fatigued. You still have a race to run that you committed yourself to.

Acknowledgements

I first would like to acknowledge YAHWEH, YASHUA, THE HOLY SPIRIT & HIS ANGELS. When so many gave up on me…you would not allow your agape love and covering to leave my path. I want to thank **my mom** for not getting an abortion and for showing me the definition of will and power. I value **Cool Cat** for never leaving me in the cold and always sharing his lunch money with me, so I wasn't hungry. I value my **Auntie Sonya & Uncle Bam Bam** for always having a warm heart and for emotionally protecting me when I was not able to. These next 2 people I owe everything to. My heart and soul, my empress **'Lois Boyd'**. You taught me and showed me that a mom could be nurturing, patient and loving even if you make mistakes. You were there to be delicate with my shattered emotions. I will be forever indebted. **'The Queen' Regina Davenport** this was the first woman I viewed as virtuous. This was the first person I felt emotionally safe with as a teenager and never believed they would want to harm me or make me not trust them. I vowed to always protect her and not allow any harm to ever approach my Big Sis on my watch. Without 'The Queen' I would not be alive to empower others through this journey. **King Robert Hector**, we met when I was about 8 to 9 years of age and you were a leader at YMCA and you took us to summer camp and I thought I could fly and tied cape around my neck climbed to the roof of the cabin and tried to fly and landed face first on a bench and busted open my lip and you cancelled all your plans and rushed me to emergency and stayed with me. You never made me feel stupid, just was always a strong community figure who overstood that you were invested in a city of broken, low esteemed boys who had the wrong imagery and definition of what a man was. Thank you and **King Larry Gray** for allowing us to have **Ella Hill Hutch Community Center**. You Gate Keepers made us feel human in the jungle. **The Colonel aka Mr. Aaron Reppert** you my heart…you have been loyal. We have made over a million together and we have struggled and lost everything. I will always be of service to you, and it will always be our family not your family or my family. Finally, I would like to thank my sisters, my nieces, legacies, and my nephews when you were young, your innocence helped me to believe the world had something good in it. I pray that after 'TROUBLESOME THE UNTOLD STORY' (OVERCOMING THE STORMS) Is read that it will empower people to protect the innocence of the innocent and to use each day to embrace who you are and take a confident step at a better version of who you want to become.

Chapter 1

Your Environment Didn't Matter So Why Should Your Life?

As kids we were asked these two questions," YOU CARE IF YOU DEAD OR ALIVE and WHAT ARE YOU GOING TO BE WHEN YOU GROW UP?" Struggling to survive and not knowing if you will have a roof over your head, food in your stomach, clothes on back or a mom around to give you affection was only half the battle. The other half was dealing with drugs around the house, and mom's physical abuse. There's no way this is living. With violence in the neighborhood, we already dead or it's just a matter of time. Feeling demonly possessed and not valuing the life of others that look like me. It's been multiple attempts to end my life: including several attempts of suicide. What would make a person want to take their own life? On this journey with me, you will be able to answer the question "IF I REALLY CARED IF I WAS DEAD OR ALIVE". Once I became a bonafide hustla and a gangsta, I moved my hustle from Prince Hall apartments and started associating myself around a more dangerous affiliation of gangstas. This crew was known as Fulton St. Mob a.k.a. Y.B.G (Young Black Gangstas). Being down with this new set meant that I would have to put in real work, and when I say work, I mean banging, robbing, and moving serious amounts of weight (drugs). This is required if you were trying to be considered a real factor in the street game. I had to prove that I could hustle just as hard as the Original Gangsters (O. G's), and that I had just as much heart as them. I joined Fulton Street Mob, which was one of the hardest Mobs in San Francisco at the time.

This gang was filled with fly dudes who looked smooth but were dangerous as hell. I was building my loyalty to Fulton Street Mob, when it was time to pull drive-by shootings on our rival sets, I was suited and booted for wartime.

Chapter 2

Gangsta!! Gangsta!! All That They're Yelling

ONE NIGHT WE decided to ride on some rivals in Hunters Point, which was an area located in the southern part of San Francisco. This was the point of my initiation into the gang; we stole an old beat-up car and rolled through Hunters Point searching for rivals to decimate. To make sure no fear was visible, we got high on a mixture of cocaine, weed, and Grand Marnier liquor. We were ready to ride on our enemies, but we had one problem—nobody was hanging out on the sets.

My heart was beating fast and sweat was dripping underneath my jacket. I was nervous but I was ready. I was holding a 12-gauge shotgun looking for marks (which is a term that means sucka's). I never shot a shotgun before and never thought I would have to until that very moment. After driving around, we still didn't see anybody hanging outside. I thought I was in the clear; I figured "hey, I showed up, I was in the car, I was down to dismiss our marks", but that was not good enough for these OG's. One of them in the car saw how relieved I was and turned to me and said, "Don't worry baby boy, we have some marks for you!" We drove down to a different rival set, which was named Third Street, and unlike Hunters Point, those sucka's were all hanging outside, which was a perfect opportunity for us to catch them slipping. The Third Street Gang were out there playing loud music, smoking dope, and getting drunk; looking like they didn't have any cares in the world. One would think since it was late on a Sunday night that pretty much all the rival sets were sexing their main girl, at a movie or a restaurant having dinner. As we begin to drive the car at a caterpillar's pace, we were coasting down the hill in this old beat-up car in neutral because we didn't want them to hear the engine. My O.G. turned to me and said, "Little n***a, you better lay these fools down!" The closer we got to the marks, the more I was shaking.

I had to think about something that would prepare me for what I had to do. I channelled all the hate I had towards mom from the abuse, neglect and not pouring love into me and guess what-it worked! We rolled up real smooth, before they knew what hit them, I yelled out, "FULTON STREET MOB B***H!!"

I started blasting the 12-gauge. It was so powerful that it jerked me back real hard. I hit one of the marks on the shoulder, but I couldn't tell where I hit any of the other targets because the buckshot's spread all over the place. I was filled with a high level of adrenalin, I said to one of the O.G.'s "Let me out real quick, I seen someone from Third Street that I had a fight with not too long ago trying to run off. I took three steps on foot and shot in the directions of his body. I did not wait around to see if I got him or not because they were yelling for me to get back in the car. We took a low-key route back to our set and burned the car. It was a surreal moment, and I was numb to what had just taken place. Everyone was praising me. I barely even noticed what was going on because it was all a blur. I replayed that night in my mind repeatedly, and from that day forward, I could no longer sleep at night. I was known as "silent but deadly" and my loyalty was never questioned again, or at least I thought. I became heavily involved with the street life. I mean, I was banging hard, especially during drive by season. It seemed like we were shooting up sets every Sunday and Wednesday nights. It didn't matter if they were gang rivals from our side of town, the other side of town, or from way out of town; we never knew who our enemies were. The only thing that mattered when wartime took place; was that we all used the same tools: guns, ski masks, and beat up cars.

I knew years ago that I was going full fledge with this street life. I just needed to assemble all the pieces to the puzzle to become who I felt I was destined to be. I started investing in some serious tooly's (guns) just in case someone tried to rob and kill me.

Chapter 3

A Dance With Beelzebub
I Would Never Forget

FOR EXAMPLE, THIS street kid by the name of Ramon came over and said, "You better move your dope. E-Dub in there." E-Dub was always on the prowl trying to intimidate dope dealers so he could rob them later. Ramon was a troublemaker always getting into stuff. One time, he threw some DD batteries at some patrol cops and hit one of them in the head and just laughed and ran off as if he didn't care what the consequences were. Later in the story more will be revealed about Ramon. Back to E-Dub, he was a short, gorilla looking, muscular dope fiend who was dark skinned and had a curly black Afro. His eyes were the evillest shifty eyes that I ever saw in my whole life. To be a dope fiend, his teeth looked better than mines, but when he was high off that dope, he would be tweaking and twitching his body, and real edgy and scary aggressive. E-Dub was 5 feet 7 inches tall and intimidating. When he spoke, it was always hyper with a con artist mentality. I ran fast towards the gate and climbed up moving my hand around trying to feel for my dope, my heart began beating real fast and heavy because I thought E-Dub robbed me. I turned and asked "E-Dub have you seen my dope sack?" He said to me, "YOU BETTA LOOK UP THERE REAL GOOD AND WHEN YOU FIND IT, YOU GO GET STABBED AND I'M GO TAKE IT FROM YOU." While E-Dub was talking, I was still reaching my arm through the gate trying to find my sack. I finally felt it! Somebody had pushed it further back from where I originally placed it. Once I came down off the gate, E-Dub tried to snatch my dope out of my hand, but I was not about to just give it up like that. People were trying to separate us because he had pulled out a knife and was trying to stab me on the side of my stomach. I didn't have my hand piece on me because it was Tuesday, and the drug task force raided heavy zone areas on Tuesdays and Thursdays.

Chapter 4

A Tribute To Jay Stone
Who Yahweh Use To Save Me

ON THESE DAYS you had to be cautious because the DTF (Drug Task Force Unit) would try to make as many arrests as possible to meet their monthly quota. It was through the Grace of Yahweh, The Creator Himself that I didn't get stabbed and lose my life. That experience taught me to always be ready and to stay on my toes, and to be the sharpest Ponne I could be. I felt like the whole world was against me and I wanted to die. My motto was "F**** everybody because they will always betray you." Later that night, I went down on the block to hustle, and I ran into my general Jay Stone. The background on Jay Stone was that he was one of the original members of Fulton St. Mob. Jay Stone and I have a bond to the grave...we both were cut from the same cloth. Dangerous, ambitious, and stand-up dudes. He never backed down from nobody but still received love from everybody. He was the type of general that everyone respected or feared. The choice was up to you in what reaction you brought out of him. Jay Stone was 5 feet 9 inches and built like those dudes who had been in and out of the penitentiary, where they originally developed their muscles. His mannerism was engaging, and he was somebody you rooted for to win. His body type was solid. He was muscular in the right places and toned in the chest. He was not real big and definitely not small. His arms were 22 inches wide; he wore his hair real low brush length with little sideburns; his eyes were wide like an owl and shapely with long eyelashes. He had a goatee moustache, with a defined forehead; his voice was real raspy like an old man, and you can hear in his voice that he's been through 5 lifetimes of pain.

He was a figure of danger but at the same time had a tremendous heart for everybody and carried himself as a respectable person. He also lived on his own at a young age as well, we had so many common struggles. He's a TRIPLE O.G. and for him to take a liking to me was special but also the fact that he recognized that I was a leader and a G as well. His face was the same as mines because we both been through so much that our natural demeanor looked serious and stone. This moment solidified my allegiance to Stone as long as Yahweh continue to Bless a soul and spirit inside me, he will always know I got him. This particular night there were no dope fiends out looking to buy any dope. So, Stone and I went to the liquor store and brought two of everything from 40 ounces of 8 ball, Seagram's Gin, E&J, Grand Marnier, Cognac, and Donald Duck Orange Juice. I mixed it all together, rushed it straight down my throat and got a sharp rush. Then I smoked a sweet b***h to numb my body because it was freezing cold outside. I was already at a point where I didn't want to live anymore and feeling down and depressed. How did I end up having a dope fiend pointing a gun at my face? What led to this moment? I wasn't getting any sales so I couldn't make any lootchi. This dope fiend happened to come on the block wanting a fifth teen shot of crack for five dollars; the crack head stuck his hand out and it was filled with dimes, nickels, quarters, and pennies. I said, "what is this s**t? You know we don't accept this change around here! DO I LOOK LIKE I'M A F*****G LAUNDROMAT?" I slapped all the change out of his hand, and it fell to the ground and rolled under a car into a sewer drain. The smoker was real dark, stood at maybe 5 feet 7 inches and had on a knitted blue cap, with a curl cap underneath. He had on a pair of oil-stained pants and a big dark blue coat; it was dark so I couldn't make out his features to a tee, but I wasn't too worried because I knew his cousin.

His eyes looked like an alligator because of all the dope he's been smoking but also, he looked homeless. He was angry and said, "I'm getting tired of getting played as a p**k," and pulled out a gun from behind his back (so much for me thinking he was homeless, what homeless person you know pulls out a strap?) … It was a 9-millimeter Beretta style gun and he put it to my head. I said, "This is Fulton St. Mob b***h you beta blast me and make sure you kill me!" Jay Stone said, "Get on Ponne, this n***a got a gun." I said, "Naw, I'm not going nowhere, this b***h a** n***a beta kill me." I continued to dare the dope fiend; testing him to see how much heart he really had. All he kept saying is he tired of getting played as a p**k and cocked the gun back to kill me. I continued to dare the dope fiend. I said, "Look I got my back turned to you." All he kept saying was "I'm tired of getting played as p**k". There was this fat man named Paul, who knew my family and my sister's dad they use to hustle ounces of weed together. Paul was just sitting there quiet and was about to just let me get killed. Jay Stone knocked the dope fiend out with one punch, then knocked fat a** Paul out for just standing there. Jay Stone went in Paul's pockets and robbed him for his lootchi, took the gun that the dope fiend had, then went in his pockets too, and told me to leave. What normally was a ten-minute walk home felt more like an hour. I was paranoid and felt as if a rival set was going to roll up on me and blast me. I was disillusioned and everything was a blur. I was walking crooked but trying to walk straight. I damn near just got my life taking away by a crack head. I finally made it to Ms. Mylene apartment at 4 am, Little Marcel and Jim Burt was up playing video games. I went into the room and just collapsed. It was the hardest I ever collapsed on a mattress in my life! The way I dropped down on the mattress is how I felt about the problems of my life that were weighing heavy on me.

Chapter 5

Yahwehs Revelation, Can You Handle It?

I WAS LAYING on my back in the dark, but that dope fiend scene kept playing over and over in my mind and I realized out of all the people that could have killed me, it was just about to happen by the hands of a fiend. I began to reflect about how reckless I was with my life and started thinking about all the battles with rival gangs that we shot at and people who were a part of my heart who died. I was burning internally inside as if YAHWEH was working in me. The realization of my actions became so unbearable that I cried silently for 30 minutes. Suddenly "YAHWEH" voice said, "Atlanta" like a strong whisper that was so clear but at the same time only for me to hear. I begin to feel confined like that time when I was in juvenile hall from my moms calling the police even though she was the one that physically assaulted me. This was my first real time in juvenile hall I didn't know what to expect or what enemies was coming at me, so I didn't let my guard down or allow myself much time for sleep. While the other inmates were asleep or looking at dirty magazines, stroking their penises for cheap thrills, I was doing fist-ups throughout the night and every morning. The next day a short Mexican and African descent dude squared up on me asking me where I was from. He had a deep hyper voice; he was built like a gorilla in the chest and arms, he stood at maybe 5 feet and 4 inches, he had an afro that was real kinky and wild, and his eyes were real tiny and slanted. Vick (R.I.P.) was the kind of dark that, if there were not enough lotion applied, his skin would become ashy black.

Chapter 6

Vick R.I.P. Showed Me
It's About Who Got Your Back

HE WAS FROM Army Street Projects but grew up in Harbor Rowe, which was located on our enemy's territory. Fulton Street Mob had a few war sessions with Army Street but, (not to the degree where we felt they were equal or even a threat to us). I squared up in his face and said, "I'm from Fulton Street Mob B***h!" He said his name was Vick and that he just wanted to know where I was from and there was no beef. He seemed to be a little shook because of the way I responded to him. In fact, the whole time I was at Y.G.C. he was the only person I became real cool with. I think we clicked so well because he had family issues just like me.

No one in his family believed that his life had any value, kind of similar to what I was experiencing. A lot of people knew I was in there for fighting with my mom and a lot of them thought I was some kind of cold-hearted person, but Vick and I could relate to one another, he would tell me how his mom used to smoke crack in front of him and force him to buy more drugs for her. He said that she used to beat him because when she looked at him, she saw that he resembled his dad. He also told me that his dad used to beat his mom so bad that he would bust open her lip and give her black eyes. His dad eventually left so his mom took her frustration out on her son. Vick and I always tried to keep each other strong but the issues he had inside were eating him up real bad. Even though I shared those same feelings, I was fighting myself to not give in like he did. I would often find myself encouraging him to be strong, because that was the only way we can make it out of Y.G.C in one piece.

It was real difficult because I felt the same way he did, with my own family who turned against me.

Chapter 7

Broken Emotional Dark Pieces Out Of Place

MY MOM HAD painted this picture to everybody as though I deserved to be in jail. The worst part of it all was that nobody was sending me any food, money or even a letter. Thinking about all of that further fuelled my hate and anger towards my family. Vick cell was right next to mine, and we would whisper to each other at night to try and keep each other strong. We talked about trying to escape together and what it be like when we were out. I never would have thought in a million years that I would ever be close to someone from Harbor Rowe, since that was one of Fulton St. Mob's rival sets, but there was something different about Vick…he was more like a brother to me than an enemy. One day he received a personal call from home. It turned out that his mom died from a drug overdose, and even though Vick hated his mom, he took the loss real hard. I overstood exactly how he felt because, even though I said I hated my mom and I wish she hurry up and die, I would have been crushed if it really happened. Vick came to me crying and said that he didn't want to live anymore. When he said that to me, I hugged him and told him to stay strong and that I'm here for him. I thought that I was getting through to him, but I learned the next morning he was found dead in his cell. He tied a sheet around his neck and tied the other end through the vents and hung himself from the ceiling of his cell. I was devastated and numb at the same time. I started to focus more and more on Beelzebub thoughts. I would draw pictures of Beelzebub smoking weed with all my rival gangs inside his body. I got a call from my Aunt Stacy (R.I.P.) one day, telling me about all the rumours that the family was saying about me.

Aunt Stacy was short about 5 feet 5 inches chocolate complexion, she had a nice body shape, heavy up top, small waist, dressed fashionably, but she had a very bad attitude.

Aunt Stacy voice was real snappy, and she was easily irritated. When she called me, she said that the family was saying that they think I sexually violated my sisters—hearing that ended everything for me. My sisters were the only two people I truly felt safe around. I was more than a brother to them; I actually protected them! Later on, that night, I tied a sheet around my neck and climbed up on the window frame to tie the other end to the ceiling vent to hang myself like Vick did, but I didn't have the heart to go all the way through with it. I took the sheet off my neck and cried all night long. Everyone wants to know the mental breakdown on how a person can become a killer, rapist, drug dealer, violent and abusive or just a gangsta who had to survive in an intense dysfunctional jungle. This story will compel you to see that everyone has a little boy and little girl in them and based upon how that soul is curated…will form their reality. When a newborn enters the world, it should symbolize the joys of life and form a bond of happiness between a man and woman who came together to conceive a child. Unfortunately for me, my life never had a symbol of love, joy, or even a happy foundation. If you let my mom, tell it, I should have never seen the light of day. My mom often told me that throughout her pregnancy she heard the voice of Beelzebub telling her to kill me, "just get an abortion," but she could not bring herself to do it. According to my mom, this was a frequent occurrence in the early stages of her pregnancy. Beelzebub was trying to kill me off, but she would cry and yell out, "No!" Fortunately for me, I guess. My mom was gorgeous. She stood at 5 feet 8 inches, with more curves than Lombardi Street in San Francisco. Her complexion resembled rich chocolate; eyes were real big and brown but pure white like the wings on an angel.

A beautiful smile that lit up Vegas. Mom took great pride in her teeth. When she smiled, it literally compelled you to smile. Her hair was beautifully textured, which I loved to touch. I was always upset that it wasn't a trait that was passed down to me. I would have to say my mom had a movie star style and personality. She enjoyed when people would give her compliments. The tone of her voice was loud, aggressive, and fiery, but delightful when she was in that mood. It was hard growing up with a part-time mom. Between the drugs and partying all night and sleeping all day, she never seemed to have time for a child who desperately looked to her for love and attention. Since no dad ever claimed me, Mom never did make the transition from being a "single party girl" to a mom with real responsibilities. Instead of being a nurturer, she would always pass me off to one of my aunts so she could hang out with her friends. Mom came from a big family; she had plenty of options. My Aunt Maxine was usually her go-to person. Aunt Maxine who stood at 5 feet 6 inches, had a light complexion, broad shoulders, and loved to press her hair with a hot comb. She was a remarkable cook and could make anybody feel welcomed. Aunt Maxine took a real liking towards me and spent a lot of time around me when I was a baby. She would always tell the story about how I had a big peanut head and would always throw my bottle out of my crib. I loved to hear my aunt tell stories. When she spoke, her voice was very laid back and had a harmony to it. Aunt Maxine loved to collect greatest hits albums, CDs, and DVD's. She had one of the (largest) greatest collections. I will always love and appreciate my Aunt Maxine for the time she spent with me. Another option for mom was my Aunt Camille. Aunt Camille stood at 5 feet 6 inches, had a deep bronze complexion, and a button nose, shapely lips, and had eyes that were big and wide as an owl.

Chapter 8

Family Doomed To Drugs, Women, Clubs And Superstars

AUNT CAMILE STYLED her braids that went down to her ears and would always wear a scarf folded across the front of her forehead. She wore her scarf the same way gang members did, but she wore different colors to match her outfit for the day. The coolest thing about my Aunt Camille's outfits was that she wore these Indian moccasins shoes. She wore them with so much comfort. Camille was cool to hang out with and talk to. When she spoke, it was slow with a harmony. She was not confrontational and was a very private person who took care of her nieces and nephews. I remember being over her house with my cousins. She would comb our hair and make sure we had Johnson & Johnson Baby Oil on our face before we went to school to keep our faces from being dry in the cold weather. Aunt Camille was the greatest lunch preparer of all time. Our lunch bags would be filled with salami and cheese sandwiches, and not those Po' boy sandwiches either. Our sandwiches would have lettuce, tomatoes and be on a soft roll. She would pack Doritos chips, chicken and the biscuit crackers, lemon sandwich cookies, a big Rome apple, and a fifth-teen cent crème soda or our flavor of choice. She took care of all of us and made sure that when we were at school that we were not hungry. I will always remember and love my Aunt Camille for the sacrifices she made to help take care of her 17 brothers and sisters and their kids. She couldn't get a job because she put her life on hold and poured her soul into taking care of her family. Later in life, she finally began to live for herself since the family didn't return that feeling of appreciation. For that very reason, she will always have a special place in my heart.

Aunt Jasmine (R.I.P.), who stood at 5 feet 8 inches, was really cute. I mean she was like cheerleader cute. She had a caramel complexion, deep, brown-circled eyes, a defined nose, beautiful lips, and a remarkable smile that seemed to turn night into day. Aunt Jasmine was very cool and could hang out with anybody. When she spoke, it was like she was always ready to have a good time. Aunt Jasmine could relate to anybody. She never judged a person. She just made you feel better. Aunt Janiece, who was more like the second mom when adults weren't around, was very responsible, had a tremendous heart, and wore her emotions on her sleeves. She was very loving, compassionate, and would stand up and fight-till the end for what she believed was right. She stood at approximately 5 feet 5 inches and wore her hair short at the top and long in the back. Aunt Janiece had these deep captivating eyes that were big and brown, but shapely and hypnotic at the same time. She had a defined nose with lips that were very full and shapely, and she had beautiful pearly white teeth. When she spoke, it was from the heart. Aunt Janiece was very headstrong and loving. Her and my other two aunts, Maxine, and Camille were my favourite. They really cared about my pain and was there for me. My mom would rotate me in between her sisters and have them watch me while she would travel down to Los Angeles to party with legendary R&B singers like Marvin Gaye, The Temptations, The O'Jays, and The Whispers. In 1976, a couple of years after I was born, my mom met a guy named Mr. Marcel (R.I.P.) He was a very handsome man, who stood at a towering 6 feet 3 inches tall and had a nice smile to go along with his charming personality. Mr. Marcel was light skinned and wore a goatee beard. He smelled good, dressed well, and you could tell he thought he was YAHWEH'S gift to the ladies.

Mr. Marcel possessed a Hollywood look, like a Clark Gable or Billy Dee Williams, and carried himself as if he was the leading man from an old classic movie like "Gone with the Wind" or "Mahogany." Mr. Marcel was dressed like a typical womanizer of his era. He had a nice suit perfectly coordinated with his shirt. He wore his collar flipped out over his suit jacket and kept his shirt open to show off the "taco meat" (hair on his chest). He wore a couple of chains around his neck, a pinky ring, and of course, his shoes matched his entire ensemble. As I got older, I remember listening to him speak. He spoke with a temper, but with a sense of humour behind it. Having him around I thought I was getting my first opportunity of experiencing a male figure in my life. Mr. Marcel was one of those guys who knew he was a handsome man and he considered himself to be a magnet to the ladies. Mom and Mr. Marcel would argue all the time about him being with different women, when all she wanted was for him to step up and be the man of the house. She would constantly have to deal with rumours in the streets about his womanizing ways. But of course, when mom would confront him about it, he would ultimately deny it. Mr. Marcel would leave the apartment early in the day and stay out all night. That made mom more furious and in doubt, because she never knew if he was out with another woman or not. In 1977, a year later, he impregnated mom, and my sister Naomi was born. Naomi looked picture-perfect. There was always a light beaming over her. She was born with short curly hair, the most beautiful bronze complexion in the world. Her cheeks and thighs were chubby. I would tickle her, and she would laugh so hard and open her mouth so wide. When I look back, I realize those were real precious moments for me because we used to be really close.

Early on Naomi spent a lot of time in the hospital because she had complications breathing. She was asthmatic.

It was an extremely emotional time for me having to see all that my sister was going through and all the breathing machines that were hooked up to her. But even with her medical issues, there was so much joy and happiness surrounding her birth. Naomi got the love and support from her dad that I longed for from my mom and biological dad who didn't bother. The 70's pulled a lot of the fathers away from being a responsible family man in the home to getting sucked in by a conscience-free era that was taking place, a.k.a. "FORGET ABOUT EVERYTHING IT'S PARTY TIME". It was the birth of the disco era that was married to the club and dance scene. The clubs were used as a platform for drugs to be introduce to people so they could become addictive and bring that addiction back to their respective communities and get more people hooked. People were being tricked into thinking that by taking the best drugs on the market, that not only would they experience something never before in their lives, but also, it would turn your sexual experiences into something out of this galaxy. Many could not describe what they experienced, but they refused to live without it. People would get so high they would do interviews and say it felt like they were being sent to another world that was far beyond existence. They called it "BEAM ME UP SCOTTIE". The club scene characters were so predictable. You had your psychedelic acid click; your angel dust click…who see everything in colors as if the whole world was a giant bag of skittles. And then you had the petty street hustler click who made themselves bigger than what they were by pushing 8 balls of cocaine, heroin a.k.a. smack, and pills. These guys were really cool with everybody from the DJs to the bartenders and especially security. They would always use their sense of humour to make people laugh and feel comfortable with them and offer free drugs just to get them hooked. Now the petty street hustler is making a name for himself in the dope scene with hopes of becoming the club's number one supplier.

His "office" was usually located in the restroom or back alley of the club, where he performed his transactions out of his pimped-out Cadillac Eldorado. You would have sworn he was right out of the movie Super Fly. Then you had the celebrities who act like they were "different" from everybody else because they were well paid and had fame, but usually, they were the biggest dope heads. The celebrities included models, actors, athletes, singers, and the people that made them rich, and of course, the fans. Everybody came to the clubs to lose themselves in the music, bright lights, and back rooms where they could bring their true inner person out. People could be who they truly wanted to be when drugs were placed in the equation. For example, if you were a married man but deep down you liked men, you could go to the clubs and be with the same gender and blame it on the drugs. If you deep down wanted to experiment with drugs, you went to the clubs and justified your actions by telling your conscience, "I only do it when I go to the clubs since they offer it for free." Finally, the punk rock click. They wanted to rub their "dare to be different revolution" in everybody's face with their spiked purple, yellow, and green Mohawks, their spiked leather jackets, and gloves, looking like they're about to perform with Billy Idol " In the Midnight Hour," "She Cried More, More, More." The similarities of all these different characters were that they all had a motive. Which was to make a red-carpet appearance, and to be noticed for attending premiere star studded, social events across the nation. This experiment with a culture on drugs really seemed like if you didn't do drugs, you were not considered hip or groovy. There were all kind of drugs from cocaine, heroin, crystal meth, angel dust, uppers, and downers just to name a few. As I got older, I was told after the night clubs closed at 2:00am, if people still wanted to party, do drugs, or find a sex partner for the night they would go to The Speak Easy which was located in different neighborhoods.

The admission was $5.00 which was considered high at the time, but at least you had a place to continue the party.

The Speak Easy in Fillmoe was located on Divisadero Street in a large Victorian style apartment building with multiple rooms. You pay your $5.00 at the door and then walk up a flight of stairs to the first floor. There was a long hallway with different rooms. The front room is where they played music. There was a room where if you wanted drugs you could request to purchase drugs and then go to another room to get high. The other rooms were reserved by pimps who sold prostitutes to tricks for sexual services. When Mom could not find someone to babysit me, she would take me to The Speak Easy and sit me in front of the speakers. This is one of many events that created my lifelong love for music. One night Mom took me to The Speak Easy, but she didn't stay long. Right after she left, The Speak Easy was raided by the Task Force and everybody was arrested from the party crowd, drug dealers, pimps, and their prostitutes. This was the beginning of a police crackdown of after hour's party spots in San Francisco. The Speak Easy was shut down. Furthermore, what was becoming more evident in the 70's along with drugs was "pimping. There were so many people trying to remake movies like "Super Fly," "The Mack," and even "Dolomite", that it seemed like every neighbourhood you walked through, guys were doing their best impression of Ron O'Neal, Max Julien, Rudy-Ray Moore, just to name a few. What these films did for the 70's era was create a newfound culture of making sure that your hair was fried, dyed, and you know—laid to the side! However, processed hair was not the only trend of the '70s, Afros were just as popular. While some were focused on how perfectly picked his/her Afro was, the streets were being flooded with violence, drugs, sexual exploitation, and unemployment, all at exponential rates. Hard times always seemed to be the motivating factor of why people were looking for other ways to escape from their misery of everyday struggles.

Chapter 9

Reaganomics And Its Iron Fist Agenda

THE '80S, WAS referred to as the "Reaganomics Era." African decent communities in the U.S.G. (United States Ghettos) called it the "Crack-a-nomics Era. Everybody knew that the government was flooding streets with drugs. Hard times begin to nurture an environment of addicts, especially African decent families, and what better drug than an affordable one that can be purchased for as little as five dollars. People depended on this drug to help them escape from their everyday depression or suicidal thoughts.

Crack cocaine was the drug of choice due to its affordability and powerful effects. Crack is cocaine with baking soda mixed and cooked to a rock form that gives off this ultimate high. African descent people in America that were already poverty-stricken and desperately looking for a way to escape, took to the drug which became a global epidemic that turned the world upside down. During this time, government agencies was reducing its workforce by eliminating many jobs and allowing big companies to close. A lot of manufacturing plants that created millions of jobs were now being relocated overseas. These jobs were providing people the so called "American Dream" for their families and empowering a lot of people of African descend to become business and property owners. The "IRON FIST AGENDA" was designed to target people of African descend and dismantle the family structure by getting the father's out of the house. To successfully execute that plan the father had to become jobless and an addict. Which created an environment of a single mom, who's now the head of the household. At the same time, the men who supplied the drugs were being locked up with unjustifiable long prison sentences.

Chapter 10

Egineered Systemics To Isolate The Family Man

THE MAN OF the house is now reproducing children excessively with multiple women…with no way to support them. Rewinding back to slavery, the slave master would have the slave, who was a male stud from the "Mandingo" tribe and other tribes as well…sleep with the women to impregnate them and once she became pregnant, they would make sure the father was taken away from the family and not be able to raise his children. He was only able to breed them so they can become good stock for slave masters. The government figured out once the man, who represented the strength of the house was removed; that the family foundation would collapse. Absentee fathers became a pandemic and in turn, the kids were exposed to an environment filled with drugs and eventually, will grow up either doing drugs as well or hustling drugs for lootchi or both. People began to lie, steal, cheat and sell their bodies and material possessions just to feel the same sensation that they experienced when they first got high. Both men and women began to trade in being socially conscious of the injustice of the government that had taken place for so long, in exchange for sex, drugs and partying.

Men were cheating on their women, getting other women pregnant, and not being around to help raise their kids. African decent families were in a state of demise. Many fathers in "Fillmoe" (the Western Addition of San Francisco) were all trying to be the next "Fillmoe Slim." He is more of an urban legend now but back in the day, he was a bonafide pimp. Instead of people going out to the clubs, they would just bring the club to their homes, apartments, or anywhere that they considered home and turn it into a crack party house.

Chapter 11

As A Man How Do I Lead A Family Without Seeing One

WHAT KIND OF strength can you receive from a leader when the leader is an addict. Mr. Marcel who suppose to have been a father figure who was a bus driver and hated being one except when he got his paycheck. He started experimenting with crack and became hooked. He eventually introduced mom to the crack game, and she became hooked as well. Mom never did mind when Mr. Marcel would bring the party home because he was the love of her life and it also kept him at home, which meant she knew she didn't have to worry about him running the streets with who knows who and doing who knows what. Mr. Marcel was never consistently around so I began to think I needed to step up and become the man of the house and focus on taking care of my sister. Once Naomi got older, we developed a bond that could not be broken. I would take care of my sister whenever mom was too busy partying or just sleeping in late from being up all night. Naomi and I would just watch mom and Mr. Marcel looking like the drunken version of Peaches and Herb or better yet the "high" version of Ashford and Simpson. Naomi and I would watch as they tried to mimic the songs that were being played on the record player. Mom and Mr. Marcel would sing all kind of songs as if they were expecting a knock on the door from the Motown founder himself, Mr. Berry Gordy. With all the late-night partying that was going on Mr. Marcel began to focus more and more on doing drugs and partying, and less and less about how he needed to show up for work and continue being the "man of the house" mom longed for. Due to his drug addiction and partying, he soon just stopped going to work all together and ended up getting fired.

Chapter 12

Life Imitating Art To It's Demonic Destruction

THE '80S DID more than just bring crack cocaine into our worlds; it created a lifestyle that went right along with it. Normally the saying goes "Art often Imitates Life," well; in this case, it was the other way around. Crack brought characters like Tony Montana from the movie Scarface, played by my favourite actor Alfredo James Pacino, to the forefront. If you don't know the story or haven't seen the movie, Tony Montana was a poverty-stricken Cuban who would do just about anything to get a green card so he could become legally accepted in the United States of America, you know the "Land of the Free, the Home of the Brave… (so we are told)" Once he received his green card, he immigrated to the United States of America so that he could be freed from the communistic rule of Cuban President, Fidel Castro. To put it in his own words, "To get what was coming to him chico". Scarface had such a huge impact on the World at that time because it showed how a man could exercise his underworld resources as a self-made multimillionaire from operating a drug cartel. With drugs being so sensationalized, it destroyed our family by Mr. Marcel choosing crack cocaine as his source of comfort in his life, causing him to be with no job to go to, a massive addiction… and if that's not enough Mr. Marcel got mom pregnant again. On June 15, 1983, mom gave birth to my baby sister Cherice. She looked so adorable and innocent. Her hair was the same length as my other sister. Mom would use the same type of style and barrette, which she would place in the middle of her hair just like she did with Naomi.

Chapter 13

Papa Couldn't Afford To Roll The Stone But He Did It Anyway

MY SISTER CHERICE complexion was a little bit more of a lighter caramel complexion than my sister Naomi, but they pretty much had the same features except my sister Cherice eyes were a little deeper and circled but both my sisters looked the same as babies. This time around Mr. Marcel was not the same dad who celebrated the birth of Cherice as he did Naomi. As a matter of fact, it seemed as though Mr. Marcel was oblivious to the newest addition to our family, simply because it was rumoured that he had stuck his temptation into another woman who became pregnant with a son. As with every other situation concerning Mr. Marcel's cheating ways, he would again emphatically deny any involvement so mom would not find out the truth. Just as the Good Book says, **"WHAT'S IN THE DARK…WILL COME TO THE LIGHT"** and yes, the baby was his! Not only did the birth of the child make him out to be a stone-cold liar, but also his actions cut mom's heart into a trillion pieces. Mom was probably asking herself a million and one questions: "How could the love of my life be so cold?" He left the family when I was ten years old. Although I was only ten, I was wise beyond my years because I had to endure so much as a little boy. In addition to my experiences maturing me mentally, I didn't feel like a little boy anyway because I had to be the man of the house and help mom out. Mom had me doing everything from babysitting to cleaning the house, to preparing meals for my sisters to eat. I had to make sure that we were being good so that mom furniture wouldn't get tore up by us playing recklessly in the house. Mom would give me her daily "to do" list, which seemed to never have an ending.

Chapter 14

No Man In The House, So You Go Be The Man Of The House

NEVER WAS I able to have a real childhood because mom had me being "man of the house". I had to take care of the house and my sisters. My sisters became my world. I felt like I had to protect my sisters with everything and give Cherice the love and attention she didn't receive from her dad. Cherice and I had an unbreakable bond because neither one of us had the love from our fathers. When Mr. Marcel got kicked out of mom apartment, for his countless cheating, Mom started beating me like Beelzebub possessed her. She developed so much fear inside me that I used to think that she hated me and wished I wasn't born. Even though the love of her life, Mr. Marcel was gone, that definitely didn't stop mom from always having company over at the house to drink, smoke crack, and listen to music until the sun came up. Mom was in a constant battle between what she knew was the right thing to do, as far as her being a mother, or continue to party with her friends. As long as we stayed in the back room and didn't come in the kitchen, everything was fine from mom perspective. I used to wonder why mom always felt like her friends were more important than the kids she birthed into this world. Mom had a rough past. She's the second oldest out of eighteen kids and had to endure a great deal of darkness, heartache, and pain growing up fast. She left home when she was sixteen because she probably thought it was much safer running the streets than to be at home being molested by different family members…while also having to take care of her other 17 brothers and sisters. Mom encountered many wolves dressed in sheep's clothing while on the streets. The streets stripped mom from the little bit of innocence that she had left.

Chapter 15

A Mom Can Repress Pain So Much Til No Love Is Available

She felt that her only refuge from all the hurt, pain and emptiness was P.D.M. (partying, drugs, and men). I wasn't' fully aware of the extent of my mother's pain until I became an older adult. Mom stored all of her hurt and disappointment inside herself for years without having any positive outlet to pour into. For her hurt and broken ness, she used me as a punching bag when I would get in trouble. Mom anger was so destructive that she would beat me with anything she could get her hands on. I mean she used broomsticks, extension cords, and she would always make me feel like I had no worth. I spent many nights crying in the dark, not wanting to come out of my room because I was more comfortable just keeping to myself. I wouldn't come out to get any food most of the time. I would just wait until she was in her room or if she called me to do something. The rest of my family didn't make life for me any better because every time when we all would get together, all they did was bring up something I had done in the past just so they could get a laugh when mom would haul off and whip me in front of everybody. I remember being twelve years old and I accidentally spilled some bleach on the carpet and then lied and said it wasn't me (this is probably one of the most defining moments of my life). When mom found out that I was lying, she immediately yelled for me to take off all of my clothes and then she put my head between her legs so I wouldn't move while she was whipping me with an extension cord on my naked behind. Mom whipped me over the smallest things and the horrible thing about it all, was that she had no remorse.

Chapter 16

What Mother Carries So Much Hate In Her Heart For Her Son?

THERE WERE TIMES when I would call out to YAHWEH "PLEASE MAKE HER STOP!" But that only made her anger rise for me bringing YAHWEH into this matter. As she was beating me like a never-ending drum, I remember yelling out "I want to run away!" Mom yelled out, "Oh yea you little n***a, you can go stay with Mama (R.I.P.), you want to stay with Mama?" (Mama was my Great Grandmother). "I would rather be with Mama than with you" is what I said in my head, but I replied, "YES!!" Mom was furious to the point she took my head and rammed it into the side of the wall and just watched as the blood ran down the side of my face. She then told me to go turn on the water so that I could get in the tub and then said, "YOU NOT GOING NOWHERE!" I spent that night in both physical and emotional pain. I told myself that no longer would I be around a mother who wished she never had me; I was going to run-away. I started school at Benjamin Franklin Middle School in 1986 and got exposed to a whole different crowd of kids. Kids from the projects and ghetto kids like myself. I mean there were fast girls who were sexy and very well experienced. On the first day, I met this dude by the name of Marquez. Our first encounter with each other, we clicked immediately. We both had the same astrology sign, which is the twin sign Gemini and we both thought we were members of the hip-hop legendary group, Run D.M.C. Marquez was short, he was 5 feet 5 inches, brown complexion, low haircut. The girls loved him because they felt safe with him and thought that because he was so small that he was cute. Plus, he always had on the latest trends in clothing.

Chapter 17

Exposed To The Jungle Now, How Long Will I Remain A Cub?

MARQUEZ AND I had the same classes, and we would always chill after school together. He had a lot of freedom to do most of what he wanted to do. I only could dream of that same type of freedom. One morning while I was on my way to school, I ran into Marquez and he saw me crying a little he said, "WHAT'S WRONG?" I didn't want to tell him at first, so I just said, "nothing." He knew me well enough to know that something was wrong, so he said, **"WHAT HAPPENED?" YOUR MOM AGAIN?** I told him, "She wanted me to wear some cheap Payless Shoes that I didn't want to wear, and I tried to sneak out of the house real fast with the shoes I wanted to wear.

Mom caught me and hit me with the broomstick twice. I tried to block the hit with my hands, but the broomstick hit me across my wrist instead and now my wrist is swollen." Marquez said, "Ponne, man, you can't' keep coming to school crying and s***. If you ever need somewhere to sleep, I can sneak you into my aunt's house when she goes to sleep." We had so much in common, even to the point of him being abused by his mother too. That's why he was so thankful for his Aunt D. As we walked and talked, Marquez brought up the big party coming up, I immediately got nervous and thought about how I would be able to get my mom to give me permission to go. Mom never let me go anywhere! I wanted to go to this big party at Hamilton Gym so bad because I knew that everybody was going to be there. Hamilton Gym is a local recreational center that was about fifteen minutes away from where I lived. I asked mom five days in advance if I could go to the party and she said, "I don't feel comfortable with you being mixed up with that crowd." I said, "Mom, Marquez will be there and so will other people from school.

Chapter 18

No More Abuse Means The Courage To Not Endure Anymore

SHE THOUGHT ABOUT it for a bit and then finally said, "I have to see how good you will be and see if your attitude is going to get you in trouble." Since the party was on a Saturday, mom had me doing all kinds of stuff for her just to see if I would give her any kind of attitude or get into any kind of trouble that would give her more of a reason to not let me go to the party. I did any and everything she wanted me to do. From Grocery shopping, washing dishes, mopping, and I even vacuumed the whole house. Whatever I could do to get her to say yes, that's what I was going to do. When Friday night came around, I asked mom if I could still go to the party, and she said that I couldn't go. Mom claimed she found out kids were being jumped by gangs in that area and also being kidnapped by homeless people (Hamilton was across the street from Kimball Park where a lot of homeless people were doing drugs and sleeping in the park). I begged her to let me go. I said mom, "I did everything you told me to do all week!" Mom In her mean way said, "I told you, NO! I just don't feel comfortable."

With all of my anger and frustration, I felt the only way I could respond to her was to say, "I never get to do anything! All you do is party all night and sleep all day and you don't let me go outside or anywhere!" Mom didn't like what I said, so she yelled at the top of her voice and said, "You better watch your m***a f****n' mouth before I get that broomstick!" As I headed back to go to my room, I mumbled under my breath, "I hate it here, she make me sick!"

Next thing I knew, mom got off the couch so fast to the point I didn't have time to react, and she said, "You think I'm playing with you LaPonne!" Moms went straight for the broomstick and hit me over my head and body more than I could even count. I went to my room that night more vexed than I was physically hurt.

Chapter 19

Sufforcated By Pain & Adversity A Manchild Was Birthed

I THOUGHT TO myself that I wasn't taking this anymore of mom abuse. I made up my mind that I was running away. I called Marquez and asked if he could sneak me into his Aunt D house and he said it would be cool as long, as we were extra careful and didn't make any loud noise. I packed what I could and waited until mom bedroom door was closed and snuck out the front door. I was so scared, but it was a good thing that Marquez only lived about ten minutes away. The next day, I went to the party just like I planned, but had all kinds of emotions tugging at me. I was confused, homesick, and most of all, I missed my sisters. I was thinking about all that had transpired the night before with mom. I ended up not having a good time at the party. I called mom the next morning, crying, apologizing, and asking if I could come back home. Mom asked, "WHERE ARE YOU?" I told her that I was at Marquez's aunt's house. She said with not one ounce of sympathy for her only son, "Well, you can just stay there!" I started to beg, "Mom, please, I don't want to be here! She replied, "Hurry up and get you're a** over here so I can whoop it!" Just as soon as I got home and walked through the door, mom told me to strip and take off all of my clothes. Mom whipped me so bad that, (I'm having flashbacks just thinking about it), and as if that wasn't enough, also she put me on punishment for a month. A year had past, and mom was not treating me any better. I was always getting into trouble for lying about this or that, so she never trusted me. I started to at least focus on making my own lootchi. I was so serious about making lootchi that I started washing people's cars, going grocery shopping for them, cleaning their houses, and whatever else I could do just to keep my pockets flowing with lootchi. I kept a "hustla's" eye, but as soon as I got home, mom would take all the lootchi I earned for the day.

Chapter 20

From This Point On I'm Enterprising The Best I Know How

THE FACT OF the matter is that mom wasn't just taking away my lootchi but was taking away my freedom as well. The only time I ever felt good about myself was when I would listen to music in my room in the dark. That was my "**FOUNDATION**."

Since mom would always take away my lootchi I earned doing it the right way, I began to ask different family members for lootchi and would not tell mom about it. I remember asking my Aunt Rasheeda, who got tired of just giving me lootchi, and decided, she will just give me a half ounce of weed and told me to get lootchi that way. I had already sold a few bags of weed at school before, but Aunt Rasheeda gave me more so I could really get my hustle on harder for myself and keep some lootchi in my pocket. It was at this very moment when I realized that, when I ran away from home the first time, I wasn't really homesick I just didn't like the fact that I ran away broke and hungry. I had a plan to run away again because me and mom relationship was not getting any better and I knew it was just a matter of time before I would have to run away again. I knew this time around that I had to be smarter about my plan and just make sure I would have lootchi to survive off. Mom would still have her friends come over to the apartment, a couple of times I tried asking her not to have her crack-party friends come over to our apartment and she would agree, but then a few hours later they would all be at the house playing dominoes, cards, smoking crack, listening to music, and getting drunk. Mom had one friend who I really loved; her name was Aunt Simone (R.I.P.); she was like another aunt to me. She looked like a vintage model. Aunt Simone stood at about 5 feet 9 inches tall, she was fair skinned, had wavy shoulder length hair, and the tone of her voice was sexy.

Aunt Simone was so helpful to my cousin Damarcus and I by helping us get a paper route job. I would sell newspapers everyday while selling weed on the side. Mom would take the checks I was earning from the paper route job, thinking that she was leaving me with no lootchi. I got fed up with having my lootchi taken. I was tired of mom beating on me, and never showing the love that a son should receive from his mom. My plan to run away was in full effect, and this time it was going to be a success because I learned what it meant to "survive off the streets!" I was selling weed non-stop and was able to stay with different friends. Something was happening to mom; she was tired of living the empty life of partying all-night and sleeping all day. She started focusing on getting off welfare and establishing a relationship with YAHWEH. She eventually decided to move us out of the ghetto. Mom started doing different things with me that she had not done before, like enrolled me in Pop Warner Football League named the San Francisco Seahawks. There were two coaches, Coach Greg who coached the junior midget level of football and his lovely wife Sofia who coached the cheerleaders. My coach was a real man and an unsung hero, he worked in the day-time as a postal worker, and he coached us in the evening. He sacrificed his married life to give us fatherless children a male figure to learn from. Coach Greg was 5 feet 9 inches tall, light complexion, shapely eyes, with long eyelashes for a man. He had a defined nose, and a full beard perfectly groomed that connected with his sideburns and his hair was a small afro that was thinning a little up front with a nice handsome smile, and a nice, pleasant tone of a voice but when you didn't show any discipline, responsibility, or didn't think of your team and was selfish, he fried that tail as if it was the catfish of the day. Coach Greg taught me a lot. I was observing him; without him even knowing. I was learning how to develop myself as a man. He was a coach who really cared about people.

Chapter 21

No Role Models, So I Observed Roles Of Men On My Own

HE WASN'T JUST your average coach who didn't know how to lead or the only reason why he became a coach was because he had a son who wanted to play football. Like most dads who prefer to coach their son only...to ensure that his son receives a lot of playing time on the team. Coach Greg truly cared about the development of people; his wife was the same way. Mrs. Sophia was very delightful, she stood at maybe 5 feet 4 inches, loved to smile, wore glasses, and brown complexion. And you could tell that they really loved each other and respected each other. Mrs. Sophia trained and coached the cheerleaders the same way her husband approached the football players. That's with love and compassion. To truly get the picture of how much they had a huge influence over our lives, you would have to witness it for yourself. It required a heart-felt approach with us, not just a mindset thinking that "okay I will just teach them how to play football or learn cheerleading routines," but to realize that they were feeling the voids of kids who were not receiving this type of attention at home. They wore that responsibility so gracefully and that's why over twenty years later, I'm acknowledging them because even though I haven't talked to Coach Greg in person since 1994, and really haven't established a phone relationship but when I called him from Atlanta and asked him if he could write me a letter of recommendation so I can try to get accepted into college, he didn't hesitate to write it. Coach and I hadn't spoken in years prior to me making that request. That's what kind of person Coach Greg is…a man who helped people better themselves…if they really wanted to.

The philosophy I adopted from Coach Greg, now that I'm older and can reflect on it now, is that he didn't believe in only developing the naturally talented players and forget about the people who required more development.

He believed in the team as a whole and if one person made a mistake the whole team paid for it. In return it created team accountability and a sense of brotherhood. Anytime a person did not execute a play he made us run the same play until we executed it with perfection. If we complained, he would have us continue to run 10 laps or more. When we were done, we had to jump in a puddle of mud because he wanted us to feel and smell how much we stunk as a team in the previous football game we played. Coach Rodney lead the midget level of football for the San Francisco Seahawks; which was more advanced and more power hitting; Coach Rodney didn't take no mess, he was more of a disciplinary figure, who knew martial arts as well. Coach stood at maybe 5 feet 8 inches, brown complexion, had a small Afro cut into a shag almost. Most of the time he wore shoes that looked like night slippers to the practice field that were for an old man. They were butterscotch colored and covered the whole foot but was shaped funny like two boats and he would yell at us at the top of his lungs. Coach Rodney taught me without him even knowing also, that if you made your mind up to do something, take what you do seriously and perfect it. Coach taught me a lot of mental toughness and, also about how to not be weak. I remember it was my first season on the highest level you can play on, with this organization. It was our first game against a team named Ukiah and they were known for having real tall corn stalk fed players that were bold, big, and strong. I played offensive Tight End, Kick-Off Team, Kick- Off - Return, and Outside Linebacker on defense. My first play on the kick-off team; my kicker punts the ball off and I run 90 yards down the field at top speed. I saw how towering and strong their players were but I could not show any weakness. I ran full speed and made contact with the player's helmet and pushed him into his teammate and then he stumbled and made it easier for me to tackle the player.

The part I left out is that when I made helmet to helmet contact, the colors I saw were black, purple, red and a flash of light, so I was dizzy (TODAY a.k.a. a concussion) from the hit caused by me running into the player…who also ran into the ball carrier. Everything was a blur; I was not able to see where I was going because of the concussion. However, to my coach it looked like I planned it that way to tackle the ball carrier. The coach was yelling saying "that's what I'm talking about make sure you keep that up!" The whole time I do not know, if I'm seeing 2 coaches or 3 or if I'm Batman or Wolverine. I'm disoriented real bad but trying my best to play it off. It was the mental tuff-ness that Coach Rodney instilled in us; to be mentally tough and to never quit on a play. The Coaches were very encouraging and saw things in me that others didn't; they said I had talent, great hands, and that I was tough. Sadly, but not surprising, out of the four years that I played football, I think I can remember mom being at maybe two of my games if that. Football became my second passion. My first was music since the age of five. I became a Pittsburgh Steelers fan in 1979. I know…I know… you say how you can be from San Francisco (a.k.a. Sucka Free) and be a Steel Curtain fan. Well three words (Mean Joe Green) real name Charles Edward Green was somebody unreal to me, but I identified with him.

He was a former all-pro American football defensive tackle he played for the Pittsburgh Steelers of the NFL. Throughout the early 1970s he was one of the most dominant defensive players in the National Football League. He was considered by many to be one of the greatest defensive linemen of all time. He was the cornerstone of the legendary "Steel Curtain" defense. He is a member of the Pro Football Hall of Fame and a four-time Super Bowl champion. His nickname, "Mean Joe Greene" stems from his alma mater, the University of North Texas' athletic team, which was where the nickname Mean Green was birthed to life.

Chapter 22

Turning 14, What Pain . . .
I'm Fearing Nothing

GREENE IS ALSO well known for his appearance in the "Coca-Cola Hey Kid, Catch!" Coca-Cola commercial in 1979, widely considered being one of the best Super Bowl commercials.

When I saw that commercial it showed Mean Joe Green as a ferocious demon on the field but off the field it showed him as a gentle giant. So, for me he represented the complexity of my upbringing and what I struggled with inside myself. How I can be nice and charming but if somebody challenged me or presented themselves as a threat; then that naturally takes me to another level of becoming really cold hearted.

I loved the colors of the Pittsburgh Steelers. The black and gold made me think of myself. The colors represented…that I was African descend & with richness inside me. Pittsburgh Steelers was a hard nose defensive team. As I got older, the team reflected my personality even more. I was tough but I also have a caring heart for people. Mom at some point did work for St. Mary's Hospital where the San Francisco Forty-Niners use to get their physical treatment, surgeries, and other medical attention taking care of there. Mom would get autographs of the players for me, so I did support the home team but I'm a Steel Curtain for life. I was just about to turn 14, I had ran away so much that mom could predict when I was running away. She was at the point of no return with me. She would say from time to time that I'm no son of hers because I would lie about everything, sneak off and get into trouble. On a lot of occasions, mom would say; "I don't trust you, LaPonne." Believe it or not, knowing that she felt that way about me really hurt me, but it did not destroy me! I had a new mindset. I no longer cared about receiving love from mom or anyone else! I stopped caring about other people feelings and focused on inflicting pain.

I barely graduated from middle school but that did not matter to mom, she was just so happy to see me graduate.

She was very confusing to me; one minute she'd be happy when I did something good but as soon as I did the slightest thing wrong, she would beat the heart and soul out of me.

During the summer, things began to look good for me. After I graduated from middle school, I got a summer job and I felt good about making some lootchi. However, there was one major problem in the eyes of mom; the job was back in the ghetto. Mom had gone through so much to move us out of the hood only for me to return. I was young and fearless! Lootchi, designer clothes, and good food to eat were the things I wanted, and I was going to get all of it. I decided to make Prince Hall apartments my "home base" because that's where I grew up since I was 6 years of age. I felt like I could do anything. I was working a summer job, hustling in the streets, and ran away whenever I wanted to go somewhere. I was out with Marquez, Lil Ray (R.I.P.), and my cousin Bay (R.I.P.). Lil Ray stood at 5 feet 5 inches, was built like a small point guard; his complexion was brown, big shapely eyes, goatee style of a moustache, and wore his hair low and somewhat wavy. Ray was a real flirt with the girls, and he spoke like he always needed attention. My cousin Bay, who stood at 5 feet 7 inches, was built like a full back football player, his complexion was brown, wore his hair low brush length, and like to play around a lot. One thing about Bay though, if you made him mad, he would dig all in you. In other words, he could fight really well. Bay spoke in a way like he was always trying to play with you but test you at the same time. Another member of the crew was Zeb, he stood at 5 feet 6 inches, he had two sizeable teeth in the front of his mouth, like a rabbit but the rest of his teeth were small. He wore his hair low brush length; he had slanted eyes with long eyelashes; he also had an athletic build. Zeb spoke like he was always plotting on something or someone. Ramon, stood at 5 feet 5 inches, he was chubby, and had these shifty eyes. He looked like he couldn't be trusted.

Chapter 23

Double Salute To My Falling Soljahs, You Will Live On

WHEN HE SPOKE, he always whined with anger if something didn't go his way. Pearl (R.I.P.) stood at 6 feet 3 inches, dark complexion, was real tall but a little chubby at the same time. He wore his hair low brush length and was very quiet and sneaky but would react quickly when there was any type of drama popping off. We were the "YG's," which meant that we were "The Baby Boys" on the block in the hood…in the eyes of the "OG's" (Original Gangstas). We weren't considered serious factors in the game at that point, nor were we real G's or respected as real hustla's. We were just some young, poor, and wet behind the ear teenagers on our own. The police began patrolling the hoods more frequently due to increased drugs and gangs' activities. Drive-by shootings became the leading contributor to homicides, which was increasing at an alarming rate. I guess the police thought that by having officers patrol on foot and posted up in a small makeshift office inside the hood, it would help decrease the violence: NEGATIVE!! All that did was make us more vexed that they were so visible. With the increased presence from San Francisco's finest, and the recently revamped drug task force, we had to worry about how to get our "hustle on" without getting arrested. One day these two cops were patrolling the streets and one of the dudes I was with took a few double D batteries and threw them and hit one of the officers in the back of the head. The officer called for backup and started to chase us. Everyone ran their own direction, but somehow Lil Ray and I happened to choose the same direction. We tried to cut through an apartment complex to lose them.

Chapter 24

The Very First Moment F*** The Police Was More Then A Song

LIL RAY PROVED to be too quick for the officers and slipped through their fingers—I wasn't as lucky. The officer's tackled me from my blind-side and placed a knee in my back and a boot on my head. As the cops took me to a small dark room which was used as an office, my entire right eye began to swell. The captain came right up to my face and spit out, "WHAT'S YOUR NAME!" He stood at about 5 feet 11 inches and looked like an ex-marine with this box haircut. His moustache was thick like a lumberjack; it looked like J.J. Jameson from Spiderman (Peter Parker's boss), and his voice was hard and raspy as if he smoked five cartons of Camel filtered cigarettes daily. I answered his question, "Lamont"; I knew it was a lie, but I wasn't about to tell the cops my real name. The captain said, "Lamont who"? You YOUNG BAS***D!" I yelled back at him, "Don't be calling me NO BAS***D!" He then grabbed me by my jacket and pressed the jacket against my throat to the point the zipper began to choke me. The captain shoved me against the wall and with his cigarette laced breath said, "I'm an F**KEN' CAPTAIN, don't you ever talk to me like that!" I quickly replied, "Don't talk to me like that!" The captain kept going on and on with his questions, "What's your last name?" I lashed out and replied, "Johnson" out of my mouth real quick.

"You threw the batteries?" he asked again, and I replied swiftly, "No captain." "Who threw them then?" he continued, I looked in his eyes and said, "I don't know, I was around the corner." Of course, I knew who threw the batteries, but I learned a long time ago from my mom you don't volunteer information, and what goes on in the house stays in the house. The officer asked, what were the names of the people who were with you? I replied forcefully, "I don't know Captain; I only knew one of the boys his name was Lil Earl."

I could tell by the look on the captain's face, he was getting extremely vexed. He yelled "This is B***S**T!" he continued ask, "What is Lil Ealr last name?" I stuck to my guns saying, "I don't know him good enough to know his last name" Before I could finish my sentence the captain says, "I know you're lying, we bet not catch you in this area again. Now call your parents or guardian to come and get you!"

I have to say that throughout the whole interrogation there was not one ounce of fear that rested in me, but when he mentioned I had to call somebody to be released from their custody, the first person I feared they would contact was my mom. My heart felt like it was going into cardiac arrest. I asked the unthinkable, "Is it possible for me to call my girlfriend Algeria to come and get me?" I already knew the answer to that question, but I was willing to try anything at this point. The officer looked at me and said I could only be released to a parent or guardian. I've never been so scared to dial a set of numbers on a phone until then, but I knew I had to call or else they would not release me. The officer gave me the phone to call mom and the phone began to ring; mom picked up, and I said in a loving tone, "Hello" Mom, it's Lamont" I suspected she would say, "Who?" Before she could, I said, "It's me, Lamont! Mom, they got me down in this little dark office for something I didn't do". The captain took the phone from me, and started talking to mom, "Yes Ma'am, this is Captain Richardson, we need you to come and pick up your son." I could hear mom through the phone saying, "Well you can keep him." The captain said, "Ma'am, we have no evidence that your son is the one that did it." Mom eventually agreed to come and get me. The whole time I was hoping and praying that she didn't ask for me by my real name; instead, she said, "I'm here to pick up my son." Mom knew how and when to be polite; it was something she had mastered over the years.

She was real polite to the officers but cut a look at me so cold that I knew what plans she had for me when we got home. The captain told mom to make sure she kept me out of the bad areas, and to make sure I stayed away from the wrong crowds. Mom turned towards the captain and said, "You don't know how hard it is being a single mom; my son keeps running away and he sneaks around doing all kinds of stuff." After mom poured out her heart to the captain, he pulled out a business card from his pocket and said, "Call me if you ever have any problems with him and we will put him in jail." While all this was going on, mom never once commented on how big my eye was looking. I thought if I mentioned it, I could get some kind of sympathy that would replace the rage that she was waiting to release on me. I said, "Mom, you see what they did to my eye?" She looked down at me and said, "Shut Up! Don't try to get no sympathy from me boy; you shouldn't have been hanging down on Virgo's anyway. I told you LaPonne there's nothing but trouble down there." Virgos was the name of a little Mom & Pop store where Fulton Street Mob set was located at. When we got home mom looked at me and said, "I should tear your behind up, but the captain didn't say it was you, but you're on punishment for a month for being down there when I told you not to be in that area." I was shocked! Just when I thought mom was going to kill me, she said, "How do you think it makes me feel as your mom having to come and get my only son out of police custody." With everything that was going on, I felt good that this was one of the few moments I wasn't confused about mom love and concern for her son. Mom was turning into a new woman. She was always giving praise and glory to YAHWEH, YASHUA & THE HOLY SPIRIT as her saviour for delivering her from her sins, and blessing her with Grace, Mercy, and his Unmerited Favour. Mom had a determination that she was not going to give up and she definitely was not going to be denied.

Chapter 25

Mission To Be Freed
From The Hurtful Past

MOM DECIDED TO join Mt. Vernon Missionary Baptist Church under the leadership of Pastor Reverend L.V. Lattan (R.I.P.) Mom was also applying to work as a bus driver for the San Francisco Municipal Transit Agency. Mom journey to embracing the Holy Trinity was learning the power of forgiveness. Mom had to face all of the hurt she was holding inside herself. She was learning how to forgive herself and others. Mom started calling people that had hurt her in the past and expressing to them that she forgave them and asked them to forgive her. One Saturday evening Cherice was getting her hair done at the salon by the owner, Sunshine. Ms. Mylene was also getting her hair done by her daughter in law, Jamila at the same time. Mom came in and for the first time the two of them were in the same place at the same time. At this point Mr. Marcel was no longer involved in either of their lives. Mom was a devoted Christian and Mr. Marcel continued to use drugs and alcohol. Mom had finally turned her life over to the light, the truth; she was determined never to return to darkness. Even if it meant disassociating with people she loved. Mom stated it really pierced at her heart how she wasn't proud of the old person she was and that for her to be delivered from her past, she had to address it and apologize to the people she hurt or disrespected with her actions. Remember Ms. Mylene? This is the lady my mom directed her hurt and anger at because she believed this was the woman that stole her knight and shining armor from her. The hurt I saw my mom foster day in and day out begun to breed into us as kids. Years later, once mom became reborn and saved, she wanted her life to be led by the spirit and not by the flesh.

Chapter 26

Renewing Your Mind
Begins With Your Environment

MOM WAS YOUNG in her infancy stages as a woman of Faith and it's one thing to say you saved but it's another thing to show that you're saved when obstacles attack your flesh.

Ms. Mylene was preoccupied by the planning of a busy morning the next day, so she really wasn't present at the moment. Mom said the spirit pulled her to express how sorry she was for how much hate she had in her heart for Ms. Mylene. Mom said, "She's now saved, and that the old person no longer exists and would you please forgive me ". Mom gave Ms. Mylene a hug. Who would have ever believed that anger and hurt that once consumed this spirit of my mom and how YAHWEH got the victory and used it for his glory to show the example of grace and the power of his forgiveness that was giving and received by both of these Empresses. Nothing ever came easy for mom. She always struggled to make a better life for herself and for her kids. I remember when mom was trying to get a three-bedroom apartment for all of us to live in. She had to harass the property owner Mr. Henry because her name was at the bottom of the waiting list. Mr. Henry was a shrewd man who stood about 6 feet 3 inches and had a short coarse grey Afro. Mr. Henry always looked as though he never washed properly; nor knew what it was like to have teeth in his mouth. Mr. Henry's eyes were gray, his skin was wrinkled, and his fingernails were always filthy. Mr. Henry looked like one of those people who never went home, they just took naps in their office, and never bathed or ate properly. Mom kept begging, pleading, and saying Mr. Henry, please have compassion in your heart, I'm a single parent with three kids and we do not have anywhere to stay. Please allow me to use my Section 8 certificate!" Section 8 was a government-subsidized certificate that reduced the market rate on the rent to make housing affordable for lower income families. Mr. Henry replied, I don't usually accept Section 8, but for you I will make this exception just this once."

Mom knew it was nobody but YAHWEH blessing us with shelter. Moms signed the lease, and we were in our new place. When we moved in, we had nothing, and I mean nothing. So here we are in this big new apartment to live in but no furniture at all. We didn't even have a bed to sleep on, so we all had to sleep together in Mom room on the floor. We kept warm by sleeping next to each other. We were like sardines packed in a can. Mom left everything at the Prince Hall Apartments because she said that everything was infested with roaches and their eggs, and she didn't want them to follow us out of the ghetto. Mom was also having a hard time dealing with her new Christian identity. She was going to church, meeting new church friends, and seeing old friends who had turned their lives over to Christ. Her new focus was to live a YAHWEH life and to atone for her sinful past. It was not an easy road for mom but at no point would she give up. Since my sister's dad and my dad weren't around, mom had no other financial help to support us. Not only did mom have to put the pieces of her life back together but also, she had to raise three kids on her own while also trying to find a job and stay faithful to YAHWEH. Mom found out that there was a bus driver position available with Muni, but that they were only accepting a limited number of applicants. Mom would stand outside in line for an application from 10pm to 6am hoping and praying that she would be blessed with a job opportunity. All she wanted to do was to provide a better life for her family. Mom prayers were answered; she got the position and was working part-time. As a driver, Mom struggled so hard because the hours were crazy. She would have to work three to four hours and then have a two-hour break and then would have to finish two more hours to complete her shift. It was challenging, but mom trusted that YAHWEH would make things better and that he did. The job didn't pay all the bills, but it helped mom pay whatever she could for the moment. Not long after, mom started working full time as a driver for Muni. It was good to see mom with her head held high with confidence that comes from being able to support your family.

Chapter 27

My Hustler's Ambition Was Always All Gas No Brakes

MY LIFE WAS parallel to mom; she left home at the age of 16, (like I mentioned before) I left home at the age of 12, mom did drugs, I did drugs, mom was molested by family members, I was molested by family members. I always admired the strength that my mom carried, I just couldn't figure out why we could never connect in a way a mom and son naturally should. Although we were out of the hood, the same problems followed us like a hungry lion chasing after a helpless antelope. I decided I was going to show mom that I'm a different kind of antelope. I made up my mind that I was not going to let mom control my life the way she wanted to anymore. Mom always wanted me to do what she wanted and go wherever she said go. She still wanted me to stay in the house unless I was going to church with her.

Mom never wanted me to play hip hop/rap music in her house, but I did it anyway because music was my first love and still is my FOUNDATION. By the time I turned 15 years old, I was breaking free from the shackles mom had on me. Although, she changed some areas of her life, I did not. I was still hustling down in the hood, yeah, I was going to school, but would cut class if I needed to make lootchi. Hustling was one thing but having a gang to protect the territory you hustle on is another thing. Fulton Street Mob/YBG was the most notorious gang in San Francisco! There was another treacherous set in San Francisco called O.C., which stood for Out of Control. They were located in the projects and there was nothing smooth about O.C. They were straight cut throats that would f*** your sister and kill her afterwards if needed.

The hustling that I experienced from hanging on Prince Hall set was not going to cut it because that set was not a set that was a threat to anybody at the time. It was filled with a bunch of cool people who just wanted to make lootchi, and not cause problems with no other sets. In fact, they were such a non-factor that people from other gangs would pass through without feeling intimidated. Prince Hall was a neutral ground for new hustlers and people who lived in the apartment complex. However, their game had to be real tight because gangstas from other sets, and even dope fiends would come and rob them. I was in the hustle game to build my name, and to be respected as a certified Gangsta. I couldn't be associated with a set that was not viewed as a threat or even dangerous. I was making lootchi from hustling summer jobs, and from hustling in the streets. I also stayed true to my friends even though I had gone another direction by becoming a full-fledged "Gangsta", I had a nice line on how to get a purer grade of cocaine and I learned about the different weight sizes to purchase, and how to sell a quarter ounce, a half-ounce or just an ounce. I had a dope fiend teach me how to turn cocaine into crack. We used dope fiends houses to cook and rock up the dope. Rocking up crack was easy, all I needed was a saucepan or coffee pot, a stove, some baking soda, ice cubes, and a big sized pickle jar. Dope fiends didn't mind anyone using their houses as a "dope re-up" space, as long as we left the shake for them. (shake was just pieces of dope or crumbs that were left over from cooking the dope. I was all about making lootchi. I developed a strategy to pull other hustla's clientele away from them. I realized that all I needed to do was to have a stronger product that was better than everybody else and the addicts would promote my product to the fellow dope fiends and that would translate into my pockets being on swole.

Chapter 28

What About My Mom Hurt, Relationships Formed Anyway

I LOST A lot of dope trying to perfect a real potent product, but I wanted as many dope fiends to know that when Ponne was on the scene, Ponne was serving that real s**t. Not only did I have a stronger product but also, I was giving deals to build my name. I was respected as the young G known as "silent but deadly" or CaPonne. Marquez and I remained close friends throughout the years. We were so close that Marquez's family knew me, and my family knew Marquez, and that made us family for life! One day Marquez started mentioning a dude named Romel to me. He said that Romel was a cool dude and that he had two little brothers, one of which his name was Little Marcel. Marquez also mentioned the name of the other brother, but I didn't pay much attention to the second brother's name because I was too busy thinking that this kid had to be Mr. Marcel's son. As soon as I heard that information, I started remembering how devastated mom felt when she found out that Mr. Marcel cheated on her. I had no choice than to share the same anger that mom felt because as I said before, Mr. Marcel was my chance to have a father figure around and he just up and left me. Marquez kept telling me about Romel and how both of us are real cool people. He said that Romel and I reminded him of each other. I told Marquez, "I'm not feeling that idea, and I think his mom is the woman who my sisters' dad cheated on my mom with back in the day." I don't think Marquez was paying much attention to what I was saying because he kept telling me that I had to meet this dude.

When I first met Romel, it was during "Turkey Day" which was a San Francisco's high school championship tradition."

Every Thanksgiving the top two teams competed to become the "Turkey Day Champion," and it was one event that no one dared to miss. Turkey Day attracted everyone from all walks of life: drug dealers, killers, fly girls, football coaches and players (past and present), and those who were just looking to get noticed. Mom had no problem with me going since it was football related. She always wanted me to become a famous football player so I could buy her a big house and drape her with mink coats and diamond rings. I met up with Marquez and Romel was with him. Marquez introduced us to each other by saying: "My n***a Ponne meet my n***a Romel," we both said a short what's up and went on about our business. Romel was probably 5 feet 9 inches, had a brown complexion, slanted almond shaped eyes, a real mischievous smile, and always was smelling and looking good. Romel was a west coast kid but wore a flat top like he was from the east coast. When he talked it was real smooth and cool. I looked over at Marquez and he was smiling. I knew exactly what his smile was saying, like "Aaaha, you said you didn't want to meet but it's too late now!" When we went to grab our seats for the game, Marquez made sure that he sat on the far-right side of me, so Romel was the one sitting next to me; we had no other choice than to talk to each other at some point. Every time I turned my head away, I would notice Romel checking me out, and every time he turned his head, I would do the same thing; we both were trying to feel each other out, just checking to see what kind of vibe we were getting from each other. I had this feeling that Romel knew the whole story about the situation involving both of our moms and Mr. Marcel. We were watching the game and this player on defense came from the other side of the field, full speed and blind-sided this player so hard, he flew out of bounds. Romel and I just looked at each other and said, GOD D*MN!

Chapter 29

Yay Area Love Was All Shook Up On October 16, 1989

AFTER THAT WE started joking around and we were cool with each other, I asked him if he knew anything about the Mr. Marcel situation and he said, the only thing he knew was that my two sisters were also his little brother's sisters. Since they all have the same dad, it became apparent that Mr. Marcel was the type of man that always avoided his responsibilities when it came to taking care of his children. When the game was over and we were all going our separate ways, Romel and I exchanged numbers, and when I got home, I told mom the whole story, but she didn't really have much to say about it. I remember when I was younger, I would go to my grandmother apartment who we all called G-Mama (R.I.P.) and it turned out that Romel mom lived right next door to G-Mama. It was so hard for mom to go over to see her mom because sometimes Mr. Marcel would be next door just sitting in the window with no shirt on, smirking at my mom, but being who she is, she kept going to see her mom even though she had to keep reopening her emotional wounds each time she saw Mr. Marcel. My whole life felt like a moving earthquake until October 16, 1989. California had one of its historical earthquakes, the 'Loma Prieta Earthquake'. It started off as 6.9 and the magnitude of the wave grew to 7.1 on the Richter scale; the earthquake killed 63 people, injured more than 3,500 and left almost 12,000 people homeless. The earthquake caused power failures throughout the Bay Area, and even a section of the Bay Bridge collapsed. I just had crossed that bridge 15 minutes prior. No one cannot tell me YAHWEH is not real.

If I had been 15 minutes longer traveling on that bridge, I definitely would have been a part of the lives that were lost by the collapsing of the Bay Bridge. When night-time came around, more problems began to erupt. Gangs decided this would be a good opportunity to go to the rich Caucasian neighbourhoods and rob them. It was a rare moment, to see all these different gangs take a break from killing each other because the earthquake opened up an opportunity for us to come together and steal from the rich. We were pulling people out of their luxury cars and driving them back to the ghettos. We terrorized many people, but we still were not satisfied with the loot we were getting. We decided to break into a record store. Now, while everyone went in a different direction trying to find anything valuable, I headed straight towards the cash register. I was trying to bust the register open when I looked out the window and saw a police car making a U-turn to come and arrest us. We were all trying to jump out of the window and run in any direction just to escape. I ran for like ten minutes at top speed and ended up getting a cramp on the side of my stomach. I hid in a residential alley and threw some nasty garbage bags on top of me and covered myself with a garbage can lid. Just as I was doing that, I noticed that there was another guy who was very dark, stood at maybe 5 feet 8 inches, had on all black, and had a short curl for his hairstyle that was hidden under a Los Angeles Kings baseball cap. He was hiding right next to me, but he was not covered up as well as I was. The cops rolled their cars past the alley that had a big searchlight on it, I heard one of them yell, "We have two suspects over here". When I heard the cops say that, at that point I knew they had us. I wasn't trying to get shot by some cops, so I came out of hiding with my hands up.

Chapter 30

School Of Hard Knocks & Steel Toe Boots Up The You Know What

ONE OF THE officers took the handle of his Billy club stick and hit me over my left eye. The hit cut the skin and blood immediately gushed out. As the blood was pouring out, it was burning my eyes and my vision was blurred. I could feel the swelling closing my eye, at that exact moment the second officer decided to punch me in the ribs. I punched the officer in his stomach immediately after he hit me, they smashed my head on top of the car and then threw me in the back seat of the police car. I was a little dazed, but my anger blocked out the pain. I was booked at Kezar Police Station by Golden Gate Park, which happened to be only ten minutes away from where mom lived. Since I was still a minor, guess who had to come and get me out? You guessed it! I called mom and told her they charging me with several different counts, but one of the main charges was a 211-felony charge, which means a robbery charge for you non-felons. The officer called mom and told her she had to come and pick me up. I was not as nervous as I was the last time mom had to come and get me out of police custody, but still it was a fraction of fear in my heart. I had no idea what mom was going to do or how she was going to react towards me since she was now living a saved life and trying to repent for her sins from the past. When mom arrived at the police station, I was prepared to hear more of the same yelling and see her face more disappointment than ever, but to my surprise, mom started yelling at the officer saying, "Look at my son's eye and head, was this really necessary?" The officer replied, "Ma'am, I apologize, but your son was resisting arrest and he had us chasing him for ten minutes." I replied, "He's lying; I was hiding in an alley, and I even came out with my hands up!".

Chapter 31

Mama Was The Foundation Once It Crumbled Family Never Solid

I SAID IT with every emotion I could muster up trying to get mom on my side, she yelled "Boy shut up and come on!" During the whole walk home mom had been yelling and pointing her finger at my face saying, "You up here robbing stores and people and running from the police. Who do you think you are? You better be thankful they didn't shoot you while you were running." The next day, my face was looking like the elephant man. I was still going to school, hanging in the streets looking deformed, and mom had put me on punishment for getting into trouble with the law. Mom had it with me! She didn't want to put up with me anymore. I had to keep going to court, had to check in with my probation officer on a regular basis, and I was still running away from mom's apartment. Mom finally realized that I was out of control, and she could not take it any longer. She didn't know what else to do with me, so she called up my Great Grandmother (R.I.P.), Mrs. Wickett, whom we called Mama. She stood at about 5 feet 9 inches, light complexion and looked Cherokee Indian. Mama wore narrow glasses over her big eyes, and she kept foam small rollers in her black hair. She was a very successful property owner, who owned a family home in Arkansas and in San Francisco. Mama was very strict. She was one of those grandmothers who meant what she said and said what she meant. If you didn't do exactly what Mama said, then her wrath would come down on you. When she got upset or laughed her voice sounded like an old squeaky door, kind of like Vicki Lawrence from the television show, "Mama's Family." I remember one weekend when I stayed over at Mama's house, she pulled out this nice comforter for me to use as a cover, but then she handed me two Sunday newspapers that was covered in plastic and told me to lay on them because she didn't have extra pillows.

Chapter 32

Why Are You So Troublesome Forced To Look In The Mirror?

I SAID "AW Mama! I don't want to use this as a pillow." Mama turned and looked at me and yelled in her squeaky voice, "Boy, you better do what I say now!" Even though I was young, I knew it made no sense making me use a Sunday newspaper as a pillow. I was not going to rest my head on a stack of newspapers all night, so before I fell asleep, I devised the perfect plan; I was going to wait until Mama was asleep and then I would take the newspapers off my neck, but there was one flaw in my plan; I forgot that a lot of seniors wake up around 4 or 5 o'clock in the morning. Not too long after I had fallen asleep, I heard a voice in my sleep yelling "GET UP! I SAID GET UP!!" It was none other than Mama; she was standing over me in her old pink robe, with rollers in her hair, and a curl cap on her head. Mama gave me a right punch and then a left punch straight to my jaw. My Uncle Apprentice had to jump up out of bed to get Mama off me. I heard him tell Mama, "You can't hit that boy like that Mama!" I'll tell you for Mama to be a woman in her eighties she sure did pack a mean right/left hook. If I didn't know any better, I would have sworn that she used to spar with Muhammad Ali. Mama was very unpredictable. Like, one time Mama came into my room, and she never comes into my room at mom's place. She said, "Well, how you doing?" I calmly replied, "Alright Mama." She then began to ask me all sorts of questions, "Why are you such a bad boy? You are always so quiet but angry. Why are you so TROUBLESOME?" Mama continued, "Don't you know there is a whole world waiting to use that TROUBLESOME spirit against you to destroy you? You better be good." Those were the last words Mama said to me as she left out of my room; a week later she passed away in her sleep.

Chapter 33

The Lioness Shows The Lion He's Really Just A Cub

MY EMOTIONS BECAME like stone. I had built up such a defense and felt as though there was no one who was there for me. When the time had come for us to bury Mama, I didn't shed one tear until I arrived at the funeral because her words "YOU BETTER BE GOOD" kept playing over and over in my head. I tried to refocus my life for the good, but things between mom and me were getting worse and worse.

I would ask mom if I could go over to Romel apartment to play with him and his brothers just so I could be in a different environment. Mom said she was fine with me spending time with Romel and his family because she said that she was done worrying about Mr. Marcel, and that Yahweh had delivered her from him and the hurt and vexation she had for him, was no longer in existence. By this time, mom was saved. I guess she didn't feel negative about the matter like she once did. I asked mom if I could go over to Romel, and it was like déjà vu all over again. Mom replied, "Let me think about it". In my mind all I was thinking was "here we go again." Mom told me to give her until Thursday evening.

I started doing everything mom wanted me to do and when Thursday came, mom arrived home and was already in a bad mood from a hard day's work. I gave mom some space and asked if she needed anything. She looked at me and said, "No I don't, and I know why you being all nice, but the answer is no LaPonne, you cannot go and spend the weekend over at Romel, maybe some other time." I started thinking about how mom was probably feeling; not only did the love of her life leave to be around this family and now her son wanted to be around this family. Although mom may have felt that way, that still didn't stop me. I asked, "Why not mom?

"BECAUSE! I said so, maybe another time" I turned all red inside and yelled out, "I'M TIRED OF THIS!" mom yelled back, "WHAT?" next thing I knew, mom got off the couch charged at me, "DO YOU THINK I'm one of these b*****s in the streets you be dealing with?" She started to choke me and scratched my face and neck. I pushed her off me. She got back in my face and said, "Oh, so you want to fight me?

Come on then." I was so hurt, upset and said, "No, I'm not trying to fight you." I started crying to my Aunt Janiece who had been staying with us for about three weeks, who came and got in the middle to separate us. Aunt Janiece said, "Madid, you know you wrong." Mom turned and looked at her and said, "Stay out of it Janiece." Aunt Janiece replied Madid, "you didn't have to do all that to that boy!" Mom began to ignore what, my aunt was saying, she said, "Janiece, don't you ever come between a mother and her son." That made Aunt Janiece vexed at mom, so she said, "You have lost your mind! So, you are telling me, that if you saw our brother Dontay put his hands on our mother; you are just going to let him, do it? You are wrong Madid." Mom was huffing and puffing and pacing around the living room floor, she said to me, "La Ponne, put my keys on the counter and wait right here while I call the police." I walked over and put her keys on the counter and then bolted out the door. My heart was racing; I never ran down a flight of stairs so fast in my life. I was so scared because I thought there was going to be a big police unit like a SWAT team waiting outside for me like I had just robbed a bank with hostages inside. While mom was calling the police on me, I had already been running for a good ten minutes straight. I jumped on the Five Fulton Bus and ducked down in the back seat so the police would not see me. I was paranoid, scared, and hurt. I got off the bus at McAllister and Webster Street and headed toward Virgos; that's when I saw my Uncle Dontay and ran towards him.

Chapter 34

A Grandson Love Infintely Engraved In My Heart

MY UNCLE DONTAY also known as Shu-Shang was a cold piece of work. He was slick like me, but more of a con artist. He could knock almost anybody out with just one punch. He was dark skinned, slim, stood at about 6 feet 3 inches, with a thin basketball build, and he had the most intimidating voice and eyes that were fire brown. Uncle Dontay and Uncle Apprentice used to make me fight them like they were my enemies in the streets. They wanted me to be mentally and physically tough. I told my uncle that me and mom got into a big fight; he looked at the scratches on my face and said, "My sister did that to your face and neck?" I started crying and told him "I have nowhere to live. Mom told me she was going to call the police, so I ran out the door!" He put his hand on my shoulder and said, "Don't let these n****s see you crying out here, you can't afford to show no weakness in these streets; it's like blood to a piranha, they will eat you alive." I was slipping and I knew it, so I hurried up and wiped my face. Uncle Dontay lived with G-Mama who was his mom. He said I could stay with them, but I didn't think that was such a good idea since G-Mama was the one who my mom got all her habits and beliefs from. G-Mama had a real lovely voice when she was in a good mood, but if you messed up in anyway, she did not play. G-Mama stood at maybe 5 feet 6 inches, a rich Cherokee bronze complexion, with high Indian cheekbones and deep round puppy eyes. She wore her hair in a natural curly afro. Her personality was a velvet touch with an iron fist all at once. Dontay Sr. (R.I.P.) he was and still will always be my everything. He told it like it was, just like G-Mama but he was straight raw no velvet touch. Dontay Sr. stood at maybe 5 feet 5 inches and was a chef. He and G-Mama worked for Shriners hospital in the laundry department.

Chapter 35

Iron Fist Titian
Always Challenged Me Mentally

DONTAY SR. HAD a hazelnut complexion with deep circle eyes with freckles on his nose; he wore his hair like Richard Pryor did on the movie "Which Way Is Up "an afro stuffed in a blue knit cap; he was very small in build but was a titan and true general who was no joke. When I think about my grandfather who started a relationship with my grandmother who had 10 kids before he came along, and he still fathered those kids as best he could. The big captain owned his own restaurant with G. Mama. He also was one of the first African descent chefs to integrate the Fairmont Hotel in San Francisco. Dontay Sr. and G-Mama (R.I.P.) were homeowners and ended up having a total of 18 kids, with 3 sets of twins. They worked hard and partied even harder. They would pull out that big gallon of Carlos Rossi wine, some E&J brandy mixed with some Coke-Cola, and throw on some B.B. King, Temptations, you know that golden school soul music; and Dontay Sr. and some of my great Uncles would put on those old man boots that were black and narrow, with the long zipper on the side, and cut a rug. They would break out all kind of dance moves until the sun came up. It was priceless. All this would take place in a Victorian house at 1800 Turk Street San Francisco, California. It was a six-bedroom house where all eighteen of the kids had to cram into at one point. When I was 11 years old, I would hang around with both my uncles, Dontay, and Apprentice. Every time I would be with the two of them someone was always getting hurt and we all knew who that somebody was. They played so rough. They called it playing, but it was more like torture for me. I think they called me out all the time because I would never back down. We would run around G-Mama place and always ending up getting in trouble for breaking her stuff.

Chapter 36

I'm Go Skin Y'all Bottoms Like Last Night Catfish

THERE WAS THIS one time when Dontay and I were throwing some toy bowling pins at each other, and we had accidentally broken this glass picture frame. G-Mama heard the glass shatter, and yelled, "WHAT WAS THAT NOISE!" Both of us just looked at each other like deer's in headlights. We tried to clean everything up before G-Mama got closer to us, but it was too late, as she was approaching the room everything slowed down and all we could hear was her deep, footsteps sounding real slow, as if it was a scene from Jurassic Park where you could hear the Tyrannosaurus coming but not able to see it yet. When she saw that the glass was broken, she yelled, "WHO DID THIS?" just like two kids who didn't want to get into trouble by their mom/grandmother, especially G-Mama, we blamed it on each other. She said "You little n****s think you slick, and she grabbed a broomstick and hit us both upside the head, hips, and wrists. I figured mom had to get it from somewhere and it had to be G- Mama. So, when Dontay suggested earlier, I go visit G-Mama, I was hesitant. That was the first memory that came into my mind about G-mama. I went to G-Mama place anyway and I explained all that happened and wanted to know if I can live with her. I didn't feel comfortable bringing that type of drama around my grandmother's apartment because my Uncle Dontay had the Task force at my grandmother's apartment before. Shortly after G-Mama moved to Eddy Street, her neighbour was Ms. Mylene. Their bay windows faced each other. Ms. Mylene would choose that location to read her books daily. This particular day Uncle Dontay came running into the building with undercover police officers chasing him. Ms. Mylene ran from the bay window to look out her door peep hole.

Chapter 37

You Don't Bring Dirt Home Where You Rest Your Dome

UNCLE DONTAY RAN up the stairs to the first floor and instead of going to the right to G-Mama apartment, he ran to the left which led him to the back stairs. At the bottom of the stairs there was an alley with doors at each end of it. One door led to the front of the apartments and the second led to the backyard of the apartments that was fenced. Uncle Dontay could have hopped over the fence and possibly escaped. Ms. Mylene ran into another bedroom to see if Uncle Dontay would get away. As Uncle Dontay tried to run down the back stairs, there was one older Caucasian task force with a bald head, slightly overweight and stood maybe 5'4". The other task force was African descent who stood at 6'3", slender built with dark skin. The Caucasian task force was yelling to the younger African descent task force, "that'a boy; go get'em." As if he was talking to a blood hound dog chasing a slave. Uncle Dontay ran down the back stairs, but the African descent task force caught and handcuffed Uncle Dontay. While the task force was bringing Uncle Dontay back upstairs, the Caucasian task force kept saying, "That'a boy; Good job!" When they brought Uncle Dontay to G-Mama's apartment, one of the task force kicked in the door. Ms. Mylene ran over to G-Mama apartment and saw that the task force had handcuffed her in the kitchen. G-Mama was pleading for the task force to inform her on what's going on. The Caucasian task force yelled, "Shut up." G-Mama kept asking, "What's going on? Why are you in my house? Why are you doing this to me?" The task force slammed her head into the kitchen cabinet to shut her up.

She screamed in pain and fell to the floor with the task force holding the handcuffs. This caused her to scream in pain again because the task force was holding the handcuffs in place while she was falling to the floor, her weight caused the handcuffs to pull her arms and shoulders backwards. This was so shocking to Ms. Mylene she yelled, "Why are you doing that? She's a senior citizen and you have her in handcuffs." The Caucasian task force yelled back at Ms. Mylene, "Shut up or I'll arrest you too!" The African descent task force brought Uncle Dontay from his bedroom. Uncle Dontay sees G-Mama and starts yelling, "Let my Mama go! She didn't do anything!" The Caucasian task forced yelled, "She resisted arrest, and you're both under arrest." The task force starting walking G-Mama and Uncle Dontay out of the apartment to take them to jail. Ms. Mylene asked G-Mama "Who can I call? Give me a telephone number." G-Mama told her to go get her purse and call her daughter Stacy. Ms. Mylene rushed home and called Aunt Stacy. Aunt Stacy rushed to Ms. Mylene apartment and picked up G-Mama purse and got the details of the arrest. When G-Mama returned home she thanked Ms. Mylene and told her she was a good neighbor. G-Mama filed a lawsuit against the San Francisco Police Department and Ms. Mylene was her witness. As I headed over to G-Mama new apartment on Eddy Street, because the house located on Turk Street had caught on fire a while back because somebody had thrown a cigarette into a vacant house next door. As an adult, I found out that the fire was the result of arson. The word on the street was a developer that was building a large condominium apartment complex next to the vacant house ran out of lootchi and couldn't complete the project, so he had the complex torched for the insurance money. Uncle Dontay came home late that night and saw the fire and was able to pull the whole family out of the house before it burned down.

Chapter 38

Who Would I Be If It Wasn't For The Foundation

I'm taking Uncle Dontay advice and I'm headed over to G-Mama new apartment; when she saw me, she smiled and said, "Hey fella, what happened to you? You been fighting with some girl? Why you have all those scratches on your neck and face?" I started crying again. After I told G-Mama she decided to call mom and all I heard was mom say to G-Mama, "No mom, just stay out of it, he hit me and I already have the police looking for him. I'll just tell them that he's over at your place." G-Mama hung up the phone. I told her that mom was telling a story. Growing up around G-Mama she didn't let us just say anything, so, to say that my mom was "telling a lie" would be grounds to get that broomstick beating. G-Mama didn't allow us to say the word lie or to speak with bad words. I said, "I didn't hit her, I only pushed her because she came in my face and scratched me up." G-Mama said, "Well fella, you're welcome to stay here but your mom has the police on their way to come and arrest you." I didn't want to put G-Mama in the middle of what mom, and I were going through so I told her I would just leave but thank you. I asked for some lootchi because I only had a few dollars to my name, G-Mama gave me $20 and said I could come over anytime for food if I got hungry. When I was walking out the door, G-Mama said, "You need to talk to your mom." I gave her a kiss on the cheek and left. I didn't really have too many options at this point since my lootchi was left at mom apartment due to how quick I was trying to escape. G-Mama was truly my everything. She made me feel beautiful in this ugly world I was stuck in and cared for me. She treated me more like her son than her grandson.

Every time I cried or felt like I couldn't go on any longer, G-mama knew what to say to me, and how to reach me. She just knew how to make me smile. I will always cherish those moments because all my life I never felt a part of the family. Regardless of what was going on in my life… I always called her and acknowledged her to let her know how much she meant to me. In 2011, I planned a surprise trip to visit her because at this point, I'm actually living in Toronto Canada, married to a Canadian woman, and wanted G-Mama to see that I'm trying my best to not throw my life away. A few months in advance I said to my wife I want her to come with me to California so she could meet G-Mama. The plan was to just show up un-announced at G-Mama doorstep with gifts and for her to meet my wife and tell me what she thought about her. I was so full of passion and excitement because I really wanted to have that moment with G-mama. I had 14 days left and counting before lifting off on the airplane. I get a call from my sister Naomi that G-Mama had passed away. I took it very hard; I'm still effected. I always wondered why, when I have good intentions on being happy and making other people happy, it never goes as planned? I began to question my life and why I can never be happy? All I wanted to do is have a happy moment with my grandmother, who was my everything, the one person who was responsible for providing me with a warm heart in this cold world. The one person that helped me with dealing with my mom, family, gang wars, drugs, and just overall survival… the one person who never judged me or exiled me. I just wanted to give back the gifts she gave me, and to show my appreciation, and to let her see the success I became. I will always cherish G-Mama like no other person because she knew how to reach me, when everybody else gave up on me and put me down, she always said "Hey fella, you need anything, how are you doing?"

Chapter 39

First To Stick That Blade In Your Back . . . You Gussed It Family

RETURNING TO THE night my mom had me arrested. Since G-Mama lived next door to Romel, I decided to pay him a visit, so I could at least be in a fun environment and take my mind off all the drama that I endured with mom. I spent the whole day and night over there. They asked what happened to my face, but I just changed the subject. I loved being over at Romel family apartment because they treated me more like a member of their family than my very own. I had brothers to play fight with and we competed on video games. I even helped around the house by taking out the trash and helping their mother, Ms. Mylene, who I began to view as my mom as well. Ms. Mylene stood at 5 feet 5 inches with beautiful, slanted eyes, and creamy complexion that looked Polynesian. Her hair was real thick but fine at the same time, and a smile out of this world. Ms. Mylene was shapely but a little stocky as well and when she spoke it was a delight to hear, minus when she started cussing. When she needed to address an issue with you, she could do it without raising her voice and you still respected her. She was a real nurturing woman. As the night was coming to an end, Ms. Mylene received a call from my mom asking about my whereabouts with out me knowing. Now keep in mind these women never uttered one word to one another, because of Mr. Marcel. My mom had the audacity to call like they were girlfriends who get mani and pedi's every other Saturday. She asked Ms. Mylene to not inform me that she was coming to get me. There was a knock at the door; Romel mom asked, "Who is it?" It was my mom. She asked in the softest voice possible, "Hi is my son LaPonne here?" The whole scene was crazy.

I was with a family that actually showed me love, and there was my biological mom at the door with two police officers.

As soon as she saw me, she told the cops "There he go." We were only on the first floor, so I thought about just jumping out the window, but a Christmas tree was blocking the window and I was stuck. The fuzz (cops) handcuffed me while everyone was looking at me in a state of shock. Nobody knew what was going on except for my mom, the cops, and me. Mom had been playing the victim role and playing it very well. The officers put me in the police car and mom whispered in my ear, "See La Ponne, you have to respect me, I'm your mom." With all the anger that was steaming through my veins…mixed with a little bit of hate, I yelled, "YOU NOT MY MOM!!! What kind of mom does this to her child?" The officer tried to make the situation better by saying, "You seem like a good kid, and I have your football picture right here." I just sat in the back seat looking at that vindictive look on my mom face. The police dropped her off at her apartment, as she was getting ready to go inside, I asked, " Can I at least see my sisters, for the last time before I go to jail?" Mom gave me this real cold look and said, "I'm not going to let them see you like this!" It broke my heart and tore me into shreds. To know that so much hate and evil lived inside the woman who gave birth to me, that she would deny me the right to see my sisters. This made me feel like there was no reason left for me to live. After the cops dropped mom off at home, they took me to Y.G.C. (Youth Guidance Center), which was a jailhouse for minors. I had to be taken to the Receiving Unit to get booked and processed. Captain Partez ran my prints, and it showed my 211-felony charge as well as some other misdemeanour charges. For him to be a Captain he was real short but carried himself big.

Chapter 40

Emotionally Dark & Heart Shattered While In Shackles

HE STOOD AT 5 feet 2 inches, real chubby, with a bushy moustache; he lost his hair at the top but had 8 strings of hair that he brushed over the bald area. He wore these big glasses like he was an inventor from the 1800's and he filled the lenses with big blue eyes. His teeth were stained like he drank 15 cups of coffee per day. He looked at me with his coffee-stained teeth and said, "It says here you put your hands on your mother?" Before I could even reply, he turned his attention to an officer and yelled, "Get Him Out of Here!" I felt like a hundred razor blades were slicing my heart. The officer took me to get my jail uniform, toiletries, towels, pillow, sheets, and a cover. He told me to hit the shower. As I was going towards the shower, I heard a familiar voice, I looked around the corner it was O.C.O. (Out of Control Ozzie); he was from the O.C. projects. O.C.O. stood at maybe 5 feet 11 inches, his skin was dark, and his facial features were very strong like the African warrior Shaka Zulu, his nose and lips were very thick and shapely, his teeth were pearly white, he had a Jeri curl that was halfway to his shoulder. Ozzie's body type was thin but very strong at the same time, he had a serious personality and made sure people respected him. When he spoke, it was with a low tone but with force. He was one of those dudes who could charm the pants off you and still be a cold-hearted killer. I was a gangsta but O.C.O. was on some other level.

I remember seeing him like two weeks prior because I had been looking for some dude who had been throwing dirt on my name and saying I'm never consistently around in the streets and that he was indirectly calling me a coward. O.C.O. was the one that told me about this person who was speaking reckless about me. His name was Boo (R.I.P.), he was about 6 feet 2 inches tall, real skinny and had a whiney voice, and he always sucked his thumb like a baby. Boo would always have on the freshest gear. When I went to confront him, he said, "Ponne, you know it was nothing like that." But we all knew he was lying. I figured if he could only stick his chest out and talk about me when I was not around then, it was not worth me digging in his chest; plus, I knew O.C.O. had to be like Ponne is sick, he went to another gang set solo to fight another dude on his own turf. Me and O.C.O. talked about that story while we were in the showers. He asked what I was in there for, and I told him that me and my mom got into a fight, and she had the cops track me down and arrest me. I was still real hurt about the whole situation, but I knew better than to start crying in front of O.C.O. He heard the story he was like, "But that's your mom though." I was like "I DON'T GIVE A F**K! I wish she would hurry up and die." I couldn't believe that even he thought I was in the wrong. It was one thing for the cops to take mom side, but not him, of all people. He had so much dirt under his nails you swore he planted tomatoes all his life. We chopped it up for a little bit more and then we went to our bunks for lights out. I was laying down on my bunk trying to figure out how everything got to this point with mom and me. All I could think about was my sisters; I tried so hard to forget about what happened, but nothing worked. Finally, I just broke down into tears. I had a one level bed, so I didn't have to worry about having a cellmate.

Chapter 41

Don't Nobody Care About What Your Mom Did You In Jail Fool

THE NEXT MORNING, I didn't know what to expect so I had my war face on since Fulton Street Mob was one of the most notorious gangs in the Bay Area. I knew a lot of our rival gangs would be in the same unit with me. At 6:00 am every morning, all the inmates had to line up for roll call to make sure the head count was the same from the night before. I told myself if anyone approached me trying to test me, that I was going to knock their f****** front teeth out. Not only did I have to condition my knuckles, but I also disciplined myself to be ready to brawl at any given moment. Breakfast was something I never looked forward to, simply because all they served was oatmeal every day, and I hated it. The only thing that I would eat was fruit and cookies and crack jokes with Vick. But since he's no longer here, I'm left alone and I'm feeling depressed and hurt about Vick committing suicide. I received a phone call in jail, and it was my Aunt Stacy, asking if I wanted to live with her just as long as I went to school and got my life together? To know that someone cared enough about me to help, made my heart glow with joy. I told Aunt Stacy that I tried to hang myself last night and she said, "Don't give up nephew; I will get you out of jail in two days from today." I began to feel like there was hope for me finally because I knew I had a reason to believe that someone really cared about me, or so I thought. Aunt Stacy had to get my mom approval for me to be released, since I was still a minor who was 16 years of age and still under mom guardianship. Surprisingly enough, mom agreed to let me stay with Aunt Stacy. She came to Y.G.C. and picked me up after I was locked up for 7 months.

Chapter 42

Never A Stable Foundation It Was Always Built On Quicksand

IT FELT LIKE I was in jail for 7 years. I was processed and released. Once I got out, I realized that the air smelled different, and everything looked real bright. Aunt Stacy was waiting there for me. When I was released, she had open arms to greet me with. I thanked her for getting mom approval for me to be released into her custody. While we were in her car, she asked how I felt? I said "Hungry!" She said, "I bet! Being locked up is not a vacation spot." I explained to her what all goes down in jail and how they tell you where to go and where you can't go, what to say and what you can't say, and what to eat and what you can't eat. On top of all that… you still have to deal with the survival wars between predator vs. pray." Aunt Stacy had only been driving for 7 minutes and immediately she informed me of her house rules." #1. Clean up behind yourself. #2. Do not have any of your guest over at my house. #3. Make sure you go to school. #4. Provide your own food. #5. Be in my house by midnight during the week but, on the weekends, I don't care." I felt real uncomfortable with all these rules, and I felt like I had to make sure I didn't do anything to mess it up because I knew Aunt Stacy would kick me out regardless of if I had somewhere to stay or not. I was only 16 years old with so much pressure on me to make sure I made a way out of no way. I had no job; I had to get back in school; I had to find ways to hustle some lootchi to take care of myself, and I had to think about how I was going to get back on my feet. I had no physical, mental, emotional, or financial support. I could be homeless at any given time. I wasn't trying to flip the pages of my life backwards.

I needed to move forward! There was this time when I was about 12 or 13 years of age, and I was running away a lot from my mom apartment. I used to sleep in other people cars or my partners who were selling dope, would rent out motels and have dope fiends or prostitutes come through to the motel to do sexual favours in exchange for drugs. I would sleep on the floor or sometimes they would let me sleep on their couch. In my mind I didn't want to put myself in that position again. I never showered regularly, nor did I have any home cooked meals. There would be times I would go 2 to 3 weeks with no shower or a bath, and with no lootchi for food, I would be hungry all the time. While Aunt Stacy was telling me her house rules, my mind started drifting back to that time in my life. To think that at any given moment she could put me out if I break one of her rules.

Survival mode kicked in real fast because I knew that the only person, I could depend on to not let me down, was me. It was 2 months left before summer was ending and I was determined to get my hustle game strong and get my feet underneath me, so I could get ready for school. I needed lootchi by any means necessary. The first thing I did was go back to Fulton Street Mob, my family and everybody was like "Where have you been?" I said "In Y.G. C." People were real happy for me to be out, just like the night of the earthquake when I got caught and I didn't snitch. I had people giving me hundred-dollar bills here and fifty-dollar bills there. I was so thankful and overwhelmed with the respect and love but, I needed one of these big-time drug dealers to front me some real dope. I saw D.J. he was this short Filipino/Hawaiian looking dude, who stood at 5 feet 3 inches, had straight black hair cut real low, tiny slanted eyes and a baby face. DJ dressed like a middle school student minus the backpack and wore a ring or two and was always high. He spoke calm and slow, and his money game was right.

D.J. had a few cars and was pushing serious weight of cocaine, in powder form or rocked up already. I remember I got into a situation with D.J. and I was the one who got caught and I took the wrap for everybody who was involved. I was in need of help, I thought I'll ask D.J. to return a favour and front me an ounce of dope. I said, "I'm bleeding out here and doing real bad; I'm hungry and don't have no lootchi to my name." He told me to meet him at a specific location at 10:00 pm and he would take care of me this one time. I was getting nothing, but love shown to me from the people in the streets. By the time all was said and done, I ended up having $300 in cash and was about to have an ounce of yayo to rock up. I would be able to make at least $3,000 to $3,500 off it. I met D.J. at 10pm on the dot and we hooked up. He wanted me to kick it with him and smoke a sweet b***h with him (which meant weed and coke mixed together). I said, "You know I'm fresh out of jail. I have to make sure I don't produce a dirty drug test when I check in with my Probation Officer." He treated me to some Brother in Law's barbecue restaurant on Divisadero Street. Since it was a weeknight, I had to make it to Aunt Stacy house before midnight. I ran to her house since it was 40 minutes away, but I made it in 20 minutes. I was running like my life depended on it. I said, "D.J., I love you for doing this for me, for real." He said, "You a REAL YOUNG N***A! PONNE" and we departed from each other. I ended up not having any time to rock up the coke, so I had to bring it with me to Aunt Stacy house. I arrived at her house at 11:22 pm. I came in quietly every night on time. I was never really there because the only thing that I needed to do was shower and lay on the floor in her daughter's room to get some rest.

Two months after moving in with my Aunt Stacy, one Sunday morning at around 7am; she yelled, "LaPonne!" I can tell by the way she was yelling my name; she had been calling my name for some time; her voice had this kind of frustrated 'I'm fed up with constantly calling your name and you not responding' pitch like my mom normally do. As I opened my eyes, I said "Yeah." She said, "LaPonne, I can't do this anymore; my daughter wants her room back and you need to go back to your mom." I said, "You know I have nowhere to go and me and mom have our problems." Aunt Stacy said, "Well, I don't know what to tell you, but you have to leave right now!" This was the main reasons why I was a little sceptical about moving in with her in the first place; she was a very moody person who throws a lot of fits. She wouldn't even let me change out of my pajamas I slept in. She just kicked me out. I was so thankful I had some lootchi in my pocket, I called a cab and had the driver take me to my Aunt Rasheeda house. Of course, I arrived unannounced. I had to be very careful because Aunt Rasheeda and Aunt Stacy had similar personalities. They would fight with anybody at any given moment. The only difference between the two of them was Aunt Rasheeda was skinny as a pencil. She had a beautiful bronze complexion and stood at about 5 feet 7 inches, had a nice grade of hair that she wore in a ponytail every day, with some beautiful full lips. Aunt Rasheeda had a real bad temper and loved to fight. No matter who it was or where she was. She was the one who gave me the half ounce of weed to sale because she was tired of giving me lootchi when I was younger. Aunt Rasheeda lived across from O.C. projects. I showed up at her front door at her apartment around 7:40 in the morning. I kept ringing the bell until she answered, "WHO IN THE H**L is it!" I said, "Ponne." I was crying and angry that Aunt Stacy pulled that "my daughter wants her room back, you have to go"(type of mess on me). When Aunt Stacy knew I had nowhere else to go.

Chapter 43

Hard Hearts Will Not Heal If You Can't Heal Yourself

I TOLD AUNT Rasheeda what Aunt Stacy did, and she said "That B***H Stacy is so cold! How could she do that to her own nephew, especially since she is the one that got you out of jail in the first place?" As my aunt was pointing out everything low my Aunt Stacy did towards me, I begin to build up a deep hatred towards her. 10 years I didn't speak to her and didn't care to hear anything that was associated with her name. Until year 2000, I was living in Atlanta, Georgia and somehow Aunt Stacy got my phone number where I was living at and left a message on the voice mail for me to call her. I played the voice mail back like 5 times because I was very sceptical, and the reason why is that my family only calls me on 3 occasions. #1.) Want or need some lootchi. #2.) Trying to start some drama or update me on some drama that happened in the family. #3.) Somebody had passed away. When Auntie left a phone number for me to call and said it's urgent, I had my defense up before I even spoke to her. Through the family grapevine the word was that Aunt Stacy had turned to prescription drugs and was causing a lot of fights in the family. My mind began to play back all the drama I went through with her, and to think now she's addicted to prescription drugs. I thought about it for a long time, and I began to have a heavy heart. I felt guilty because she did get me out of jail, and she was family, so I called her. Auntie answered the phone, I said Aunt Stacy "How are you feeling?" She replied, "I'm not doing to good, and I just want to get my life back together and was thinking about relocating to Atlanta."

She wanted to see if she could stay at the apartment I was living at. I kind of brushed her off and was like, "If you keep in contact with me, we can talk about it to see if that's an option." I never heard back from her, and I was relieved to be honest. I knew that my whole reason for living far away, and starting my life over in another state was, so I wouldn't have to dwell in my past or be haunted by it. Now fast forwarding 11 years later I see my Auntie Stacy at my grandmother G-Mama funeral in 2011 and we hugged, and I couldn't believe how different my auntie looked because of the pills she was taking for years began to take its toll. She was the one who was always impeccable with her style and had to have the best of everything. When I hugged Aunt Stacy it truly hurt my heart to see her looking like that. I really didn't have much to say, but to give my love. I was really devastated by G-Mama passing away just 14 days before my surprise visit. Aunt Stacy reached out to me through Facebook asking me to receive her as a friend 2 years later which again I was sceptical. I didn't want to deal with my past all over again. I really wanted no parts of dealing with my family, only for the dynamic to reach a point where we are arguing or physically fighting. If that wasn't what their motives were; it would be to manipulate to get lootchi out of me. I broke down and accepted her as a friend on Facebook, and 33 days later she passed away. A couple of days right before she passed away, she sent out this cry for redemption on her soul on Facebook on March 09, 2013. She wanted to make peace with Yahweh, Yahshua and The Holy Spirit and her family and friends. As I return back to the time of being kicked out of Aunt Stacy apartment and now, I'm at Aunt Rasheeda apartment and she's encouraging me to not worry and said, "You can stay here as long as you want; you are welcomed to everything just go to school and do good. She also reminded that whatever goes on in my house stays in her house."

Chapter 44

C-Moe Helped Me Not See The World Ugly All The Time

I STAYED WITH my aunt and her two kids Snuggles and Cuddles who were really cute; each of them had an adorable smile that was infectious. Snuggles was I believe 5 or 6 years of age and spoke very calm and a little deep at the same time, with a brown complexion, deep and impressionable eyes, black wavy hair that was above her shoulder and looked very girly girl. Her mom kept them dressed very clean and adorable. Snuggles just loved to smile. Cuddles I believe was 2 or 3 years younger, she had a light complexion they both had a skinny body type, but Cuddles was skinnier, she also had impressionable eyes as well, but cuddles hair was a little thinner and came to her ear. Cuddles had a lot of energy.

She was very testy but also like to have a lot of fun. They truly were some good girls. I stayed light on my toes because I didn't know if Aunt Rasheeda would switch up on me like Aunt Stacy did. Aunt Rasheeda had this boyfriend named C-Moe (R.I.P) He was about 6 feet, 3 inches tall, brown complexion with short wavy hair that he brushed to the side with an old school part on the side of his head. He was lanky but chiselled with muscles. C-Moe was a classic old school hustler with one of the warmest hearts I had ever known anyone to have. The relationship between C-Moe and my aunt was crazy love and volatile. When they would have physical episode and my aunt would be jumping in his face and putting hands on him, I would try to get in the middle to break it up and my aunt would say, "Ponne keep your ball headed a** out of it!!!" C-Moe and I became the ghetto version of 'Batman and Robin'. We were married to the game till death do us apart.

There was nothing that he and I would not do for each other, we robbed people; we hustled together, and got dressed up like two Mack's ready to tear down the streets. Meeting C-Moe could not have come at a better time in my life. I was becoming an angry monster from the core of my spirit. I actually got a selfish gratification from inflicting pain on the lives of other people. I was Mr. Beelzebub best servant because he knew that he could count on me to showcase destruction without remorse. When C-Moe would see me act that way, he told me that I needed to find a much smoother approach to the way I handled situations. He would take me to nightclubs where the age group was 30 and up. It was nothing but high rollers and pimps on the scene. C-Moe had 10 to 12 years on me, and he was very knowledgeable of the street game, but he loved how I was so young but wise. He used to always say he loved how I kept him on his toes. Being around him every day it allowed me to have a free pass to hang around different gang sets because he was an O.G. I soaked up so much old school game, while at the same time handling my own as well. By this time, I was back in school, and my mentality was, "I don't give a f**k" about nothing and no one! My number one focus is to ball hard and do things my way and never be broke!" My Aunt Rasheeda moved out and left the apartment to me. I stayed there to maintain everything. C-Moe and I would rock up dope there and make certain sales to dope fiends we knew. We would come in like 3 or 4 o'clock in the morning and be so high off coke and weed that we would have the munchies. We would heat ourselves up a couple of hungry man pot pies. C-Moe would act like he was some kind of gourmet chef, sprinkling different spices on the potpies, while crooking his right foot back and forth with a clean pair of K-Swiss sneakers on. I'd be laughing so hard to the point my stomach would hurt.

Sunday through Thursday was "Kung-Fu" nights at the movies, and we would go in the living room and watch it on the television while eating our hungry man pot pies. This was something we practiced religiously, and we would watch the martial art movies until we both were knocked out sleep.

My mom and I were still not on good terms, and apparently, she was not on good terms with Aunt Rasheeda and Aunt Stacy as well. I started to notice how both of my aunts wanted to get back at my mom and show her that my relationship was better with them, then it was with her own son. No doubt it was hard, but I stood tall and dealt with it all. I would hustle in the streets until 2 or 3 in the morning, and then sleep for a little bit and then wake up to make sure I was at school by 8:15 or 8:30 am. I knew if it was something in class I didn't overstand, I would pay some square girl to do my homework or I would put the pleasure pipe on her so she would do it for free. I never spent time on homework; the only thing I had to pay attention to were test reviews, which meant that a test was coming the next day. Here I was sixteen years old and balancing school, hustling, gang wars and trying to survive by not getting busted by undercover cops who was determined to catch me slipping. C-Moe became my number one guy, but he was having too many verbal and physical altercations with my aunt. It began to weigh heavy on me and I didn't have any peace of mind. The cold part about their situation was that my aunt would be more physical with him, and most of the time he was just trying to calm her down, but that was making her more vexed. She would be out of control. Several months had passed by since I moved in with Aunt Rasheeda, and things seemed to be falling apart right before my eyes. The reason I ended up at my aunt apartment with her and the kids is because the landlord tore down the other apartment that she left for me to stay at.

Chapter 45

My Brother's Keeper
Or Was It Cain Vs. Able?

I HAD TO move back with my aunt, and it was the same drama between her, and the boyfriend and I was not getting any peace. C-Moe and my auntie would continue to fight as if they were enemies in the streets. The landlord said we had to move because the building was getting tore down and rebuilt. I also came to the conclusion that my piece of mind was in jeopardy. I started hanging more and more over at Ms. Mylene apartment to see my brothers Romel, Little Marcel, Jim Burt, and my other mom. At first it was at a point that I would spend the weekends there and when I thought Aunt Rasheeda and the girls were asleep, I would come home late at night. Aunt Rasheeda got tired of me not really being there, saying that I was trying to have two homes and told me to get out. I wanted to be at Ms. Mylene apartment anyway. When my aunt said get out, I replied "That's how you go treat me?" I asked Ms. Mylene if I could stay with her, and she didn't have a problem at all. I was already staying there anyway. I introduced Romel to some of my dope contacts and we were going to take over the underworld, at least that's how I envisioned it. I was really feeling connected to Ms. Mylene. She was a gorgeous woman like my biological mom and had a natural inner beauty like Clair Huxtable from 'The Cosby Show'. Ms. Mylene was a great lady; I grew to love and respect what she stood for. Romel started hanging around Page Street and Hayes Valley Projects. My plan was to have him hustle in those two areas and I would continue to hustle in the areas where I built my credibility and still be apart of putting in work when duty called for me to gang-bang.

Romel was more of a ladies' man than a hustler.

He was a nice guy, who had style and most importantly he cared a lot about women and loved to sex females; they really were attracted to him. Women would say that he was a good lover because he paid attention to them, and they definitely paid attention to him. When I brought Romel into the next level of the game of hustling, I did so in mind thinking he had lootchi on his mind like I did, so we would each go in half on purchasing large amounts of dope. I was a slave to the lootchi, so I was looking to make a large profit for us. He would give so many deals so he could hurry up and get rid of the dope. We were getting into arguments because things were not going the way it was designed. It had gotten to a point where we could no longer be partners. Romel still my brother and it will always be STONE LOVE, but his grind wasn't serious enough for me. One time, I got so devilishly vexed at him that I cocked a pistol at him because of how nonchalant he acted towards losing our profit and not taking this hustling seriously. He was always arguing and cussing at me in my face. When I cocked the gun back, he said, "You betta kill me then!" I was out of control! To know that I pulled a gun on my own family, my brother, hurt me to the core of my soul. I cried to Romel, and I apologized because I knew I was wrong, and violated the code: 'Never pull it, if you not go use it!' I felt real bad showing that side to my family. I really loved my brothers and my other mom with all my heart. I was getting older, and my gang affiliation was becoming stronger and stronger, and I was constantly risking my freedom. The task force was raiding different gang sets all the time. If they couldn't catch you with their undercover tactics, they would set you up by planting dope on you to legitimize their arrest.

Chapter 46

One More Sale Or Trust Your Instincts Fool

I REMEMBER WHEN I was fifteen years old, and I came back to live with my biological mom to see if we can finally get our mother & son relationship healthy. I started working as a Teen-Counselor for the summer. As I mentioned early in the story, this is the job that brought me back to the hood that mom moved us from. My job was located at Ella Hill Hutch Recreation Center. I worked from early morning to mid-afternoon. I showed up to work every day at 8:30 am and left at 12:30 pm. After work I would grind from 1:00 pm to about 5:30 pm. I could only hustle for a few hours because I had to hurry home to clean the house before mom arrived from work at 7:00 pm. I made two dope sales, and something didn't feel right; I got this strong feeling not to continue hustling for the day. My instincts were becoming more dominant, telling me to stop; something doesn't feel right. I happened to look out of the corner of my eyes and thought I saw a couple of Task Force Officers staring at me with a pair of sunshades on, posted in a light blue Ford-Monarch edition car. Since I was not 200% sure that the Task Force was exactly looking at me, I sent my girl friend at the time Algeria to check and see if that was in fact the Task Force sitting in the car. I told her to page me 911 from the bus stop pay phone and just as I had imagined it was them. I had a half-ounce of crack on me that I was trying to get rid of before I re-upped. I gave it to my cousin Marvin and my pager very discreetly and told him to hold this for me because I'm being clocked. Marvin was a teenager; I think he was 18 but he carried himself like a grown man. He was well groomed; he wore his hair low with a duck tail in the back, had a nice muscular build but couldn't play a lick of sports to save his life.

Chapter 47

A Gentleman Or Gangster Maybe I'm Both, What You Think?

MARVIN HAD A mid-sized face (not too long, not too small), a shapely nose, medium eyes, and smelled good. He stood at maybe 6 feet 2 inches and when he talked it sounded like he was always trying to charm women. He said if he sold anything, he would give the bread back tomorrow. I said don't worry about the lootchi. I saw the 5 Fulton bus coming, so I ran and got on it. Next thing I knew the Task Force cut in front of the bus and pulled me off in broad daylight. The drug task force said that they saw me making drug transactions, so they made me lay face down on the ground in front of everybody and told me that I was under arrest. They started to search my pockets looking to see if I had dope on me but couldn't find anything. One of the officers' asked, "Where's the dope?" I replied, "Officer, I don't know what you are talking about, I work at Ella Hill Hutch Recreation Center as a summer Teen Counselor." I could tell they were real p*ssed because they shoved me against the wall and took the handcuffs off; they knew they had nothing on me. I was 10 steps ahead of them. At that point I felt like Michael Jackson (R.I.P) dedicated the song 'Smooth Criminal' to me because that's exactly what I felt like for that short moment until, my bubble was busted because of my cousin Tevin, who was on the same bus as me. Tevin was 5 feet 10 inches, dark complexion, had a long peanut head like me, big eyes round shaped and two bunny rabbit teeth in the front. He wore his hair real low. I guess he was getting off work from doing construction based upon the paint and dust that covered his clothes and boots. I believe he was maybe 23 years old at the time, and when he spoke it was real sarcastic. It just so happened he saw everything that went down.

As soon as the Task Force Officers let me go, I rushed home to mom apartment, to clean her place before she got home.

I'm feeling so scared and humbled at the same time, because I'm playing everything back in my mind while there's a sink full of dishes for me to wash. I just gazed down into the soapy water and begin to say to myself: (P.O.N.N.E.) =POWERFUL, OVERCOMING, NASTALGIC, NEVER DEFEATED, EMOW-

ERING). You just almost was arrested, and your freedom would have been taking away by the Task Force who would have sent me to jail; I would have done some serious time because I was already on probation for the felony charge from the robbery case. At this point it didn't matter because, I beat the system. Mom came through the door tired from a long hard day at work. I usually stay in my room because the first thing mom would do was yell at my sisters about their room not being clean and the house being a mess.

This was one of those times when I didn't want to give her any reason to say absolutely NOTHING TO ME! Mom was relaxing while sitting on her bed in her room. Everything was looking pretty good for me until, the very moment the phone begins to ring. I couldn't hear the conversation from my room, but I did hear mom say, "Hi Cousin Tevin! I haven't heard from you in a long time." I started thinking, it's not a good sign when mom voice goes silent. I knew he was calling to tell her what happened! For about ten minutes, silence penetrated throughout the apartment, and then I heard "LaPonne!!!" Mom yelled from the highest scale note from her lungs! I said "Huh." "Come here now! Tevin is on the phone and said the police pulled you off the bus and arrested you." I said, "They did but it was mistaken identity." Mom said, "You bet not be lying." I was trying my best to get her to believe me over Tevin, so I had to think fast; "Mom, I would be in jail right now if I did something wrong."

The look on her face was saying that she didn't believe a word that I was saying, but at the same time I can tell she thought; he got a valid point. What I said made more sense than what Tevin was saying. Mom wasn't going to let go questioning me that easy, "Why did you hide what happened? How come you did not tell me?" I said, "I didn't want you to start yelling at me as if I did something wrong. I was coming home from work, and they pulled me off the bus." Mom said reluctantly, "Okay, you better make sure you are being careful and go make me something to eat." My soul burned in the highest grade of fury that I vowed to never talk to Tevin ever again for the rest of my life for snitching on me. I don't hold a grudge anymore currently but, I just don't speak with him. The day came in December 2011, I saw Tevin at G. Mama funeral and I went the other direction, to avoid speaking to him. So, when my Aunt Stacy had passed away, I had the same scenario happen again. I saw Tevin coming towards me, and I felt like Yahweh was letting me know to free myself from that past anger and let him know how I felt. At first, I was resistant, but I thought to myself how could you be at a family members funeral and still holding to bitterness in your heart towards other family members. I decided to not give people power over me and to free my spirit and let Yahweh use me through his son Yahshua and The Holy Spirit, by being the example now and not the victim. For my family members to know that I'm very dedicated to make peace with my family and just standing on Stone Love. I approached Cousin Tevin and said," How you feeling family?" I said, "Do you know I been mad at you for like 22 years?" I told him why and he said, "What! I don't know if I remember or not." He was like cousin, "I'm just trying to be cool with family and have good energy around me. I'm not trying to be in no mess, so anybody I did wrong in the family, I'm sorry and let's move past it, because now I'm just traveling and enjoying myself."

Chapter 48

What's Worse Than A Loser? One With An Anger Problem

I APPRECIATE THAT, was my response. I asked about his kids, and he asked about mines and then we hugged, and I felt an emotional load lifted off me. Now going back to my relationship with my other mom and brothers was beginning to strengthen me. I was officially staying with them, and for the first time in my life, I had a real strong family dynamic, even though, I thought about my sisters and my biological mom a lot. It was a feeling that followed me through whatever I did. Like for instance, I remember when Fulton St. Mob would go to the local basketball games at Kezar Stadium to fight one of our rival gangs like Third St., H. P. (Hunters Point), Harbor Row, or Lake View because they would be the rival team that we played basketball against in the championship game. Instead of it being about basketball it always got turned into a turf war, which meant that their turf was on our side of town violating our space and now they had to pay the consequences for it or vice versa. I hadn't seen my mom in about two years, and although we lived in the same city, not one time had we run into each other. Whenever I would take a cab, I would have the driver take a route that would past by my mom apartment hoping I would get a chance to see her. After months of driving past with no success, at this particular time I asked my home soil (another word for my partna in the streets) for a ride. Although, I didn't expect to see mom, she happened to be outside checking the mail. I got so emotionally scared when I saw her, I ducked way down in the seat on the passenger side; my heart start pounding so loud I could no longer hear the music playing. To this day I can honestly say, I still don't know why I was so emotional scared.

I felt real sad about not saying anything to mom and not seeing my sister's, but I didn't have time to stop anyway, due to having to be at Kezar for our championship basketball game. Upon our arrival, we saw Lake View Street Gang go inside the stadium 8 gang members deep; we didn't have everybody with us, so only five members of the team were there. Nevertheless, regardless of the fact that we were outnumbered in bodies, in our mind, we didn't like the fact that these sucka's was on our side of town, so we rushed them.

I was already battling with a bunch of emotions; trying to process seeing mom after 2 years and not saying anything to her. I was totally off balance and ready to explode. The opportunity to inflict some pain on somebody could not have come at a better time, and Lake View was my target. I grabbed a folding chair and charged at a gang member named Blue Bear, he was about 5 feet 9 inches, chubby, had a long curl as his hair style. Blue Bear always wore a black hat that had Lake View engraved in red letters in the front; his eyes were bubbly but to me he looked like a blowfish. Blue Bear always wore a long blue puffy triple goose coat with fur on the inside of the hood. The coat was so big and bulgy, I wouldn't be surprised if he was trying to hide a 12-gauge shotgun in there. I grabbed the nearest chair, swung it, and hit him on his face; his nose gushed out blood. I snatched the hat off his head, spit on it, and threw it in the trash can. Pandemonium broke out in the building, and everyone began to run for safety. Fulton St. Mob was beating the living daylights out of Lake View. While Blue Bear was holding his nose; he was getting even more p***ed off. I saw two members from our team in a corner being kicked on the ground by 3 Lake View dudes. I came up from behind and hit one of them with the chair on the back of his neck, and I watched him fall to the ground, that's when another dude from Lake View knocked me down with a hit to my jaw.

I got up and was feeling a little dizzy. I refocused and a member from my gang hit the guy in the eye, and he also fell to the ground. I started stomping on his face trying to drive it into the basketball court. I saw pain and fear in his eyes and that made me stomp that much harder. I think I scared a member who was from my set because he said, "Look at all the blood, you about to kill him in front of all these people!" The police arrived and pulled their nightsticks out and started spraying mace on everybody. I started thinking like, here I go again, running to get away. Those types of battles were the story of my life. I was no stranger to warfare, and I loved to inflict pain that I had bottled up inside. I never cared if a situation was small or great, it was just an outlet for me to channel the hurt into a destructive action. When I was fourteen years old, I played basketball for Hamilton Recreation Center, which was the local gymnasium and playground. I remember this guy named Lawrence; he was probably 6 feet tall with the 'boy next door looks.' You know the kind of guy girls wanted to take home to mama. Lawrence smile was contagious so much that you swore he did Colgate toothpaste commercials for a living. Although basketball was his sport, he had a running back built, with calves that resembled the bottom of bowling pins. When he played, he could do a 360 dunk over other players. Lawrence was basically our coupon version of Michael Jordan. As a kid, I always had a competitive nature and wanted to be carefree and do things when I wanted to do them. However, the only time mom would let my freedom soar was when it was school, or sports related. I played on the 13 to 15 age group team for Hamilton. There were eight of us on the team who hustled dope but played sports in between. There was my cousin Damarcus, B. Shaw stood at 6 feet 2 inches and due to his hair people thought he was a mixed race, certain parts of his hair were thick and wavy, while other parts were puffy and curly (he had like 3 different hairstyles all in one).

B. Shaw had a brown complexion and eyes that made him look innocent and trustworthy, and he loved to smile. B. Shaw had a very competitive personality and was very good at all sports. He was respected as being a great athlete even though his body type looked more like a tennis player. He was a cool kid he never got in trouble and only cared about playing sports, which later in life, lead to him playing professional football in the NFL as a Wide Receiver for my Pittsburgh Steelers from 1998 to 2001. We knew he was destined for greatness. Another player who went by the name JB just knew he was a sex symbol ever since he was a baby. He stood at 5 feet 7 inches; had a real rich brown blemish-free complexion, a nice grade of wavy hair, and the body type of a chiseled wrestler. JB was a character and when he talked it was like he was laughing and whining at the same time. Terrell Jackson kept a real dark and serious demeanour, he had a dark complexion, and really short coarse hair that resembled be-be gun pellets because he didn't brush his hair. He didn't smile much and when he did you can tell it was sincere. Terrell stood at maybe 6 feet 3 inches, had a bad attitude, little eyes, and was built like a bear. Tyree Jackson was Terrell's brother; he stood at 6 feet 1 inches, his face was slim, but his forehead and jaws were puffy like a blowfish. Tyree wore a mid-size afro that he tried to put a S-Curl in himself but the way it came out, some parts of his hair was curly and other parts were an afro. When Tyree spoke, for some reason it always sounded like he had a stomach-ache, or he was constipated. Zay stood at 5 feet 7 inches, with a dark complexion, lizard-like eyes, and a chipped front tooth. Zay had a basketball star upper body built, but he had these skinny linguine noodle legs; he had a big alpha male personality, and when he walked one of his legs were bow-legged. When Zay walked, he led with his chest out but overall, he was a cool person.

The last person on the team was none other than a real good partner of mines who is no longer living. D. Sess (R.I.P.) he was all kind of people in one. He could sit down with your grandmother and be granny's baby; he could sit down with your mom and be offered a hot plate of food as if he was part of the family, and he could be in the streets too. If you needed him to come ride with you to take care of some dirt, D. Sess was always down. D. Sess never looked like a thug, he kept a clean cut, the way he dressed was very clean but with a street edge, and his demeanour was very approachable. D. Sess was a prankster, you know a jokester, and he played all kind of tricks on me. I will share a story later about our journey. D. Sess had a caramel complexion, and soft brown eyes and his teeth were slightly crooked. Although he was chubby, he could move very quick and was very agile. He stood at maybe 5 feet 6 inches but talked mess as if he was a giant. His voice was slick and calm at the same time, but he could get rowdy if he needed to. When he wore his clothes, he would always have to cuff his pants at the bottom because he was so short. He had a real playful personality and was good people. Now our basketball team is completed. Nobody took our team serious and underestimated us because we were a group of unorganized kids who were from the ghetto. Our Coach George was a Caucasian man who looked like the famous film director Woody Allen. His hair was salt and pepper and was beginning to thin out a little at the top. He stood at maybe 5 feet 5 inches; his body type was thin, but he had a little belly. His eyes were slanted a little; his teeth were dis-colored heavy yellow probably because of all the coffee; he was soft spoken until he really had to get in your behind. For the most part he was a calm coach who had great people skills. He didn't take any mess but was easy going at the same time. Since we were from the ghetto, people knew not to disrespect us, or else we would knock their F****N' front teeth out and stomp them into the ground.

We made it to the championship game, and we had to face one of our rival gangs from Hunters Point. We literally hated each other with an intense passion. We both had close members killed by each other gangs, so I was furious to know that we had to play against those marks— meaning "suckas." Before the game started, we rushed towards each other, and the coaches ran in the middle as well as the referees. They were finally able to get everything under control and told us to "take that animosity out on the court." That was exactly what we did. We did all sorts of dirty things to each other like, kicking the back of their legs when they tried to drive the ball to the hole and score. Extremely hard fouls and everything in between. The referees would call a flagrant foul on each team but that did not prevent us from trying our best to seriously hurt them and believe me they were doing the same to us. Once the referee realized that our intentions were not about basketball, he blew the whistle and said if we didn't keep our focused-on basketball that the game would be cancelled. We became more discrete with our dirty moves. The score was 45 to 38 in our teams favour when the referee started calling all kind of ridiculous fouls that was putting Hunters Point on the free throw line with a chance to catch up. We had been leading the whole game and now the score was tied at 45 points. There were 49 seconds left in the game, Hunters Point had the ball, so our coach called a time out and switched our defensive play call from zone coverage to man to man. Coach George was making each of us responsible for not letting our man get open and score. The player I was guarding was bringing the ball down the court when he did a crossover dribble and drove the ball to the other direction, his teammate who played the center position set a screen on me that freed up my player to make a play. The guy that was playing the center position was big, and strong and looked like a malnutrition version of Shaquille O'Neal. I blindly ran into him and fell to the ground hard.

Nobody on my team yelled out backdoor screen to alert me that they were bringing another player over to screen me, so the player I was guarding had a clear shot and made the game winner on me. I ran so fast and hard into the screen nose first, that it was nothing I could do. Tears started to fill my eyes because of the pain that was swelling inside my nose. They started yelling "HP! HP!" They were pointing and saying, "We told you fools", meaning that they told us they would beat us! I started turning red inside, so I told D. Sess that when they hand out our second-place trophies, I was going to crack one of those HP bi****s in the face with my trophy. I'm a person of my word and when they lined us up to shake hands to show good sportsmanship, I took my trophy and broke it over the eye of one of their player's. Chaos broke out immediately and fights were breaking out everywhere. I escaped away from the scene ran to my biological mom apartment. She asked, "How was your game?" I told her that we lost, and then she asked, "Where is your trophy?" I told her it fell out of my hands, and the base of it broke! Mom replied "Aww, LaPonne. That's too bad." How I ended up at my biological mom's apartment was because things were starting to fall apart in my life while living at my other mom and brother's apartment. I began to spend more time with my other mom's mother, who we all called Mother (R.I.P.) she stood at maybe 5 feet 8 inches and when you looked in her eyes you saw a sweet loving woman who was strong. No matter what she went through in life she kept this grace about her, and you saw this strong faith in her eyes, she wore a mid-sized afro, deep captivating brown eyes, and a very defined nose and lips but when she spoke, she sounded like a country woman slash Irish woman all in one. Her body type was very strong, she had broad shoulders and every-part of her body looked durable and tough but she was a pleasant lady at the same time.

Chapter 49

Thick Game Death Effect On Me That Twisted My Phschy

THE LIFESTYLE THAT I was living was no longer appealing to me. I wanted peace in my life. I didn't want to have to run from the police anymore and I didn't want to participate in anymore drive-by shootings. I just wanted to have that peace of mind that I longed for from the very beginning. I started thinking about a friend of mine named Tanisha (aka: Thick Game R.I.P.) Hardy who was killed as an innocent bystander. Thick Game and I would confide in each other about our bad relationship with our mothers and all the drama that came along with it. We would go back and forth about the pain we were feeling inside. There were many times when I would ride the 21 Hayes bus around nine in the morning and see Thick Game sitting all the way in the back on the bus crying about how she and her mom got into a terrible fight. I'd gave her a hug and let her know how I was experiencing the exact same thing with my own mom.

As she was crying, she told me that she had just ran away and had nowhere to go. I told her just to hang out with F.G.G.P. (Fillmoe Girls Getting Pumped) so she can take her mind off her mom. F.G.G.P. was a female gang who formed their own sisterhood and loyalty to each other. It was a way for them to have their own sense of family unity. I gave Thick Game a few dollars and said I would see her down at Virgo's. I saw Thick Game later that evening, and asked how she was doing, she said, "I'm good, but I'm real f***ed up though I was drinking my a** off all day." Thick Game said she was going to the movies later, but she was going to get her ticket early. In 1989, Spike Lee produced and directed a movie called 'Do the Right Thing' all the gang sets from my side of town were planning to go to the late show.

I said I was headed to the Kabuki Movie Theater as well. We all arrived at the movies, and everybody was making jokes about Rosie Perez the leading actress big chest. I started looking for Thick Game at the movies, but I didn't see her, after the movie was over, we all went back to Fulton St. Mobb only to see people crying and an ambulance in front of Patrice and Mannie Pooh's apartment on Webster Street. It was Thick Game lying on a stretcher with her eyes closed. She had been accidentally shot by someone who was trying to shoot someone else. Everyone was pushing the paramedics and cursing at them saying if they would have hurried "The F*** Up" Thick Game would still be alive. I just stood there, right in front of Thick Games body, surrounded by all the crying and chaos. I was just playing back our last conversation in my mind when we were on the bus together. My face and body were like cement; I couldn't move. I couldn't believe that only twelve hours earlier, I was telling her to go hang with F.G.G.P. and then go back home.

When her mom got the news, she broke down physically and mentally, and was never the same. The reality of me staying in the hustle game for life was coming to a drastic end. People who I considered to be family and more than just friends were getting killed one by one rapidly. I knew I needed to do something completely different with my life or I'm next! I needed more for myself, but I just didn't know what that would be. I was tired of the street life. It has been my means to survive for most of my life, so to let that go, was impossible to do or at least that's what I thought. So, to go back to expressing my benevolent love for my other mom and brothers, you guys just don't get it as readers. I literally adopted this family as my own because I genuinely have a deep love and respect for them and the way they treated me was something that I really needed in my development.

As time progressed, I realized that I was forcing the acceptance of Ms. Mylene love to compensate for the love that my biological mom didn't fulfill. I wanted that feeling so bad, but it wasn't the same feeling one would get when it's the love from your own mom, I had sunk deep into a state of depression. I began drinking all the time to the point that I could not get drunk anymore. I was mixing all kinds of alcohol together like: Old English Malt Liquor (8 Ball) with Seagram's Gin, Grand Marnier, E&J, a little Jamaican Rum with a little Donald Duck orange juice, and still couldn't get drunk. I figured if I smoked some weed and drank a lot of alcohol, then I would get high and be taken away from my depression. The next best thing was to mix the weed with cocaine. I remember when Marvin and I went to this boiler room that was downstairs from Miss. Mylene apartment. I had like 3 ounces of cocaine on me and we snorted cocaine from 11pm to 630 am, no lie! Right before my cousin came over, I had this dude sister who was a dope fiend come over to the boiler room. She wanted a twenty-dollar piece of crack, so she let me f**k her in the a**.

Her name was Constance; she was a person who used her body every day to get drugs with everybody because she no longer had any lootchi. She would perform all kind of sexual favours in exchange. She was a popular dope fiend. If she would have taken care of her body and her soul, she could have been a model. She stood at maybe 5 feet 10 inches, had a real nice grade of wavy black hair that she wore in a ponytail; slanted Egyptian eyes; defined nose and shapely lips; her complexion originally was smooth darkish brown but living on the streets in crack houses her body begin to quickly let go. The most disgusting part of it all was the fact that she was on her monthly cycle while I was sexing her. I had to be high as hell and out of my mind to allow myself to do something like that! I was totally out of control; I had no respect for my temple.

I was humping on dope fines left and right and would just give them a thirty shot of crack ($ 30.00 dollar of crack) and didn't think twice about the consequences for my actions. That continued to tear my soul down. There was a new dope fiend on the scene named Pumpkin who was a butta-head (meaning everything was shapely and beautiful butt-her-head). Her a** and legs were thick, and she had a shape on her, except for her face and hair looked like one of the monsters from 'Tales from the Crypt' movie; however, I didn't mind getting down with her, because she was a fresh dope fiend who was newly strung out on drugs and had a nice shape on her. She never cared about her face or hair only her lower body. She stood at maybe 5 feet 7 inches, she had big owl eyes, small nose, thick lips, but her hair was very short so she would always try to keep it wrapped in a scarf, with a couple of fake braids hanging out but, since her hair was so short the braids never stayed in. When she spoke, it was always freakish, and she didn't mind letting 4 people run a train on her all at the same time. I really was out of control with my life. It was as if, I was begging Yahweh to take me out of my misery. I was in a state of self-destruction. I believed nobody was in my corner, I missed my sisters; I felt as though no one gave a dam about my welfare. I began to focus more and more on physically delivering pain to others because I felt why I had to be the only one to carry these feelings of pain & torment. I would become even more demonized and refuse to let anyone become close to my heart. I became notorious for having one-night stands with females and then find ways of getting rid of them. I continued to sleep with dope fiends because I knew all they wanted was drugs and they would do anything I told them to. I loved having that control. I would eat at some nice restaurants, smoke a few sweet b*****s, and then f**k a dope fiend in her a**, sometimes with no condoms on.

I was never taught the meaning of safe sex let alone about the birds and the bees. I knew that it was nothing but the grace and mercy of Yahweh that I didn't contract H.I.V. or A.I.D.S. I was real depressed and lost. I remember one Sunday, my cousin Damarcus called over to Ms. Mylene apartment looking for me. Just a quick story about our relationship, my cousin and I were more like brothers, one could not say Cousin Damarcus without saying Ponne in the same breath. Damarcus and his mother Camile lived with my mother and I at one point. My mom is the oldest sister and Cousin Damarcus's mother is the second oldest. His mother's birthday is January 1ˢᵗ. my mother's birthday is January 2nd. Our mothers were kind of close but not like we were. When Cousin Damarcus and I got together, we would always come up with different schemes and plots to out slick the next person, regardless of who the person was. It could be our mothers, teachers, the police, you name it, and we out slicked them. Cousin Damarcus was 6 feet 2 inches with a bald head and baby teeth. His personality was real cool and laid back, and he talked with a real deep and slow tone. His skin complexion was real deep bronze; his body type was like a college basketball shooting guard. He had broad shoulders and a defined chest; no stomach and had a real strong passion to play professional basketball. The way he dressed was like a college athlete. His mother was somewhat like my mother, except she was not loud. Aunt Camile was very quiet and private. As I mentioned earlier in the story, but there was also another side to Aunt Camile as well. She was sweet but will cut any communication off at the snap of a finger with you. You would never hear from her again until she was ready to talk. If any of her nieces or nephews happened to be by her apartment and needed a drink of water or needed to use the restroom, she wouldn't open the door, even though we could see her little head peeking through the curtains.

One of the other things that Mom and Aunt Camile had in common, was when Cousin Damarcus and I had lootchi, they would always take it away from us. My Mom friend Aunt Simone (R.I.P.) was a supervisor at the San Francisco Examiner newspaper company. She got Damarcus and I a paper route delivery job. We got tired of our moms taking our pay checks so my cousin came up with a brilliant scheme that would combat when our moms took our pay checks so we could still have lootchi in our pockets. He was the brain behind the operation, I was the muscle and the fearless one that would pull it off. Damarcus had this idea that instead of delivering our newspapers to the customers, we would sell them directly to the corner store that was owned by the Arabs. Since they knew our mothers, it made things move along much smoother. Our plan was to take the papers from other paperboy routes and deliver them to the customers we knew would call in and complain about not receiving their papers. When our mothers would take our checks, we still would have lootchi because the store would pay us in cash and give us junk food as well. This was the day a true 'DIPLOMAT' was born. I've always known from a very early age that if a person threw fifty cents my way, I could get them to throw me a dollar. Cousin Damarcus and I were real competitive with each other from sports, video games, to who can get the most lootchi, to as little as who could get out of trouble the most. He was always the family favourite, and his mother was the cool mom, and my mom was considered the Mafasa of the family (you know S.S.D.) Serious, Strict, Disciplinary. Cousin Damarcus was the first grandchild/cousin of the family—there's so much to say about the history between Ponne and Cousin Damarcus, but back to the story. When he called me at Ms. Mylene apartment, I dropped everything and grabbed the phone.

Chapter 50

All It Takes Is One Person To Be A Light Mr. Belesco Was It

HE ASKED WHAT was going on with me. I said, "Nothing, what's was going on with you?" There was seriousness in his tone. I never heard this tone in him before. Normally when we talked it was never intense, he told me that he was tired of me dealing drugs, banging, and taking my life and driving down a dead end. He said would I do him a favour and just jump out the window, so I wouldn't delay my death. He woke me up with that statement! I mean he really got my attention, however, at the same time of getting my attention, his words hurt me all the same and I hung up the phone on him. I was already feeling depressed and empty inside, so the comments that he made about my life, only added salt to the wound and stomped on the last piece of my heart. His words begin to have me reflect on what I really want to do with my life. So the next day, I went to the Employment Development Department (E.D.D.) I met this Caucasian man named Mr. Chris Belesco (R.I.P.), who stood at maybe 5 feet 6 inches, had white hair, with a full white beard, and his teeth were yellow from the cigarettes. He had big blue eyes that always looked like he was always overworked; and his body type would be compared to an old, retired detective, who had been eating unhealthy food that clogs your heart for over 40 years. While at the same time he was not fat but was somewhat a little wide in his upper body and had a medium size belly. He was a man who had compassion for me and wanted to help me get a real job. Mr. Chris Belesco was nothing short of an angel that Yahweh placed in my life at the right time. He helped me get a job bagging grocery that would give me school credits so I could try to graduate from high school on time.

Chapter 51

How Your Life In A New Direction With An Old Compass?

THIS WAS NO summer job I was working; even though I was thankful and have nothing but love in my heart for Mr. Robert Hector who was my Summer Camp Director and he was the real deal. Mr. Chris had arranged for me to schedule an interview with Safeway Inc. I got the job for part-time work after school. I was so happy that Mr. Chris Belesco took time out of his life to invest in me, by showing me how to do a resume, teaching me how to interview for a job and some other key factors that helped me become successful even up to this point in my life. As soon as I got the job, I went to purchase a gift for him and bring it to him, but they told me he passed away and no longer was with us and they could not tell me the nature of his death. I didn't know how to feel. It seems as if the people I care for we're being taken away from me. I made a vow to always acknowledge him, even though I didn't really know him, but he took a chance on me to see if I wanted to do better with my life or become another statistic. I worked at Safeway for about a year and realized, I was getting fed up with the way people were talking crazy to me. They were treating me like I didn't deserve any respect because I was a bagger. I was cleaning toilets in the men and women restrooms, mopping the whole store, bagging groceries, and running for price checks for items that didn't scan at the cash register. I was really fed up, I was 17 years of age and although I was a grocery store bagger, I still couldn't let hustling drugs on the side go. I would hustle dope after I got off work and do some house calls to people, I knew wanted to buy a half ounce of dope or more.

My brother Romel would hustle in the daytime after he got out of school, and I would work part time at Safeway after school. We would meet up after I got off work and go over the plan for the night and see how much dope we had left and how much we needed to try and sale before we headed home for the night. There was a problem though, so at this point my mom and I got into another fight so I'm back staying with Romel and my other Mom and Brothers. They moved out of Fillmoe. Their new location was now close to my rival gang side. Romel and I would travel home late by bus, which was the 15 Third bus line. I didn't want to take a chance on being blind- sided and caught slipping, so while at work I carried a 32 handgun in my pouch with hollow point bullets, because most of the time you had to wait a long time on the street corner for a bus to come and your enemies could drive by and remember your face and easily catch their target.

My mentality was like if they ride on us, I'M MAKING SURE SOMEBODY MEETING THEIR MAKER! I made sure that I was never getting caught in a situation where I'm not able to protect me and mines. I used to carry a black pouch underneath my uniform, and I would make sure it was a little unzipped, so I had easy access to my 32. If anybody saw me at work or if we were going home and somebody recognized me, we weren't going down easy. Romel and I was on the bus going home, which raised the possibility for anything to go down. Rival gangs were located on this side of town, for example. Third Street, Hunter's Point and Sunnydale. Sunnydale was kind of cool with us most of the time because some of the people who were from Sunnydale a.k.a. (Swampy D) used to be from my side of town. Also, like North Beach Projects and Prince Hall Apartments, some of these dudes from these sets you knew since you were kids. Like this dude named Tony, he stood at maybe 6 feet 2 inches, light skinned complexion, his eyes were always puffy because he had bad allergies, but he also stayed in a lot of fights as well.

His hair was a low afro, and he talked like he was trying to sound hard, but it always came out laid back with a slight raspy-ness to his voice. He smiled a lot but had a temper at the same time. The way he dressed, was as if he was always ready to fight, like he would have on sweatpants and maybe a hoodie and sometimes you would see him with a cast on his arm. Then sometimes you would see him with a black eye. His body built was like an amateur boxer who never trained in years, certain parts were toned, and some parts were a little flabby, but overall, Tony had a cool personality and was adventurous and like to get into anything; so, we were cool for the most part. Sets like H.P., Third Street, Oakdale, Harbor Rowe, Short view, and other sets would drive down this long strip called San Bruno Ave. I remember one night some guys hopped out of their car on me and Romel and said that we look like some of those "Fillmoe N****s"; they said, "This is H. P. M***A F***A!" I had my pouch on me, which meant I was strapped but it was on the main street of San Bruno Ave, and we wouldn't have gotten away with it, plus they weren't trying to shoot us they were trying to jump us with 4 of their guys against me and my brother. We broke out and ran up a one-way street and kept running all the way home. We realized we definitely can't stand at that bus stop any more. I decided that if Romel and I got stuck in Fillmoe from hustling, we could always call Ms. Regime and get a ride from her. I let her know how the rival gangs jumped out on me and my brother and she was like anytime we need a ride just reach out to her. I just always felt her, and my other mom who were my ghetto angels. My mind set is that I can't be broke bagging these groceries and taking this crap from customers.

Chapter 52

One Foot In And One Foot Out, What Is That Really Go Do?

I STARTED ASKING my store Manager if I could get promoted to the Meat Department because they had a better union and got paid more lootchi, I saw this African Decent Man named Jeffrey, who stood at 5 feet 5 inches, and looked like he played bass guitar for Kool and The Gang or Earth Wind & Fire. He had natural curly hair that he wore short at the top but a little long in the back, he had a light brown complexion, and had this jolly presence about him. He always greeted you with a smile and this thick moustache, he had a chubby little built and was 40 years of age, he was always in a humorous mood. He was a Safeway employee who drove a Corvette sports car. I was still tied to the hustling game and gang wars, but I wanted to make real lootchi the legit way and not get these small crumbs at a slow pace and take a whole bunch of mess from customers talking crazy to me. I easily became dis-interested and felt as if they didn't want a young African decent man making real good lootchi; they wanted to continue to get that cheap labour off me. I know I just finish saying that Jeffrey was African decent as well but it's like when you young you don't always overstand why you can't have what you want, and you feel you have to fight for everything to prove you are deserving of it. I became real frustrated; I was back hanging in the street's real tuff. Great! My timing couldn't have been better, because now my set is headed to go and street brawl with East Oakland Set. Which was something we did every 4th of July. We would meet up with some Oakland Gangs at the Pleasanton County Fair.

Sucka Free would meet Oaktown and we would fight in the parking lot or inside the Amusement Park. We created so much chaos that the police would try to hit us with their night- sticks and spray us with mace or both. I remember one episode where this dude named Double K who was from Fulton St. Mob, socked some dude in his eye for hollering, "Felix Mitchell rolling. Felix Mitchell (R.I.P.) who was considered an underworld icon, a legend in the drug game. In fact, one would say that he was the drug lord of the underworld from Oakland, California. Many of us strived to take our drug operation to the level that he did.

It was compared to the Italians or the Columbians, and Felix was the one who reached that status. He was African decent, young, flashy, and ambitious, and did everything his way no matter who got hurt or whatever the casualty was. His "kingdom" reigned strongly for about six to ten years until he was caught by the feds and stabbed to death in a Federal Penitentiary. His legacy is carried out through the new generation of G's from Oakland. So once Double K socked the Oakland dude in the eye, everybody found somebody to match up with from the rival set to fight. I got hit from the back and then T.B. (R.I.P.) hit the dude on the side of his jaw who had hit me, and then I ran up and punched the dude in his nose. We were in a slugfest for about ten minutes. Cops were showing up about five cars deep and they were running with their nightsticks out. Double K and this other dude named C Mack was the only two who got caught from Fulton St. Mobb. We stayed and waited for them because our motto was 'no family member gets left behind' period! We waited forty-five minutes to an hour and C Mack came out, people was happy and then Double K came out. We all went off celebrating that Double K didn't get taken off to jail because he was on probation. We got back to our turf, but we knew the battle was not over.

Oakland and San Francisco had the same area code (415)at one point of time. We were a little better with each other, especially when we were behind the walls in the Penitentiary together fighting against the skinheads or other rival sets. When Oakland became (510) area code and the Oakland Rapper Too Short put out this song titled "Cuss Words" which had a part in the song where he said "Worse Than a Fag or A Frisco Dyke" everybody from The Sucka Free wanted Too Short head on a platter. I guarantee you if you come to "The Sucka Free" with that mentality that a whole city represents a homosexual lifestyle, I ensure you, that you would have wished you could rewind and erased that statement. How convenient it was some people from O. C. Projects caught Too Short at Santa Cruz Beach Boardwalk, which is an Amusement Park located in Santa Cruz, California. They beat him down and snatched the chain that was on his neck. The violence between the Sucka Free and The Town was very deadly, and it didn't stop. It makes me think back to when D Sess, and I got into a lot of stuff together. We would fight each other; pull pranks on each other and combine our lootchi together to buy large quantities of dope. Just to give a little more background on D Sess; he was always in and out of jail, he and I had a lot in common. We knew each other families; he was the oldest and had three younger sisters; I was the oldest and had younger sisters as well. We were approachable, clean, and dangerous. We both played football for the San Francisco Seahawks Pop Warner League. I remember one time while at Ben Franklin Middle School, I just bought a camping style trench coach, now this was one of the few times my mom didn't take my paper route check; maybe it was because I had to buy my own school clothes. I also purchased a Seattle Seahawks Knitted hat and some Blue/Gray Nike Air Max shoes that were suede. I was color coordinated and dressed for the rain at the same time.

I guess D. Sess, and his partner named Silence, who was real dark and skinny but had pink shapely lips and brown slanted eyes that were barely opened because he had allergies. He stood at maybe 6 feet 3 inches. He played a lot of pranks as well, but he was very quiet and low key at the same time. They must had made a bet that the next person who came up the stairs on their way to class was going to get an egg thrown at them and then they would run afterwards.

YOU GUESSED RIGHT? That someone had to be me, I was their victim! After I was hit with the egg, I was looking to see who threw it. Everybody who was around felt sorry for me except for D-Sess; I was so vexed, I called him a "Chubby b***h." Then I grabbed him, and he started laughing. I said, "Break open your pockets, you better give me the lootchi to get this cleaned!" He said, "I really wasn't trying to throw an egg at you! It was just aimed for the next person who came up the stairs." He would always challenge me because we were the same kind of people. He felt on girl's bodies. I felt on girl's bodies as well. I even did the same thing to his sister Tina. She was cute dark and feisty, which made me attracted to her. She had the perfect upper body and her legs they were long, which seemed to never end. She stood at maybe 5 feet 8 inches, wore her hair styled in a curl, and dressed very cute. She wore a lot of red. Her eyes were kind of slanted and when she talked it always sounded like she was laughing and smiling at the same time. She would fight you though if you messed with her. She tried to be real tuff, even though she had a real sweet personality. D-Sess and I messed with each other on every level possible. So going back to the story about the rival between The Town and The Sucka Free. I remember after that fight we had against Oak-Town at the Pleasanton Fair, a month later, D-Sess picked me up in his yellow El Camino and we was listening to Public Enemy's 'It Takes a Nation of Millions' tape and he pulls out a stick of dynamite. I asked him where he got that from and he said, from his "Chinese connection."

He asked me if I was down to light it, so we can throw it at those Oaktown fools. Knowing me, I was like I'm ready; I said, "Let's get them!" We drove all the way deep into East Oakland and a police car was on the side of us, as well as five other police cars in the direction that we were headed to. I said to D Sess," Turn down the music. We should turn around." He said, "Ponne, n***a are you freezing up on me?" "F*** Naw!" I replied. "I just feel we gone get caught." He agreed with me, so we turned around and went back across the Bay Bridge. Rap music was becoming more and more popular and eventually the voice of the youth. There were so many artists from the Bay Area making beats and finding artists to rap to them. Just like how you had everybody back in the day who thought they would be the next 'Super Fly, The Mack. The new generation were trying to be the next Run DMC, Too Short, MC Hammer, Huey MC, Rappin' 4-Tay, Kurtis Blow, L.L. Cool Jay, Ice-T, N.W.A., Slick Rick and Big Daddy Kane in the rap game. Furthermore, the rap music started to become the new form of hustling and many gangstas and drug dealers started to focus on getting their lootchi that way. Gangstas played a major part in funding local rap artists or just music in general, hoping to legitimize their hustle. It also helped to calm down a lot of the gang violence that was erupting on the streets real bad, because different rival sets would get on each other songs to try and expand their fan base which would translate to more exposure in different markets and more lootchi in the end. As I reflect on my life, I realize I'm still at a point in my life where I really don't know what side I'm standing on nor what direction I'm going in with my life. I just felt so alone and had to try and figure out everything for myself. I was still working at Safeway and not progressing financially.

I asked the manager again about me being promoted to the meat department, but he transferred me to the deli department, which I hated working over there and it only increased my pay by 75 cents more per hour. The manager, Mr. C. H. was very shrewd, with a no-nonsense type of attitude. He stood a little over 6 feet 4 inches; weighed like 250 pounds and looked like a cross between Hitler and Super Mario Brothers all rolled into one. Working in the deli department was a very hot and itchy area. The work area was so small it was hard to navigate around six other people working in that same department, while sliding on a greasy black mat on the floor, that would not sit still on the ground for nothing because of all the grease. I stayed in the deli department for about six months and realized that the manager was not going to promote me to the meat department. At some point I knew my days were numbered there. However, four months prior to me quitting, I started speaking with mom. Although, I was still staying with Ms. Mylene and my brothers, I never stopped keeping in touch with my sisters. My sisters were my world. They stayed on my mind all day and night. Even though I was not living with them, I made it a point to see them as often as I could. Even if it meant me going up to their schools to give them lootchi for lunch or buying them some clothes or shoes for school. As the days, weeks, months, and years continued to pass by, the pain of loneliness was eating me alive. I really appreciated my other mom opening her heart and home to me when I needed someone to give me that motherly compassion, but those feelings of me trying to ignore the pain I felt from my biological mom, begin to affect me stronger and stronger even when I tried to block it out of my mind. Romel and I would fight all the time, and my other mom was beginning to feel uncomfortable because of her being Romel biological mom, it created a lot of tension in the house.

Chapter 54

Self-Destruction Mental State
But Yahweh Had Plans For Me

WHEN WE FOUGHT, I thought for the most part, Romel and I were at odds because I viewed myself as the big brother whom he was going to respect. When you think about it, we were no longer just friends but family. I don't think I allowed myself to see it from Romel perspective, being that before I entered his family, he was the big brother and here I come along acting like I have been with them since day one. Maybe it just felt so good to be a part of a family that I truly loved, but I felt they respected me as the big brother when they wanted to, but my position was like I'm the big brother all the time. I start thinking that we really needed to get a car, because commuting on the bus or paying people for rides was not cutting it anymore. I brought a nice 1990 Toyota Corolla that looked like a BMW with tinted windows, a detachable steering wheel, and a sports kit on the body from a Filipino man who I worked with at Safeway named Dave. He stood at maybe 5 feet 9 inches and was very slim, but his body type was very toned, with a bronze complexion and a whole bunch a veins popping out of his body. His eyes were medium big and almond shaped; he had a bushy moustache and he smoked cigarettes like a chimney. His hair was jet black and he always looked like he never got enough rest. His personality was very low key and when he talked it was very serious at the same time. Dave always had a complaining look on his face, which in reality, he always did complain. One morning my family and I were headed out and running late for school (I was attending George Washington High School at the time).

I was already downstairs honking the horn for my brothers to hurry up so I can drop them off at school, while at the same time trying not to be late for school because I didn't want to have any problems with Mr. V., the school's principal. Mr. V. was no ordinary looking principal. He was tall maybe 6 feet 5 inches, a Caucasian Man. He had a nose like Richard Nixon, a belly like Santa Claus, and looked as if he was an ex-military reject who was mad at himself for not making it to a high-ranking Commander. I remember when he tried to kick me out of school for three possible reasons: first, I think he knew I was selling drugs at school but he had no physical evidence; second, I never acknowledged him the way other people acknowledge him, and thirdly, when it came to rival fights at school, he thought I was involved even though I would be far away from the scene before school security would come. Principal V. knew I was not just some innocent kid. He knew there was something behind me. It seemed as if he came to a conclusion in his mind that he had a clear view of everyone who he considered 'troublemakers' but he couldn't figure out why they respected me and wanted to be around me. In addition to all of that, I was also really cool with the security guards and was never seen causing any trouble. There would be times when Principal V. would try to take the lootchi that was in my pockets, saying that if I didn't tell him how I made that kind of lootchi, he would kick me out of school. Remember me saying that I always stayed ahead of the situation; I showed Principal V. one of my check stubs from my job that I strategically placed in my backpack for moments like that. The look on his red face! I could tell that he was getting sick and tired of trying to get something on me, so he could have a reason to kick me out of school, but he kept coming up completely empty.

This one time he did something that even I didn't think of; he brought my counselor in and said let's see his attendance record and tardy record. Finally, he had something that could stick. I saw Mr. V. face shine with a smirk and said, "If you keep missing days out of school or continue to be tardy, I will personally kick you out myself." At this point of my life, I had a world wind of emotions going on. There were so many different things dancing around in my mind that nothing seemed to be working out the way I planned. I was still staying with Ms. Mylene and loneliness remained a constant friend of mine. 'Troublesome' thoughts kept creeping up in my head like a midnight stalker. My mind was slipping into a dark direction; it was like I wasn't in the present moment. Each day seemed to be a repeat of the day before. I'm still downstairs waiting for the kids for about ten minutes and thinking about the warning the principal gave me if I'm late again for school. I'm in the car still waiting for everybody to come down so I can make it to school on time. I was in a hurry and put my foot all the way down on the accelerator. However, there was one problem, I didn't realize that the car was still in reverse, and I crashed into a neighbours Cadillac and then drove off. When I got to school, I received a page from (Ms. Mylene) letting me know to call her, she said that the next door neighbours called her and asked if someone in her house hit their car. It was obvious that someone saw me hit the car, because why would they even call and ask my other mom. The neighbours began to make threats that they were going to press charges against her for the hit and run and sue us for a host of other damages. Mom told them that I didn't stay there, and she didn't know when the next time she would see me. Pressure, pressure, and more pressure from everywhere was surrounding me. I felt like life was closing in on me faster and faster.

Chapter 55

Demons Of The Pasts Creep Aggressively At Night

I WAS GOING in circles with trying not to get kicked out of school. I was unsure about how many more credits I needed to graduate on time because I never took being in high school serious. The neighbours were looking for me to cash in on damages done to their car and if that wasn't enough, I had to watch my back, so I didn't get caught slipping by any rival gangs or arrested for hustling dope. The more I stressed, the more my problems seem to climb in my life.

I was back involved with cocaine heavily and would snort for several hours straight. After getting high, I felt real good and would start dancing, and just as soon as I started enjoying myself, my high wore off and I began to feel worse than before I got high. I was so pitiful that Romel tried to cheer me up, but it wasn't working. When he gave me a 50 sack of cocaine, I would go in the bathroom to snort it, and then start dancing and making jokes and feeling good. Again, it would ware off and put me deeper in darkness. I was so deeply depressed; I filled a bathtub with water and stuck my head in to drown myself. I wanted to die! I needed to die! I tried twice and was not successful. I just stopped and brought my head out of the water and dried off, sat in the dark and cried. By the time daylight arrived, I just laid in the bed looking at the ceiling. I was so tired of feeling the same way every day that YAHWEH voice played in my head saying, "IF YOU DON'T SUBMIT TO STRESS, IT DON'T EXIST, YOU CREATE YOUR OWN STRESS." I had to stop telling myself I'm stressing, I'm stressing, I'm stressing, I'm stressing. The more I said it the more miserable I was becoming. More negative things kept happening to me; more evil thoughts were coming into my mind.

Chapter 56

Forced Religion Will Only Force The Person To Disconnect

WHEN I TURNED seventeen, I made a covenant with YAHWEH and myself that I would not use those words "I'm stressing" because by me saying that it became my state of mind and opening the gateway of bad spirits to follow me and bring bad experiences around me. It would have continued to exist if YAHWEH didn't make me conscious of knowing I had to make some changes in my life and be more conscious and over-standing that YAHWEH is in control of everything. Having that as my everyday thought process, in my lifestyle, and in my heart. My willingness to want to change, I ended up moving back in with my mom to see if our relationship could get better. Mom and I apologized for everything we put each other through. I explained to her that I had a job working at Safeway in the deli department and I hated it. I told her that I requested to be promoted to the meat department and instead, I got transferred to the deli, and just like a religious mother, she simply responded be thankful that YAHWEH had blessed you with a job. Mom relationship with YAHWEH was apparently growing because everything out of her mouth was "YAHWEH this YAHWEH that." Her house rules were I had to go to church every Sunday, no rap music, no videos, and "LaPonne, you need to give me some lootchi while you are staying here, nothing is free." In my mind, I was like, 'Here we go again!' Mom with her list of demands. She would force me to meet the pastors at the different churches she fellowshipped with.

Chapter 57

No Power To Put Me
In Heaven Or Hell Yet You Judge?

THEIR RESPONSE WOULD be "Ooh! We heard a lot about you," I'd would just say, "Ummh!" Mom would cut her eyes at me with that 'I'm going to get you soon as we get home look.' I didn't want any more problems added to my life. I already had a mountain high of problems that my mind consumed every second around the clock. My focus was to make sure that I graduated on time. I knew that I had to meet with my counselor to find out all that I needed to do to make sure I had enough credits to graduate with my class of 1992. My counselor informed me that I had to go to summer school, take some extra classes and use my job to get more credits for school. Although, I was happy to be home with mom and my sisters, when the problems kind of decrease in my personal life and a little with mom, it picked right up with mom and my sister Naomi. I mean they would fight, verbally and physically. I remember one time when I was walking up the stairs to mom apartment complex, I heard all this commotion going on. I came through the door and saw mom on top of Naomi beating her and my sister was kicking her back. Mom yelled, "Don't be kicking me!" I picked mom up off my sister and expressed how we can't repeat the cycle that you and I been through mom. There was another time when I came through the door high, and the police were there to put my sister in jail. I pleaded with mom not to put Naomi in jail and said, "You see how it messed me up mom." After about twenty minutes of talking with mom, the police took the handcuffs off and left out the door. The relationship with mom and my sister continued to be up and down. Mom was beginning to force her Christian beliefs on me more and more and it just made me more distant.

Chapter 58

Where You From Don't Matter But Your Heart & Character Does

SHE WOULD TELL me that if I didn't go to church, I had to get out of her house. The first thing I did was look to see if my lootchi was still stashed in the room. All of my $8,000 was still in the same place, stashed deep down in an old box that was filled with old clothes and my sister's old toys, in my old room, in the closet. The quarter ounce of weed I left was there as well. I was attending school on a regular basis, but that didn't stop my hustle. I kept making house calls from my pager, regardless of if they wanted crack, weed or cocaine. What my customers wanted, I had it available. No matter what was going on, I had to maintain my focus. I wanted to meet mom demands, hustle, and make sure I was handling my business in school. However, every time I put forth my best effort, I seem to always find myself in a situation, whether at home, at school or in the streets. One day while at school, I was going to gym class and right before I arrived at class, some students and I stopped to mess around with each other, as we were playing, I saw Romel at my school and I was surprised because we went to different schools. Romel said he was there hanging around because he was dating this girl named Dawn, when suddenly some Asians were playing football and the ball hit Romel while he was drinking a cup of punch while talking to Dawn. His back was turned in the opposite direction from the Asians. The cup of juice spilled all over Romel when the football hit him. He was immediately vexed. He said, "You need to watch where the f*** you throwing that football!" As I was trying to pull Romel away the next thing we knew we were in a bull ring circle, surrounded by the Asian Mafia Gang.

They were known for jumping a lot of African decent people, and it was just Romel, and I surrounded by nine of those suckas. Then out of nowhere this person who looked like he was an extra for Will Smith the famous rapper turned actor from the TV show 'Fresh Prince of Bel-Air' jumped in to help us fight. I didn't know him from a can of paint, but it was no time to get acquainted, we had these chumps closing in on us. Then out of nowhere school security came and broke up the crowd. I'm from the 'concrete jungle' (the streets) so I learned at a young age to salute a person who has heart and is a stand-up person. I found out that the Fresh Prince extra name was Cashmuir. He was a free-spirited person, who was easy-going and loved to laugh and clown around. He was 6 feet 3 inches with a voice that was slow and calm. He was built like a basketball player and had that 'Taye Diggs' kind of swag, you know the kind of guy you can bring home to Mama. Women knew they didn't have to worry about getting shot messing around with Cashmuir because his grandmother made sure he had a descent upbringing. Although our backgrounds were nothing alike one thing was for sure, 'real recognize real.' He showed me heart, so I was loyal to him. Cashmuir and I went to summer school together and ended up having the same classes. We did so much together that, we tried to see who could 'Mack' the most females. He thought I was crazy at the mouth, because I would say anything and not give a flying f*** on what anybody thought, especially a female who was trying to clown me by not giving up her phone number. During one of our summer classes, we went on a field trip to the George Moscone Center Museum located at downtown San Francisco. We were bored out of our minds until we saw about four females walk into the museum. Out of the four girls, only one of them looked official and the other three looked like extras from Michael Jackson Thriller Video. Cashmuir said, "Those breezy's is checking us out."

I was trying to see if they were for real or were they just playing the pick-a-boo game, you know, checking us out when we were not looking and then when we look, they turn their heads in the opposite direction to make it look like they not noticing us. They kept doing it again and again. They did it for about forty-five minutes, so I told Cashmuir if they looked at us again, I was going over there to clown them. He didn't think I would do it, and when the girls looked at us again, I went over and said, "Why you peeking but not speaking?" Instead of answering my question, they walked away so I yelled out "Didn't we graduate from this?"

Cashmuir started busting out laughing loud and hard. Things began to turn around in Cashmuir life, when his grandmother who meant everything to him, passed away. He had unresolved issues with his dad, who had already passed away when Cashmuir was young in age. His dad was shot to death by a woman he use to date, and Cashmuir mother never really made his life a priority, so his grandmother stepped in and saved his life by taking him out of the hood and raising him in the suburbs of San Francisco known as the avenues. If you drove all the way to the end of the avenues, you would arrive at the San Francisco Ocean Beach. Cashmuir was really searching for an outlet for a lot of things he had repressed inside him. He started paying more attention to rapping and listening to different kinds of music that would spark him artistically. I started co-producing beats for him, even though I was trapped in so many different worlds, I always found a way to make music and be around the artistic process of it, which I loved (It's) "My Foundation". I was always fascinated with the process of creating something that requires you to take something in your mind & heart and bring it to life artistically by one's creative imagination.

Chapter 58

I'm Finally A True Chameleon
No Matter The Trubilation

THAT'S WHAT CAPTIVATED me about Cashmuir, he could freestyle a whole song about anything a person wore or about anybody and go deep with the description of different words that would paint a complete picture that you could close your eyes and envision, he was truly a wordsmith. This church that he used to attend with his grandmother in San Francisco, the pastor of the church use to date gospels iconic singer Ms. Yolonda Adams. For a short stint Cashmuir, actually performed on a gospel tour with her doing gospel rap as an opening act before Ms. Yolonda became the global symbol for gospel music. Cashmuir was a reclusive renaissance man, with so many gifts that the world never got a chance to bear witness to. Like I was fortunate enough. Summer school was finally completed and there wasn't a week that passed by that me and Cashmuir didn't hook up with my cousin Damarcus as well as B-down (who stayed in the same apartment complex as Cousin Damarcus). When we got together, all we did was play hoops so hard, we swore we were getting paid in the NBA. Our ritual was smoking weed and buying the latest hip-hop cassettes of the next great self-proclaimed rapper who would release their music in the record stores. The relationship I had with Cashmuir, Cousin Damarcus and B-Down gave me the feeling of a brotherhood. The situation with mom and I was still on uneasy terms because I felt more like the man in her life as opposed to her son. She made me pay her lootchi for living with her. I could never save any lootchi because she always cried the 'I'm broke blues' when there was no music playing in the background.

Chapter 59

The Proclamation Of Emancipation Within Self

I FELT MORE frustrated because I was taking care of the needs of everybody in the house, so when I needed to take care of myself, I had nothing left. My mental state was no longer about I'm just a 'gangsta' but more along the lines of 'there has to be more to my life than just this!' I was trying to make my way of hustling more legitimate. I started applying for jobs at temporary agencies, but my main focus was to graduate from high school. I would be up late at night playing back all those devilish deeds in my head. I was never able to get a good night's rest. In fact, for some reason, I would go days at a time when I couldn't rest except for when it was raining real heavy outside. I spent over 20 years of my life being haunted by my demons. They tormented me to the point where I would wake up in a cold sweat, while my body would be jerking like I was getting shot by an Uzi machine gun. I used to have nightmares about getting caught slipping without having a weapon on me. When I was sixteen, I said if I make it to the age of eighteen, I was going to run outside butt naked, shooting a gun up in the sky yelling at the top of my lungs out of happiness that I made it this far. When I turned seventeen, I was my own man. I vowed to never let a female get close to me because my mom made it difficult for me to trust them. They say that a boy's first example of a woman is his mom and based upon how the mom treats her son, will determine how the son treats women. The same thing applies to girls, her first example of a man is her dad and if her dad treated her with no love or did not build up her self-esteem then she would do almost anything to get that attention elsewhere.

By subjecting her body to be objectified. Regardless of if it's through being promiscuous or being abused. My view on women was that they were all b***ches and could never be trusted. Those thoughts were based on my experiences of observing how women could be sweet and refreshing as a sunny Sunday morning in the spring, and then, at the snap of a finger would switch and become so evil like Beelzebub lover. It really messed me up socially because I would sleep with a woman only one time and feel like as long as I did not let them get too close to me, I had the control over not only myself but control over the female as well.

Mom had instilled so much fear in me from a child and into my teenage stage. The fact that I was molested as a child by family members and that my kindergarten to 5th grade principal would always call me and my cousin Damarcus to the office and have us sit on his lap all the time. He gave us candy while he touched us in our private areas and our behinds and would put my hand on his penis, according to what my cousin said because I didn't remember. All these traumas didn't help how I viewed sex and how my hormones were out of control, or how confused I was in trying to love a woman from a healthy state of mind, when I didn't even have a healthy state of mind or knew what that was. When I didn't have sex physically with a female, I would masturbate until I reached the climax I was looking for. I would easily masturbate 4 to 5 times in 15 minutes and still have a strong appetite for that feeling. I was very compulsive. Even when I had sex with a woman, I always felt like it wasn't enough. The complexity of my feelings about not trusting any females with my emotions didn't mean that I didn't feel comfortable having a female sell dope for me or having one nightstands. I remember on May 28, 1993 (Friday) a day before my 18th King Day, Cutty Bang was like let's go see the movie 'Menace to Society' which was released on May 26, 1993(Wednesday).

Chapter 60

The Moment I Realized My Life Should Be On The Big Screen

I WAS LIKE let's make it happen captain. The movie was directed by Allen & Albert Hughes-their respective directorial. The movie budget was $3.5 million but grossed $27.9 million. It stared the likes of Samuel L. Jackson, Jada Pinkett, Larenz Tate, and Tyrin Turner as the lead (who was in Janet Jackson, oh excuse me 'Ms. Jackson if you nasty' Rhythm Nation video prior). 'Menace to Society' was coming off the heels of John Singleton (R.I.P.) movie' Boyz N The Hood', which garnered $57.5 million, which afforded Menace to Society the opportunity to be, green lite (which means New Line Cinema agreed to develop and distribute the movie worldwide). Boyz N the Hood was ground-breaking and really helped Menace to Society immensely. All the movie theaters were sold out in the hood, I was like "Let's go to the avenues" in San Francisco. We should be able to find tickets available there. We went to the pay phone and called the Coronet theatre, which was located at 3575 Geary Boulevard, San Francisco, Ca. As I imagined the employee answered the phone and stated that the late show has tickets available. We arrived at the movie theater and while watching the movie; I'm just seeing so many aspects of my life in this film. I was in a state of shock. I'm looking around and saying in my mind all these people who purchased tickets to my life, are sitting in this theater, who don't look like me and don't have my background, are sitting here with their jumbo popcorn and Slurpee's and are so captivated about my life and this is on the silver screen! I was mind blown.

I spent so much of my life ducking and dodging the destructions of the street life and trying to hide my background from people who would judge me or not give me a chance at a fresh start with life, and now it's being celebrated and supported. You can tell that the content was so raw to the audience that they didn't want to move. They just finished a large Slurpee and you telling me they didn't need a bathroom break. The movie was so captivating that they were getting pulled into a world they had no knowledge about. After the movie me and Cutty Bang was walking out of the theater conversing about the movie, and we saw 2 Sista's come out of the movie theater with us. They stuck out like a bunion on bad feet because it was no

African decent people in this theater. I spotted them and was like Cutty look. He was like, "Umm hmm, I saw them." Tameka and I checked each other out at the same time. I initially knew I better react in the moment or there was not going to be another moment. I conversed with her and stated, "You use to live in my apartment complex?" She was like, "You remembered me from back then, that was Hella long ago." She had a dark complexion that was Carmel in certain areas and stood at maybe 5 feet 4 inches and body type was a little thick in the upper and lower, to say the least she was cornbread fed; (you know a 'Brick House') in my Lionel Richie voice. She wore vibrant colors to compliment her complexion. She wore some yellow guess shorts in an overall style, with one of the straps from the shoulder un-strapped, which was the fashion at the time. She had on some bamboo earrings, like the iconic rap duo Salt-N-PePa. She had on Cross Color shoes that were Yellow & Green and her eye shadow was like a bronze cinnamon color which sparkled. She smelled really good! I hugged her and we talked a little about the cinema, but she had to go so, we exchanged numbers and I said I will call tonight. I know she didn't believe me.

Most people wait a few days to call a person to make it look like they not concerned if they speak with the person or not, but I don't play with people emotions. A person never has to guess if I'm into them or not or what my intentions are; I'm very direct. I called her and we had a warm and engaging conversation to the point we both didn't want to get off the phone. Daylight was about to come up and I was like, "Let's go out today." She said, "If I didn't mind meeting her over at her friend's house we could." I said, "Consider it done." Where we had to meet was literally 7 minutes away from where my mom stayed; off Page Street & Clayton. Martin Scorsese couldn't have directed a better scene. I went to get my car cleaned inside and out, so it would be smelling good for her. It was a 1994 Volkswagen Cavalier, and the color of the car was champagne with BBS rims. The sunroof looked real sexy with a light tent on the windows. I arrived with a bouquet of yellow roses since she had on yellow when I first met her. I pull up to this steep hill located off Haight and Ashbury and low and behold it's the legendary actor/activist Mr. Danny Glover's house. His daughter was friends with Tameika. She looked just like here dad. She was slim with a ballerina built, real sizable lips and nose, she was very intelligent but in a self-assured kind of a way. This is crazy because I remember mom just telling me a week prior, that she was at Cala Foods which was a grocery store located across the street from Mc Donald's and Amoeba Music Store at Haight & Stanyan. Mr. Danny Glover was flirting with mom, but she claims she didn't pay it no mind, because she was a born-again Christian. So now I'm talking with Danny Glover's daughter and Tameka, we talked for a few minutes and then I took Tameka to this Italian restaurant called Little Henry's.

It was located right around the corner from George Washington High School. I used to take certain dates there, because later on at night I would stroll the beach with them. Tameka enjoyed the meal, we talked about life and future plans, and we enjoyed laughter with each other. She wanted a bottle of some Strawberry Bacardi Dakari and I said, "I also have some blankets in the truck; let's go to the beach and play some romantic music and acquaint ourselves better." She said, "Look at you trying to use different words to impress me, talking about acquaint; just say talk (N*GG*)." We stopped at the store to get the drinks and by now, it's nighttime. I had rubbers already in my pocket just in case. Strawberries, 2 wine glasses, everything is going according to plan. Except for one flaw, because it's like midnight and we actually on the beach, sitting right in front of the water on blankets bundled up; we're shivering our tails off. I begin to massage her and kiss her and then caress her breast. Once I get to the breast you are under my spell. I was so tender with her breast but stimulated her nipples with my tongue, she begins to climax! I said in my head B-I-N-G-O and bingo was her name. I wrapped her up in the blankets; while at the same time un-buttoned her pants and gently slid her panties down, which looked very sexy, and she smelled good. The only thing is that I like to kiss a woman ear and her ears had splits on each ear lopes, which was a turn off for me. It's like taking off somebody socks, and you see they have 6 toes on one foot and 5 on the other. It just was an awkward look, but I climaxed anyway quickly, and we begin to leave because we been on the beach for about 2 hrs. As we were walking, we saw a pregnant woman lying on the beach. I said, "She dead." And Tameka said, "That pregnant woman is not dead." But of course, she didn't know my background; I can spot a dead body.

Tameka and I are going back and forth about this pregnant woman lying on the beach dead, as we got closer, "I'm like we need to go before they try to put this on us." Again, here I am still in my street mentality state of mind; instead of trying to call for help I'm concerned about us being African decent and young getting away from the scene, so we not charged with a redrum case (which means murder).

We standing over the body and we see blood and a stainless steel 45 magnum gun. I said, "I'm leaving!" we left, and I dropped her off at home and never met with Tameka again. For some reason we just started arguing over the phone from her trying to be bossy. I just don't vibe right with bossy, loud people. I went back home, and I just thought about the pregnant woman, and I prayed for her even though I didn't know what to say really but it looked like it was suicide. I really felt bad for her. But for some reason, I didn't feel anything for fleeing the scene.

I think because of what was going through my head was, how am I going to explain two African decent kids in an all Caucasian, Jewish, Russian, Asian rich district, finding a Caucasian woman, better yet a pregnant Caucasian woman, and trying to explain to the police we don't know anything. All I can think about was the more I tried to get away from death it doesn't want to get away from me. I was starting to see my life in a different light because I was getting older and maturing in many different areas. As the days were getting closer towards my eighteenth 'King Day', I felt invincible! I began to feel a strong sense of being more responsible for who I was and who I wanted to become. When May 29th finally arrived, I said "A king is born!" I felt as though my life was just born or maybe just finally had purpose. I've been in jail, pulled drive-bye's, had lootchi. I had my own car and my own apartment before I was 17 years of age! My life was still incomplete; I wanted more.

Chapter 61

Knowledge Of Your Culture Empowers You & Exposes Deception

GRADUATION WAS ONLY a month away I had to set up an appointment to speak with my counselor to know if I had a chance in hell to graduate from high school. Although I was much closer than I was when I first spoke with her, I still needed four credits from my job, and I also had to take a 'Step to College' course which would give me the other four credits I needed in order to graduate on time. Step to College was a program that gave you an overview of what the college experience would be like from an academic perspective. I went there and was nervous because there I was this street kid whose quiet and who did not feel comfortable letting just anybody get to know me. I met this professor who was teaching the course his name was Dr. G. V. He was about 5 feet 7 inches tall. He had short curly hair, and his face was filled with freckles. He actually looked like an island version of the legendary Grammy Award Winner Lionel Richie. The first time in my life, I was learning about how powerful and influential African decent people were in Africa, America and throughout the world. This information was mind blowing. One of the first things that Dr. G. V. had us do, was each day we had to grab a classmate hand and look them in their eyes and try to explain each other's personality and characteristic traits. That exercise was not only powerful but inspiring to me because it taught me how to pay attention and read people in any environment that I found myself in. Of course, I had my street training, but this class helped me to develop mentally and learn how to think critically and be more informed about the truth of my African decent culture.

I was so deeply involved in the 'Step to College' course that the professor recommended that we buy a book entitled, 'Introduction to Black Studies' by Dr. Maulana Karenga. Reading that book helped me to know who we were as (African decent people) and what we had as a culture; we had our own spiritual beliefs and economic wealth; we had our own cultural identity, self- taught knowledge, and most importantly, we were the 'Originators of Civilization'.

That's right we were the Original Kings and Queens of the earth and not some self-destructive, incompetent, ignorant savages that we mostly portray or get portrayed as. Once I finished reading that book, I had to do a research paper and it was so hot that the professor needed a pair of heat resistant gloves just to touch it. I had the top paper in the class because I did my own personal research outside of the book and filled it with questions like "Why African decent people worship a blond-haired, blue-eyed Jesus?" Another thing that had a major impact on me was when I had to do a report on 'The Old Ancient Egypt and The New Egyptian Rule.' With all of the new discoveries I was learning about African decent people, my mind was becoming more stimulated with compassion and concern. In fact, it made me take a deeper look at myself as a young African decent man, my race, and Africans at large. I begin to develop a conscious of not being quick to shoot or possible erase lives. I stopped hanging out as much as I use to and was not banging or fighting with rival sets as much. I looked at the world with a new pair of eyes! Being a part of the 'Step to College' program also helped me to realize that I shouldn't be so quick to bring harm to my own people; I slowed down selling crack to my own kind. I could feel the shackles breaking off my mind freeing me from my 'dumb, deaf, and blind state.'

Dr. G.V. probably didn't know how his class changed my life! I went from thinking like an 'animal' or an 'n***a' to becoming the king I was born to be. I did so well on my report on the Ancient Egypt and The New Kingdom of Egypt, that it inspired me to read other books like Malcom X, Harriet Tubman, The Soul of Black Folks and A History of African People, The Art of War, The Bible, The Qur'an (a little), and The Theory of Evolution. When I started reading the Bible, I was reading the King James Version, but after learning so much about him, I no longer trusted his version, or 'his-story.' I knew I had to go into deep dark aspects of knowledge to bring truth to light. I would ask mom, "Why she had a Caucasian picture that depicts Jesus on the wall, when the Bible said Jesus had a bronze complexion, hair of wool like sheep skin, and eyes that were fiery red." Mom said, "It's just a picture LaPonne; you need to stop being so militant." For the first time in my life, I felt like I had value and meaning. People who were strangers, would approach me and start talking to me about their lives. To see the growth in me in how I would show compassion in my heart, mind, soul, and even with my lootchi. I completed the 'Step to College' course and we had a ceremony held at Phillip Burton High School. The professor gave me two choices because we had to do a play and I didn't want to act in the play, (that's the shy part of me I never conquered). He said either act in the play or I have to say the introduction speech for the play, which was like five minutes long. So, I was so excited and nervous at the same time because both choices were very foreign to me. I chose to read the opening to an African Spiritual Hymn. I was so nervous to the point I was shaking and sweating under my armpits. I took a deep breath and looked at my grandpa, mom and my sisters and I began to speak.

Chapter 62

Grandpa Distant But I Cherished It For What It Was Worth

ONCE I WAS done, I received a standing ovation. Grandpa was very proud of me, and I gave him this African scarf that Dr. G.V. gave me for completing the program. He was the first and only person who took me fishing; he was the only person who let me use his car to take my driver's test. He was the first person that made me pay attention to how you communicate and carry yourself as an African decent man. Grandpa Burton was 6 feet 3 inches tall, slender built and brownish complexion but on the dark side a little. His hair was really fine texture that was soft, curly, low, and wavy. He always wore a fedora hat, that reminded me of Langston Hughes, a famous poet who wore different fedoras. My grandpa had circle shapely eyes that were hazel, and all his other features were not dominate. His nose was not too big, not too small; he had small ears but, had very long arms and legs and when he came into the room you noticed he had a quiet presence about himself. You would always see him with blue overalls on or a blue jumpsuit because he was a painter for the shipyard, and he also worked as a street cleaner. My grandfather Mr. Jewel Burton (R.I.P.) was born on October 25, 1923, in Center Texas. His Grandfather named Mr. John Carter owned 268 acres of land and that's where my grandfather would learn everything about working on a farm. Mr. Burton left Center, Texas with his mom at 15 years of age. His father was abusive towards his mother, so the father left, and it was just mama and son. They picked up and moved to Portland Arkansas for a short while, then they relocated to Greenville, Mississippi.

They moved around so much, because his mom could not find a good job, so they had to go where the job opportunities were. They relocated to Pine Bluff, Arkansas, which became the turning point for his life; that's where he learned how to build concrete, at the age of twenty. Grandpa and his mom left Pine Bluff, Arkansas, and moved straight into the projects of Double Rock located in San Francisco, California. He immediately found work in South San Francisco as a Concrete Builder. His superiors were immediately impressed with his work ethic. One day the company was short staffed, and the supervisor had to go on a 3-week vacation; the employer of the company asked grandpa to fill in for the supervisor until he came back from vacation. The supervisor came back off vacation and observed that grandpa had everything in order, so he transferred him to work in Marin County on the shipyard. He then begun to increase his value by learning everything there is to learn on the shipyards. Learning how to paint the ships, label them and clean them. Whatever was required of him, he did it all. He eventually worked for another company named Bethel & Steel back in San Francisco, which worked out better because it was better pay and was closer to home. He eventually got promoted to supervisor. He would work 12 hours days and save his lootchi for 10 years and purchased his first home at the age of 33. After working for Bethel & Steel for 15 years, he applied to work for the city of San Francisco, which was a government job that provided more security. Working for the City of San Francisco involved him cleaning the streets and anything that was required to help keep the cleanliness of the city. My grandfather went even further and was the first person in San Francisco to start cleaning the parking lots of grocery stores and collecting the abandoned shopping carts. He was so diligent in the work he performed; he became the most sort after contract worker.

He owned a couple of houses and had 3 Cadillac Eldorado's and paid for his two granddaughters to be educated at the top French School in California; he also paid for them to attend college as well. One attended Stanford, located in Northern California and the other granddaughter attended UCLA located in Southern California. One granddaughter became a lawyer, the other became a journalist and they both made grandpa feel like the proudest human alive. When I became 18 to 19, I would see my grandfather around different parts of San Francisco, and when we talked it was brief, but it felt organic; he would tell me how extraordinary his mom was and stories about how the women really paid attention to him and how he would wine and dine them. He told me his mom snatched him up and told him "ARE YOU STUPID, DON'T YOU KNOW THESE WOMEN ARE LAYING DOWN WITH YOU AND GETTING UP WITH SOMEBODY ELSE". She said, "You think you Yahweh's gift to these women?" She said, "Listen son, go get you that one wife and go build your empire." And he changed immediately. When Grandpa was back in Arkansas, he met this young woman named Mrs. Bobbie (R.I.P.) and each of their families knew each other. I really didn't have a relationship with my grandfather. If I did, maybe life would have turned out different for me, who knows but the reason why our relationship was not consistent was because he never made my mom feel a part of his other children's life. My grandfather had an affair with my grandmother while he was married with Ms. Bobbie. Mom feelings were that her father didn't really want to have nothing to do with her, because she was a reminder of the mistake he made. When I talked to grandpa he said, since my grandmother had 18 kids total, he would ask her for custody for my mom, but my grandmother would not give him custody. He really wasn't involved in my mom life until she got older. If mom got into a tough financial jam, she sometimes would call her dad.

Chapter 63

I Graduated, Did I?
Why Do I Still Feel Trapped Mentally?

THEIR RELATIONSHIP BECAME based on if mom seen him around, they would talk, and mom would try and see if he had some lootchi to give her. As the years have progressed, mom tries to do a better job of mixing it up with grandpa and not asking for lootchi only but by trying to communicate with him more frequently and checking on him because his health was beginning to decline. I was not able to continue a relationship with my grandpa because he kept being 2 different people with me. One moment we would be close on the phone but when I would come in town, he would not always keep his word to meet with me like we planned. He passed away and my mom and I didn't even know until maybe 5 months later. As I'm contemplating being able to graduate from high school, it would have been significant to have my grandpa there. I have successfully accomplished all that I needed so I can graduate from high school on time, I'm just waiting for June 15th to arrive, so I could walk across that stage with my graduating class of 1992. I started making big changes in my life and other people were noticing it. I had so many people in my corner at this point in my life that I never had before, they started telling me how proud they were of all that I was accomplishing. Yes, I was the same person, but I had more things that my life was associated with other than drugs and gang banging; although I still sold drugs, I limited myself to only sell to clients I knew well enough to make a house call; making lootchi was something I couldn't let go of so easily.

I went to have a talk with Fulton St. Mobb to let them know, that I decided to lay low from hanging on the block, and that didn't go over too well. They started saying things like "aww, that n***a Ponne trying to square up on us." They went as far as to put doubt in the minds of people from Fulton St. Mobb saying that I was snitching on people! And if, they found out that it was true, that they were coming for me. It hurt me to the core, that these heads would respond to me in that manner. Labeling me as a snitch was something I didn't ever think my street family would ever consider calling me, but I guess from their vantage point, they were wondering why they wasn't seeing me as much. I just kept popping up infrequently on the set, so maybe they thought something was not right. With that thought in my mind, I went to my double O.G. at the time, Jay Stone from Fulton St. Mobb. To let him know, not to ever let nobody take away my loyalty and the work I put in for Fulton St. Mobb. I was tied to the Mobb until my dying day. I also told them how much the mobb meant to me because when I had no mother and father to be there for me, they were all I had; after I said what I had to say, nobody said anything to me as I left. Nevertheless, no matter what those heads felt or what they thought, I was not going to allow their feelings to penetrate and kill my spirit for wanting something better for my life. I meant that to the death of me because something real deep was working inside me, and I believe it was Yahweh transforming me slowly, but he tested me to see if I would surrender to the voice. I was stubborn at times and Yahweh always punished me, but I begin to pay more attention to his voice. When I made the decision to make the transition from hanging on the block, I started to hang out with people who did not have the same street background as I did but with people who were real and squarer than a pool table with twenty-eight pockets.

Graduation day had finally arrived and so much was happening, my mom was running late as usual, and she made me late for my own graduation. I bought a car earlier in the year and mom drove it on the day of graduation. As she was driving, a construction truck hit us and dragged the car, ripping the car door from the driver's side back door to the front. I was so infuriated beyond words because mom was driving, and I didn't have any car insurance and the car was registered in my name. I had to let the driver go without reporting it because I had no insurance. We had to go and pick up my tuxedo and I had to change into my snow-white tuxedo with a purple bow tie and cummerbund and purple suede shoes. I was the cleanest "G" in the whole school. When the ceremony started and they called my name to receive my diploma, as I walked across the stage, I pumped my fist in the air. I felt like I actually did something right with my life. Mom expressed to me how proud she was of me. My heart glowed because I knew it meant everything for her to see me, her only son graduate across the stage because like I mentioned before, she had to sacrifice her own education and help take care of her other 17 brothers and sisters. Mom never got the opportunity to walk across the stage and receive her high school diploma. Now at 60 plus years of age, she started going to Seminary College to study to become a pastor. I'm very proud of mom empowerment. After the graduation ceremony, I left and met up with a good friend of mine, his name was Pretty Boy Floyd (R.I.P.) he had a light complexion, wore his hair in a short high-top fade, his eyes were very captivating, deep, and almond shaped, and his ears stuck out a little. The girls loved him. He had shapely lips, a chiselled chin with a basketball point guard type of body. His personality was a little cocky, but he was down for his friends. He really loved his friends.

I headed over to his graduation, it was located at West Moore High School in Daly City, California. After his graduation was over, we headed over to different friends houses and ate a lot of barbecues and other types of food. We went to about 4 different people houses that also graduated. We just chowed down like there was no tomorrow. At Floyd graduation ceremony he had over 50 people who came up to him and wanted to congratulate him and take pictures with him. I'm mean he got so much love; he was truly just a friendly person and mom loved him as well. After we left the final house, everybody loaded up and headed over to the Cliff House located at San Francisco Ocean Beach so we could continue the party that night. We had a thirteen-car caravan. We were speeding down the Great Highway, when suddenly another car cuts in front of me that was not a part of our entourage, and the driver didn't stop but continued running through every yellow light, while I was following close behind. Then the driver suddenly decided to stop! By me not having a lot a space in front of the car, I easily could have run into the back of the other driver's car, but remember I still didn't have no insurance, so my only option was to crash my car into the highway divider. The crazy thing about me crashing into the divider as if I was some celebrity stunt driver from an action movie, we could have had a 13-car pileup! The GREAT HIGHWAY was known for car pile ups. I could have flipped over the divider into oncoming traffic on the other side! After I crashed into the divider I checked to see if Floyd was hurt, and he said he was okay but that his ribs hurt. No one was hurt! I got out of the car to assess the damages and the only problem was that the parking light busted on the side as well as some damage to the front end of the car. I was just happy it was not as serious as I thought, so I yelled at the car "THAT'S MY N***A HANK."

Chapter 64

Can Only Eat Off The Streets
For So Long, What Else You Do?

TWO ACCIDENTS IN one day!!! I named my car 'Hank' after the television show 'The Fall Guy' starring Lee Major because I was a fan of the show. My car was tough, and it deserved a tough name. We arrived at the Cliff House and the party was on until the break of dawn. We started drinking, bumping, and grinding on females and listening to music. However, after a while of being there, I was not in the partying mood; I think I was beginning to feel emotionally down because every time I tried to be happy about something good, I had accomplished, somehow or someway, my happiness would be taken away. I went home crying and thinking to myself, "Why can't I just be happy? I just turned eighteen; graduated high school and can't be happy." It wasn't like I didn't have anything to be joyous about because where I come from boys were hardly even making it to the age of fifth teen. Imagine making it to high school and on top of that graduating. I couldn't overstand where these emotions were coming from and why I felt so sad, maybe it had to do with the fact that I struggled all my life trying to find out who I was and now that I was officially a man, even though I always had the responsibilities as a man since the age of 10, I really needed to be a man more then ever now. I didn't have any plans to go to college because I couldn't see past my street life or my battered childhood, which left me torn and confused. I never wanted anybody to be close to me because I didn't trust his or her motives.

Mom was constantly screaming at me about how I needed to help her out in the house paying more bills, go to church, do not play no rap music or music videos in her house. I had gotten to the point of being sick and tired of all the mess that was going on that I just wanted out! Out of my moms house and out of the deli department at Safeway because they never did promote me to the Meat Department. I believed in my heart that they were not going to give a project kid like me that type of promotion. I would have been earning $25 an hour to start with and as an eighteen-year-old that's considered real good lootchi. The Store Manager Mr. C. H. was just stringing me along to keep me in the Deli Department or bagging groceries.

I was not going to be anybody's lollipop, no matter what I did to try and focus on finding happiness, everything kept getting in my way. No matter what I did right, it always seemed to go wrong. I had it with Safeway and enough is enough, so I resigned from Safeway. Mom hit the roof! She said, "You not going be sitting up in here like you King Tut and thinking you're going to get a free ride around here." She could be so cold at times. I just thought about how much she gets underneath my skin. I didn't know what my next move was going to be. All I knew was that I needed to find some happiness in my life. I was tired of running away and living on the streets; I was tired of feeling as though there was nobody in my corner; I was tired of trying to legitimately create a positive livelihood for myself and at the same time feeling intimidated because I had nothing to hide behind. I knew people would look at me and view me as this 'ghetto child' when they looked in my eyes and judged me according to their point of view. I had made up in my mind that I was going to treat this corporate hustle like the street hustle.

I learned that whatever one pursues in life, he/she needs to find out what are the necessary requirements needed to apply in order to manifest that into a successful reality. Since the job market was not doing a lot of direct hiring, Temp Agencies were taking in a lot of job seekers. I equipped myself with the proper uniform which showed that I over stood 'Corporate America.' I dressed in a suit and tie, even if I was just picking up applications or just asking questions about a job position; I came 'dressed to impress!' For me, it wasn't that much different from the street life because it was always important for a hustler to show that the product, he had was better than what the next person had. Every Sunday, my eyes were stuck in the 'classifieds section' looking for a job like my life depended on it. I called employment agencies, no luck; I prayed to Yahweh to please rain down his Blessings and to help me. Mom continued to yell at me about not bringing in any lootchi and eating for free, which increased the level of pressure for me. I went to one Temp Agency named 'Personnel Pool' located in the Embarcadero District in San Francisco (the experience was so foreign to me). I walked into the agency and the staff looked at me with all sorts of scepticism written on their face (even though I looked professional). I felt like they could look into my eyes and see that I was a kid from the ghetto or a kid with a rough background. After seeing that I was serious, the recruiter drilled me with so many questions about what skill sets I possessed, as though I was in an interrogation room. I didn't have any computer skills, such as typing, 10-key or any other office skills; however, the one skill I did have was 'people skills.' I was gifted with being engaging with people and problem solving.

Once I began to speak, they respected my keen mind and my sense of humour. I believe that's what convinced them to hire me to represent different job assignments. I did all kinds of assignments that I didn't like; one of my first assignments was moving furniture for a furniture store.

I really hated backbreaking jobs because not only was I under paid but also, I'd leave work with every part of my body screaming like James Brown for taking it through so much torture. Mom stayed off my back just a little bit because she knew that I was trying to do the right thing, although, I kept my ears to the streets and dibbled a little in certain illegal activities. I would hear about people who were dear and close to me getting killed; and those that were getting sentenced to life in prison; and my enemies were speaking bad about me and were trying to find out where I lived, so they can catch me off guard and get at me. It was so much that I was trying to figure out about my life like 'Who I wanted to become? What do I let go of? Or Can I make it totally without doing anything illegal?' My heart was different by now and my mind became conscious of all my devilish deeds. The 'Step to College program left an everlasting effect on me; I no longer looked at African decent people as a race that had to live in inferiority but more of a culture of people who were enriched spiritually and who were the creators of civilization. The assignment from the temporary agency with the furniture store, only lasted two weeks and then it was completed which meant that there was no more work for me, which meant I had no more lootchi coming in. It was back to the drawing board. Three weeks went by, and I had no lootchi and no new job leads.

I continued to pray to Yahweh to please rain down his blessings upon me and let a job call me with a new opportunity. Yahweh heard my prayer because a week later, I received a call from the Temp Agency asking if I was interested in a job assignment with Wells Fargo Bank as a Data Distribution Clerk. My heart leaped with joy for two reasons; one, my prayers were answered and two, my pockets were no longer going to be empty. The job duties and responsibilities included processing everything for the banks so when they opened all documents like mortgage loans, credit card statements, investment statements were processed and prepared to be distributed out to customers and merchants before business hours resumed. I worked overnight to process heavy bags for the trucks to come in the morning time and pick up the supplies that were to be delivered to the banks. I worked extremely hard to make an impression; if they offered overtime, I took it because I knew I could not get ahead by financially just working the standard normal hours. I knew I had to go above and beyond to compete with what I was making on the streets. When I was hustling crack, I made about $1,000 on a bad day, so it was obvious that I had to make huge financial adjustments on how I would spend my lootchi. The fact that lootchi was now coming much slower than before, I had to start making my pennies make a whole lot of sense! The trade off with working for a corporation was that I didn't have to worry about a rival set coming to gun me down or the police trying to arrest or plant drugs on me. The corporate office had its own set of drama; people were judging because of my youth, my skin color, and because I was from the streets. I had these square a** people trying to test me because they thought they were better than me. They had their parents lootchi, which allowed them to have more access to resources than myself or because they had their college education and knew that I was uneducated. I never carried myself with a chip on my shoulder; I just didn't want people to mess with me because I didn't want to bring that other side out of me.

It was really difficult trying to move forward when everything was trying to pull me backwards. My assignment with Wells Fargo Bank was up after six months so I was back at the drawing board once again. The routine with mom was exactly the same so there's no sense in telling you what happened! Wells Fargo Bank explained to me that they were impressed with how hard of a worker I was but by me going through a temporary agency they had to allow sixty days to pass before they could hire me permanently. The manager's name was Mr. Paul, and he took a liking to me. He knew I was a young soldier who came from the struggle and was focused on doing the right thing. Mr. Paul was about 45 years of age who stood at maybe 5 feet 7 inches; had nice wavy hair combed back into a shag, with a full beard. He had a light complexion, with big green eyes and he was from Kingston Jamaica and when he walked, it was with a limp; and when he talked, he would always be observing and reading you deeply in your eyes like you were urgent breaking news. He was very wise and a smooth operator at the same time. Believe it or not, Wells Fargo called me sixty days later and asked did I still want the job, I said with all the enthusiasm I could mustard "YES!!!!! THANK YOU!" In my heart I truly believe 'Yahweh works in mysterious ways' I was just about to buy an ounce of cocaine to rock up and sale and Yahweh Blessed me with this job. I was always on time to work and could blend in with all walks of life at this time, I cracked the code. I had people on the staff who were racist, judgmental, snobbish, and spies who reported everything to management. I worked extremely hard and spent less time hanging in the streets; I still helped younger hustlers out by fronting them a couple of ounces of dope to sale for me, so they would have some start-up lootchi in the dope game.

Whomever I fronted the dope to they had to bring me 70 % of the lootchi on what was sold. I took a liking to this young kid who was about 19 years of age named Damond, he seemed real bright and was just trying to survive like me.

Chapter 65

One Foot In Corporate
One-Foot In Dope-Game

DAMOND TOLD ME how much he struggled in life and how he was trying to work part time and hustle dope on the side. He stood at maybe 5 feet 7 inches, but he was built real strong and stocky, like an amateur boxer; he wore his hair very low because if his hair grew, it looked real coarse and nappy. He had big lips with a big nose, with big brown eyes and had a real big bright smile. He bagged groceries at Safeway with me. He also sold dope in the Valencia Garden Projects before he came to work, he was a strong hustler and could move the dope fast. This young dude really reminded me of myself; he had a big head and a fore-head that was like the legendary football player Ronnie Lott from the San Francisco Forty Niners. He was a strange kind of kid though, especially when he ate; he would eat chocolate donuts, Doritos Chips, and strawberry milk all the time; at no point did I ever see him eat a real meal. I felt comfortable with him, I continued to front him dope until one day he crossed me. He never showed up for work and did not pay me my percentage from selling the dope I fronted him like we had agreed. I told another associate of mine about how this young hustler was missing and how I was thinking he was trying to hide so he didn't have to pay me. The dude I told it to name was Mike, who was real good people and just wanted to fit in with the African decent gangstas. Mike was Italian and mixed with something else, but he looked Latin; he stood at maybe 5 feet 5 inches; loved to smile; had stringy wet black hair that he kept hidden under a black beanie knit cap. His complexion was in between being pale and bronze, so it was a combination, certain sections looked Italian and other parts looked Latin.

Chapter 66

The Company You Keep
Can Help You Experience Defeat

MIKE ALWAYS WORE black Chuck Taylor shoes and Ben Davis pants and Ben Davis jacket. And he would light you up on the basketball court. Mike was a good solid soldier and was loyal. Mike was like, he would kill Damond for me, if I wanted him to. I told him that I would burn his a** alive myself. We drove around Valencia Gardens Projects relentlessly for about three weeks trying to catch the youngster and could not find him. However, I didn't even trip too much because I knew where he worked and the day he got paid on. Even if he quit, I knew at some point he would show up for his last check. It was just as I had imagined, the young dude showed up for his last paycheck and I was right there waiting. I said, "M***** F****! You know how I've been looking for you to burn you alive?" He gave me some sorry a** story about how the task force raided this house he was staying at, and how he had been trying to get lootchi to me but was unable to, as he continued to tell me what happened, my angered simmered and I wasn't as upset as I was in the beginning; he gave me about $465 and was short about $900. As time continued on, I was not able to keep up with him anymore, to collect on the debt he owed me, so I had to bill it as a lost. I was always putting myself in the wrong situations; so, I wasn't trying to press about the lootchi that Damond owed me because, a couple of days before I saw him, I just finished dealing with another episode with the police. I had gotten off work, I got a ride because I didn't have my car that day, so instead of me waiting around for my ride; I ended up getting a ride with someone who was involved in a murder case. We were pulled over by the police and they ran our information.

One reason or another I had to spend a half of day in jail because they could not verify our backgrounds and they said we fit the description for suspects in a drive by shooting. I was worried that I was going to lose my job. I called mom and explained that I was in jail and I did nothing wrong; I explained to her I was with someone who may have been involved in a crime. She said, "LaPonne, boy when are you going to learn about the company you keep? You need to call your job and tell them you're sick and will be back the following Tuesday." I did exactly what mom instructed me, and I was released from jail a day later. The police had been questioning me about my whereabouts at the time these crimes were committed and come to find out they brought us in for being suspects that fit a certain profile right. I was sure that the profile we had in common was that we were all African decent and lived in the hood. The police released me because they had no evidence that could stick. I was released 24 hours later, I returned to work on that Tuesday like nothing ever happened; everyone was talking about how they spent their Labour Day Weekend, so when the question came to me about what I did over the weekend I just said, "I took it easy." No matter what I did to stay on the right side of the law, somehow, I always found myself tangled up on the wrong side of the law, not because of something I did, like for example. I remember when I got arrested on my nineteenth birthday when this dude named Jamal, who stood at maybe 5 feet 11 inches, who had a weird body type like he was wide and chubby in some parts and then he was slim in his upper body and when he smiled, he looked like the rat mascot for 'Chuck E. Cheese Restaurant'. He had a light complexion, with a whole bunch of red acne bumps on his face; he wore his hair low in the front with a shag in the back. He saw me on the road and asked if I wanted a ride. I didn't think much of it, so I was like cool after all, it was my 'King Day' I wanted some enjoyment, you know some excitement, so we drove around listening to music and then he pulled out some weed.

While he was pulling the weed out, he looked down for a moment and he ended up missing a stop sign. So, we got pulled over by the police, and then got arrested because the car he was driving was stolen and he didn't tell me. I spent the whole day on my 'King Day' in jail until 10pm that night. My emotions were twisted because I didn't know if I was more upset with Jamal or myself for not using better judgment. I began to cut everybody off and started focusing on surrounding myself with people who were going in the same positive direction I was headed in. There was this guy I befriended and coined his name The Show Stoppa who stood at 6 feet 3 inches and built like a basketball player; he swore his hair was naturally curly with a flat top, but I caught him one time with a S-Curl kit in his bathroom, he had real deep puppy sad eyes that were brown, with a brown complexion and big lips and shapely nose. He spoke real articulate with energy but cool and happy at the same time. I would see him at school telling people to handle their business in class, which was a lot different from what I was used to hearing other people say. It was refreshing to hear someone young pushing others to be more serious about handling their business in a positive direction. We did a lot of things together; we rode our bikes from the Ocean beach in the avenues too Pier 39 and every Friday Night, we watched martial art movies religiously. I taught him about the streets, as well as helped him with his manhood. When he graduated from high school everybody was saying congratulations to him, and the first words I said to him was "Welcome to the real world and now it's time to be a man." My words caught him off guard and he responded, "Like man you couldn't let me enjoy this." We became really close I was still working at Wells Fargo Bank making pretty decent lootchi. Mom yelling almost ceased to exist because I was contributing to the household expenses more. I brought some cars and clothes because I started to change my style of dressing.

Chapter 67

Experiences Won't Change Until I Change How I Present Myself

I REALIZED AT this point that your uniform, 'meaning you UNI', 'will form people judgment of you based upon how you present yourself.' I changed from my normal 'street attire' to more of a mature Wesley Snipes style from the movie 'Sugar Hill' with the brown leather three quarter trench coat, leather vest, nice shirts, slacks, and sometimes I would wear suede low cut Timberlands that were wingtip style, along with different styles of suede loafers. I always wore leather gloves just in case something dangerous went down or somebody was trying to threaten my dwelling space, I would be ready to give them more than they could accept. Even though I was trying to change my 'circle of friends' those elements were still in my DNA regardless of where I went. I devoted so much of my character and mannerisms as a kid and a young adult to the streets that it's certain parts of me, I just have to say, 'I am who I am.' At this point of my life, it was just about work and having one-night stands with different females from different ethnic backgrounds. I tried as much as I could to get into the mindset of college through Show Stoppa experiences while he was attending City College of San Francisco; I would also visit St. Mary's College that another friend of mine named K.P. was attending, just to observe and learn a little bit about that college experience. The way it worked was that some of their courses were open lectures and I would show up to the classes; although, I was a 'street dude' who learned many of life lessons on the streets, I did have enough common sense to know that I needed to add some academic skills to my life to have a balance perspective on how to survive in life.

Chapter 68

Too Stupid For College, Why Set Myself Up For Failure?

FOR THAT VERY reason, I tried to surround myself around people who knew academic things I didn't know, and I would share my knowledge of the streets and how to survive in any situation that occurred in life. My twentieth King Day was just around the corner and if someone would have told me five years ago that I would live to see my twentieth birthday on May 29th, I would have called them a damn liar to their face. Making it to the age of twenty was like dog years in the hood; it was almost like I was celebrating my sixtieth King Day instead of my twentieth. If death had not come to sweep a young man's life by the age of fourteen, fifteen or sixteen, it meant he was locked up doing life in the Penitentiary by the age of 18. If that wasn't the case, then that person would have been to jail at least seven times by then. I began to reflect on my life, thinking how I wouldn't feel comfortable in college. It brings me back to this time I was sitting at the table talking with Ms. Mylene when she asked, "What college was I going to?" She said, I responded "I'm too dumb to go to college." My response shocked Ms. Mylene and she asked, "Who told you that? Who would tell a kid that? Why would someone tell you that you're too dumb to go to college?" I said, "My teachers, the principle, my mom and everybody says I'm too dumb." Ms. Mylene was furious and said, "There's no such thing as being too dumb to learn! You can enroll in City College of San Francisco, and they can bring you from a sixth-grade education to a college degree and you can transfer to a four-year university. All you have to do is go to the admission's department and they will test you to see what your education level is and start your classes at that level." I said, "I don't think college is for me."

Chapter 69

Cultural Iconic Explosion Was Being Birthed

MS. MYLENE SAID, "You need to think about your future, and not be afraid to go outside of this environment." The streets were calling me, and I had no strong family support. It was at that very moment I realized that I had to relocate out of state if I wanted a new start, I could not be in the same area or even remotely close to the places I performed Beelzebub work. Just as I explained before when I was fifth teen years old 'Yahweh' voice whispered in my ear 'Atlanta' and it was very clear what I needed to do. So, at this point I had been keeping in touch with Ms. Regime the entire time when she moved down to Atlanta, she told me that if I was looking to make a better life for myself, I could move out there with her, and that she would love for me to come. It may have been a week or two later, when I heard back from Miss. Regime. She was the true definition of a 'Shorty'. She stood at 4 feet 11 inches and was very kind and sweet. She had a caramel complexion, accompanied by a lovely voice. Strong in her Christian faith and was my first example of seeing a woman in a positive light that I felt comfortable being open with my emotions. I wanted to be around her all the time. Her eyes were slanted but mysterious and calculating at the same time. Her hair came right to her ears. When I first met her, she would just wear her hair pulled back in a ponytail style that came below her shoulders. Her teeth were perfectly shaped, with nice shapely lips; her built was very petite and modestly developed. We both met mutually through C-Moe, and when the two of us met for the first time, we clicked instantly.

Regime was easy to talk to and had a tremendous heart filled with compassion. Even though she was going through an emotional roller coaster with her children's father, she stayed strong and continued to progress as a single mother of two boys. I could call her at any time of the day or night, and she would take me anywhere and never asked for lootchi for gas. I would give it to her anyway.

Throughout the years, I would send her holiday cards and gifts and she would send me different artists new material like Outkast, Usher, TLC, Toni Braxton, Sam Salter, and Pink just to name a few. Ms. Regime got a job as an Administration Assistant for La Face Records (La Face Records was the Motown of Atlanta) founders Antonio 'L.A.' Reid and Kenneth 'Baby Face' Edmonds, (formerly known from the R&B musical group 'The Deele'). La Face Records revolutionized the whole music experience; no longer did an aspiring artist have to rely on moving to Los Angeles or New York in order to increase his/her chances on having an opportunity to get a recording contract. In fact, Atlanta and La Face Records gave artists just as much, exposure as Hollywood or the Big Apple. Not only was a historic movement taking place, but the 'Freaknik' was becoming a staple in Atlanta right when Spring Break occurs. The 'Freaknik' was about college students, players, pimps, macks, strippers, entertainers and athletes all coming together to express their inner freak and party animal side, which defined everybody partying like there's no tomorrow. The first time I came to Atlanta was in June of 94 and I had just missed Freaknik. My first impression arriving in Atlanta was sur-real; it was so many young African decent promoting positivity; my jaw would have hit the ground hard if it could; it was so overwhelming to witness. Young men and women around twenty-three to twenty-seven years of age operating their own businesses; owning their own homes and driving brand new Lexus's.

It was mind blowing, when I arrived at the greyhound station in Atlanta, this brother seen me struggling with all my luggage and asked if I needed help carrying my luggage. I was not used to that level of brotherly love, the fact that it came so natural for him, helped me overstand the true meaning of that 'Southern Hospitality.' I was not use to people showing or giving much respect or love to people they don't know, especially young folks. I was able to freely let my guard down and was like "Where have this place been all my life?" When I first came to Atlanta, I took a Greyhound Bus, which took about 5 days and 4 nights just to get there (something I vowed to never do again). It was a horrible trip; I sat in the back of the bus by the bathroom getting nauseated and ready to vomit. The humidity of the heat was different, it was no breeze at all, and we were making all these stops in different cities and states I never heard of in my life. I arrived at the bus terminal finally in Atlanta and Ms. Regime picked me up and then took me to get some clothes and food. I gave her $500 until I was able to figure out where I was going to get more lootchi; she took me to her house and asked if I needed anything before leaving to go to her boyfriend's apartment. I thought Ms. Regime would show me around but since she was in a relationship, working long hours at La Face Records, and having to care for two boys; left little to no time for us to bond like we did in California. My first night in Atlanta, I was watching the news and there was a report on 'African on African decent crime'. It was five males and one female, ranging from the ages twenty-five to thirty who kidnapped a girl who was 18 years of age. They gang raped her and then forced her to drink some bleach and tied her up in barbwire, connected a battery to her, shocking her with electricity, stabbed her multiple times with a rusty screwdriver, before beheading her.

It was reported, that those kind of crimes from kidnapping people, then burning them or cutting their heads off so their souls would not return, that was some demonic stuff to me. True indeed, I come from the Mecca of 'drive byes' but cutting heads off was a different type of killing for me. It tripped me out because that was not my overstanding about Atlanta. That story left my mind twisted, and yet at the same time, I knew that there was no turning back for me.

My life was in Atlanta at this point. I was having a very difficult time finding employment in Atlanta and getting my feet underneath me. What helped me to balance the tough times out was the fact that Regime would get free passes to almost every event that came into Atlanta. I mean I was meeting all kinds of people from Puffy, Biggie at the Outkast Picnic, to meeting Usher. I had an opportunity to talk with Baby Face over the phone when he called for Regime. There were times when I picked Regime up from work because she would let me use her car in the daytime to try and find employment. One evening I almost got into a car accident with Toni Braxton at La Face records company in the driveway, which was narrow. If you were driving down to come visit someone and say somebody was driving up to leave from La Face Records, there was a sharp curve, where once you made that turn around the parking lot, you were not able to see the other car approaching from the opposite direction. I turned the car to the side at the last minute to prevent Ms. Braxton from hitting Ms. Regime car. We stopped and I looked into her car like, are you crazy and then when I saw her look in my eyes; I was like oh man that's Toni Braxton! Then she looked in my face and then drove off in a Cherokee Jeep. I was around so much established and developing star power but was unfazed because I was still that street dude, with that street mentality that I'm from "Fillmoe" and I'm not go let nobody disrespect me nor am I going to be jumping on people coat tail.

Chapter 70

Crooks Don't Dwell In Cali Only . . . How The South Made Me Naïve?

I ALWAYS PLAYED it cool but missed out on a lot of opportunities with that mentality. I was denied job opportunities left and right until this packaging company named R.P.S. (Railroad Package System); this company was like U.P.S. (United Parcel Service) but just on a lower scale. I worked graveyard from 12am to 7am. I really hated this job because the heat in the South was like being in a fiery furnace. Management was running the organization like a modern-day plantation. Supervisors talked down to workers who worked on the front line by referring to African decent men as 'boy'! They had us unloading boxes from trucks, like quicker than thieves robbing a bank. Although, I hated that job; I did everything within my power just to keep the job until I was able to create other opportunities in Atlanta.

However, one night I just didn't want to go to work. I dragged myself in even though my body felt like I had been beaten. The supervisor on my shift name was Steve. He was a young Caucasian 'Good Ol' Boy' who had blue eyes, blonde hair styled like Tom Cruise from the movie Top Gun he was 5 feet 10 inches and looked like he used to play Quarterback for Nebraska in College; he chewed tobacco and talked with a heavy southern twang. He was such an arrogant a** wipe and felt he could talk to me or anyone else for that matter any way he deemed necessary. On this particular night, he said to me "Get over their boy and unload these trucks!" I went into a zone and just paused. The whole scene was like Tony Montana did in the movie 'Scarface' when the character of that guy who took Scarface sister Gina in the bathroom and was feeling on her behind.

Tony would pause and then go off. That's exactly what happened with me. I charged at him, two chubby workers stopped me, I couldn't get to him, so they fired me and gave me my last paycheck for $176.86 cents. After they gave me my last check, I went to some check cashing place the next day that was not too far from Regime's apartment. It was raining really hard, but it was that warm summer rain, nonetheless, the visibility was extremely poor. As I was getting out of the car to cash my check, I realized I was only going to have $76.86 to live off once I gave Regime $100 to help pay on something. In my mind, I started counting every penny that was to be left in my pocket because only Yahweh knew when I was going to be blessed with more lootchi and a new job. As I approached the check-cashing place, some guy was walking towards me looking like brand new lootchi. He dressed immaculate with diamond rings shining on all his fingers. He was an older man with sections of his hair gray peeking out of his 'derby edition' style of a Kangol hat. He had green eyes; he stood at maybe 5 feet 7 inches and appeared to be from another country because he spoke with a heavy accent. His complexion was deep bronze, I happened to look at both his pockets and they were stuffed with lootchi. He seemed a little anxious about something and then he spoke, "PLEASE, PLEASE, HELP ME!" I didn't fully overstand what he was saying because he was a man in distress, so I asked, "What are you saying?" Again, the man repeated, "PLEASE, PLEASE, HELP ME?!" I yelled back, "What are you talking about!" The man had a piece of paper in his hand, that the cab driver had written and gave to him, stating if the man pays him $80 then the cab driver would be back within forty-five minutes after he finish his last customer on his route. He stated that he had been waiting for two hours and thirty minutes and that the cab driver had not returned yet and begged me to please help him.

I asked him what he wanted me to do exactly, instead of telling me what he wanted, he pulled out a bank roll of hundred-dollar bills (which could have easily been about $20,000 to 40,000). When I saw all that lootchi, my hustler's appetite was being tempted! I will always be a hustler, to my grave! When I saw that wad of lootchi the old man pulled out of his pocket, suddenly my tune went from "What do you want?" to "How do you want me to help you, Sir?" The man stated that he's trying to find 'First African Baptist Church' I informed him that I only been in Atlanta for about two weeks and didn't know anything. He continued to beg for my help, but the man's accent was so strong that I couldn't make out everything he was saying. As I wrestled with the sounds of his accent, I finally overstood that he wanted me to find a telephone book, but all I kept thinking about was how hard it was raining. I started looking for a payphone and I just so happened to see one way on the other side of the parking lot. I yelled out with such excitement "There go a payphone! I hope a yellow pages book is inside." I got inside Ms. Regime car to drive across the lot when the man tried to get in the car with me.

I told him that he had to walk over to the payphone because he was not getting inside the car with me. He continued to try and again I let him know that he had to walk and meet me there, which he eventually did. As I tell this story till this day, I now realized that the other man who looked like a dark version of Shady Grady from the Television show.

SanFord & Son was waiting for me to get his attention while I was looking through the Yellow Pages trying to find First African Baptist Church. I was not able to find it at all in the phonebook. I asked the other man, "Bro! Do you know where First African Baptist Church is located?" The man replied, "No, why?" The man who was looking for the church spoke and said, "How do I know that both of you are honourable men?"

His question came out of left field and left me a bit confused. It prompted the other man to ask, "Why are you looking for the church anyway?" The man pulled out a notarized document with an ambassador's seal on it stating that he was not allowed back in his Country in Soweto, South Africa, unless he donated his American currency. The document further stated that his family would not be freed if he came back into his Country with that illegal lootchi. He said that he wanted to donate $40,000 to the First African Baptist Church that someone recommended to him. Since the cab driver never came back, the man asked, "If I gave the two of you $20,000, each $10,000 to donate to a charity and $10,000 for you to keep for yourselves, how do I know that you are honourable man and will honour my wishes?" He continued, "How do I know that you are not like those African decent guys who stand on the corner pushing drugs?" The other man strongly stated, "I can go to the ATM machine and make a withdrawal of $300 to show you I have a savings and that I am a working man, and I can be back in five minutes." I said, "You not going nowhere!" Then he said, "I promise you; I'll be back in five minutes." Believe it or not, he came back in exactly five minutes with a record of the ATM transaction in his hand. The man turned to me and said, "How do I know you are an honourable man?" I looked that man dead in his face and said, "I just got fired from my job and all I have is $160.86 to my name because the check cashing place just deducted $16.00 dollars for cashing my check of $176.86". I showed him my check stub and then said, "I'm from California, and people who know me there, know that my word is my bond. I will donate $10,000 to the NAACP". That was the only African decent organization I knew at the time that help people that looked like me. The man told us to place our lootchi in a scarf and wrap it up so we can pray over it.

He started speaking in tongues asking who ever he believed in because it definitely wasn't Yahweh, to soften our hearts and to make sure we donate the money to a charity of our choice and to honour his wishes. The rain was still falling hard as the man was praying. I kept my eyes open because I began to get nervous, but I closed them for about forty seconds just to pray to Yahweh that he does not allow any harm to come on me for accepting this lootchi. After he finished his prayer, I kissed the man on the cheek and asked if I can keep in touch with him to inform him where I donated the lootchi. He told me that I could write him but not to mention anything about the lootchi in my letter. I hurried and jumped in the car and drove off like I was in a NASCAR race trying to cross the finish line first. I got to Regime's house and ran into the bathroom, locked the door, got down on the floor and opened the scarf, and to my surprise it was cut paper from a telephone book inside!

Those crooks took my last and only few dollars that I had to my name. I began to think how they could have switched the scarf, the only thing I could think of was that they switched the scarf when I closed my eyes for those forty seconds when I was praying to Yahweh that nothing wickedly comes back on me for accepting this lootchi. For the next couple of weeks, I went to that same location strapped with a weapon ready to let them feel the way they he made me feel. I punished myself severely and did not eat for many days. I told my family back in the Yay what happened, and they laughed at me like I had no feelings, then they said, "You from the streets and you fall for the oldest con in the book?" That was a rude awakening for me because there I was all the way down in the South and got a costly lesson taught to me. I guess I thought being in the South, I didn't have to have my guard up so high because I was meeting quality African decent people, so I thought.

Nevertheless, I should have known better because I knew firsthand that broke people make the best crooks. As the saying goes 'everything that sparkles isn't a diamond' that incident sent me into a severe stage of scepticism and hard-heartedness. I began to dare somebody, anybody for that matter to try to scam or challenge me. It almost happened again, I always wanted permanent gold teeth in the front of my mouth; it was sort of like a personal statement for me saying I finally made it out of the ghetto. I had come a long way from dealing drugs, being in jail, faced with death, betrayal, neglect, and loneliness. I was in a place of gratefulness to Yahweh for Blessing me through all that I had been through. One day, I had gone to some place in the mall where they do gold grills for your mouth. There were five guys who looked like they were from Jamaica or from somewhere in the Caribbean, they all looked like bullet wound survivors; like they just got out of Vietnam right before they met me. They were big and dark like they were literally in the Penitentiary, and they were plotting on me. They told me to give them the lootchi up front and get my shaping of my grill done and then go to a different building in three hours, which was located on the other side of town. I said "No! I will give you some lootchi up front now and the rest when you are done." They looked at me and asked, "Where you from?" I replied, "THE YAY" One of the guys yelled out "Cali". Maybe they thought they were talking to some younging that was an easy target. I ended up getting a gold tooth in the front of my mouth and paid the rest of the balance at the other location. The struggle continued for me in Atlanta. I was jobless yet meeting all these celebrities and really didn't overstand what was going on with me. I went from being in control of things in 'THE YAY', to moving to a place where I felt like I was in a different Country.

Chapter 71

Anguish On My Heart That I Never Felt Before Do I Still Go?

I WAS A twenty-one-year-old Souljah who had been on the streets for most of my life; I felt alone and didn't have any real expectations for myself. Just to add more pressure on myself, before I left for Atlanta in June 1994, my sister Naomi who was only sixteen years old and was pregnant and hid her pregnancy for about seven months. Since she was so skinny like a model, no one could tell if she was pregnant or not. She wore big coats and shirts; it was easy for her to hide her pregnancy. Our mom asked her if she was pregnant? my sister started crying and said, "Yes mom; I am!" Mom was devastated and disappointed and looked as if somebody came and snatched out her heart during the night. For some reason no one informed me about what was going on for several weeks; however, I knew something was not right because the tension in the apartment was thick and uneasy. I think mom only told me because I was leaving for Atlanta soon. When mom told me, I was extremely hurt and could not stop crying from the news. I went charging at my sister ready to knock her head off, but she had this fear in her eyes, and it covered her face. I just broke down crying.

I was crying so hard to the point I remember saying, "How could you do this to me and Mom? I shared with you all my mistakes so your life could be better; I taught you about these cavity creeps(dudes)." My heart bleeds with pain even now as I tell this story. Naomi and I were just crying, I said, "I'm here for you." It really put me in a deep state of sadness. That moment reminded me of the video 'I Miss You' by Aaron Hall, lead singer from the group Guy, when the woman revealed that she was pregnant. The video had a real emotional effect on me because I didn't have any experience when it came to someone being pregnant.

The risks that were involved. All I knew was that anything could happen, and I wanted to be there for my sister. Hearing that my teenage sister was pregnant messed me up in more ways than one. I was working for Wells Fargo Bank at the time when I learned about my sister, and I just couldn't keep the tears from rolling down my face because I would break down at any moment. I remember my manager Paul coming to me trying to find out what was going on. I told him about my sister and how she was only sixteen and pregnant and hid it all this time and now I just found out a week before I'm leaving to go to Atlanta. I was such an emotional wreck that he said if I needed to talk, he was there for me, and gave me information about a counselling hotline to get some psychological support. I was in desperate need of some emotional encouragement, to rid myself of my 'Sucka Free' days in 'THE YAY' filled with guilt and destruction but to have a once in a lifetime send off, with my aunt LaToya, who is pretty much the same age as me and who is more like my sister. She stood at maybe 5 feet 7 inches and had a cool personality; she could get along with anybody. She had a brown complexion, talked real deep, with brown circle eyes, perfect white teeth and a tomboy and woman all in one. She can fight with the best of them. When it came to getting on the basketball court get ready for a serious battle because she was nice with the rock too. Aunt LaToya and Aunt Janiece, Cousin Damarcus and both my sisters we took a trip to Great America Theme Park. We wanted to bring the fun back in our lives before I left. My sisters and I took pictures with all of our faces together and we spent that day just laughing.

Chapter 72

Laying The Foundation In Atlanta But What About Home?

IT WAS JUST what my life needed at the right time. Naomi gave birth to a baby girl on August 08, 1994. Since I didn't know what would become of me in Atlanta, the words of my grandfather Dontay Sr. kept on playing in my head; "You don't ever just up and jump into a new state, always visit first and get the local newspaper to find out what is going on in that state before you commit to moving down there!" There I was again reflecting on my experiences since arriving in Atlanta. I realized that there was nowhere for me to run, I couldn't turn back to "THE YAY" because I had done so much dirt and rival sets were seeking revenge on me and Futon St. Mobb for lives that were affected when we did drive-byes on our enemies. I spent so much lootchi to relocate my life, and furthermore I was determined to learn more about LaPonne and what else I'm about. I made a commitment to myself to try to figure out who else I can be, other than Beelzebub servant. What's a trip is that I thought about selling dope again in Atlanta because I had no job and no lootchi. I started thinking about how I'm living with Regime and not knowing how long she planned on letting me stay with her without a job. Although I didn't have a job, I did cook and keep her house clean, picked her boys up from school, was assistant coach to their flag football team, as well as assistant coach to their basketball team.

I never did end up getting a job, so I ventured out on a limb trying to write rap songs about what I was going through and the pressures of what I was feeling from trying to establish my life in Atlanta. I had no female companionship and no family. Just felt so alone.

Chapter 73

The Moment I Realized
I Can Monetize My Passion In Music

I SPENT MORE time calling my family in 'THE YAY' just to see how my mom and sisters were doing, even though I was at a challenging point in my life. I still kept in touch with people as I did, as if I was still back at home with them.

I was beginning to second guess myself, wondering if I really made the right decision for my life moving to Atlanta. Until the day something exciting finally happened,

It was July 10, 1994, and Regime invited me to rap icons Outkast picnic that was showcasing the movement of Atlanta, as well as rising stars from Atlanta and New York. I was neither overwhelmed nor star struck by the event because my perspective was these Stars/Celebrities use toilet tissue to wipe their behind just like me. Being in that environment made me feel like I was just as much of a star as anyone else. I felt like I belonged there, and I could get lootchi as well through entertainment. I was kicking it with everybody from TLC, Usher, Busta Rhymes, Notorious Big (R.I.P.), Sean "Puffy" Combs, Jermaine DuPree, Ed Gordon (the host of BET News), Big Lez (who used to host Rap City with Joe Clair), Goodie Mobb, L.A. Reid, Da Brat, Kris Kross, The Boys, and the list goes on and on. Notorious B.I.G and Puffy was on stage performing 'It's Unbelievable Biggie Smalls is the Illest' and I was just observing everyone who was in attendance. I started thinking about, here I am this young street kid from 'THE YAY' hanging with people who I'm used to seeing on T.V. Now I was standing right next to them. When Biggie and Puffy finished their performance, I went to shake Puff's hand. Regime went to talk with Usher because by that time she had become an A&R Coordinator for his project.

Usher then had gone on stage to perform two of his singles 'Can You Get with It and Think of You.' He had to be about thirteen or fourteen at the time and had a real good showmanship. He knew how to engage the crowd with perfection. I remember seeing Busta Rhymes at the picnic, and all I was thinking was how hard he walked as if somebody had just let a lion out of the cage. He was very colourful, electrifying and a real animated artist that the world would begin to pay attention to. He had that kind of personality that no matter how far away he was you noticed him. His star power was shining bright. As I got close to him, I started making this dragon sound that Busta is known for making when he performs; I reached my hand out to give a pound and he stuck his finger out to me with a cup in his hand as if he didn't want to shake my hand. Now he could have easily put the cup in his other hand and gave me a real man to man handshake, so in my mind, I was like you really are a Busta and I wanted to leave the picnic because I really never outwardly expressed my emotions for someone or something and if I do, I like that same energy to be returned. I explained to others about what happened, and they were saying that I probably made him a little paranoid by approaching him in the way that I did, however, I was just trying to give him some respect on how I felt about his artistry and personality. This is the first time since I had been in Atlanta, I finally felt like I knew what I wanted to do with my life and where I wanted to be. I wasn't sure about how it was going to happen; I just knew I wanted to get paid from what I was passionate about, which was music. I got back to the house with more focus and drive trying to write flows about my life experiences. I was writing about my life in the streets and all the dirt I did, but I began to feel uncomfortable about writing about all the bad things I had done, because I didn't want to seem like I was glamorizing the pain I inflicted on others while in the streets.

Chapter 74

Atl Can't You Tell May Be What The Doctor Ordered After All

I KEPT CALLING home because certain family members were saying my sister Naomi was trying to hang around in the hood and hanging with the wrong crowds, and that my mom and Naomi were fighting and arguing. They were also saying that my sister was leaving my niece Scrappy Doo with mom to take care of, which was disappointing. I talked to Naomi, and she explained that mom was tripping with her the same way she was with me, so after many months of hearing all about the madness at home in 'THE YAY' it became heavy on my heart. After months of being unemployed and getting conned for my last check of $176.86, I finally got a job through a Temporary Agency working at South Trust Bank in the mail department as a Mail Processing Clerk. The man who interviewed me name was Mr. Johnson; he was tall and dark skinned with an instant sunroof at the top of his head (for those who do not know what I mean: he had a bald spot in the middle of his head), wore glasses, but he reminded me more of a high school principal by the way he dressed and the way he talked. Mr. Johnson was very impressed with me for being a young man leaving one state to come to another state without knowing anything about it. He said it showed that I was a man of character. I explained to him that since I was twelve years old, I had always done things on my own, with very little support from family. Mr. Johnson hired me on the spot and told me to start on Monday (this was in October 1994). Now that I was working, it sort of filled up some of those lonely spaces I was experiencing in my life; however, there was still an issue on my mind about not having any female companionship.

I wanted to get out more to mix and mingle with people, but I didn't have an opportunity to explore Atlanta in a way that I would normally explore things. Life for me in Atlanta was nothing more than work, cook, and clean; while looking for jobs in the newspaper and playing basketball in the apartment complex. What a boring life for a twenty-one-year-old. I remember one time playing basketball in the apartment complex and I got picked on a team to play five on five.

The other team had a buff face gorilla looking dude who wanted to guard me because I looked young and probably thought I didn't know anything and was an easy prey (that's why I stayed in so much trouble and got tried and tested a lot). This gorilla face dude didn't like the fact that my defense was own him real tight, like a hand in a glove, so he resulted in getting physical by bumping his body against mine real hard, but I wouldn't back down. I started to use his own strength against him and take him off his game since he was short. I would steal the ball from him, and he would say, "B**** a** n****!!!" I replied, "You a b**** a** n****; you better quit low blowing me with your body!" He didn't like what I said so he came charging at me to fight. I stood my ground because I was not about to back down from nobody! I didn't do it in 'THE YAY' and I wasn't about to start in the ATL. The other players on both teams came to break up the commotion, and it was until that very moment I realized that I was like a 'Stranger from Russia' I could have been jumped or in multiple fights with these dudes. They knew I was a foreigner. I felt like me versus Atlanta. I felt like the whole world was against me, but I thank 'Yahweh' that I had a job because I started meeting some friends who seemed to be pretty cool to hang out with. One of my co-workers looked square but he was down to earth. He resembled the guy who played Eminem manager Eugene Byrd on the movie 8 mile with the exception that this dude wore glasses and was tall and was very skinny.

He tried to sound like he was 'hood', but one could tell he was a square because he was trying too hard to be cool. He was good folks though; I think his name was Torrence and he was from Texas and was the first person to hip me to the legendary group U.G.K. (Under Ground Kings) which consist of Pimp C (R.I.P.) and Bun B. They had this song called 'I Got a Pocket Full of Stones' it was so relatable to my life that I rocked with the song and brought their CD. Since I started consistently making a little lootchi. I started hanging out with Torrence who liked going to strip clubs. We went to this one strip club called Club Nikki's (I think that was my first time going to a strip club); it was a straight up low budget joint that had anything and everything going on in there. I mean people were dealing guns, p*s*y flinging everywhere, drug slinging, and bootleg movies pushing before they were in the theaters. I can't even lie, that club had some of the most gorgeous women who had remarkable bodies and were not ashamed to share it with the public; of course, for a lovely price. I didn't like a woman who would be gyrating on one guy and then want to come over to me to do the same thing for a fee. That was a big turn off for me. Atlanta offered different things for all walks of life; it didn't matter if one was single, married, gay, single parent, a couple, businessman or woman, entertainer or athlete, there was something in Atlanta for everyone. I started getting some security and stability under my feet being in Atlanta, which boosted my confidence. I started to feel real good about being in Atlanta with my 'YAY AREA FLYNESS.' Throughout the entire process, I continued getting calls from family back home expressing to me that my mom and my sister kept fighting, and how my sister kept running away and leaving my niece Scrappy Doo with Mom. My family meant everything to me, and even though we had many problems, and I made the decision to move to Atlanta to begin a new life, my sisters always came first.

Chapter 75

I'm Going Going Back Back To The Yay, Blinded By My Heart

I CONTEMPLATED GOING back to 'THE YAY' and Regime could see it's written all over my face. My feelings were bouncing all over the place because I just hated to hear that the same dysfunction was going on with Mom and Naomi. Regime said something to me that really made sense, she said, "it seem like every time you start getting everything going for yourself and start feeling good, you get a call from a family member telling you how bad your sister or another family member is doing." However, her words were not as comforting as the thought of going back home to 'THE YAY'. Besides that, I think I just got tired of being out in Atlanta alone. Anyway, I had a long talk with Regime to let her know that I was going back to try to get the situation with my mom and sister resolved because I was the only one who could get through to my sister. Regime was concerned about what I was feeling because she knew that I was always putting everyone before myself, but I had to explain to her that I was like a father, brother, and friend to my sisters, and that they needed me. She took a deep breath and said "OK". Everything that I packed and mailed to Atlanta, I had to send it right back to 'THE YAY'. I called people to let them know I'm coming back, and they were happy which surprised me because I was not close with a lot of family members. I began to set things in motion, so when I got back to Cali one thing in particular was meeting with Cashmuir and Show Stoppa who was planning to start a rap group. That I created the name Foundation. When I arrived, I hooked up with Cashmuir to talk about some ideas about starting a record label named Foundation Records.

My Aunt Janiece and Uncle Bam Bam who was shaped just like Mike Tyson and had features like him, and he stood at maybe 5 feet 7 inches but spoke a little deep and slow. They were happy that I was coming back to 'THE YAY'. They offered to let me stay with them at their apartment and that I could sleep in one of their daughter's beds. At that point, they were the only two people I really considered to be real family, one of our favourite things we did, was tell jokes and watch the television show 'Martin', as well as my aunt cooking some of the best food and desserts ever. I would play with my two little cousins Shay-Shay and Bri-Bri.

I think Shay-Shay was 6 years of age, who was her mom and dad all in one from her looks and everything. Bri-Bri had here mom smile but had some of her own unique characteristics. I thought I would never have to worry about not having my Aunt Janiece and Uncle Bam Bam in my corner, since she had seen a lot of the abuse my mom had done to me and felt sad about how I grew up. The problems between my sister and my mom were getting heavier and heavier. Mom and Naomi would actually fight, and Mom would kick her out, but then Mom would change her mind at the last minute because my sister had a child. I think Naomi began to take mom for granted because she knew mom had a sensitive spot for her being young and having a child. I asked my Aunt Janiece and Uncle Bam Bam if my sister could stay with us?

They agreed to let Naomi stay with us, so I got a second job working at Burlington Coat Factory in downtown San Francisco to help my sister out a little. I began to use my employee discount to buy clothes for my niece Scrappy Doo. My sister did not work, and my aunt and Uncle started to feel a bit disappointed with Naomi for not showing that she had some plan to get back on her feet and getting a job. She wasn't even trying to get back in school, nor was she trying to make herself be more productive, since she was a mother now and she wasn't trying to help keep the house clean as well.

Her days of staying there didn't last long, because she too, began to feel uncomfortable because Aunt Janiece was not cool with Naomi's unwillingness to show respect and appreciation for the support that they were providing. Eventually she had to apologize to mom and mom let her come back home but the same outcome was the reality. One minute Naomi was being responsible and respectable, and then, the next minute she would be extremely disrespectful to mom because mom was arguing and yelling in her face. Mom didn't like for anyone to challenge her, especially her kids, so whenever that happened, mom would get up in the face of whomever and dare any of us to continue to be disrespectful to her. I personally did not like the way my auntie handled the situation with my sister, but I overstood their concerns and I knew it was not my apartment so it was only so much I can say or do. I also did not like how Naomi was disrespecting mom and I didn't like how mom would get in Naomi's face challenging her. I was fresh from Atlanta and started to second-guess myself once again on whether or not I made the right decision leaving Atlanta to come back and help fight a losing battle. My hands were tied, with my sister and mom, because they both were stuck in their ways, so neither one was listening to me, except when things got so far out of control. I would try to defuse the tension between them and at the same time, I was trying to launch a record company with my partner at the time Cashmuir to let the music be the Foundation to legitimize my newfound lifestyle. So now I working back at Wells Fargo Bank, but have a different position as an information clerk, which was not really making ends meet. One thing I can say about myself, I knew how to put myself in a position to get a job. It was definitely Yahweh Blessing me; I always knew how to get loot in the streets and in Corporate America now. I was starting to get my feet secured and my flow in motion.

My aunt and uncle delivered some news to me that I don't think 'Ripley's' would have believed. They said that they wanted to talk to me about how much time it would take for me to get on my feet because they wanted me to leave. I felt like they hit me with a steel baseball bat with nails on it over my heart. I was so enraged with the breakdown in our relationship, and it hurt me real bad because I constantly continue to have people be revolving doors in my life. According to my Aunt Janiece, she said one day, I asked her if I could use her car to get to work, she said it was okay to use her car since she worked in the daytime, and I worked at night. Well, one night while at work, I parked the car in an alley by Burlington Coat Factory and got a ticket. I told her about the ticket; nevertheless, my aunt and uncle were beyond angry. I'm not sure if getting a ticket is what made her that upset or if it was just the fact that they wanted their-own place back? I don't know what made me think they were any different. They begin to monitor everything and would say that I been using up all the tissue and food and had a problem with it. Now mind you, I already felt a certain way about how they did my sister because even though my sister was sleeping all day, she had a newborn baby and was giving my aunt her food stamps and W.I.C. My sister was contributing by providing extra food to come into the house that would allow my aunt to get free groceries. When my aunt said the things she said to me, and she was nit picking on things that was not all the way accurate, and how I thought our relationship was infinite stone love that nothing could come between that, especially some toilet tissue or food, I was crushed! They were the only ones I considered to be my 'real' family, that I expressed admiration earlier in the story about; I thought we were inseparable. I called my aunt LaToya and said to her all what happened; she told me that I could stay with her, which meant living back in the projects.

Chapter 76

Came Back Just To Go Back To Being A Drug Pusher Again

IT WASN'T THAT I thought I was too good to live in the projects; it was more about I didn't want to get caught up in some street drama and then I'm going backwards with my life. I really felt I let myself down! I go from being in the ATL and I'm meeting all these icons in the making and now I'm back in the projects. I went through so much to forward my life. The struggle for me was going to be much harder because the lootchi I was making to get a place of my own was not enough. I started back distributing ounces of weed and I also enrolled myself in John Adams Community College. John Adams Community College was an extension of City College of San Francisco. I was taking some basic studies just to stay sharp on the general stuff I already knew. I felt like my life had no order or purpose, I was mad at myself for putting my life on hold for people, who only disappointed me time and time again. I thought I had let go of those heavy bricks I was carrying in the past, only to realize that a thousand more had fallen down on me. It was in that moment when I knew I destroyed my life by leaving Atlanta. The worst part of it all, I had to resort back to my old familiar street hustling tactics; selling weed the same way I entered the game as a baby boy. I was getting my weed from some folks who had connections to people who grew it in Hawaii, and I started to be known as the 'weed man' because I was giving some good deals. I remember one time when I was trying to get this last ounce of weed off me, so on my next re-up, I can begin to see a profit, but things never go according to plan.

Chapter 77

Surviving With Hood Tactics Is How You Started Now U Caught

I RAN INTO a guy I hadn't seen since he was a kid (ironically, I used to be his counselor during summer camp) his name was Eddie Cheebah. He was a little chubby and dressed real nice; he reminded me of Jam Master Jay (R.I.P.) from the legendary group Run-DMC. We were at the bus stop waiting for the 38 Geary bus located at downtown San Francisco; I was going home, I knew he smoked weed, and like I explained from the beginning, I will be a hustla to my grave and will always look at everything as an opportunity to come up. I knew I was struggling trying to get this last amount of weed off so I can re-up. I knew not to be distributing all out in the open, so we went into a little corner of a wall. While waiting for the bus, I pulled out the ounce of weed and Eddie Cheebah said he wanted to buy it from me. I hooked him up with a 'pla-ya price', when in the midst of our negotiation we heard "Freeze! Put your hands up and get down on the ground". Undercover cops pulled out guns and pointed them at our heads. I remember seeing two dudes but not realizing they could have possibly been undercover cops. I just glanced at them instead of studying them like I usually do, it was plain and simple, that I was slipping.

My keen sense of judgment was put to the test, because the simple fact of the matter was, I got to ex-cited about finally having a buyer; I compromised my sense of awareness because someone was buying the ounce of weed off me and the anxiousness altered my better judgment. I was handcuffed and, on my way, to jail. No longer was I going to Y.G.C., I was going to jail as an adult.

I didn't know what to feel at that moment because all I knew was that I should have stayed my Afri-can decent a** in Atlanta; at least with me being in Atlanta, I stayed away from all the madness. Now, my mind set was of a radical tyrant, speaking out against the injustice by the government and police brutali-ty, and there I was sitting in the back of a police car saying all kinds of crazy stuff about the 'Babylonian Establishment' while Eddie Cheebah was whining about how tight his handcuffs were and how he had a dentist appointment to go to. I was totally in a self-destructive mode all over again and was relentless with my words, and sure enough, my words eventually bit me in the you know what. After a few hours they let Eddie Cheebah go and kept me. I didn't know what to make of that because I couldn't say that he snitched or not, but he was with me pretty much the whole time. The good thing about that situation was that it was my first offense as an adult. I didn't know how everything was going to unfold because I had more bags of weed stuffed inside the linen of my backpack where I kept my chrome 25-millimeter handgun that had hollow point bullets as well. I was so thankful that I took that gun out of my backpack; if I didn't, there was a great possibility that I would have definitely done some serious time in jail. Which wouldn't have been good for me at all! I would have lost everything. I was still working two jobs that definitely did not want to risk losing. The first call I made was to my aunt LaToya and explained to her what happened, and she was like "YOU STUPID. I thought you were smarter than that!" I didn't like what she said so I just got off the phone with her because I didn't need to hear all that. After getting nowhere with my aunt the next person I called was mom; I was so embarrassed and ashamed when I called her because I knew she was going to give me that same old dragged-out speech she always preached, and it goes a little something like this hit it.

Chapter 78

The Impossible Possible Through Yahweh & His Angels

MOM SAID "LAPONNE I told you about hanging in those streets, hanging with the wrong crowd, and now you got your behind locked up in jail again. Didn't you learn your lesson the first and second time?" However, her speech was laced with more wisdom than ridicule. She replied, "Awe LaPonne! You must quit letting the devil destroy you. How do you go from trying to leave 'THE YAY' to Atlanta coming back and returning to your old ways? What are you going to do LaPonne?" I was at a loss for words and said, "I don't know Mom." She was so gentle to me, and her words were comforting, 'Yahweh is trying to get your attention LaPonne, but you keep thinking you can figure things out and work things out yourself." Her words of wisdom continued, "How long are you going to keep struggling and suffering on your own? Don't you know Yahweh is your only way out? Believe me LaPonne, I have tried to do it on my own and failed every time." Tears began to fill my eyes, but I made sure to not let anybody see me cry in jail, I said, "Mom, I have to get off the phone." Mom then said, "To call collect if I needed to and to let her know how long I was going to be locked in jail." I got arrested on a Friday. I wouldn't know anything until the weekend was over. It was the Super-bowl weekend, which meant that I might not be able to watch the San Francisco Forty Niners and the San Diego Chargers fight for the championship. Thankfully, I was released on O.R. (own recognizance) that Sunday afternoon since it was my first offense as an adult. I was given a court date to report for my sentencing.

I called mom collect and she accepted the call and I explained to her that I no longer wanted to stay at LaToya apartment because I was totally pis** off at her insensitive comments. Mom said, "Okay LaPonne, you can stay here but you know how I am, and you know my rules and you have to go to church every Sunday." I never liked being forced to go to church or being forced to do anything because it made me want to rebel. The first three weeks of being back at mom house wasn't going as well as I hoped. Mom and I got into a fight because she was getting in my face and nagging me about any and everything, so I reached out to my cousin Damarcus who worked at Safeway to see if they were hiring for baggers. He said he didn't know but that I should come down and fill out an application anyway. The location Cousin Damarcus worked at was located at the Marina District where rich people lived and shopped. Mr. J. Cain was the store manager, he stood at 5 feet 8 inches and had a real shrewd look in his eyes, he was Caucasian, and his skin was always red, he had shifty eyes, blond hair that was thinning up top and a little long in the back. He had an old, retired athlete kind of built, he was about maybe 50 years of age at the time and on one of his fingers, the whole fingertip was gone. He liked to laugh and crack jokes, but he was also a crafty guy as well. I introduced myself and complimented him on how impressed I was with how positive the atmosphere was at his store location. When I worked at the Market Street location, it was very negative; there were homeless people hanging around, heavy drug use, thefts, fights, and stabbings. I was just released from jail. I was broke and really needed a job because mom and I were back on 'shaky grounds' with our relationship. I did and said whatever I needed in order to get something going for myself. I kept calling and finally the hiring representative called me in to take an online test.

I took the test, and they offered me the position and asked if I had a problem with taking a drug test right now at some clinic. I said I had no problem at all. Next thing, I was hired and working all kinds of shifts from sunup to sundown. I was doing all kind of duties from mopping floors, cleaning the public restrooms, bagging groceries, running to get price checks and escorting customers out to their cars. I was cutting Christmas Trees and tying them on top of customer cars during the Holiday season. It was such a strange feeling because I was just released from jail a month ago, and now I'm working around all these squares that had no idea of what my world consisted of and where I come from. I felt like people were always looking at me with negative thoughts in their head. I started using my cousin Damarcus name a lot hoping that people would stop looking at me with scepticism, since he was the 'big man on campus' who had all the friends and girls who liked to talk and hang out with him. My reality was totally different from the average twenty-two-year-old; although I had a job, I was making about $8.25 an hour. Nevertheless, the good thing about it was that I was working full time and was able to give Mom some 'Get off my back' lootchi, while trying to save at the same time to get my own place. $8.25 an hour seemed impossible for me to have my own apartment anytime soon. I was doing everything I could to survive because I was in desperate need. I had no car to drive because I sold it when I moved to Atlanta, so that meant I had to ride the bus to get to where I needed and wanted to go. I was talking to a partner at the time name KP, and he told me that he had a friend he was going to school with named Jack. He said Jack was looking for a roommate to help with the rent. My heart leaped for joy! I spoke with Jack over the phone and the conversation went smooth.

I met with Jack, and he was this crazy red head dude who stood about 5 feet 5 inches with freckles all over his face and neck, he had brown eyes and was built like a junior college middle linebacker and his mannerism was very carefree and brut at the same time. He was a cool fiery dude who suppressed a lot of his pain; since we both clicked with one another, three weeks later, I moved in. When I moved in, Jack had a pit bull named Cognac who looked like a panther; he was black as midnight with white fur on his stomach, Cognac was very strong and aggressive, but playful at the same time, and knew how to push both Jack and my buttons. The dog was as smart as a human; he would do things to make us mad and knew exactly what he was doing. Like he would knock over his water bowl or food bowl if he couldn't get none of our table food. There were times when he would make Jack and me so mad, but we couldn't stay mad long because Cognac would put his head down as if he was saying, 'I'm sorry that I made you mad.' I would be eating some pancakes and Cognac would always come by my plate and stick his tongue out begging. I began to develop a real strong connection with Cognac. I would run with him up hills with a heavy chain around his neck so that we both would stay in shape. Things seemed kind of steady between Jack and me; however, in my mind I kept thinking, 'How long would this last?' Soon after those thoughts began to swim around in my head; the reality of it came crashing down with so much truth. One night Jack came bursting through the door talking about how he had just disfigured somebody's face with a broken bottle, and that the police looking for him, and he's scared, and he must leave now. No matter what I did to keep myself surrounded by positive thoughts, my peace of mind was constantly being disturbed by someone else's 'Troublesome' behaviour. I vividly remember how his eyes looked as if it was yesterday.

He told me that he had to go to Hawaii as soon as possible and that his mom and Stepdad would pay for the next two months of rent, but then I would have to get a new roommate. Jack also asked me to take care of Cognac until he found someone who could keep him. He and I had become such good partners, that I hated to see him like that; I began to worry about him, but soon realized that I had to move on with my life. I did not want to get myself caught up with not living my life because of other people problems. I did that before when I left Atlanta and was not about to do it again! Jacks activities put me in a terrible position, which caused me to start watching my own back. I began to see unmarked cars with detectives inside who were staking out in front of my apartment with a sketch of Jack profile. They started calling and harassing me about Jack whereabouts and to give them whatever information I had. I told them I did not have any information other than the fact that he came in two nights ago and stated he had to go and how sorry he was for having to break our lease agreement. I believe the detective's name was Sergeant Kennisaw, but he acted like he was 'David Caruso' from CSI: Miami, but short and pudgy with a long nose that looked like the barrel of a gun. I think he was Scottish; his hair was gray combed back but missing patches of hair, with a bushy moustache and he dressed like a retired shoe salesman, his breath, oh my, his breath smelled like he had just finished drinking an onion milkshake with hot diced garlic blended with skunk juice. He tried to be intimidating by speaking hard and aggressive. I guess he believed that was the way he needed to talk in order to get respect and be taken seriously. His 'short mans' complex got the best of him. I was real upset because I felt like my privacy was being violated, my own criminal past was going to attach me to Jack crime.

Days later, I learned that the girl Jack was dating told the police that he fled to Hawaii, and that the guy whose face he slashed was sleeping with her. They began the process to extradite Jack back to 'THE YAY' to arrest him. With everything going on all at once, I was left in a position to figure out quickly what am I going to do next. I didn't know how I was going to maintain paying all of the rent, keeping food in the house, and other unforeseen expenses. At that point, I was frustrated with all the bull that was happening and started living life carelessly. I was at a point where everything was beyond serious with me. I tried to stay on top of everything and kept things under control; I was working harder than I did before; coming home cooking and working out with weights and running with Cognac outside.

I had no transportation and relied on public transportation. Which was MUNI and BART (Bay Area Rapid Transit System) to get me from one side of the city to the next. As the days were approaching for me to go to court for the drug possession charge, that I was busted for with Eddie Cheebah, I had to go meet with the Public Defender appointed to me named Ms. L. D. She was a sister who worked really hard.

Her body was shaped like R&B pioneer Ms. Patti Austin and her face kind of looked like an African decent version of the Broadway Legend Liza Minnelli, and her voice sounded as though she was always out of breath. Ms. L. D. seemed to be a very caring woman because she had a passion for the kind of work she did. She didn't look at me as just another case to process, but a young brotha she could help turn this negative situation around and how I deserved another chance with my life. Once she got to know me, she saw that I was a good kid who happened to make a very bad decision. They say that we should count our Blessings every day, and believe me, that was a Blessing from Yahweh. I also think that because I had a 'baby face' it kept me out of a lot of trouble.

Ms. L. D. fought for me to get probation, pay some fines, and go to a drug diversion class, anything was better than having to sit in a cage like a wild untamed animal. The day finally arrived for me to appear in court, and as I stood before the Judge, my Public Defender Ms. L.D. laid out her recommendations for me to the judge, and they were accepted.

The Judge asked if I overstood what those recommendations were and I said, "Yes, Your Honour, I overstand what was required of me and thank you Your Honour." I was put on probation for two years and had to pay $1,000 in fines, which I did not know how I was going to pay. I was already in a tough financial situation with Jack going bloody 'Rambo' on that guy behind some girl, and although his parent's was going to pay his half of the rent, that still meant I had to be responsible for all the other utilities in the house. I wanted to get the court fine out of my way as soon as possible because I did not want it to linger over my head. To save lootchi, I started eating 'Hamburger Helper' until it came out of my ears. I would mail in $200 here and there every chance I got. I was still $500 short; I needed $345 to enter into the drug diversion class, which was included in that $500. One day while I was at work, depressed about how I was going to get the $500 that I needed to put this terrible mistake behind me, I met this lady named Ms. Betty Stuart (R.I.P.). She had to be about seventy-six years old, struggling carrying her groceries. She had very pale white skin, with a warm and silky voice that was like melted butter being poured over a short stack of pancakes, and a spirit of a young cheerleader. She looked like she could have been a character on the television series 'Golden Girls'. Ms. Stuart would wear a rain cap over her head and a light trench raincoat, whether it was raining or not. I remember her always saying, "Each time I come to Safeway, I didn't mean to buy all of this stuff" and laugh, which was something she loved to do.

Chapter 79

Ms. Betty Stuart
Let Me Know Angels Do Exist

MS. STUART WOULD try to give me $3 to $5, and I would refuse it; even though I was a hustler, I never hustled or conned people. I would always put myself in their shoes, because if Yahweh Blessed me to make it to a 'wise age' I would hope that someone would share that same kind of good fortune for me as well. Another time when Ms. Stuart came to Safeway to shop, I walked her home with her groceries because she lived directly across from the store. She knew I was not my same joking self and asked what was wrong with me; I said, "I'm just tired of my life being so TROUBLESOME. Every time I try to get my feet underneath me, I get knocked back 5 steps more." She then said to me, "There's something special about you, and don't lose sight of your gifts." Her words brought some comfort to me, but I told her that I've been doing everything on my own for a very long time and didn't have the support I've been needing my whole life; I've been fighting an uphill battle. When we arrived at her apartment and she opened the door, it was filled with cats. I don't like cats! Not only did I not like them, but I'm also allergic to them; nevertheless, that did not stop me from helping Ms. Stuart. Thirty minutes later, Ms. Stuart came back to the store, and while I was helping someone else, she had an envelope in her hand and said, "Yahweh Bless You! Yahweh is watching over you" and put the envelope in my pocket and left. I ran and gave her a big hug and a kiss on her cheek. I did not open the envelope right away. I just really appreciated Ms. Stuart not judging me as some ghetto child without any value.

Chapter 80

After This I'm Giving Myself Permission To Live For Today

I WENT TO a private part of the parking lot and opened the envelope; it was $500 wrapped in a letter that said, "I wish Yahweh to bless you, Sincerely Miss. Stuart." I have that note still this very day. I never told her the amount of lootchi I needed or what exactly was my problem; Yahweh used her as my angel because the amount she gave me was the amount I had left to pay for my drug diversion class. That was no one but Yahweh Blessing me. I remember everything like it was yesterday. My Drug Diversion Counselor, Ms. Mary Williams was a very spiritual person; I found myself being very honest with her about me working and not earning enough lootchi, and that I just made a bad decision. She took an immediate liking to me and said that I had no business being here and would discharge me as a successful completion a few months earlier than the court ordered. I believe it was November 1996 when I got off probation; it seemed so surreal to me because of the stupidity that I put myself through. Again, it was an on-going battle I was having with myself; trying to get my life together, while fighting off the old ways of my past. During the middle of the year in 1996, Safeway began hiring younger and fresher looking people to work for them. I met this guy named Z-double, who worked in the Winery Department. He was a cool Caucasian dude who reminded me of a cross between 'Jack Tripper' from the T.V. show 'Three's Company' and Ted McGinley from the show Married with Children. Z-double was about 6 feet 2 inches, he had slick black hair that looked like he came fresh out off the waters of Acapulco, Mexico. He always had this accommodating spirit and loved to chill and smile.

His eyes were very engaging that he used to captivate women with a voice like 'Shaggy' from Scooby Doo but with a cool twist to it. We bonded instantly; in fact, our interest in music gave us that immediate connection, and the fact that we both loved the Pittsburgh Steelers. His mom was an artist and would draw pictures of Malcom X and all different types of prominent figures. Z-double and I studied the legendary, revolutionary rap artist Tupac (R.I.P.) like he was a science project. We shared each other's clothes and took turns cooking for each other. I remember when he worked at some home supply store and let me rob it while he turned his back and looked the other way. He knew I needed supplies for my apartment but knew I didn't have the lootchi to purchase any of it. Trying not to get caught doing illegal activities, while just getting off probation, was an obstacle in itself. He became like a brother to me; I mean, we really hung tight, and although our background had no compatibility, our medium was music, sports, food, humor, and women! Z-Double's favourite woman of all time was R&B singer Aaliyah (R.I.P.). Z-double has always been more than a real good friend to me. We always had each other's back, and we are family for life. Since we both love The Pittsburgh Steelers, we would throw 'Steelers Parties' and invite other friends of ours to come. As I said before, Safeway was hiring new people left, and right, those new recruits sparked an era, which changed my life. There was this guy Safeway hired named Teese; he was 6 feet 3 inches tall and had a dark complexion, with the perfect 'Morris Chestnut' smile that a woman looks for in a man. He ended up being friends with Cousin Damarcus, and apparently told Cousin Damarcus that he knew C-Moe, and that C-Moe was his cousin. Knowing that he was closely related to somebody dear to me, I felt it was only right that I bring Teese into our family, our unit and bond. Teese would be hanging out at the house with us and I would fix a big breakfast for everyone who was there.

Chapter 81

A Bright Star In My Dark World
So I Thought

I MEAN I was throwing down in the kitchen with pancakes, four egg omelets, turkey sausage and chilled orange juice. There was a turn of events that had taken place that caused one of the greatest divisions of my life. One day, we were all at the job, Cousin Damarcus, Teese, and me; were known as the 'Three Cousins.' We were the same, but with different characteristics: Cousin Damarcus was the cool one to hang out with and smoke weed with and have a good time; Teese was the one a girl wanted as their boyfriend and take home to meet mama, as for me, I was the one people loved to talk to and help solve their problems. You know 'The LessonStresser I am' I filled them with lessons on life. There was a new girl who was hired named Ms. Star; she seemed very outgoing and wore her hair slicked back with gel and attached a ponytail hair piece. It was the popular hairstyle at the time. She could get just about anybody to engage in a conversation with her even if you didn't want to talk at the time. She had a caramel complexion and had some nice lips; she looked exactly like the female hip-hop artist named Miss. Jones, who had the song 'Where You Gonne Be Boy' who later became a radio personality. I didn't think much about Ms. Star in a sexual way or had any attraction towards her, but she had nice legs with shapely calves and a nice high behind. Her eyes were almond shaped and had a look about them like 'If you do me wrong, I will gut you open.' She had great potential to become a marketing representative. I would hear her change people minds on how they would say they wanted one thing, and she would convince them to choose something completely opposite. I never did say much of anything when I was around her, and I definitely minded my own business.

She would always speak to me and say, "What's going on with you, Mr. Burton?" I would be kind of shy and in her eyes be antisocial; no matter how short and boring I was with my replies to her questions, she would continue to speak to me.

Since she wasn't getting anywhere with me, she started talking with Teese, and the next thing you knew they were involved with each other. I wasn't involved with anyone, per say, other than talking to a couple of females from Los Angeles, but nothing serious. I was pretty much a loner. I was hustling illegally just a little bit in the streets, but I really was trying to shed that part of my life completely. I was trying to find myself. I definitely would not be good for anybody. I always felt nobody could ever overstand me or care about the ugliness I've experienced. Things started to become a bit tense for me while working at Safeway. I was no longer hanging out with Cousin Damarcus, and Teese as much anymore, but they would hang out with Ms. Star, and they would all hang together a lot. I was in my own world trying to build myself. Cousin Damarcus would call to check on me, and every time he did, Ms. Star would jump on the phone and ask how I was doing. At first, I looked at her as my little homie but then started to view her as my little sister (she reminded me of my sister Naomi). Teese and Ms. Star were a couple (or at least that's how it appeared), the subject came up about what she thought of me, and she was like he's a good dude and she wanted me to meet up with her play cousin. I really didn't feel comfortable with that idea but did not object. Ms. Star told me about her cousin who just moved back to California from Texas, and that I seemed like a cool dude who could take her cousin around to show her a good time. I think I made a joke like "She bet not look like no extra from Michael Jackson's Thriller video!" everybody laughed. There was some dude who was the frontend Supervisor (at Safeway), as well as a party promoter on the side. He told us about an event that he was throwing and wanted all of us to come.

Ms. Star thought that it would be good for her cousin Shanika to come so we could meet each other (I'm not going to lie; I was feeling myself a little bit). I was like okay that'll be cool; a female coming down to meet me at a party and my folks Ms. Star had already done the groundwork for me; and if we hit it off, I could explore her treasure later on in the night. When Shanika came into the club, she looked good and smelled real good. She appeared to be full of herself as well and acted stuck up, we finally met and did not hit it off; she was more interested in my cousin Damarcus; so, from there, I didn't pay her any mind. She was African decent but looked Latin, she was pretty tall probably about 5 feet 10 inches which I loved, and she was very beautiful, but her personality made her appear ugly; she had a beautiful hazelnut complexion, beautiful piercing brown eyes and hair was very soft and nice lips and nice breast with some beautiful long legs, but she just carried on as if the world revolved around her as if it owed her something. Furthermore, she spoke with a bad attitude and had anger issues; our personalities clashed like titans; we just did not match. I was not engaging in conversations with her, and it made her upset, and she spoke to her cousin about it and Ms. Star came over to me and said that Shanika told her that I wasn't really talking to her. I was like, "She's feeling my cousin Damarcus, and she acts like her stool don't stink!" Ms. Star went on to say that her cousin is funny like that sometimes, but she was overall a cool person. To try and break the ice, I started forming a 'Soul Train' dance line and had everybody in the club following me; we had a ball. I think the fact that I was fun and exciting caught her attention and she wanted to get to know me. Later that night, after leaving the club, we all went over to my apartment. I had food and drinks there and plus, no one really had any lootchi, but it was all good, I had everything supplied at my house.

We dropped Cousin Damarcus off at home because he had to get up early for work. Teese, Ms. Star and Shanika headed to my house to spend the night. Everybody was feeling good from drinking at the club and having someone to lie next to for the night. Teese and Ms. Star had their own room and Shanika, and I had our own room. I went into the one bathroom to freshen up, while Shanika went into the other bathroom and put on her 'night attire' and I turned on some music to relax and smooth us out for the night. Although we were not really feeling each other however, it was just one of those situations where we were making the best out of the night. To see how we would feel about each other after that. As the night progressed, I began to lace her with my literature from my mouthpiece in order to please her mind so that way she would feel more comfortable being with me. She took a very strong interest in what I was saying that within a moment we began to kiss; her lips were soft as cotton, and she smelled like paradise! I could not escape her remarkable scent. To be very honest, I truly appreciate when a woman takes time to adorn herself as a beautiful rose. The kiss was so intense that my nature began to take its course on the both of us. I began to swirl my tongue around the nipples of her breasts, as I slowly lowered my hand to explore her treasure beneath. She began to moan in a way that it felt as if she had been waiting for a real man for a long time. Once I knew the 'sex gauge' had reached its boiling point, she was ready for my caramel stick to swim in her 'pool of paradise' and I was ready. Now, making love is something that I take very serious, and I'm not that kind of dude who just takes a 'tasting' to any woman's 'undiscovered treasure.' However, this girl smelled and tasted so good that I wanted to please her on every level as possible. Her treasure was warm and wet; I knew I wanted to explore, and I dove right in (I went against my code about tasting a woman's treasure which was something I really did not do but she smelled so good, I couldn't resist). I reached my climax and then got off of her.

There was no emotional, physical, or sexually connection at all, I was not about to risk getting 'blue balls.' My long tongue traveled up her long legs and then I finally arrived at the place of paradise; she was feeling real good by me tasting her nectar so when I got to the point where she wanted me to put my communication piece inside her. The interaction became boring because there was no sexual chemistry between us. It was just alcohol! I hurried and soon after our 'sex scene' was over and she was not pleased, and I was not pleased. Teese and Ms. Star got into an argument about her flirting with some guy who worked for Seven Up Bottling Company. They were getting on my last nerve with their arguing. I told them that they had to leave my place with all that arguing going on. On top of that, Shanika was angry, which caused Ms. Star to ask her what's wrong, and she said, "Nothing! I'm just ready to go." It was about 4 am and she was getting ready to walk to the bus stop, which was crazy because there was all kind of rapist outside in the area, including the Mexican gangs. I didn't want her to walk out during that time of morning, but if that's what she wanted to do, I wasn't going to stop her. She started walking, so I ran down to catch her to try and talk some sense in her head. I didn't know what her problem was but as we were conversing, she started getting angry and cried. Maybe she felt like I did not show her enough attention, or she was not sexually pleased. I don't know what exactly caused her to just up and leave. Neither one of us appreciated each others company, but since she had a nasty attitude, my mentality was as long as I got mines. Ms. Star told me some months later that it was just a game Shanika was playing on me with the fake crying; I said to her, "I didn't care if it was a game or not it did not work. I just loved the way she smelled and was able to get her to my bed." All four of us were in the same bed together; Teese and Ms. Star was having sex and Shanika and I was not having the best of time because she had a real negative attitude.

We got into another argument, and I kicked her out of my apartment; Ms. Star was like "you can't kick her out!" I told her "She is serving stress to me, and I am tired of her different moods already, so I kicked her out." Since it was the afternoon, this time around the girl would not have any problems walking to the bus stop. After the interaction with Shanika, I reflected on my life and realized that I have no more tolerance for drama. I had just turned twenty-three years old and at that point I was still hanging out in the streets, but not as an active banger. I was still a young O.G. but feeling empty and alone and looking for something to fulfill those hollow spaces in my life. I was always true to Fulton St. Mobb and anytime any drama jumped off, I had a lifetime allegiance and loyalty to my street family. My emptiness was being replaced with my excitement with Italian cooking Cuisines and drinking expensive bottles of wine that Z-double would hook me up with. I would flirt with women occasionally, but nothing serious to the point that I would let them get too close to me; my social skills towards women were tarnished because of the relationship I had with my mom. I thought since I did not trust my mom and didn't have a loving upbringing that I could never trust women. My functionality with any female was twisted and was not getting better due to my family turning on me and doing n shady things to me, which continued to add fuel to the fire. I didn't socialize with anybody, so I spent my time being 'troublesome.' I didn't overstand why I continued to be so confused and frustrated about knowing what things to handle, as if I was in the streets and when not to. I had no clue about what to do. I would have at least thought by now at the age of twenty-three, I would have some things figured out, but I felt alone and hopeless. I was being haunted by those unsettled demons of my past. I was waking up in cold sweats thinking that someone had found out where I lived and started shooting me to death, to the point where my mom could not identify my body. I mean those demons were waking me up out of my sleep at four or five in the morning.

I had so many terrible nightmares of seeing skulls of people and of people killing me, that I used to think that someone close to me was going to set me up to be killed by a rival gang. I could actually feel my body being shot and would be moving and jerking my body in my sleep. I continued to go through this cycle of my life for about ten to 15 years. There would be times when I would stay up for two days not wanting to go to sleep. I was surprised that nobody ever associated my devilish past as being the reason I could not sleep, they'd just say 'Oh you have a bad case of insomnia' not realizing that I had a lot of pain, loneliness and darkness going on inside me. My life felt like it had no purpose. I contemplated and realized, that I left Atlanta like a fool only to return to a place of loneliness and incompletion. I was feeling like no one knew me or could overstand where I was in my life or what I wanted and needed. The only thing I was kind of sure about was that Yahweh was responding to my pain and my emptiness and did not want me to feel alone anymore. I could start to see things turn around in some of the relationships I was in. One in particular was with Ms. Star, she and I began to form a solid brother and sister relationship; she showed a tremendous amount of care and concern for me and would make me laugh. She was somebody who always asked questions and listened to every word of wisdom I gave her. I would listen to the issues she was dealing with in her life; hoping that I was saying something that would help her out so she could be happy. She had a troubled upbringing like I did. She did not know who her dad was and lived with her grandma. The environment she was raised in was real bad as well; her mother treated her horribly like my mother did; she called her all kinds of "B****HES" and would show favouritism towards her other sisters and treat Ms. Star like she was not her own flesh and blood. Her Mom would make her watch her sisters and leave her to do the cooking and cleaning, so she was never able to go anywhere.

I guess to get back at her mother; she would steal her mom car as well as her lootchi. Her life was rippled with a lot of pain as well, and the way she dealt with it was to physically fight any and everybody who got on her nerves.

Ms. Star and I were more alike than we thought; we even had the same sense of humour. Some people thought that we looked like brother and sister. The situation between Ms. Star and her mom got so out of control with physical fights that she started to sneak around with boys and would get in trouble when she got caught. She was sent to live with her grandma. Which didn't make life any easier because her grandma had her brother living there, who was Star unclean ex-military uncle who was mentally affected from the war and who always felt as though someone was out to get him; extremely paranoid. In addition to the grandmother's brother living there, she also had her son there who was a 'professional dope fiend' who was in and out of jail and was a 'kleptomaniac.' Ms. Star would open up to me about being unhappy. She said that she was throwing up a lot and didn't overstand why she was always tired. I remember while at work, she would go into the lady's restroom at work and go to sleep. She eventually went to the doctor only to discover that she was pregnant, and the only person she was really involved with sexually was Teese. Things seemed to get worst by the days for her as she found out that Teese had another woman pregnant at the same time and he denied it. Ms. Star went into a state of depression. I tried to be a friend to her and wanted her to smile and not cry. I sincerely viewed her as a little sister and wanted nothing but the absolute best for her; but as time continued on, things did not seem to change for her. Many problems that she was facing sparked some deep concerns for me. Everyday conversation between Ms. Star and I did not change.

She was tired of dealing with the uncomfortable feelings about her uncle who was always stealing her stuff and then finding out that Teese had another woman pregnant at the same time. I seriously thought that with that level of depression, she was going to either kill herself or her unborn child was going to be a miscarriage, because of her not eating nor keeping a healthy diet for herself and the baby. Her lack of focus at work also affected her sensibility. I remember when one of the managers had another co-worker spy on her to see if she was going to the bathroom to sleep; when the report came back to the manager that she was sleeping on the job they fired her. At that point, I opened my doors and told her she could stay at my apartment to be in a more positive atmosphere. I told her that she could have my room since she was pregnant, and I would sleep on the couch. I also said just bring your VCR so we could watch movies. I lived near the top of the hill in Daly City, and it was a huge hill to climb; I told her to meet me at the train station and I would walk up the hills with her.

As we were walking up the hill, I started cracking jokes just to keep her mind off her troubles, and especially that steep hill we had to climb. When we got to my apartment, I had everything arranged for her to feel comfortable; the bed was ready for her to relax and to be at peace. She felt guilty about taking my bed and said, "You don't have to be on the couch; you can come and lay in the room in your bed." She repeated again, "You do not have to be on the couch." I was like, "Nah! I'm not going to have you on the couch." She said, "Well, we both can lay down in the bed." She was not going to stop with the guilt, so I said, "Okay, I'll sleep at the bottom" but she insisted I sleep at the top. I was laying next to her, and I felt a magnetic connection; I didn't know if it was just me, or if it was her or both of us. All I knew was that I enjoyed having her company.

She put her hand on my penis (which shocked me completely). I immediately pushed her hand away, she did it for the second time, and again I moved her hand away. I thought to myself, "If she does it again, I'm going to leave her hand there." The next thing you know, she put her hand right back on my penis, and I left it there. I wasn't sure if that was her way of thanking me for being there for her when no one else was or if we were responding to some unspoken feelings that she had for me. The connection between us at that moment was special, which propelled us to having sex! Now don't get me wrong, I've had a lot of one-night stands, but being with her was different. It was like we were in a serious relationship! After that night, our friendship/relationship was more than I expected because every morning when I got up for work, she would get up and pack a lunch for me. I thought it was real considerate of her to do that, and it felt good to have somebody around who really cared and thought the world of you. She was a shining star that illuminated my dark world. Since no one knew how far we had gone in the relationship, we were now telling people that we were brother and sister. Yes, it felt real awkward saying that we were 'brother and sister' when I knew

I wouldn't be having sex with my sister. One day we had gone to visit her mom and we just happened to have on the same color shirt; her mom knew that there was more going on between us and started saying, "Brother and sister? Humph! You both come in here looking like the Bobbsey Twins Whatever?" The next morning, after that trip to her mother's house, I played a sweet song and dedicated it to her and expressed my appreciation for her, and to let her know that she was the first woman I ever let get close to me. I said I wanted her to know that with all the love and care she showed me, she made me feel like I had a right to know what love was all about. I wanted her to be my wisdom, I expressed to her that I play for keeps, so losing is not an option; I will do right by you, and we are going to build this Burton Empire.

It was a good feeling and crazy at the same time because here I was with a girl who was pregnant with another man's baby and loving both her and the baby as if it was my very own child. I felt as if it was my responsibility to be there for her when she had been left on her own so many times before. We were an inseparable pair, and we did everything together. Things were going good for a while; however, things began to change with us financially because I was laid off from my job with the Seven Up Bottling Company. I was not trying to be hustling in the streets full time, but that 'old nature' of mine was biting me in the behind. The next thing I knew, I was back hanging with the O.G.'s. I always made sure the house was together and food was cooked and that she was taking care of. I always knew to take care of home before I left for the night. Although, I was trying not to be in the streets at night, little by little; with neither one of us working, it was a real struggle trying to make ends meet. We were struggling so hard, that this 1999 Hyundai car I bought for her didn't even want to stay around. We called the car 'Bertha' and it made screeching sounds in the engine that sounded like James Brown was yelling. The car had some serious axle issues, and a flat tire. We did not have the lootchi to get the car fixed, nor was it worth fixing. So back on the bus we returned. Traveling on the bus was a problem. I was going to her doctor visits with her to make sure the baby was fine and healthy, as well as attending her prenatal classes because I never looked at the baby as if it was not my own; that was the bond Ms. Star and I had with each other. No one had ever made me feel comfortable with opening my heart and be committed to any relationship the way she did. In fact, what we shared was so special that she even infused my name into the baby's name. She was judged by a lot of people because she was young and pregnant. They also felt that I shouldn't want to be committing myself to that kind of obligation.

What people did not overstand about her was the fact that, I knew the 'quality of the person she was' and grew to love everything about her; she was such a sweetheart who thought the world of me, which really overwhelmed me. Believe it or not, we were having the best time of our lives; we were so close that we began to know what each other was going to say before it was even said. Things Started to become a bit scary for her and me as the baby was growing inside her. One afternoon, we wanted to be intimate, but it was hard because her stomach was beginning to really develop, and we were not able to easily find a comfortable position. She would say, "She can get on top as long as I don't go in real deep." At first, I was like "Naw"! You can't get on top of me you are four months pregnant." She replied, "I have it under control, just make sure I was careful." She got on top of me, and we were in the moment; the more she was riding on me the deeper I was penetrating, while trying to pull back at the same time. However, something was just feeling a bit strange, so I said, "Something doesn't feel right." She got scared and jumped off me and said, "It feels like something is coming out of me!" She ran to the bathroom, and then, she yells out "PONNE! COME HERE" in a scared and crying tone. I ran into the restroom and was like "What's going on?" She yelled out "I think the baby fell out into the toilet!" I said, "What are you talking about?" I told her to get off the toilet so I could see what was in there, all I saw was a bunch of white stuff with some pinkish red color of blood in the toilet. She continued to explain that something didn't feel right and that it felt like something was trying to come out of her. I said to her call the advice nurse at Kaiser Permanente Hospital, so that they could tell us if we had anything to worry about. We called and were on hold for about twenty minutes when she started to feel some extreme pain in her stomach.

A representative finally answered, I began to explain all that took place. They told her to elevate her legs and put an ice pack on her stomach; that didn't make any sense to me, I was like "WHAT?! That's no advice!" I said, "Something's not right; we have to go to the hospital." We had to take that broken down car to the emergency department, only to be waiting for hours to be seen by a doctor. Once the doctor came out and they ran some test on her to see if the baby was all right; they gave her an ultrasound and discovered that the baby was not alive! The baby was stillborn at four months. My heart stopped in the middle of its beat. I felt totally guilty and responsible for taking her through so much devastation. I had broken her bond with our daughter; I didn't know how to handle that stage in my life. Her mental state of mind changed immediately before my very eyes. I felt as if she did not want to live anymore. I was really nervous and scared and thought that I would have two deaths on my hands.

The death of the baby and from her taking her own life. I was wrapped in complete devastation and found it extremely difficult to forgive myself for taking her through all of that emotional torture; it was one thing just having the baby prematurely, but she had to give birth to a baby who was no longer alive; the thought of that still makes me sad today. Ms. Star pain and depression was so deep that it was preventing me from helping us move forward from that heart wrenching experience. I tried to get her to overstand how the loss of a baby, my baby, our baby, affected me just the same. She looked at me with the evil of death in her eyes and would not let me help. Every day I watched as she cried and held a baby photo album in her hands, and she would fall asleep with it at night. I sat for about six months in sorrow and darkness, helpless for myself and for her as well.

As I watched her light dim, I knew I had to be a light in her dark world, but she was making it difficult for me because of the hurt she was feeling. I felt so torn inside. I felt like I had nothing more to offer. I wanted my tears to be seen but I could not break down because I had to be strong for her. While in the midst of my own shattered emotions, I was determined to keep things together for us because if I didn't, the loss of the baby would have destroyed all that we were building. We were approaching our one year of begin together and she still had not fully recovered from losing the baby; however, she was making great progress towards getting herself together (I guess she got tired of the unhealthy way she was dealing with the loss). She started putting the pieces of her life back together by looking for work and allowing me to help her in whatever way I could. She thanked me for enduring everything and for being by her side. She eventually was hired to work at the Warehouse Music Store where they sold CD's, VHS, DVD's, Video Games. She also got a second job working for Macy's in the appliance department and would steal expensive appliances; she would take lootchi from the cash register and steal movies, CD's, and video games for me from her job at the Music Store. Every time she would steal stuff for me, I would give her some dry thank you and it really hurt her. I wasn't doing it deliberately, but she felt that because she was going through some extreme measures to make me happy, I wasn't giving her that 'happy reaction' that she was looking for; it made her real upset. I don't know if I was going through my own emotional distress from losing our daughter or if I was just in a place where I really didn't know how to truly be happy unconditionally.

The more she hustled for us, the more my love for her grew stronger and stronger. She was the first person I ever met who gave me back the love and support that I gave to her. While going through the midst of everything with her, I got a strange phone call from a security guard who used to work at Safeway where I worked. I remember when I worked there, he said to me that people used to call him 'Mad Dog' when he was in the military; he was a short and very muscular guy who lived in a motel paying large amounts of lootchi on a weekly basis. He also told me that he didn't like living there. He called me in regard to a vacancy ad that I placed at the Safeway grocery store before I resigned stating that I had a room for rent. I took Mad Dog through a couple of tests before I allowed him close to me and he seemed cool. In addition to that, I empathize with his story he had two kids and was working hard and did not have anything to show for his labour; he had no lootchi, no car or a place of his own. Since I had firsthand knowledge about that kind of struggle, I was willing to open my doors to give him the opportunity to at least have a place to call home. It happened to be one of the biggest mistakes I ever made, although Ms. Star was living there before Mad Dog came, I needed some additional help with paying the rent since I was only receiving unemployment bene-fits due to losing my job with Seven Up Bottling Company. Ms. Star and Mad Dog are now living in the apartment with me, and things are starting to become a little suspicious to me. Something was revealed that I didn't know. Mad Dog had a thing for Ms. Star, when she worked at Safeway, and he did security there.

After Mad dog was staying with us for about three months, Star was getting upset that Mad Dog was living there and the fact that he was eating her food and drinking all of her grape juice and using it to enter-tain his lady friends, which really just irritated her. He would put water back into the container of the grape juice so no one could tell he had been drinking it. When she told me that her juice had been tampered with, I confronted Mad Dog and he denied touching any of her stuff. Problems upon problems began to brew in the apartment with Mad Dog being there. He would bring real heavy set Mexican women to the house at like three or four in the morning who would have on narrow 3 quarter inch high boots on walking real heavy and drunk making all kinds of noise on the fragile hardwood floor with no consideration. They'd be drunk, having sex, and making me so vex that I wanted to go off. I was extremely fed up with all that he was doing. He was always bringing heavy-set woman who would walk so hard you could feel the vibrations throughout the apartment, it would always be like 3am or 4am. He would try and copy some of the things that I would do for Ms. Star such as cooking nice candlelight dinners and other romantic things as well. I remember Ms. Star telling me one time that she overheard Mad Dog saying that we were some roommates living with him in his apartment temporarily. Knowing that information sent my temper level to the fiery pits of hell. There was no way in the world I was going to let this dude take for granted my kindness in my apartment like that. One day, just like clockwork he had a different heavy set Mexican woman come through the door while both of them drunk, at the same time as always. I talked to him once before and yet, he made up in his mind that my words were coming in one ear and going out the other.

Chapter 81

Fragmented Emotions Fueled By This Thing Called Love

AT THIS POINT, my 'man to man' talk did nothing and it just ushered in the invitation for him to see the other side of me that I tried to grow from. Personally, I live life by this rule: If I have to talk to a grown adult more than two times about a problem or situation and they refuse to adhere to it, then I have to unleash that Beelzebub side out of me. Mad Dog and this girl was getting louder and louder. Ms. Star kept trying to pull me back from going towards his room. She knew what mental state I was in. I yanked my arm away from her and said "Mad Dog! I need you to keep the noise down." He replied by saying, "Okay, my bad." I went back to my room and fifteen minutes later they started back up. Ms. Star again tried pulling me from going back out there. I yelled, "Dude! I asked you to keep the noise down, if you can't then you need to tell your company to leave." Prior to this incident, we had an arrangement that if any one of our guests was causing problems, we had to respect the other roommate request to have that guest leave. He did not respect what I said, so I told him that he needed to have his company leave within thirty minutes. He didn't like what I said so he yelled, "Who you think you talking to? Telling me that my company has to leave. I pay rent just like you!" My mind was like "You Must have Forgot whose house this is. This is MY M**** F*****"!!! House and you and that fat B***h can get the F***out right now!"

I went back in the room and dude, and I were yelling at each other through the door. The woman leaves and we are still arguing through the door at this point. I stopped responding to what he was saying and just left him arguing with himself. Mad Dog was saying things like "Go f*** around and get killed up in here." I don't play with words that threaten to take my life, so I called a good partner of mine and told him that I needed a firearm that didn't have any body counts on it. That morning, I went to meet up with my partner to get his '9mm Beretta' style handgun with a scope on it. I let Ms. Star know not to come out of our bedroom while I was gone. I also explained to her that we were going to kick Mad Dog out and if he wanted to wage a war then I was ready. I got the gun and returned home; I put on all black and stayed up all night sitting and staring at the doorknob waiting for him to try and get in. My mental state was like tonight is the night he's about to feel my wrath. I didn't care because he was so scandalous at times that he would have women call me, trying to flirt so that Ms. Star and I would start arguing and have problems in our relationship. I asked the females why are they calling and how did they get this number; they told me Mad Dog gave it to them. I sternly expressed to them that I already had a lady and for them to stop calling my phone, but they replied, "What she don't know won't hurt her!" I knew everything had reached an all-time low because I felt like I was sleeping with the enemy. He was such a low-down snake in the grass, that he would even try and get another woman to talk to me to cause problems with me and my lady. Nevertheless, no matter what he did, I never ever let him see any weakness in me. To take Mad Dog's life was not what I wanted to do, but he was pushing me in ways I hadn't been pushed in a very long time.

Chapter 82

Time Doesn't Heal Wounds
On Its Own . . . Put That Work In

IN ORDER FOR us to just go our separate ways without anyone getting hurt, was to let him know that we were getting ready to move and he had to find another place to live. I told him that I couldn't believe that things had gotten to such a point that my 'peace of mind' was at stake; I couldn't afford to go backwards again. He told me that he felt bad because I was like his brother; however, it didn't matter to me what he felt because I was as done with him like an over cooked Salmon steak. My goal was to keep things kosher so we could just go our separate ways in peace. Once Mad Dog moved out, two months later the landlord said that he was going up on the rent, so we started looking at apartments in Oakland, California where the rent was more affordable. Ms. Star was able to find an apartment in East Oakland for us (an area that's known as the murder dubs) which use to be a rival set at one point. We moved into the apartment complex, which was okay; nevertheless, we were more excited that we didn't have anybody living with us. We wanted to focus on building our relationship. Now that things seemed to be going as planned in Ms. Star and my relationship, we still had a lot to struggle with, one thing in particular, a car named Bertha. That car was in such bad shape, it was worse than a 'second hand car' she was more like a car that was passed down from five generations. We struggled so hard to the core of our being. We were so in love, like the ghetto version of 'Romeo and Juliet.' Three months after moving to East Oakland, we both started looking for jobs.

It was kind of hard because we had one car that was in real bad condition that made a lot of noise. The approach I took with finding a job and trying to get hired was going to the grocery stores trying to meet employees who worked with either Pepsi or Coca-Cola Beverage Company. I met this one guy who worked for Coca-Cola, and I asked if the company was hiring, he said that they always hiring. I was so appreciative of the fact that the guy could have been a hater like 'Darth Vader' and been negative about the situation and said nothing. He was willing to be honest with me. I began to thank Yahweh for allowing me the opportunity to pick that guy's brain to find out about Coca-Cola products. I can apply my previous experience when

I worked with Seven Up Bottling Company. I felt like that put me in a great position to possibly get hired. The man gave me all the information that I needed to pursue a career with the company, including which days to pick up and submit my application. I didn't know if I had one or two felony charges under my belt, but all I could do was to put my trust in Yahweh and pray for another opportunity to better my life. There headquarter office opened at 8am, I was there at 7:30am. I was dressed like a broker active on Wall Street. I met with this manager named Mr. Michael B.; he was a character, he stood at 6 feet 4 inches tall and had a brown complexion; his voice sounded like he was always exhausted, we hit it off instantly, he looked like the lead singer JT from the Pop funk band Kool & The Gang. He asked if I had a problem showing up for work at 4:30 in the morning and how often I called in sick to work. I politely said, "Mr. B., you have to realize that I totally overstand what you are looking for; I worked for Seven Up Bottling Company for a year, so I am very familiar with the Coca-Cola Brand."

My interview was going so well that Mr. B. asked if I could take a drug test right after the interview and if I could start work on Monday; I said, "I most certainly can!" I looked up and gave thanks to Yahweh for Blessing me again; it was and still is important to me to give honour and praise to Yahweh for every accomplishment I've ever had in my life. It was moments like this that made me know that it was not by my own doing that I had made it thus far.

I was so happy and couldn't wait to tell Ms. Star that I finally had a job. Ms. Star and I were both working now. She had a job working at Boston Market and there were times when she would have to walk to work and the sun would be beaming on her fake braids making her hot, sweaty, and vexed. She unfortunately had to walk pass the street blocks that were filled with pimps and prostitutes who would try to recruit her to join their family. I was furious, I told her she did not have to go back to that job and that I was just hired to work for Coca-Cola. I told her to just focus on finding a better job so that she wouldn't have to go back there. She ended up getting a job at Albertsons grocery store bagging groceries and I was working hard as well; pulling in 70-hour work weeks, which also included overtime. Although we were making some lootchi, we started to argue because she was just about talking on the phone with her friends, I began to feel like I wasn't 'number 1' in her life anymore; plus, she was becoming controlling, and I had a toxic attitude. My approach was very demanding and possessive. I was really just being overprotective with her, but it was all coming out the wrong way. I was just making situations worse. Since I'm working now, I knew that I could not continue to allow us to be without reliable transportation. Before the weekend ended, I had to find a car before I went back to the job game (work).

I wanted a car with a manual transmission (stick shift) because they were faster and much cooler to drive and good on gas. I went to a Honda car dealership to get a car and had to get it financed, since I didn't have any credit. They charged me 24% interest rate on a 1995 Hyundai Accent, which for me was like paying for two cars but was only able to drive one. I was so upset; however, I was just happy to turn in Bertha and get a new car that I named Nubia. I don't think Ms. Star was feeling the car I purchased, because it was rumoured from her family that I got a stick shift so she would not be able to drive it. She was the one I spent all my time with. I thought she knew me better than that. I never been that kind of person who beat around the bush; I say what I feel, and I feel what I say! I could not believe she took what her family and friends were saying over my word. She should have just stood by her man! With unwanted 'third party comments' coming from her family and friends, it caused a lot of drama between the two of us, which eventually led to our demise. I can't say exactly what happened to her, but we were no longer treating each other as his and her #1. I was so sick and tired of arguing about a bunch of nonsense that I would leave home at 4am for work and I would not come back until 8 or 9 at night. When she wasn't working and would be home alone all day, I thought by the time I made it home, she would be excited and ready to take care of her king. Honestly, I missed those special moments we spent together, when we were not working, we had a lot of time for each other and when we both started working again, we were not around each other like we once were. We were constantly getting into arguments all the time, so when I wanted to make love to relax myself from a 15 to 17-hour workday; she would not be in the mood. We came to a mutual decision that we would go our separate ways.

Chapter 83

Daddy Creating
A First Lady In The Womb Of A Star

IN ORDER FOR us to try and stay cordial, she was going to have to move out of the apartment. I kept telling her to get out and every time, she would yell out "I'm the Boss!" She would walk up in my face wanting to fight (I guess she was used to bossing other guys around); however, my mentality was different because I said to her, "If anybody was going to be the 'boss', that someone was going to be me." I'm not sure me being twenty-three years of age and she was just turning twenty played a factor in our separating, but whatever the case may have been, we were both ready for it to be over because she wanted to experience things as well. However, sometimes when a person want something so bad, it doesn't necessarily mean it will happen right then. What I mean is this: One day, I happened to come home early from work on a Wednesday because she had already agreed that she would move out by that Friday; there was nothing there to keep us together and our relationship was done. Nevertheless, when I walked into the kitchen, she was eating a pickle with a glow on her face; I said, "ARE YOU PREGNANT?" She looked at me with a scared look on her face and said, "I don't know." The first thing that came to my mind was "AWW Man! What is going on? How are you pregnant and you are moving out on Friday?" I went into the living room and didn't know what to do. I was already battling with my emotions about us not being together anymore after being with somebody who I opened the doors of my heart to (which I swore not to open up to anybody), and now after almost two years of being together we were splitting up. Ms. Star said she did not know if she was pregnant.

Chapter 84

Symbol Of Definite
Love Caught Between Broken Hearts

I KNEW IT! Because their were other woman I saw pregnant before who I had no involvement with, so I knew what the symptoms were. So, the first thing I asked was what are we going to do since you moving out? "Are you planning on getting an abortion?" She looked at me and started crying and then went off by screaming, "I'M ABOUT TO CALL MY MOM!" She called her mom crying and screaming saying, "I'm pregnant and I need to come home!" I told her to hang up the phone, she was not leaving because the situation was between us. She kept on crying and crying because she thought I was telling her to get an abortion. "I said, I did not say I wanted you to get an abortion. I just didn't know what we we're going to do since you are moving out on Friday." She said, "I'm not going to be with you because we have a baby!" "This is not about us being together because we have a child on the way." I replied, "Listen I have stone love for you, and I want you close to my heart." After arguing back and forth for some time, we kissed and made up; however, about two months later, we were back fighting. She was the type of girl who likes to get up in a persons face ready to fight; I didn't know how to deal with a girl like that. I didn't believe in hitting a female to get her to shut up or take me serious as a man, so the best thing I could do was to tell her to "Get Out!" She would then say, "You would kick me out while I have your child inside me?" I replied, "Yeah, I'm telling you to get out!" She was very confrontational, and my thing is this: I don't believe in letting a man, woman, or anybody for that matter disrespect me in any form or fashion without correcting that immediately.

One day while we were at the house, she allowed her mouth to become extremely reckless and disrespectful, and even though she was pregnant, I still told her to "GET THE F*** OUT AND I HATE YOU!" As I was talking, I bent over to pick up an object off the floor and she tried to push me into a bookshelf that had a nail sticking out of it. Just as she did that, I turned my body in an awkward direction so my shoulder would hit the nail and not my face. It was weird how I was able to maneuverer my body in a way that I missed hitting the bookshelf with my face, but it knocked her off balance and she almost tripped and landed on her stomach with my precious First Lady inside her. I was so vexed and felt betrayed; I told her to "Hurry up and get the F*** Out!" She moved out that same night. I was mad at myself and crushed at the same time because I had grown so close to my unborn child, my daughter had grown so much inside her stomach. I started thinking about the times when I would bath Ms. Star and wash her body, rubbed her stomach, and sing songs to my daughter. I'd cook breakfast, lunch, and dinner for Ms. Star, because I wanted to make sure she was well taking care of. If she wanted me to get up in the middle of the night to get her favourite juice, I did it! I spoiled her like she deserved. For those reasons it crushed me that I wasn't able to experience the whole pregnancy stage because of the many 'break ups to make ups' moments that we had during her nine-month pregnancy. To be very honest, we probably spent about three to four months together; if even that. What was even crazier, was the fact that, the more we fought, the more we realized how much we loved each other. Every time I told Ms. Star to leave, she would pack all of her belongings only to return back three days later because our hearts would hurt from missing each other too much. When she came back, she apologized, and I apologized to her as well.

Chapter 85

A Baby Can Mask An Unhealthy Dynamic For Only So Long

WE ONLY HAD a month left before the baby was scheduled to come. Early in the pregnancy, I just knew I was having a son, so I went and bought a host of boy clothes; however, to my dismay, when the first ultrasound was performed the doctor said the baby was not faced in the right direction and we was not able to determine the gender. I believe it took the third ultrasound, which they are not ethically allowed to do, but we begged, and the doctor said, "There is no third leg it's a girl!" I was extremely shocked because all this time I've been yelling out "Souljah Boy" the baby would move, and I always would talk to the baby as if it was a boy. Either way, I was happy and excited about the birth of our baby. One night, after we made love, she started having contractions and said she needed to go to the doctor. I said, "You do not need to go to the doctor, we've been to the doctor a lot already" (she had so many episodes about thinking she was going into labour, but they were false alarms). I was so tired because I had been working and had been up for like twenty-four hours. Prior to that, we were living in Oakland and the doctor was located in Vallejo, California. I told her to just drink some warm milk and elevate her feet. She said she had already tried that and that the milk made it worse. I tried to lay down to rest for a while when she said, "I'm leaving with or without you! Something is not right." Next thing you know we're driving to Kaiser Hospital in Vallejo, and after waiting for a long time, the doctor finally admitted us, and we learned that she was already four centimeters dilated. She said, "I told you something was not right."

Now, as you read this, I would like for this to be kept in mind: I had not had any sleep, I left the house with an old shirt and some wrinkled pants, and my hair was nappy. Anyone who looked at me could tell I was a rookie father because an experienced father would have made sure he had himself looking together because he knew pictures would be taken. There I was looking like an extra out of the movie 'Night of The Living Dead.' I was there helping her every step of the way with breathing and counting how far the contractions are apart, so she could get ready to push for the baby to come. We kept trying to make sure it was a natural birth, but the pain was getting the best of her to the point I thought I seen Beelzebub in her eyes. She transformed right before me; she tried to put her claws into my skin and gave me a look like 'You, M**** F*****; you did this to me!' We got to a point where the pain became unbearable for her, so they gave her an epidural. She was begging for some relief, I personally didn't agree with the shot, but what can I say, I was not the one on the delivery table, nor was I the one who was feeling the pain. I just didn't like all the side effects, which were, headaches, irregular periods, back pain, and the list goes on. Once the medicine from the epidural began to take effect, she was able to fully dilate. Then soon afterwards, about an hour later, my daughter First Lady was born—weighing in at 8lbs, 5 ounces, and 22inches long. Ms. Star had been in labour from 8:30am to around 11:30pm. Witnessing the birth of my child was an amazing sight to see, although the process was like me looking at an alien from another planet with all sorts of multi-colored fluids flowing out of Ms. Star. My baby didn't even cry when she came out. She looked up at me with a vein over her eye and did a little cry and then I started talking to her and she went quiet.

She was listening to me as if she remembered hearing my voice from when she was inside the womb. There is no amount of lootchi that could substitute that feeling of holding a life in your arms that you are responsible for helping to create. I was so honoured and proud of the fact that Ms. Star gave me the greatest gift I could have ever hoped for. I wanted her to know how much I appreciated all that she had gone through for me. After everything was over, she wanted about eight (8), yes eight cans of Root Beer Soda. I went out to get what she wanted, as well as a dozen of roses, a nice cuddly teddy bear, a card, some balloons, and a baby photo album to begin building memories; that was the least I could do for her. When I first spoke the name First Lady, I wanted to make sure that my daughter would be the first lady, in my life. That I could teach how to be trustworthy, loving, honest, respectful, and always aim to be the best at whatever challenges she decided to tackle. This was one of those rare moments in my life that changed my overstanding and perception of how to value something or someone. My appreciation and admiration for women changed as well. It grew into a more infinite love and humble respect for how a woman could have that intimate relationship with Yahweh and the baby. Which was something that a man could not have in that intimate way. Ms. Star and I were in a new space in our relationship after the birth of our daughter. I made a covenant with her that I would remain by her side no matter what. Being a family was a rewarding feeling for both of us since we lost a baby prior to the First Lady being born, and to go the full 9 ½ months, that's right 9 ½ months, maybe the First Lady knew something about this world we didn't. She did not want to come out at all. All in all, it was a tremendous blessing from Yahweh! I went and bought my First Lady all kinds of baby stuff that was nothing less than the best.

If people were looking for the definition of a proud father, they would have seen my nappy head and long face in the Webster's Dictionary posing. I would show anybody who I would talk to a picture of my daughter. That moment was very transforming for me because I never looked at myself as a confused emotional person anymore, who did not have anyone to pour my emotions into. My daughter validated my life, by giving me a sense of innocence that I couldn't identify with before. When the time came for Ms. Star to leave the hospital, we stayed with her mother who lived close to the doctor's office for a couple of days since the baby tore Ms. Star through her vaginal area and had to have an episiotomy (a surgical procedure which helps to open the birthing canal) and stitches are required. Ms. Star was healing right on schedule and the doctor gave her a clean bill of health report. I was ready for us to be at our own apartment in Oakland, anyway, to get back to doing some of the things we were doing before. I wanted her to be a 'stay at home mom' so she could breastfeed and take care of our daughter.

One thing in particular we started doing was going to IHOP (International House of Pancakes) almost every morning for breakfast as a family. We were mesmerized at the fact of having our daughter right there with us. Taking care of my family was more important to me than anything else at that point. I wanted to make sure that we had the financial stability we needed. I would work any and all extra hours at Coca-Cola that was available for me. When I came home, I would stay up at night with the baby so that her mother could get a break and a chance to rest. However, the relationship between Ms. Star and I was beginning to drift backwards. Yes, we had what one would consider a 'partnership' but the intense arguments that we were getting into were a bit too much. We would try not to argue in front of the First Lady, but not with much success.

We both were emotionally undeveloped and mentally wounded because of the 'individual and family baggage' we both brought into the relationship. Neither one of us knew how to effectively deal with hostile and aggressive situations in a healthy manner. I was demanding and possessive, but was caring, loving, and I took care of my family and the house. On the other hand, she was very confrontational and felt as though she was the boss of me and everyone else for that matter. Therefore, my perception of her being the 'star in my dark world' was beginning to change. I'm sure her perception of me being everything for her changed as well. She started letting other people's opinion dictate our relationship by putting the wrong kind of information in her head, which caused us to forget about the foundation we built our love and union upon. Which eventually led to us having a big fight and her moving back with her mom. Ms. Star and The First Lady not living with me anymore, it tore me up inside and out! Not having my daughter in my life every day was not making life feel comforting or purposeful at all. I would tolerate so much from her mom because I wanted my First Lady to have both of her parents in the same household, but her mom and I, together, was not a healthy match. My daughter personified the definition of 'Stone Love.' I watched her leave with her mom and my world returned dark. I fell into a deep state of depression. I didn't go to work, nor did I eat or drink anything for about five days. I just sat from morning to night in the dark, drowning in my own pain. I was so hurt that the pain I was experiencing in my head felt as if someone heated up some screws and began twisting them in my left and right temple.

Chapter 86

Never In My Life Was Their One Person I Can Always Count On

I HAD NOBODY there to take care of me, I'm not sure if I wanted anybody to take care of me anyway. I didn't know what was wrong with me. All I knew was that I no longer had anybody I could count on. I called one of my partna's named, KP. I got to a point where I lost my voice and could not speak from crying all day and night. I was hurting! When I tried to speak to KP, he thought I was playing on his phone, I told him that I lost my voice and had not eaten or drunk anything in five days and wanted him to bring me some Gatorade and food so I could rehydrate my body. KP told me he was waiting for his girl to come back with the car, and he would be at my house in thirty minutes. I was so relieved knowing that I had at least one person who I could rely on. However, it was getting close to thirty minutes, and I hadn't heard anything from KP. I waited another thirty minutes and still no call, no show from KP. I called his phone and didn't get an answer. Now, at that point, I was hotter than hell! Another thirty minutes had passed when I decided to call KP's phone again and he finally picked up the phone saying "Sorry P, I'm on my way now! My girl is right around the corner with the car." In my heart I knew that he was lying, but I needed some food and drink to get some energy, so I felt comfortable enough that he would come through. Just as I thought, another hour went by, and I called, and I got no answer. The fact is, that KP only lived about fifteen minutes away from me, so for him to be taking as long as he did, meant that he didn't want to come in the first place. I called that dude's phone relentlessly throughout the night and he didn't pick up. I could have died waiting on his a**. The next morning, I called KP and finally got him to answer. I said, "what happened?" He was like, "P, I'm sorry I fell asleep."

I was crushed! He tried to explain himself, but I just hung up the phone and changed my number so he could never call me again. I called my sisters as my last resort and they came through for me, being that I had not showered or brushed my teeth or cleaned myself up for five days, my apartment smelled like the Serengeti with a touch of ten-year old sh***y diapers! I looked horrible! When my sisters came over to help take care of me, I could have cried like a newborn baby. It was one of the saddest moments in my life. My pride got the best of me once again and I would not bring myself to ask any of my female friends for help. I had to rely on my sisters. My daughter mom never realized not having my daughter around, how it made me feel. Through it all, because she got herself a good paying job, she begin to meet new friends and also begin to attract a lot of male interest. One particular male interest would be one that she could never escape. My world was cold and alone. I felt as though life was not as meaningful to me anymore because I didn't have my daughter around me every day. What made everything even worse, was the fact that she didn't see my viewpoint of how I felt. I guess that's because she found a job that paid well and was beginning to meet new friends, and new males, and I guess she was blinded from all the attention. She had no time for me anymore. I begged her to come back to me! I told her that I needed my family back, and I was really weak right now. I continued to say to her, "You know I never had my dad in my life, nor was my mom in my life the way I needed her to be." She just ate my emotions for breakfast, brunch, lunch, dinner, and a late-night snack. While at the same time, looking me right in my face in broad daylight and telling me that she didn't want a relationship and that it was just about her and her Cita's (that's what she called our daughter).

Chapter 87

Role Reversal When Your Not Special No More To Them

THE TRUTH OF the matter was that she was making her own lootchi and did not need me anymore! I allowed myself to go through so much emotional torment by showing weakness to a young woman who really did not overstand my value. I would surprise her with large teddy bears and roses. I was willing to do anything to get my family back and all it did was make things worse. One of the most difficult things about trying to get my family back together was that she did not look at me the same as she once did, and it was hard to accept. We both knew that our situation was unhealthy, but everything within me was willing to try harder than I ever had before. I think I was going through an identity crisis again. I went from being a respected O.G. to trying to work in Corporate America, and then trying to become a family man and failed at it all except for the street life. I began to believe that I was only good for doing the wrong things in life. I went through a phase that I did not believe anything good could come from my life. I spent a lot of time praying to Yahweh asking him to let me know where my daughter was located and to give me the strength to fight in court to get custody of her, so I would not have to see her mom again, and just deal with her on my terms. I ended up having to pay child support even though I was taking care of my daughter. It was just another blade stabbed in my heart. I was so enraged! I would leave all sorts of hateful messages on her mom voicemail and on my own voicemail about her! I would record some painful songs to vent my anguish and leave them on my voicemail like 'You Can't Handle a True Man' by one of my favourite groups Jagged Edge.

Chapter 88

You Don't Like How It Feels, When It's Done To You?

I ALWAYS HAD been able to avoid being hurt by a woman since receiving my bachelor's degree from my mom 'Cold Hearted Abuse University.' Again, if I ever had a downfall in life, it was letting a woman be sweet in the beginning, just to get close to my emotions and also putting people before me.

I remember one time when my Uncle Apprentice (R.I.P.) and I were watching the Super Bowl when I got a call from a dude telling me that this Asian girl said she was going to kill herself if I wasn't going to be in a relationship with her. I was just cold hearted, telling him, "Don't be calling my phone with no S*** like this." I could not believe what he was saying. I told this square, "To get off my phone! And I let her know we could just be friends." And the girl was in the background crying her heart out as if she was taking her last breath in pain, and the cold part about it all was that, not even one cell in my body was affected. I don't know if she really committed suicide or not till this day.

I had an introspective moment as I begun the writing process of the journey of this story. I was reflecting on my mom; how she would inflict so much evil and fear upon me and not have a second moment of guilt for none of her actions. I was wondering if that's why I justified my behaviour to be harsh and normalized it by being desensitize in situations. Not caring, nor investigating if the young woman really killed herself or not. It's crazy because I wanted people to sympathize with my hurt, but I wasn't giving it back to the universe.

Chapter 89

It Hurts To Deal But She Still Has Your Daughter

I TRULY THINK the hurt that mom put inside me gave me a stern exterior. I finally made time to go to Family Court to find out what I needed to do in order to get full custody of my daughter. I was already paying child support, so that was not an issue. The issue was that I wanted my daughter to be with me full time. The courts told me that just because I was paying child support, visitation required a completely separate court order. The person who was helping me told me that, if the mother was neglecting the child, harming the child, providing a bad environment for the child that was putting the child in harm's way and I could prove it, then I had a case. I knew within my heart that Ms. Star loved our daughter and was providing her with all the love she could offer. My greatest concern was that she had our daughter growing up so fast and exposing her to certain adult situations. Since I was running into so many brick walls, I made my mind up, I just needed to block out what happened with me and my daughter mom and just focus on our daughter. I started just focusing on having my daughter all the time with me so I would have a strong influence on her life. I think it was also because I was trying to heal my hurt through my daughter. Me and her mom would still get into big arguments over our daughter and how she thought she could control the situation. What she failed to over stand was the fact that I was not that kind of father that was weak and just let the mother control everything. I didn't care that our daughter lived with her mom fulltime, she wasn't about to come at me like I'm a dead beat. I made sure I was not going to be anything like my dad and just let the mother of the child shut the father out or just only involve the father when it's time to get lootchi for the child.

Chapter 90

Ignoring Your Own
Hurt For A Person Who Needs You

I'M WILLING TO admit that we still had feelings for each other, but she wanted to explore her options and I was trying to finally settle down. One day she called me and was saying things like how she was tired of arguing with me, and how she wanted to know if she could come and change her clothes at my apartment and spend the night after she left from some concert. Our relationship was as dysfunctional as one could be! We would always let each other back into each other's lives and be cool for a few weeks, just to return to what was more familiar; arguing! While she was getting ready, I noticed that she had a different level of confidence about herself that she didn't have before. Since she was getting all sorts of attention from her male counterparts, her head started to swell. I tried to caress her, but she acted as though my touch was the worst feeling she ever felt in her life! I realized that she just wanted to keep control of the matter. When she returned back from the event, she pretended to be tired. I guess trying to let me know that nothing sexual was going to take place between us two, but we manage to do something when she came back anyway. Her plans was never to bring the family back together but to make sure I did not put a tombstone on her head and try to bury her completely out of my life. After that incident, a couple of weeks went by, and she came by my apartment; crying saying I got her pregnant and I was like "WHAT ARE YOU TALKING ABOUT!!" I said we're going to Planned Parenthood to take a test and get an accurate count of the days she been pregnant.

We arrived at Planned Parenthood and when they completed the pregnancy test, it was discovered that she was already pregnant before we had sex! At that point, I was through with all of her antics and schemes. I was like "I don't want to have anything to do with you. I HATE YOU SO MUCH!!!" Then she was like "Why you can't just say the baby is yours and we be together?" When she said that, I was thinking; "This broad is truly crazy!" I was destroyed! I never did view her in the same way as before. She no longer represented any positive light in my dark world; in fact, I think she dimmed every light I had left. Every weekend I would go and get my daughter and would not say anything to my daughter mom. After a month of me just focusing on my daughter and not saying anything to her mom, I think it began to affect her. I know for a fact that it did bother her because about a month later she called me and was crying and apologizing for everything she took me through. She also told me she lost her job because the person she was pregnant by worked with her and was sexing other females on the job and was trying to force her to get an abortion, and then at the last minute was saying not to. I felt sorry for her and for the situation she was in, but I just focused on my daughter, even though it was hard for me to see her pregnant by somebody else. I tried not to look at her stomach all the time because it would make me feel more hurt. My only concern was to put more time in with my daughter and treat her as the 'First Lady of my world.' There were people Ms. Star, and I knew who wanted nothing but the best for us and would come up to me and say that I needed to step in to rescue her from her situation and to take back my family. My heart was no longer in love with her as I was before, I just didn't feel the same as I once did.

When she gave birth to her baby, she called to share the news with me and I said, "I'm glad that you had a healthy baby and congratulations on your delivery." I didn't want anything to do with her, I told her that she better not ever have that baby around me when I come to pick my daughter. In fact, I said, "Just have my 'First Lady' ready at the door."

I knew that I let my crushed and troubled heart get the best of me, but to shake that feeling of being hurt so deep, was like when I saw how hurt my mom was when she found out Mr. Marcel was having kids by another woman. Five months passed after Ms. Star gave birth to her other baby, she was going through a tough time because she needed to move out of her mom's apartment, and she needed to get a job real bad. She had nobody to help her with the baby while she went to look for work. At the same time, when I injured my knee from working at Coca-Cola and had surgery, she was there for me when nobody else was. I felt in my heart I should be there for her because, for the most part she has always been right there for me. Even by my side while the surgeon put me under Anaesthesia to perform surgery on my knee. Thinking about it makes me remember when I was looking up at her and forgetting about all the pain she brought into my life and was like "Thank you for being here, would you marry me?" Next thing after that, I was knocked out and I woke up from surgery sore. Her face was the first thing I saw when I opened my eyes. I didn't know what to make of the relationship between us. I think for the most part, if one is fortunate to meet someone who could have such a profound impact on another person's life, whether love, pain or perhaps both, it's not easy to just erase them from your life. I was released from the hospital and the doctor stated that I needed somebody to take care of me because I needed to stay in bed and have the ice for my knee changed every three hours, to help keep the inflammation down.

Chapter 91

Stone Love Means
Being There, When You Really Don't

THE DOCTORS INVENTED a new treatment with some new ice pack devise that had a tube connected to a cooler so when it was filled with ice, coolness would circulate around to heal my knee quicker. Ms. Star was a good sport about taking care of me in the beginning, but I think by me being impatient, she would take care of certain things for me and then she would develop an attitude quickly. We would start to argue, and I would tell her that she didn't have to do anything for me, if she didn't have it in her heart to help me with my recovery. At this point of my life Ms. Star and I are going through one of our 'up and down spats.' While at the same time I'm going through the recovery of my knee my partner B-Down was graduating from San Jose State University. He was receiving his Bachelor of Science degree in Criminal Justice. I had seen him go through so much, from losing his mom, getting jumped by the Chinese mafia and his head getting bashed open, to being arrested while in college and he was not guilty. I guess the only thing he was guilty of was being associated with melanin. Having his dreams of playing professional football got derailed because of a lot of politics that came with moving from high school level to the collegiate level of football. Knowing that I witnessed all of his madness, I was like a proud big brotha who seen this one-person battle storm after storm and carry everything on his shoulders and still persevered through it all. I only had one good leg, from the surgery which was not going to stop me from missing a huge milestone in his life.

I was having the spirit of Kunta Kinte from the movie 'Roots running through my veins!' There was no way I was going to miss my family paramount moment of his life. I was not cleared to be out of bed, so I wrapped my knee underneath and had my crutches and represented for my family. As I'm driving down to San Jose State for the graduation, I had so many things playing in my mind about my different experiences while B-Down was attending school and how it was a blessing that Yahweh had brought us this far in life.

I was a street disciple, but I had friends who went to college, so a lot of us hood dudes would go to college parties trying to find nice looking 'L 7' women (meaning a nice-looking females who was a square and not street at all). Like this one time I was just trying to get some air and party a little because at that point I had been hustling extremely hard and taking care of my daughter. When we arrived at the party at San Jose State, Cashmuir, Griff a.k.a. Cousin Damarcus, ShowStoppa, B-Down and a couple of B-Down partners who were ex-Crips from L.A. but attended college with him. We all arrived only to discover that the party had reached the maximum number of capacity. We were all thinking we drove this far to just be standing outside of the party looking through the window seeing people dancing and partying having a good time. B-Down partner name Lil Devil was an ex-member of the Crip's in East L.A. He had a bald head, 5 feet 6 inches muscular guy who looked like a fullback for a football team.

Chapter 92

I'm Not An Active Gangsta No More, Why Does It Follow Me?

LIL DEVIL HAD a nice look about himself that no woman would complain about; he had a brown complexion and a clean baldhead with a full goat tee moustache. Lil Devil had a warrant for his arrest and the police were able to catch him slippin at the party and arrested him! We're looking at B-Down partner get arrested, and we all were vexed. It was one of those nights where nothing was going right. The fuzz (police) is walking Lil Devil out of the party in handcuffs, and it was like 6 dudes laughing about Lil Devil going to jail, B-Down yelled out "What's so f****** funny about somebody going to jail?" We later found out that the people who were laughing were with this set called EPA (East Palo Alto); which was located south of the peninsula in San Mateo County. At that time, EPA was leading the nations murder rate in 1992. B-Down and this E.P.A. dude, who had to be like 5 feet 5 inches. He was dark with some real short course hair and had this real shady hyper voice and had on all black, they both started exchanging words and the next thing you knew security was forcing us away from the college premises. Next thing, some EPA dudes were waiting for us around the corner; I believe it was about 10 of them and six of us. B-Down and the main dude who started the problems were in each other's face exchanging words again.

B-Down put on these gardener gloves to cover his knuckles and I was right by his side. I heard one of these pranksters from EPA yell out "F*** THESE B****** THEY F***** AROUND AND GET SOME HOT ONES PUT INSIDE THEM!" I jumped in and pulled B-Down away, and then said, "These sucka's ain't talking about coming from the shoulders and fighting. They got a tooly (gun)!" I was so vexed because I had been trying to stay away from drama and trying to stay alive and keep the gangsta on ice and just be a family man. I just had a daughter and finally had decent employment so I can just lay low like 'Al Jarreau with a round fro.' We went to downtown San Jose hoping that we could shake off that negative moment with those pranksters and get into a nice club. By that time B-Down had been drinking that 'Hen Rock Tuff' (Hennessey) to the head by himself, and once he gets that dark drank in him, he'd turn from being Bill

Bixby to David Banner in lighting speed. As we were walking, I could smell that some drama had jumped off or was about to jump off. It just did not feel right. So here we are in the heart of San Jose, and I said let me check on my daughter, and I called her mom and let her know what's going on with me, so she doesn't think I'm fooling around with some bumble bees (females).

I got on the phone and she and I started getting into an argument. As we are getting into this argument over the phone, I'm looking at B-Down leaning over on the passenger side of the car that had these 2 women who were real big and husky. They looked like they ran straight out the house and hopped in the car with one thing on their mind and that was to stump a hole in somebody. Their hair was bushy all over the place and they were ashy and gangsta looking; they had this look in their eyes like they were looking to jump somebody and beat them down. B-Down goes over and yells out "WHAT'S GOING ON BIG DRAWS?" He was drinking that Hen Rock and rapping to the females, and I was observing all this while my daughter's mom and I were going back and forth on the phone. I think she was just mad because she was home alone with the baby and here, I am out roaming the streets.

This man had to be only like 5 feet 2 inches and was real black with a bald- head and had a body that was in real good shape. He looked almost like a little person but gorilla strong. He comes to the car and tells the woman who was driving, "To pop the trunk." He was on edge, antsy and enraged and was looking as if he was trying to get a gun out of the trunk. The woman was taking too long to open the trunk and he was getting impatient, by the time he looks up, he sees B-Down hanging on the car door. The dude comes over to B-Down and says "DAWG THEY COOL"; and B-Down looked at him and gave him a look like this man is not talking about nothing and waved him off with his hand. The guy comes back over to B-Down and say's "DAWG! I SAID THEY COOL." I was still on the phone with Ms. Star while all this was going on. I told my daughter mother to hold on and I yelled out,

"Y'all pull B-Down away! The dude said they cool." Somebody from our side pulled B-Down away and I ended the call with my daughter mother. The next thing we knew the dude got mad at B-Down. As this guy is brewing steam out of him! I'm actually walking towards B-Down; the dude started shooting at us. Everybody was running! It was so much pandemonium going on; everybody trying to run away from the bullets, and since B-Down was with me, the shooter was shooting right at us. We hid behind some cars and bullets were ricocheting off the cars. B-Down white jacket made us such easy targets. The gunman kept shooting towards the area we were trying to hide in. I'm certain that if he would have came closer, I would not be here writing this book. B-Down yells, "Let's hit this fence!" I said, "You have this big wind breaker white jacket on that makes noise and is noticeable, and you think I'm about to jump over with you?" But he did not pay any attention to what I was saying. B-Down jumped over the fence without a second blink while the guy was still shooting at us. I got to the point where I was like he just going to have to kill me in action trying to get away, than me sitting still waiting for him to get closer to me to shoot and kill me.

As we were running, we tried to run into Taco Bell, but they locked the door and would not let us in, so we all just kept running until we were far away from the scene. We were dog tired, but we all made it and waited at one location to make sure none of us got hit and that we all survived. While we were headed back home, no one was saying a word; everyone was p***ed off at B-Down for letting things get that far. I tell you one thing, it was a reality check for me, because I was not banging anymore, nor was I hanging in the streets all the time; I was just trying to square up a little bit, work hard on the job and take care of my daughter. So that is just one of the insane in the membrane episodes with B-Down. I told Ms. Star what happened, and she replied, "I knew something didn't feel right about you going out!" Yahweh kept providing me with revelations throughout the night on what could have happened to my life. I made it urgent for me to become conscious of the decisions I make. When I finally made it back home from the traumatic night, I realized I'm at the age of twenty-five and the way I envisioned my family life, was definitely not my reality. Back to B-Down graduation day. I had to drive a stick shift with one good leg for 3 hours round trip. Made it just in time to hear his professor call out his name to cross the stage. I jumped up on my good leg, clinging on for dear life to my crutch and yelled out "BUCK, BUCK!" so I stayed to make sure B-Down saw me and we hugged, and he was just so humbled that I would be fresh out of surgery and still dedicate myself to honor my word and be there for him and he talks about that very moment till this day. So now I back to my reality in my life with Ms. Star that's going nowhere. We continued to argue, and we tried our best to keep it away from our daughter, but the environment was getting more and more unhealthy. I started reflecting over my life and the things that I had to endure in the past year.

Chapter 93

Never As Good As The First Time . . .
Time Would Reveal

WHAT ACTUALLY TOOK place in that year, was that I just got injured on the job; I had been fighting to get Worker's Compensation for about a year in a half, and if that wasn't enough, Coca-Cola tried to fire me. While getting injured on the job that required me to get knee surgery. They were trying to string me along by having me come to an arbitration to get my supervisor to lie and make it seem as if I did not follow the correct protocol when I was working, I had documents to support my actions, phone bills to show when I called in the injury and the location of the store where I got hurt. They really thought they could eight ball me because I was young, African decent and from the streets; What they did not know was that I was the young Johnnie Cochrane Jr. (peace to his soul) I knew how to handle my business. Fooling around with them, I lost almost two years of my life because by me being injured, I had to make sure that the investigators that they sent out to spy on me to see if I was faking my injury did not see me lifting items that I was not allowed to lift, or I would lose my Disability Claim. They tried to throw everything at me to make me lose my case, but Yahweh is good. I ended up being rewarded with $43,000, and, after paying the lawyer's and the advance that I received, I think I pocketed around $32,000. Right before I got the lootchi, Ms. Star didn't have anybody to watch her second child so she could look for employment, so I ended up watching our daughter and her baby, who would holler all night long as if somebody poured some volcano hot lava on her. Now, remember this was the same baby I told her that she bet not have this child around me ever, but I knew she had nobody, and she really needed me. I prayed that she got the job, and she did. I was so happy for her.

Ms. Star was still living with her mom, and they still would get into arguments. Since I was off work and just going to vocational school; I wasn't able to return back to my old job. I would take the girls to their Yahweh-mother's house every morning, if I had any appointments and if I didn't, they would just be with me all day. This one particular time, she ended up moving in with me again, so she traded in her car to get the vehicle she always wanted which was a 2001 Silver Honda Civic. That's one thing about her, once she put her mind to something, she always got what she wanted. I didn't even know that she was getting a new car (that's how she operated; she always had separate plans on the low). I found out that she was getting a new car when she didn't come straight home one Friday. We talked about not getting no new cars because we was going to move to Atlanta, Georgia and hustle foreclosed homes with a subsidized government certificate that we could use out of state. I wanted us to keep our overhead down. This one occasion, she did not come home on time and was not answering her phone and I had both of the kids all day. It was getting later in the evening, at 9:00 pm, she walks through the door saying, "I'm sorry for taking so long." Now remind you she has been gone since 7:00am. She yells out, "I have a surprise, look out the window." There it was the Honda Civic; she sweet talked me with something and was like, "Let me take you out to dinner and let's go see a drive-in movie." I was hot as a firecracker, but by now, it shouldn't be a surprise to anyone, that we ended up getting into an argument at the drive-in.

Chapter 94

The Star You Knew Is Dead Fool You Must Love Being Hurt

IN HER MIND she was not too concerned about us anymore because at this point, she was now focusing on building her own independence; she would not have to rely on me for anything! She started looking for her own apartment in Stockton, California. At this point, I knew we were no longer the same people to each other that we once were. She started feeling herself; she had her new car, a stable job and calling her own shots. I paid to go to Computer School and once I graduated from school, I was moving back to Atlanta, Georgia. I felt nothing was going the way I had planned for my family, and she was wilding out and enjoying all the new attention and her new male and female friends all over again. By this time, my daughter was three years of age and beginning to look 50% like me and 50% like her mom; straight down the middle. Normally when you see a child, they look like both parents but always looks like one of the parents more than the other. My daughter 'The First Lady' had a beautiful bronze complexion, with big brown promising eyes like me, she had deeper dimples in her face then me, a gap in her teeth like her mother, her hair was thick and coarse like her daddy (I'm sorry) and her body type was kind of thick that she got from my family side. She was a happy baby and made me want to have 17 more legacies. Before I left for Atlanta; I brought my daughter and her sister some Bunk beds with their favourite cartoon characters comforter sets and about $3,000 worth of gift cards for different children stores so whenever The First Lady needed clothes her mother could use the gift cards to take care of my daughter. I also opened up a mutual fund account for my daughter that she couldn't touch until she was eighteen years of age.

Chapter 95

Accept People
For What They Show You Not Tell You

THE SPECIAL LADY, my daughter sister had a light skin complexion, who looked exactly like her dad but acted like her mom. At one point she viewed me as her dad at the time because her biological didn't bother to show her any attention. I was the one taking 'The First Lady and The Special Lady to school, to their doctor's appointments, buying pampers, medicine, milk and helping with everything else they needed.' So many trials and tribulations in my life that was making me depressed, and I needed to restructure my mind back in the right direction. I told Ms. Star that I was leaving on this date to Atlanta, and she did not believe me because she thought she had a hold on me because we had a daughter that I loved dearly. When we broke up, I had to deal with other dudes being around my daughter, had me losing my mind. I would drive out to Stockton trying to fight the dude who were around my daughter. I told them they bet not put their hands on my daughter and they bet not raise their voice at my daughter. She has her father to discipline her. It was important that whoever was around my daughter new who I was and that I was no one to play with. My over protectiveness had a lot of triggers due to my childhood traumas and the hurt. Seeing how Ms. Star just moved on with her life, like it was nothing and how I laboured for us because I thought this was my star in my dark world. I would drive al the way out to Stockton, California to get my daughter faithfully. I didn't want anybody else but me around my daughter and the only way I could control that is to try and pick my daughter up from her mom as much as possible.

Chapter 96

Hurtful Decision I Made Was Leaving My First Lady

I WOULD PICK The First Lady up and we would do everything together and go visit everybody, I would buy her clothes all the time. That was truly my partner. As the days were counting down for me to leave for Atlanta, I would explain everything to my daughter about why I was leaving and that I'm trying to make sure she has a bright future. I remember it was a time, when I had a false imagery of family security when my daughter turned two. Her mother and my sister was staying with me, so we brought in Christmas together. This was a proud moment for me, as an African decent man and a father, to be able to go and shop for a tree, gifts, and decorations for Christmas; since I had never done nothing like that before as a man because I had stop celebrating the holidays because it was birthed by paganism rituals. Nevertheless, it was something I had seen as a kid when my mother would celebrate with us. My sister Naomi cooked Gumbo for the first time; she put everything in there from, chicken, shrimps, sausages, crab, bay leaves, filè, and the list goes on. My sister also made some sweet potatoes pies from scratch and Ms. Star made her Macaroni cheese from scratch and we had a blessed meal. While they were in the kitchen throwing down, I had to go to the corner store to get more filé for the gumbo and this homeless man was laying on the ground asking me for lootchi. I gave the man some food and about $200. I was curious about how ended up in that position. I like to try and overstand people's thought process and what got them to the point of being in a state where they have no other option but to be homeless.

Chapter 97

First Time In My Life Focused On Being Happy Am I'm Worthy?

NOT HAVING ANY friends or family to work with you while you recover from whatever unforeseen knockout punch life throws at you. During my encounters with different people who were homeless, I learned that many of them had a great amount of wisdom, but who let their circumstances of life dominate them and they were not able to recover from that curveball that struck them out of the game of life. I got back to the house to chow down and enjoy all of the Christmas festivities. I don't know if I was just reflecting too hard on my life with my daughter's mother because of the 'craziness of our relationship' at the same time, Brian McKnight had this song called 'Crazy Love' and we thought that song was personally made for us. We went from being 'tweedy birds' in the tree K.I.S.S.I.N.G., to her family members trying to get people to come after me trying to hurt me, but I was not the kind of person who would just sit and take any type of abuse. When we first was living together for real for real, she was arrested and taken to jail for an old warrant she had as a teenager, then the next episode was her being pregnant by somebody else, and I still established a committed relationship with her. Now at this time in my life I finally got it through my thick head that it won't never be the same between Ms. Star and me. Before I left for Atlanta, I realized I can't throw myself away or put my life on hold and that's what I had to keep telling myself. I'm young and fly and it's time to mingle with the ladies. So finally, I met somebody and at first, she was kind of sceptical about getting involved with me because I never hid the fact that I had a daughter. The woman's name was Sheila, and she did not want to be caught in some baby mama drama.

I told Ms. Sheila I feel that the people who have that kind of situation are people who haven't let go of the hurt of not being together with the mother or father of the child or the children that are involved are having a real challenging time with adjusting to not seeing both parents together. I express to Ms. Sheila, "Me and my daughter mother is no more." I had to really show Sheila that I was truly about getting to know her. I was like I finally met somebody I can move on with my life; she was gorgeous but very apprehensive.

She said her brother had a baby-mama and she was crazy; so, when he would have a new girlfriend, the baby mama would fight the new girlfriend and cause all kind of problems. Sheila experienced firsthand because she was in the middle of all the drama, and it really made her dread dating a guy who had kids. Sheila was Puerto Rican & African decent, she stood at maybe 5 feet 3 inches but had the perfect body and well put together as if I dreamed how I wanted my queen to look, and it came to life! She had a small waist, with curvy hips, with juicy breast and an apple shaped behind that looked so juicy. Her lips and eyes and mannerism was so seductive and passionate at the same time; she had a bronze rich complexion and she said when it's winter her skin changes colors. How we met was when B-Down invited me out for his King Day to this club called Riffs, which was located in Milpitas, California. B-Down was feeling like the President, I mean he was dressed shark-fin sharp, while at the same time putting the letter 'D' in the word drunk. He was trying to talk to every woman in the parking lot and the women was just smiling at him but not giving him the time of day. Sheila comes out and he start trying to get her number aggressively, but she kept trying to exit away from him. B-Down was trying to get some action but she was like you drunk and you should have your friends make sure you safe.

B-Down kind of fanned her off with his hands like 'whatever anyway.' She kept walking away, so in my mind, I was like I can get her; I just had to finesse the approach to her. I told myself in my mind, I could get her, and I want her, so I came to her and said, "That's my family right there it's his King Day and he's just enjoying himself, sorry if he was a little aggressive." Then B-Down yells out, "F*** these stuck-up broads, man!" I was like, "Hold on I'm trying to see what's up real quick." I ended up finding out a little about Sheila. Her career choice was to become a computer engineer I believe, but she was very fascinating, and we just had magical chemistry. She gave me her number and I told her, "I'm going to call you; you have my word." And she was like, "You better!" And she faked like she was going to punch me in my stomach. She was extremely cautious, but I can tell she was a keeper, and it was gonna take some work, but I can have her. We were making progress at a snail pace! We talked about everything under the sky; she told me that she worked for Hewlett Packard in San Jose in the marketing department and how much she loved Hershey's kisses but the white chocolate and milk chocolate with almonds inside. I really wanted to experience falling in love with her. It was a weird space I was in, because after Ms. Star and I experience, which was a horrible disappointment for each other, I was like I never want to fall in love again. I never trusted love to ever last for me. I researched Sheila job and sent her a special delivery to her job. It was a music cassette of all her favourite songs mixed with different songs of me expressing how I feel about her and also, a beautiful teddy bear that was covered with white/chocolate Hershey's kisses with almonds, with a beautiful poem and some long stem roses. She was blown away and was now open to explore the romance I had to offer.

Chapter 98

Escaping Situations To Fall Into A Pit Of Betrayal & Pain

JUST WHEN ME and Sheila was developing our romance, I'm on the phone with Sheila and I get a call on the other line it's Ms. Star talking about how she apologize and that I was right about a lot of things and that she wanted to come back into my life, so we can rebuild our family. I was like why Yahweh? To myself. I put in all this work trying to move on, which sucked every ounce of blood out of my heart, and just when I finally met somebody who I really enjoyed, my daughter mother comes back to me, what do I do? I wanted Sheila so bad but, I wanted my daughter 'The First Lady under the same roof as me.' I had to put my daughter first and make a call to Sheila even though I didn't want to, but I had to let her know I'm going to try and rebuild my family and she replied that she respected me for letting her know and she wish me the best and I just complimented her on how breathtaking she was on all levels. I looked at it like my daughter was back in my life every day and her mom who was my everything is coming back, so we can be who we originally were to each other. A lot of physical fights, hurtful and destructive word play (all in the name of love, I guess??). I had four more weeks to go before I would leave for Atlanta, so Ms. Star and I got back together, and she was like, "You were right about everything you said, and I really miss you!" I didn't feel as though she was manipulating me in any kind of way, it was just that I missed her and my daughter so much that I wanted it to work. Since we made the decision to reconcile our relationship, we ended up going to Reno, Nevada trying to rekindle our love again.

We took my car that had never been driven anywhere far and went to Reno for the first time. We went there with $500 and left with like $800 believe it or not. Ms. Star and I were really good at hustling together and knew how to work together to get lootchi or run a scam to get whatever we wanted. When we arrived in Reno, it was not a good first experience because we arrived so late at night, that we really didn't have much time to enjoy because the next day I had to get on a plane later that evening. We made the best out of everything and I think we were back in love with each other, and she cried real hard because she did not want me to leave. I told her to focus on getting the government assistance voucher for foreclosed homes and then we will unite in Atlanta. She continued to cry her heart out, but I knew that I had to leave, and I didn't want to get caught up in the moment. I told her to stay focused and try to get through this. A month had not passed, and she started talking about how much she missed me, and how she felt as though she was never going to see me again. The more I listened to what she was saying, the more concerned I was about her hanging in there and being faithful to us, and just overstanding that this is just temporary. Unfortunately, I got proven right, she started getting numbers from guys, after I guessed it, she eventually confessed and said that some guy stopped her on the freeway and was begging for her number. She started getting phone numbers from other guys; I called her every word that would give an explicit definition to describe a garden hose. I was emotionally turned upside down because I never overstood how I could do the right thing with the wrong people. I stopped speaking to her and would just send payments for my daughter.

Before I left Ms. Star, I gave her the security deposit to move from Stockton to find an apartment closer to her family in Vallejo and if everything didn't work out in Atlanta, I would have a place to come back to and lay my head. Now that I was back in Atlanta, nothing seemed to be going the way I planned! Everything had changed with my friend Ms. Regime and her two sons. They were no longer doing the things that she taught them and things I was teaching them when they were younger. In fact, they were doing all the wrong things from smoking weed to being sexually active and not attending school like their mom raised them. They wouldn't listen to anybody, which really shocked me because I was in their lives on and off since they were two and four years of age and, now they were around twelve and fourteen years of age and they felt like they were men. I was assistant coach for their basketball and flag football teams for the Boys & Girls of America Association. I was trying to use that as an opportunity to bond with them, but they did not want to listen to the coach, nor hustle hard on offense or defense.

It had gotten to the point where they were taking their mother for granted and being disrespectful towards her; that didn't sit too well with me. I had to step in, and I ended up having to punch the oldest one in his ribs and chest to show him that he was not going to be disrespectful because he challenged me as a man and disrespected his mom. He called some of his relatives on their dad's side of the family to come and fight me; I was not backing down from a fight, so I told them to come on. I started running towards the door and Miss. Regime pulled my arm and was ripping my shirt saying, "Don't go out their Ponne please!" Next thing I knew the police came and pulled me outside and questioned me; they told me that if they had to come back, I was going to jail. I believe Ms. Regime had a lot of family problems and failed to inform me of what I was walking into.

Chapter 99

False Hope In ATL Only To Return Back To The Yay Unwanted

I WAS VERY disappointed at Ms. Regime and was not in a happy place with her. I had nobody in my corner and did not know what my next move would be. I left to see my partner K.P. who had been living in Huntsville, Alabama. Now, originally my purpose for going to Atlanta this time around was to meet up with K.P., who had a business venture to run a Sports Agency and that he has a very rich third-party person in mind that's going to invest majority of the capital into the Sport Agency. The other investor who K.P. mentioned ended up cancelling his financial commitment after I had already dedicated my life to move to Atlanta and paid all this lootchie. Me moving back to live with Ms. Regime again this second time was only because K.P. didn't stay in Atlanta and wait for me to arrive. He was staying with a friend temporarily in Atlanta until I arrived and then we were going to buy a house together but, the place where he was staying, his friend had him sleeping on the floor and it was very uncomfortable. I advised him to maybe go and visit his female friend in Alabama, since it's driving distance.

But stay tuned this will be explained later in the story.

I reached a point that enough is enough! I am not about to continue to be miserable living with Ms. Regime. That's when I decided to leave to go to Huntsville, Alabama. I refused to spend my 27th birthday around Ms. Regime where I was unhappy and disappointed. Being in Atlanta kept proving to me that I didn't belong there. I packed all of my things and stuffed them into my extremely small car and drove all the way to Huntsville, Alabama. Once I got to K.P.'s house, I told him that he could keep the car if I could keep my things in his storage.

He said it was cool for me to keep most of my stuff in his storage and then I left from Alabama. I brought a plane ticket headed back to the YAY AREA. A ticket that happened to be another great mistake of mine! I arrived at the Oakland Airport and Ms. Star was there to pick me up. However, seeing her didn't leave us with the feeling of 'Aww, I am glad you are back!' The feeling I got from Ms. Star was more like, I got my own thing going on and I don't need you coming up in here trying to mess anything up I got going on. I was so happy to see my daughter; she had grown up so much! It didn't take me long to get back into the swing of things with my First Lady. I would go to school with her and go over her homework with her and her sister. I know that her mother loved me, but she was doing what she wanted to do and, she didn't want me to be cramping her style. It was a strange position to be in because I was so used to leading the house and now, I had to be kind of cool because I had nowhere to go, and I knew, me being cool would last only for so long, if I'm being honest about the Alpha Male I am. It was certain things had drastically changed between the two of us and it bothered me to the point that I felt I needed to say something. Of course, we would get into fights, and then try to get things back on track as long as it was beneficial for her and on her terms. For instance, like watching the girls and helping take care of them while she goes and hang with her friends or dudes. I could not and did not want to be there anymore. So, after 2 years, I was challenged by extreme poverty and shelter issues and became homeless and had to sale my daughter stocks to have lootchi to survive. It was an insult to my manhood! I ended up begging my sisters' grandmother Ms. Herbert (Peace to her spirit) (who was my grandmother as well) if I could stay with her. I really didn't have any lootchi to pay her because I was waiting to draw my unemployment benefits.

When I got some lootchi, I gave her $500 to live in a room that the walls were filled with mildew and mold. The curtains, and the windows were covered with cigarette stains. I had to clean so hard to get things somewhat descent; I was just thankful to not be out in the cold on the streets. I would call Ms. Star like 3am because I was out in the streets trying to get some kind of lootchi so I could get something to eat. I sold everything I had to my name from; DVD's, CD's, clothes, everything. I was desperate and she was so ice cold because she was determined to let me know that she had moved on with her life. However, I was not going to be out done with her antics, so I said, "I F***ING gave you the security deposit! I'm out here sick with no food and you go treat me like this?" She didn't take anything I was saying to heart! I would hear a guy's voice in the background, and I would get even more enraged. I said, "You got somebody around my daughter?" She said, "You need to be focusing on taking care of yourself, don't worry about what's going on in my house. Now if you want this $1000, I could give you that back but, you can't stay with me." She was making me dig deeper and deeper into hatred towards her. Things were real horrible at grandmother's; she had Alzheimer's and would yell from the bottom of the stairs at five in the morning saying that I cooked up all the fish fry batter when I wasn't even there to cook any food! It was all bad. Grandmother who was very lovely looking lady, who had the traditional Creo French look with the hazel eyes, light skinned, lovely smile, stood at 5 feet 3 inches, can cook any Louisiana dish to perfection. Her personality was very lovely but fiery at the same time and she really could argue. I spent most of my childhood with grandmother almost every weekend in the projects where she lived along with my cousin Darrell (R.I.P.) who had a rich dark complexion, with strong brown eyes.

Chapter 100

Uncle James Will Forever Be Treasured, He Truly Cared

DARRELL (R.I.P.) HAD a good texture of hair that he wore low in a shag style, which was brushed short in the front but long in the back, he had his mom complexion Pam (R.I.P.) his body type was of a tail back in the National Football League. His personality was like the actor from the Movie 'Paid in Full' Mekhi Phifer; you know he had that borderline cockiness but confident, at the same time bravado. We always got along. His mother Pam was very sweet and mysterious at the same time. She was this beautiful rich dark woman, that was full figured but looked good and was very strong on what she meant. I was so young I don't remember everything about her, but she passed away because of cancer. I think maybe I was 10 years of age. Shan was Darrell's sister and while Darrell took after his mom complexion, Shan took after her dad complexion. His name was Uncle James (R.I.P.) who was an ex-Vietnam vet, who stood at maybe 6 feet 5 inches, and he was ever since of the word old school; the way he got his haircut, to the food he selected to eat, to even how he never wanted a bank account. He just like to cash his lootchi at a check cashing place. His complexion was more like hazelnut; he wore his hair in a short Afro shag with a part on the side of his head. I loved everything about Uncle James because he had a philosophy about everything in life and he was the only male figure in my life that made me feel comfortable about how I looked at everything in a philosophical way because he was the same way. His body type was like one of those basketball players from the Boston Celtics back in the 60's. He was very low maintenance, and he knew what was important in life.

He used to ask me if you had a choice would you rather be rich or happy and I thought both answers were one in the same (silly me right) I guess when you are focused on getting lootchi that's the only thing people respect, so you begin to think that's happiness. He used to make so many profound statements to make me re-evaluate how I thought I had life figured out. One of the most important lessons he instilled in me is quit having more expectations of people then what they are developed to deliver. I used to have my soul pinching with anger when everybody in my life would disappoint me but wanted me to be reliable.

When I was 17 years of age, he told me that as I get older, I would see my circle become very small because the way I see life is going to make people feel that they're not ready to deal with life in Black and White. It was very significant, how he shared so many jewels out of his treasure of wisdom with me. He applied and compared his whole existence of life to when he was in the war. He was somebody who always been in my corner and never turned his back on me and I will forever have Stone Love in my heart for him. His daughter, she was very cute and fun but could never be counted on. Shan loved to have fun and made sure she enjoyed herself even as a kid. She was very tall; she stood close to 6 feet even taller with heels on. She had pretty shoulder length hair and was always thinking ahead of people; she was always calculating. We were close as kids. She had these deep sad puppy eyes but in a very cute way; she loved to always look cute and at the same time loved to challenge the boys. She was shapely and a little thick at the same time, which she got from her mom Pam because her dad was skinny as a pole, but I have nothing but enjoyable memories of my cousin Shan. Now my other cousin Little Dent II kind of had this Rick Foxx kind of personality. He knew he looked good and came from good DNA. He had all the latest toys; he had a turtle and just knew his life was a little better than most people.

He stood at maybe 6 feet 3 inches, and we all thought that he would go onto to become an NBA professional player. Everything about him spelled college jock, from the way he dressed, and acted; he was the one you knew would turn out fine in life and if that wasn't enough, he had the coolest dad. His dad was very handsome and a Dentist, who played basketball and had the coolest personality. His mom Denise (R.I.P.) was a very beautiful wholesome lady. She was just so naturally beautiful; she had this Indian and African decent look about herself. I never saw her with makeup on and she just had this strikingly natural beauty and was very wholesome with her love towards me. I was around them all the time and she had this very low-key demeanor, and I never heard her raise her voice and I was around her almost every other weekend! Truly a sweet woman and I miss her till this day. She really adored her son and was expecting a new addition to the family. It seemed like the perfect family before there was a Cosby show. During her pregnancy with her daughter, it was discovered that Denise had liver cancer, but nothing could be done because any treatment would harm the unborn baby. The cancer grew all throughout the pregnancy untreated. The baby was born healthy and normal, but the delay of medical care for the cancer caused the cancer to spread. His mom passed away and it was devastation for the entire family. I was so young I didn't know if I was 11 years of age or how old I was, but my emotions did not overstand the in-depth-ness of the pain. My cousin Little Dent took his mother's passing really hard as one could imagine. My cousin Little Dent we were very close as well and spent a lot of time together but he always kind of carried himself like the big brother with me and even though we had a lot of fun together, he always laughed when my mom would beat me with broomsticks and telephone cords.

Chapter 101

Courageously Vulnerable Births Breakthrough Love With Mom

EVEN WHEN LIL Dent and I went to High School together. He would show off in front of his friends. We would go back and forth and argue sometimes but we still were close but not as close as my love one, my cousin Cutty Bang. Who was just a cool friendly person. Who always had women on his mind. He would always look crisp, like he's fresh out of your favourite expensive urban apparel store. CuttyBang took pride in how he presented himself to the world, because of his thirsts for attention from the ladies, and they definitely did not disappoint him. He stood at maybe 6 feet 4 inches and had that fully confident walk and assurance that he knew can't nobody tell him he's not fly. He always dressed sporty, I mean whatever the latest trend was, he would have it on in its first week of being on the racks or before it was on the racks. He was just that kind of person. He could draw, dress, and make people feel enjoyment around him. I just wish he could have really taken advantage of his gifts. Now that you know the background of everybody, we would always go to Grandmother's apartment in O.C. projects and look at Soul Train early Saturday. In the morning, we would have Orange Sherbet Ice Cream with Hawaiian Punch poured over it and she fried these things called Fritter's which were to die for with powder sugar sprinkled over a pastry fried, which tasted so immaculate. Later in life grandmother moved out of the projects and had a nice apartment that was left behind by one of her sons who got married and expanded his family. She lived on Divisadero Street and at first, I didn't know what to expect living with my grandmother as an adult. I didn't know she had Alzheimer's until after I moved in. She would tell everybody that I was a bum and that I did not work when I would apply everywhere trying to get a job.

I remember when she called family in Seattle, New Orleans, and Texas just slandering my name, I ended up talking to my mom and she was like, "You look bad LaPonne." I ended up moving out because I could not even take my daughter over to grandmother's apartment because it was so smoky and dirty on the upstairs level, because Uncle James lived with my grandmother, and he was a chain smoker. His room was upstairs. So, I ended up back at mom house. I moved in with my mom and I was happy to be in a cleaner environment, but my peace of mind was in jeopardy once again. Mom, sisters and nieces…were too loud and always arguing with each other. I'd be breaking up fights from sister to sister to mom and daughter. It was 6 of us in a two-bedroom house on Head Street in Lakeview, California. Mom was still strict! If anyone of us took a bath, mom wanted to see not even a drop of water anywhere. We had to take turns washing dishes and could not come into her house late. I was going back and forth living with mom and then somewhere else. She was still forcing me to go to church and I knew I had to come up with a plan fast. The first thing I had to do was get my own transportation; I borrowed $700 from Cashmuir and told him that my uncle owed me a few thousands and will pay me when he got out of the Penitentiary. Cashmuir said for me to give him a week and he would let me know. I ended up getting the loan and I got a car that was a runner but the body of it was primed down and needed a paint job. It really didn't matter to me what the outside of the car looked like, all I cared about was being able to get my daughter and move from point A to B in a timely fashion. My Uncle Apprentice got arrested, so he begged me to take over his apartment so he didn't lose his place of residency and said that he would pay me back for the expenses I paid to keep his place for him. I felt like a heavy load was taken off my shoulders; at least that's what it felt like.

Chapter 102

Born To Fail Bread To Win At All Cost, I Don't Give A What

I PUT ALL the pressure on me to find a job, so I reached out to my cousin Ke-Ke, and she said she probably would be able to get me a job interview at Kaiser Permanente Hospital as a file clerk. I didn't make much lootchi, but at least I had a steady check because I was about to go back to distributing some serious weed. I was going back by the hoods just keeping my nose in the mix of the streets. I saw D Sess, and we had not seen each other in about seven years because he was in and out of jail and I was just trying to stay on the stick and move and just moving state to state. We talked and exchanged numbers, and just shortly after our brief reunion, I got the news that he got killed like maybe 15 minutes after I had left him, from my overstanding, it was not even his bullet originally. It served as another reality check for me. I knew that I had to get out the YAY. I was living in newly 'Revamped Army Street Projects', which was in their eyes considered our rival set at one point of time, and the way the apartments were built, it was open to the streets and not gated off. Which meant anybody could come and shoot to kill. My partner KP said he had been trying to catch up to me for months and sent me an email giving me his number to call him. I called him and he was trying to see what was going on with me. I told him I was staying with my grandmother I started telling him about the stuff Ms. Star had pulled and how things were going and how I had to stay with mom. By that time, I was staying at my uncle's apartment temporarily, paying his bills so he wouldn't lose his place and he agreed to pay me back once he got out of jail. I called KP and I told him I was just with D Sess, and he died 15 minutes after I left and KP was like "How long you gone keep struggling with your life?"

Chapter 103

Wasn't For KP I Wouldnt Have Gave The South Another Run

HE KEPT ON saying things like "When I was going through hard times you were there for me." He asked me to be the best man in his wedding. I felt honored that he would ask me, I said to him, "I don't have a pot to piss in, nor a window to through it out of!" He was like, "Man, why don't you get away from that life and relocate to Alabama? You were just talking about how you almost died, if you would have stayed with D Sess 15 minutes later, so just come to Alabama and help with the wedding and get away from that madness". I told him that, "The furthest place I would go in the South was Atlanta". He said, "P just come down here; I will have my fiancé put together a buddy pass for you which would allow you to fly for free if any extra seats are available." He also told me that his fiancé said that Delta Air Lines was hiring for Customer Service Agents. His fiancée Ms. Kristine was very sweet in the beginning and hospitable. When I first met her, we naturally connected. KP also tried to arrange for me to meet with a woman when I first came down to Huntsville. I agreed to come down to help with the wedding, but I was not interested in making Alabama my new home. I arrived in Alabama in March 2002, on a Sunday afternoon. When I landed, I did not know what to expect because the last time I came down to visit, I was seeing women who were looking real outdated like they were extras from an old New Edition video performing the song 'Candy Girl.' Their hair was outdated, and their style of dressing was completely different from what I was used to seeing women wear. I said to myself, I don't know how this is going to work from a socializing standpoint! At that point in my life, I stopped drinking and doing drugs.

Herbal tea was the extent of my exotic choice with absolutely nothing in it and little 'crumpets' to eat to compliment the tea. I ran out of my Ginseng Tea (my drink of choice). I asked KP if he could take me to the store so I could get some more tea and a few other items, but he was like "Man save your lootchi. Ms. Kristine has all kind of teas at the house!" We finally arrive at their apartment, and they showed me where I was going to sleep (which was right on the living room floor), and if I had to use the restroom, I had to go through their bedroom to be able to enter into the restroom. His fiancée cooked a nice shrimp and pasta dish with garlic bread and salad. We stayed up and talked about a lot of things in life; after dinner, they showed me where I could find the tea before they were headed off to sleep. It was about 3:00 am and now I had taken a nice bath and ready to relax; I go looking for the tea in the dark and I see like 4 boxes of different tea brands. I just grabbed one of the tea bags out of one of the boxes and warmed up my banana nut muffins and brewed my hot water for some tea. I looked at this green box; it had this Caucasian girl in a ballerina outfit on her toes with a slogan that read: 'It keeps you light on your toes.' I didn't think much of the slogan that was on the box at the time because I was tired and wanted to hurry up and get to bed. I put two tea bags in the cup and was eating my muffins. I started watching a replay of the Los Angeles Lakers playoff game that I missed earlier that day because I was on the airplane. I took my first sip of the tea, and it tasted real good, so I took two more long sips of the tea and the next thing I knew, my stomach started speaking a foreign language. I mean my stomach started kicking and rumbling. My stomach literally turned upset and started growling and bubbling like boiling hot water. I got nervous because I was too old not to be able to get to the restroom in time.

Chapter 104

Live In The Ville, First Time
I Committed To Re-Invent Ponne

PLEASE KEEP IN mind that I had to go through their bedroom to get to the bathroom. I was trying to call KP's name with a whisper without waking up everybody in the apartment but, he was not budging. I tried to shake the door aggressively because the situation was becoming real urgent, and my bowels decided that it couldn't wait for me to make it to the restroom! All I could think of was how could I introduce myself to his fiancée as a grown man who needs to wear diapers! As I'm roughly shaking the door and continuing to call KP's name, he finally woke up and opened the door a little and I pretty much almost knocked him down trying to run to the bathroom. I made it to the bathroom, and I felt like I was sitting on the toilet with a white flag and a facial expression like I surrender. I ran back and forth to the bathroom all throughout the night. The next day I was scheduled for an interview with Delta Air Lines Inc., thanks to Ms. Kristine and my charisma. The people who were doing the interview liked me a lot and I ended up being offered the job right on the spot. I was really appreciating how Huntsville; Alabama was treating me. It was real refreshing for me. Now that things seemed to be going pretty smooth at this point, KP arranged for me to meet a woman. When I met the young woman, she was very smart and well endowed in the breast area. Her hair had old braids in it that were unraveling; she had on an old sweater that had a big hole under her arm pits and her clothes were looking like she kept it in the dryer too long and everything shrunk overnight. I was not attracted to her, but I thought she was outgoing, but my stomach was still rumbling from drinking the tea from the night before.

I was still running back and forth to the restroom, and I was trying not to let this woman know that I was having problems with my bowels. We went to Chick-fil-A, a fast-food restaurant because they have real good chicken strips and waffle fries. I wanted to make sure I was meeting people, so I didn't get bored in Huntsville, since it was a real small and simple city. The young lady ordered a chicken salad and wanted me to order something, I didn't want anything to eat because I didn't want my stomach to take over the date.

She asked me again to get something to eat, so I figured she did not want me to make her feel uncomfortable by just looking at her eat. I ordered a salad with no chicken, and I took a bite and the next thing I knew my stomach begin to boil over like a volcano in Hawaii! She was trying to talk, and I told her that I did not feel good I had to go. I ran out of the restaurant trying not to let a bowel movement get the best of me. I made it to K.P. apartment and I was so relieved!

I did not trust leaving the house or the bathroom for that matter. I looked at the box that I grabbed to have some tea and come to find out it was a body cleanser. I was like Ponne! What have you done to yourself? What a way to start my experience off in Huntsville. I started working for Delta Air Lines in April 2002; it was definitely the beginning of a new journey for me in Alabama. I could not believe how the stars were all aligned with me relocating to Huntsville. I struggled so much in the YAY and in Atlanta and when I made it to Huntsville it seemed as if everything fell into place perfectly. My uncle was getting ready to get out the penitentiary and we already had talks about us being roommates, but things were going good for me down in the South, so I decided to stay. I took a flight back to the 'Sucka Free' and packed what I could and brought things back with me to Huntsville.

Balancing my expenses from the Bay Area to Alabama was becoming too costly, so I decided that when my uncle got out of jail, he could just pay me the $3000 he owed me for the expenses I paid to keep his apartment. He also wanted to buy my car that I was selling for $900. I told him that he needed to pay me as soon as possible because I needed to pay Cashmuir the $700 I borrowed. If I didn't pay it by a certain time, I would have to pay him $800 for the inconvenience. I was really banking on my uncle being a man of his word. I told Cashmuir that he would have his lootchi by a certain time and my uncle sent me $1000 only and I had to give that to KP in order to get my car back so, he could use the $1000 as a down payment on another car for himself. It was crazy because here KP was 320lbs and stood at 6 feet 3 inches and was stuffing his body into this little teenage car with no air conditioning and one of the windows did not roll down. KP would get in the car, he would have a white towel over his shoulder and a big camping thermos filled with a gallon of water with ice. With him being big, that Southern heat was putting him on edge; it was so funny. I thanked my uncle and asked when he will have the next $2000 because I owed a lot of people. I had to borrow lootchi from my friends to stay afloat. The training class that I had to attend for Delta Airline was crazy because if I fail the training then I was not allowed to keep the job. I had already committed myself to staying in Huntsville, and if I didn't pass the test, not only would it put me in the position of not having any lootchi; I already had lost a place to stay in the 'Sucka Free' which would have left me homeless again. I could have easily let all of that pressure weigh me down, nonetheless, I was not about to let all that I worked so hard for this time around knock me out of the boxing ring of life. I was going to stay in the fight because I had already been beat down so many times before.

When I started the training for Delta, I had to learn over a hundred airport codes, different ethic codes, safety codes, privacy act codes, and a bunch of other codes. Thinking about all that Delta wanted us to learn, I said to myself, "Wow they don't want to pay no real lootchi but want you to take on these big responsibilities." I only made 10.75 hr. but, if flights had seats available at the last minute before a flight departed, I could fly for free. Delta's belief was that since employees were able to fly 'standby' they didn't have to pay top dollar working for them. Whoever was the brains behind that 'Einstein's logic' must have not realized that lootchi is needed for traveling! While in the training class, I did not take it serious. I was already under pressure and decided to just enjoy the ride. I thought by me reversing the pressure, I had nothing to lose because I was always working my way up from the bottom. In fact, that was my first time in my life that I was focused on laughing and making people laugh and just enjoying life and growing from my past. I started to have a flock of women trying to get to know me. I think it was something different that they've never experienced before that attracted them to me! I guess it may have been that 'Yay Swagg' that was on me but most importantly in me. I would get up at 7am get to class by 8am; class was over by 5:30pm. The training course was to last for about two months, and the only way we could stay in the class was that we had to pass our weekly tests.

I would come home and tell KP about the pressures of the class and how intense it was, and that I was not going to take it too seriously to the point I would start to worry. When KP asked me to come to the South, he made it seem like if I relocated there, we would be hustling the Sports Agency that we were all trying to get off the ground.

Furthermore, I thought, we all would hang out but all he did was work and sit in front of the T.V. with his fiancée. I became like the awkward 'Uncle' who did not fit into their family picture. I was getting that feeling of not belonging and, feeling as though my time to leave had finally arrived. I think KP fiancé was beginning to want her privacy and wanted me to find my own territory. Now, I'm a man who can respect another person's privacy and territory; however, these were the same people that gave me the invite to come out and stay with them so I could get my life together and I was being confronted with the notion of me needing to find my own space in a state I knew nothing about. I really took the news personal but, I also overstood his position, I strongly believe that if KP and I were bachelors, we would have not had that problem because we would have overstood that we were each our 'Brother's Keeper.' What was so ironic about the whole situation was that KP was scheduled to live in Atlanta and when his fiancée asked if it would be okay if she stayed at our house most of the time when she would commute from Alabama to Georgia every weekend, I said I had no problem with that. When I got to Georgia, KP decided that he was going to just stay in Alabama, and he was getting married. Thoughts started to dance around in my head, and then I realized why KP was always asking me if I had met a woman. He was sending me some subliminal message letting me know that they wanted their own space and wanted me out of the way. Honestly, I knew it was his fiancée who was doing most of the planning in his head, because I didn't overstand why she would suggest that I get my own place when she knew I just started a new job; that was not cool at all! The last thing that I had on my mind was trying to get hooked up with a girlfriend. I just wanted to focus on getting my life back in some kind of order.

Chapter 105

To Re-Invent Ponne, You Must Have Healthy Relationships

KP ASKED IF I found somebody in my training class, I told him that there were a lot of older people in my class; however, there was one young female who seemed sweet and dressed nicely and educated. In fact, she was the one who actually helped me with my class work, but I never thought anything of it. KP was like "You need to talk with her and see what's going on with her." I was like, "Naaaw man, I was not about to mess with those red bones (light skinned girls) because my experience with red bones is that they always got angry real quick, and I didn't need that in my life. Plus, I am not trying to be violent in my life no more unless I really needed to; not because I wanted to. However, there was one young lady that my eyes caught attention to whose name was Ms. Tiffany; she was very fair skinned and had the most beautiful eyes in the world if she was not mad at you. Her eyes were very rich brown but shaped like an Egyptian, her lips were perfect, her hair was very long and soft texture; she really looked like a beautiful Latina, but she wasn't. She stood at maybe 5 feet 2 inches and took pride in how she dressed. She packed her lunch, which often times was healthy and carefully put together, and she wore a lot of make-up which was a turn off for me. She seemed charismatic, meticulous, and well organized which I was really impressed with because that's how I operated. She helped me out if I had any problems in training class. I introduced myself to her and was like, "I just wanted to shake a hand and make a friend, how you feel about if we exchanged numbers to see if we're compatible or not?" She said, "That would not be a good idea because I'm seeing somebody.

Chapter 106

Example Of Two Remarkable People Hurting Each Other

I SAID, "I'M not trying to put no papers on you, I'm just trying to, like I said, just shake a hand and make a friend." I can't say that I was ever attracted to her; I was trying to have someone to converse with outside of work, since I did not know anybody. I think a week may have passed by and things didn't work out with her ex-fiancée because he got caught cheating and they were never able to get past some of their problems. I never sweated a woman if she was not feeling me; I always treated it like she just missed out on really getting to know a genuine man. We had this big exam to take in class that was going to determine whether or not we would be able to keep our job. I asked Ms. Tiffany if we could study together at her place, and she said that would be fine. Prior to that, she had a wedding that she attended over the weekend where her purse that she was carrying her bankcards and employment ID badge for work was stolen. I offered to pay for her badge and buy her lunch. She and I had a real sweet companionship. The time had finally arrived for us to take the exam and we both passed! We were so excited about having permanent employment, that I told her that I would treat her to a sundae ice cream. We went to the Dairy Queen and had a sundae and a two-hour conversation about things we would and would not tolerate in a relationship and what each of us learned from our previous relationships. We appeared to be compatible but, when the smoke cleared, we realized that we were on the rebound for each other and was infatuated with the fact that we could relate to each other's pain.

After that 'sundae ice cream date' everything changed between us; we became instantly close. We would talk on the phone for hours upon hours; she only stayed like seven minutes away from me it was refreshing. We talked so much that I just felt good about being able to have someone in Huntsville that I could laugh and enjoy myself with.

Our relationship began to bloom and blossom in ways I don't think either one of us realized how fast things were happening, but we were enjoying each other's company.

I took her out to a nice restaurant to wine and dine, and she would bring me food to work as well so we were working on a 'Two Way Street.' She was benevolent with her love and expressed a caring emotion even when she gave you a hug, it was with so much feeling behind it; I appreciated how she was raised. Ms. Tiffany was one woman; I did not look at in a way to hurry up and sleep with. I just wanted to get to know who she was as a woman. We started spending more and more time together, we did not immediately kiss or anything like that. We were both getting to know the soul and mind of who we were as people, and if our relationship was to go any further, we both needed to consider one thing; could we make each other happy? She was the kind of woman who loved to express her emotions. She showed me letters where she poured her heart out to Yahweh asking why he took her child away from her-who was no longer alive, and how angry she was with Yahweh. In her letters, she was begging Yahweh to take away the hurt and pain that she was having a hard time getting pass. I was so thankful that she would share that part of her life with me, and as I was reading the letters, I could honestly feel the exact pain she was going through. She had seen abuse happen to her mom and her biological father was not apart her life when she was younger. She just had a lot of emotional brokenness that she harbored deep down in her soul. It made her hot headed with a smart mouth.

Chapter 107

Testing The Strength
Of Our Emotional Co-Dependency

She was still a sweet person. My thinking was as long as I never lied to her and treat her as the queen in my life, we could triumph over all of our shortcomings. I always thought I had the answer, and things were looking pretty good for Ms. Tiffany and I., I had to fly back to the 'YAY'. When I got there, I would call her all the time so she would know that I was not fooling around with anybody back home; I decided on May 13, 2002, that she and I needed to be together all the way. I had been telling everybody my feelings about her and how she was a breath of fresh air for me. She was a little apprehensive about getting into a relationship with me because she didn't want to have to go through the same drama she had experienced with her previous relationships. To ease her heart and mind, I express to her, "The only way we will know if we have grown from our previous hurt is to put ourselves back into those same situations we been trying to avoid. We have to become courageously vulnerable again in a relationship." As I was speaking, she remained quiet and just listened to everything I was saying, and then, she said "Thank you for overstanding me." I said, "When I get back in town we will go to a nice restaurant, and toast to our new beginning." She was there to pick me up from the airport and we had a beautiful kiss and hug; I let her know my love for her could not be denied, nor was it fake. When I devote myself to someone, I give all the power of my love to that person exclusively. I was feeling on top of the world! I had a beautiful young woman who was just so expressive with her feelings. We worked at Delta Airlines together, so people would try and see how they could cause problems with our union.

Women would wait until she leaves and try to offer me pineapples that they claim they got from a Hawaiian trip, flirting with me trying to get me to respond. Guys would try to be all over her as well, but she did not play at all. She would go off and let them know to get away from her. Ms. Tiffany would get these migraine headaches at times and would have a bad attitude. I'm the type of person who likes to play and have fun with my girl, so one day, we were at her apartment and, I like to be spontaneous. Out of nowhere,

I said, "I will throw this 'Kool-Aid' juice on you!" She said, "I dare you to do it!" And that's exactly what I did. I told her "Do not dare me to do something especially when you say I bet you won't do it." I poured it all on her and the next thing you know we're having a 'Kool-Aid' fight in the apartment. I said to her, "I'm an ex-banger so you don't stand a chance!" She started getting upset and shaking and called me a "b****" because I was hiding so she could not hit me with the juice, like I was supposed to be a duck waiting to get pluck and just be a sitting target. When she called me out my name, it was as if the DJ stopped the music because there was no need for her to call me a b***h. 'I don't play that; we're just playing around and you getting all serious and deranged and taking it too far.' That was the first moment of me realizing that there were some deep issues going on with her. When I saw her reaction to us playing around, I begin to think to myself, 'Houston you have a problem on your hands!' I still thought I could just show her what I'm about and not to measure me by the type of guys who wronged her in the past. Ms. Tiffany emotions would go up and down, and all around; she would get angry easily and, I was at a point where I wanted to just laugh and enjoy my life. KP and Ms. Kristine's wedding date was set for June 15, 2002, and he had asked me to be the best man.

I invited my two sisters, my adopted sister Ms. Yoshi who was Korean & African decent, who had become my youngest sister best friend since they were 12 years of age. Ms. Yoshi is my heart. She was very intelligent, hardworking and was loyal and hated to disappoint. She stood at maybe 5 ft. 6 inches; light skinned; with Korean shaped eyes; that was not slanted at all but almond shaped with a 5-year-old little girl smile. Her built was a little size in her upper body but no hips and kind of had a Freshman College Cheerleader shape at the time. Her voice was like she spoke with a smile as long as you weren't on her bad side. I also invited my daughter to the wedding as well. Being with my 'First Lady' made me feel real good. My daughter was five years old at the time, I don't let any woman meet my daughter and it just so happened that since I was in the wedding and my daughter came because KP was her Yahweh Father, I thought out of respect it was the right thing for me to do was to have her there. The only problem was that Ms. Tiffany would be at the wedding as well. I didn't put much thought into if they would get along or not, I didn't believe in forcing their relationship. It just so happened that my daughter wanted to be around Ms. Tiffany more than she wanted to be around me, the nerve of them! I had to snatch my daughter away just to get a dance with her. All jokes aside, I was happy to see that they got along with each other naturally and it wasn't forced. Ms. Tiffany took care of my sisters. She also cooked a six- course breakfast for my sisters and they had girls' night out. I had my own apartment with a "55" inch big screen T.V. My apartment complex was equipped with a park, swimming pool, tennis court and a workout facility.

I said to myself a long time ago, that the next woman that I dated had to be educated or have her own lootchi, and in that situation with Ms. Tiffany, she presented herself to me as if she had it all. I paid for KP and his wife to honeymoon in Negril, Jamaica. They wanted me to house sit for them and take care of things for them while they were away. While they were gone, that was the perfect opportunity for me to spend some intimate time with Ms. Tiffany. I think our relationship was being tested in the deepest part of the waters, and it was time to take it to the next level. We went out to catch a movie and I made a special type of music cassette tape that expressed my feelings for her. She got emotional and started crying! I took her upstairs and the love making was very sweet and intense. The love making was so hot that she did some sexual move where she was faced the opposite direction and she began to gyrate her body in a circular motion, which made me want her even more. I said to myself, Man! She could be the perfect woman if she just was not a hot head and did not want to fight all the time and wore a lot of makeup. I used a condom one time but, she said that condoms gave her yeast infections, so I did not object because I preferred natural intercourse when it came to making passionate love with a woman that I was seriously involved with. I remember how happy she was and thanking me for overstanding her heart. She would get a lot of school loans which, I didn't know how in depth the situation was at the time. She brought me a cassette player for my car and treated me to dinner. She put the gas and electricity bill in her name for my apartment, since I was new to the State of Alabama. She truly showed me what supporting your man was supposed to be like. I was supportive to her as well, there were times when I didn't know if she was coming or going because she would be so moody. I remember one time she told me that she didn't want to hang out one night and that she was going to bed early.

I didn't overstand why she would make a drastic change like that when that was how we spent our time with each other after work making homemade pizzas and all types of dishes at two in the morning. We stayed up late at night watching old Butch Cassidy's movies (I love those old classic vintage movies). We would be up all night laughing, making love, and enjoying each other company. Before she and I officially became an item, I explained to her that I was very spontaneous and how I couldn't stand if I said to a woman lets pack something and go for a drive and have some fun and if the woman is giving all these problems like; "Where are we going?" or "Why do you want to do this?" or "How long is it going to be?" That's not the woman for me, I didn't like being with a woman who didn't like to be spontaneous. I wasn't sure if she really meant what she was saying, so I tested her: we got off work at about 1 am, and I said, "Let's drive to the State line of Tennessee listening to some passionate music and having an intimate conversation until we reach a point where our souls dive into each other's hearts and become as one?" She was like, "Let's go!"

At that point I thought the world of her, and never did I think we would not be together. I kept fighting with myself to be with her because her anger was just out of control and unruly and my attitude made it no better. We began to argue more and more because she was argumentative, stubborn, and liked to be in control and anybody who knows me; control should not be the word of choice you use nor the action of choice around me. She was so combative, and it began to cause gigantic problems initially. You really have to choose the words you say around me, especially when it pertains to disrespect or trying to control me. There was absolutely no way, I was going to play 'puppeteer' to anybody.

Chapter 108

Love Don't Make No Sense . . . I'm Confused

I STOOD MY ground and was not backing down from how I felt, and because I was not going to let her control situations, or me and the end result of that was that it was causing immense friction in our dynamic. I may not be an easy person to deal with but I'm the most loyal and loving person if you able to tap into that core of me. I was at a point where I was ready to go back to THE YAY. In fact, I made my mind up I was leaving. Ms. Tiffany was saying how she was not feeling well and that she had not had her monthly cycle in about three weeks. I was like "You think you pregnant!" She said, "She didn't know because she was taking birth control pills at one point but, they made her migraine headaches come more frequently." I wanted to know for sure if she was pregnant or not, so I was like "Let's go to the store and buy two pregnancy tests." When we came home from the store, she went into the bathroom to take the test. I prayed to Yahweh, "If she is pregnant Yahweh, I will stay here and do right by her." She came out of the bathroom and yelled "I'm pregnant" with excitement, I was in disbelief because I'm like I'm leaving to move back home. How is she going to be pregnant but it's like the old saying "If you want to make Yahweh laugh, Try telling Yahweh, your plan." I had to switch my plans from a person who was about to board an airplane on that Friday to go back home, to one who just received news on that Wednesday that I'm about to be a father again in 8 months. I had to make this work.

She looked at me for confirmation to see if I was happy and excited as much as she was, and I was. I started to think being in Alabama with Ms. Tiffany was my destiny.

I spent my whole life living out of duffle bags as though nothing was wrong with that; however, in actuality, there's a lot wrong with that. It finally hit me that if I kept on moving around from State to State, I would never be able to build anything strong that would last long. For much of my life, that's all I did was runaway or pick up and move. I was so used to cutting people out of my life when they did something that was contrary to what we built our friendship or relationship on. I would hurry up and remove them from out of my life without regret. Now that Ms. Tiffany was expecting our baby, and there was no way I could continue to do what I was used to doing in the past; I told her that we had to stop allowing ourselves to get out of control with each other, and she agreed with me. When we would get into arguments, I didn't overstand what I would do exactly to get her to want to become physical, so I asked, "What did I do to get you to this point that you have to be physical and yelling going all crazy?" She said, "That I came off too strong with her and always tried to force her to deal with things right on the spot instead of allowing her to deal with them when she was ready and that made her vexed." Her words threw me completely off guard because in my mind I was like 'Woa!' I thought we were at a point where we could talk about whatever problems that bothered us, as we agreed to not let them build up and create a much bigger problem in our relationship. She told me that those were her same values as well, but again everyone does not really share the same truths or values! I remember it like it was last month.

We were sitting in Dairy Queen Restaurant having our own respective sundaes and I gave her an example. I said, "I hate it when a person who has a problem with you, but they tell you nothing is wrong; I hate when a woman does that to me." She was like, "I'm not like that, I like to express how I feel." When she said that, my mind got to thinking that I finally had a woman who is courageously vulnerable with her emotions and is straight forward with honesty; however, all she was doing was masquerading herself to cater to the things she knew would intrigue me. For the life of me, I never overstood how a person would go through all that hard work turning into Ms. or Mr. Me Too (you know the person who always agreed with you until they got in good with you, and then they begin to show who they really are). We would argue over the smallest things, but I realized I had to try and change the way I was dealing with her. We found out that she was about 2 months pregnant and that her blood pressure was high. Knowing that her health was at stake, I wanted to make sure I treated her as my queen and to take care of her even more than I had been. Nevertheless, no matter what we did to stop from arguing, we often found ourselves going in circles. As mentioned before Ms. Tiffany and I worked for Delta Airlines, so we could fly for free on 'standby' as long as open seats were available. We decided to take a flight to 'THE YAY' so I could show her where I grew up in the slums of 'THE YAY AREA.' She had this facial expression of being kind of nervous but sad at the same time. I took her to the 'Old Fillmoe' at midnight because we arrived in the 'Sucka Free' late. I also took her to East Oakland and showed her some of the more treacherous areas like '69 Ville' and the 'Murda Dubs.' I used to actually live in the 'Murda Dubs' I showed her where my exact window was located.

I was hoping showing her where I grew up, would help her overstand my struggles, and that I was not like any other guy that she was used to dealing with. I wanted her to overstand that I came from humble beginnings and, how much I appreciated good people. I wanted her to feel deep down in her heart with conviction, that it's not my desire to do her wrong. I wanted her to know that I play for keeps, I don't do something just to do it as if it doesn't have significance. We were on our way to see my daughter; I have not seen her since her Yahweh father KP got married in 2002. I made sure that I gave Ms. Tiffany and my daughter mother a heads up with each other, especially since Ms. Tiffany was pregnant by me; I just wanted to keep peace all around. Ms. Tiffany was in the car with me as we are headed to my daughter mother's apartment to pick up my daughter, I called my daughter mother and let her know that me and Ms. Tiffany are getting close she yells on the phone, "Oooh hell naw! "You bet not bring B**** to my house"; I said "What you crazy? What are you talking about!" She said, "You better have her wait at the gas station, at the corner until you finish picking up your daughter; you bet not bring her a** to my house!" I said, "You deranged a** b****! Don't be disrespecting her like that!" It was crazy because she was just being real messy and negative, trying to ruin Ms. Tiffany whole trip. Nonetheless, Ms. Tiffany just sat there with so much class and grace and did not even respond to my daughter mom crazy antics. It was surprising because my daughter mother never behaved like that. To be very honest, watching the way, Ms. Tiffany handled herself made me love her that much more. Some other women I knew from the hood would have said "I know that b**** didn't just disrespect me like that? You don't have your s*** together so I don't want no parts of this drama."

Watching my daughter mother act like that was just awful and the words that I called my daughter mother was very out of control and weak on my behalf, because I didn't want Ms. Tiffany in any kind of war between her and my daughter mom, I decided not to get my daughter. Even though she had been waiting for me all this time it was very hurtful, and I was extremely vexed and I just made it up to my daughter at another time. The time had finally come where Ms. Tiffany met my mom; and seeing my sisters again and my nieces for the first time, my family embraced her with love and words of kindness. Remember, she is the same woman who cooked that big breakfast for my sisters back in Alabama and believe me they did not forget. My mom asked, "When will I be able to come down to Alabama and taste Ms. Tiffany's cooking?" Ms. Tiffany started smiling and said, "Anytime Ma'am." My mom told her, "Just call me Madid." That was the difference coming from the North. A lot of corruption came in and took away the proper respect you gave to your elders but, most of the people from the South still addressed their elders with 'no sir, yes ma'am.' We had a lot of fun and an inseparable time in 'THE YAY.' It came to an end, and we had to head back to Huntsville because we had a doctor's appointment to go to and find out what the sex of the baby was. Now by that time, I had learned my lesson from my experience with my first born. Remember when I said that I was having a little 'Souljah Boy' and went and brought little boy clothes and I ended up having a Souljah Girl, so this time around I kept saying "Man, I'm not going to have a boy" and kept trying to play a 'Jedi' mind trick with myself. After one of our doctor visits, they were able to see the sex of the baby and said, "There's a third leg it's a boy!" It was like I heard the doctor say, "It's a boy" but I didn't hear the doctor say, "It's a boy."

Chapter 109

Second Chance At Life
With My Little King I'll Do Better

Ms. Tiffany said, "Did you hear what she said?" I said, "What!" She said, "It's a boy." I replied," YES! YES!" I think I was disillusioned and really didn't hear consciously because I thought about my dad for some reason, it was weird. I remember it was this time I had to live back with my mom, and this was before I moved to Atlanta and was considering going to Skyline College in South San Francisco. I was trying to figure out how to balance the street life and square up at the same time, the two just don't go together. My mom had a split shift from her Muni job, and she came through the door and kind of had this nervousness in her voice. When mom talked like that it's like somebody died or some life changing news is about to be delivered. Mom closed my bedroom door and said, "LaPonne I just saw your dad." I said, "Who Quincy?" Mom said, "Quincy not your dad boy! No L. J. Johnson is." I was like, "Who?" She said, "Yeah L.J. Johnson." Mom begin to express, "You know LaPonne, your mom was young and foolish, and he was a merchant seaman in town, and we met. L.J. the world of me, and he even asked to marry me, but I told him no and he broke down and cried. Mom said, "I just ran into him, and he did not recognize me. I was traveling from downtown San Francisco getting on the bus heading home and out of all the people it was L.J. He could not even place my face as being the mother of his son." She reminded him of their history and who I was and told him about me. Mom was real adamant about me meeting him and I was like, "I'm not meeting him."

Chapter 110

Emotional Immaturity
Equates To No Accountability

THERE'S NO POINT meeting him because I already had it described in my book, that we never met anyway. At the age of 18 I knew I had a story and one day I would share it with the world. My belief was by meeting him, my story wouldn't be as compelling for my book. My edge has always been I didn't know who my dad was, and mom was not there for me. Mom and I argued for about 2 weeks about me calling L. J. and arranging to meet him. When mom wanted you to do something she will ride you, (for example) as soon as I opened my eyes to wake up, "LaPonne you called L. J.?" Soon as you come through the door, "LaPonne you called L. J.?" If you in the room minding your own business coming through the door "LaPonne you called L. J.?" I just gave in and called him. His voice sounded like an old timer who smoked cigarettes all his life and finally decided to stop smoking when it was too late. I was like, "L.J., this LaPonne, my mom said she saw you and I was just calling to see if you wanted to meet up." He was like, "Oh yeah, that would be good." I arrived at his apartment located off 16th and Potrero Street right at the lower corner where the shipping and mailing service UPS building was located. As I'm walking down the hill, in my mind I'm like, how long have this joka been this close to me and didn't care to check on me or help my mom out on any level. I didn't have anger in my heart anymore, but my thinking was that I just wanted to connect the dots. I went into his apartment and the first thing I notice he has small mini bit size candy wrappers all over the place in his apartment and that his apartment was extremely small. He just seemed really sad and alone and he had a terrible cough like his health was declining drastically.

I believe he was 65 years old at the time and I think I was 19 years of age. He was light skinned, with a mini afro in a cap and had diamond rings on all fingers, stood at maybe 5 feet 5 inches and had on a tan colored members only jacket and some shiny wing tip shoes that were tan as well with some slacks and dressed like he was retired. L.J. was like, "You want me to take you somewhere?" I was like, "Well I'm trying to see if I can get into Skyline College, they have an orientation for me to attend today but my car got vandalized.

If you can take me there, "I would appreciate it." L.J. took me to Skyline College and he waits in the car until my orientation is over and then he asked, "Did you want to go to Sizzler?" Which was located in the Fillmoe Center across from the Safeway grocery store in San Francisco. I said, "Okay." In my mind I'm like this is my perfect opportunity for me to connect the dots. He ordered some soup, and I ordered some Fish & Chips with some shrimps on the side. I was like, "So what happened? Why you just forgot about me? Do you even know what the hell I been through? I have been in all kinds of wars, shot, jailed, drugs, been shot at countless times, guns pulled on me, me shooting people, the police cracking open my eye, gang fights" and as I'm saying all this I'm crying. I just sat on the edge of my seat just waiting to hear his response.

L.J. says "Well You Know your mom wouldn't let me see you." I said, "You didn't have no kind of backbone for you own flesh and blood?" My words were so piercing and he's coughing real bad from aggressive declining health like any day is his last. L. J. said, "You know your mom would say she needed some bunk beds for you and would close the door on me once she got the lootchi". My response was, "Why you didn't fight for me, through the courts?" It was dead silence.

I said, "Do I have any siblings?" L.J. said I had an older brother in the South that he doesn't keep in contact with and have no information for me. In my mind, I'm like oh he just wears a costume that says gardener; acting like the seeds they plant will be taking care of and curated to blossom. L.J. informed me that his great-grandfather was from Trinidad, Tobago. I started to connect the dots after speaking with L.J. when he mentioned his great-grandfather was from Trinidad, Tobago. I see the resemblance of that in my daughter in how she's shaped and her rich complexion, it all makes sense now. We eventually left Sizzler and we went back to his place and as we got out his car to walk up the stairs I said, "Can I have one of your diamond rings?" In my mind, I'm like that's the least you can do. He said, "Aw, later you can have that stuff." I said, "I love you" and I don't know if I just felt sad for him, or I just was thinking maybe finally I would have someone be there for me. He did not tell me he loved me back and it messed me up psychologically. Then his neighbors walked down the stairs and he said, "This my son" and I had to quickly transition from my anger and just put on an empty smile. I hurried up and left out of his apartment. I went to my mom I said, "I told you I shouldn't have saw him. I told him I love him, and he couldn't tell me it back. I'm not talking to him nor seeing him again." I was broken and dismantled. The streets had been my mother and father! I had built up armour over my heart and to now have it melted away that quickly. 20 years of building up armour was melted away in 3 hours. I was back in a dark state of mind, and I didn't care at all and just wanted to hurry and move away from my mom. She forced me to do something that I didn't want to do and look at the outcome. 23 years later my wife had done some research behind my back to track down L. J. because I guess she thought knowing him would make me healthier and reduce our issues in our marriage.

My wife found out everything during her investigation of L.J. and it was identical to the information she remembered that I shared with her about the only time I met L.J. She said he had deceased in 2003 which was 10 years later after I met him in 1993. I was also informed that he was born in Troy, Alabama and that his mom was born in Georgia. When I first came to Atlanta in 1994, I would say to people I feel my ancestors pulling me and Atlanta felt like a second home. I been coming back and forth from Atlanta to Alabama for 20 years. What's so insane is that my son was born in Alabama. I don't know any official information about L. J. Johnson, but as I gradually arrive at the completion point of this book and I realized when he lived off 16th and Potrero, me, my cousin Ke-Ke and ShowStoppa used to rent this club out on Wednesday nights that we called the 'Gambit' and believe it or not why I realized later in life L.J. stayed above the club all this time and I never knew until now that he was still alive at the time. I guess I truly blocked him out so much my focus was to just re-write my past and to realize what was done to me or not done for me didn't matter. My legacies was not about to experience what I did. Now I'm in the hospital room with Ms. Tiffany and the nurse is performing the ultrasound and I get the news that I'm having a mini me. I immediately went into this zone about L. J. and how I'm going to be better, and I felt this certain urgency to not screw my son life up and to always be there for him. My young king is not going to be like me, is what I told myself. I was still in a trance. I was illuminated with joy and was glowing as if I was carrying the baby myself. I was so thankful that Yahweh Blessed me with an opportunity to correct my life through my 'Little Diplomat.'

Chapter 111

You Have A Family Now
& You Struggling What U Go Do?

AFTER WE LEFT the doctor's office, we started talking about how I should let my apartment go because it was becoming too costly preparing for a new baby and paying the expenses for both of our apartments. The financial pressure for both of us was overwhelming, especially for Ms. Tiffany because her blood pressure was continuing to get higher and higher because we would get into arguments about everything. I just wanted her to know that I was there to take care of her, but her stubbornness was winning over what I was trying to do. I started thinking to myself, this was harming our baby more than helping, she was too explosive over nothing. This is a different pregnancy experience than it was with my first child because when, Ms. Tiffany would throw up, I would throw up as well. I kept getting upset with her about not doing the right thing during her pregnancy, such as drinking enough water and staying off her feet as much as possible, because of that, my son was going to be born early than expected. Her blood pressure became dangerously high to the point that the doctors said it was deadly for her and the baby, so we had to check her into the hospital. One of the first things that the doctor needed to do was get an IV started to address the blood pressure, then they started some Pitocin to stimulate her contractions, so her labor is induced. The doctors said that once the baby was out, her blood pressure should gradually decrease. The next day, I'm still at the hospital by her side as well as her family; I had to get used to seeing strong family support since my family was not like that, especially since Mama passed away.

Seeing that strong support actually allowed me to appreciate her family bond. Especially when her Aunt Katy (R.I.P.) who stood at maybe 5 feet 4 inches and was a very sweet and private person but was a very pleasant woman that I viewed as my aunt as well. She was very beautiful inside and out. She had shoulder length hair in her mid-50's and spoke very pleasant and the way she dressed and looked as if she was a piano teacher in the daytime during the week but on Sundays, she was a bible schoolteacher. Aunt Kathy was a little full sized and had a tremendous amount of patience. She was Martha Steward before there was a

Martha Steward. Aunt Kathy had an evenly brown complexion and would also grow her own pecans so they would be ready for the holiday season. Aunt Kathy would bake pecan pies from scratch, which was the best I ever had in my entire life. I will always love her and remember her for the lovely lady she was. Ms. Tiffany's mom, Ms. Lovely was just a gorgeous lady who stood at maybe 5 feet 6 inches and looked pure Indian with very light skin and almond shaped eyes that were very engaging. She dressed very conservative but always made sure her hair, nails, make-up was flawless. I just wished I could have known her more because she was very protective of her feelings and rightfully so. This lady had been through so much with trying to put her trust in men who seem to always disappoint her. She decided to put her trust only in Yahweh and is at peace now. I truly appreciated this woman because with all she been through she was the kindest spirit you can ever meet and when it came to her cooking meals, the patience she applied to make sure meals as simple as baked chicken breast that was so tender and juicy, you swore it came out of a 10-star restaurant; I'm falling in love again as I think about that chicken. So now Ms. Tiffany was released from the hospital.

Chapter 112

Can You Raise A Prince To A King You Wasn't?

WE WENT HOME to our one-bedroom apartment, and we made the decision to stay until our Little Diplomat got bigger. His Yahweh Father at the time and I built my son's nursery that was beautiful, I felt real proud of myself building something for my son. I felt like an African Warrior building a hut for his family. I was going back and forth from home to the hospital checking on her just to make sure everything was going according to schedule. However, the doctor informed us that the baby was too small to do a caesarean, so they told her she had to push. I was right there cheering her on; I was like, "Come on baby, you can do this! I'm right here with you; I'm proud of you." Right after I spoke those words, she was pushing the baby out and the doctors were not even in the ready position to receive the baby coming down the birth canal. They were still putting on gloves and medical covers for their shoes; I hurried over to catch my son and said, "Doctor my son is coming out!" Translation, "If nobody comes over here, I'm going to be kicking some tail and taking names." Ms. Tiffany was strong; she pushed my son out with only two intense pushes. I think she just wanted the delivery to be over with. There he was, my 'Young King The Little Diplomat' although he was only 4 lbs. and 22 inches, he came out with his lips poked out like his mother. I was so happy my son and his mom were healthy, even though my son was the size of a good authentic Mexican burrito from Mission Street in San Francisco, I was humbled by the experience. All I could think of was that this is my opportunity to have a mini me to right the ship. I thought I would be there through all his developing stages, but the problems between his mom and I continued to climax with no expiration date.

Chapter 113

People Use Your Fork & Knife To Eat Your Food Then Stab You

SHE SEEMED TO have lost her identity once she became a mom and she admitted to having postpartum depression. We already had issues with co-existing with one another and the postpartum did not make matters better; I would ask her to not yell in front of our son or slam doors because it was messing with the development of his nerves. At the time when I had my daughter, I wanted to have fourteen (14) more kids but, when I had my son, I wanted no more kids because he cried all the time, and he was needy and demanding. It was too soon for Ms. Tiffany to return to work, so I had her stay off work while I worked two jobs to try to keep things together. I wasn't making much lootchi, but Yahweh Blessed me in ways that I was able to take care of my family the best I could without going back to jail. I went to New York because my partna Show Stoppa, at the time, grandfather died. It was an opportunity for me to go to New York and to also meet more of his family and get some clothes at a lower price. I brought Ms. Tiffany a lot of knock off Louis Vuitton watches & bags just to show her I appreciate you carrying our little king. I took real good care of her. I wined and dined her, even though I don't celebrate Valentine's Day. I brought her a diamond tennis bracelet and a talking teddy bear that had a dozen roses wrapped around it. I always treated her good; she was a spoiled girl who always expected things like that to be done and I still hung in there with her. Other women would see how I was treating her and would try to flirt with me. I would not entertain the idea. There was one occasion when things got really blown out of proportion with some girl named Mamie who was real train smoke dark beautiful and was real flirtatious and a sweetheart, who knew what she wanted and wouldn't be denied.

Mamie stood at maybe 5 feet 3 inches, really slanted eyes, and her personality was that she was a go getter, and she could make friends with anybody. If you came phony to her, she would check you. Mamie was very stylish and loved to laugh and quick to get in bed with you if she was curious about you. I hired her to help me decorate a surprise party for my lady's birthday party and bake a special cake that was dedicated to her Delta Sigma Theta Sorority. I didn't know anything about sororities or fraternities (I at least took time to learn about her world), so Mamie and I became cool friends, although I think she may have liked me a little bit. She would talk to me about some of the guys she would date, and we would go to each other party events. Ms. Tiffany was off work on family leave, she had all these so-called friends who were 'allegedly' keeping an eye on me to see if I was doing anything at the job to disrespect her. At the time I didn't know this was going on until it was rumored that I had a lot of women coming in my face flirting with me. One day, it was a long day at work, and I worked overtime. Mamie and I were sitting next to each other when she said that her neck and shoulders were hurting. I didn't think anything of what she was saying because my neck and shoulders were hurting as well. I went over and massaged her shoulders and neck, and people was spreading rumors around the job saying that we were sleeping together and that I was no good and how could I cheat on Ms. Tiffany while she's at home with our son. I heard the rumors, so I called Ms. Tiffany, so she could hear it from me. I said people on the job spreading gossip about Mamie and I sleeping together. She casually replied, "Why are they saying that?" I said," I don't know, but all I did was rubbed her shoulders and neck." She was like, "What do you mean rubbed?" I said, "You know like a massage minus the affection or intimacy." She went off on the phone yelling, talking about "You only told me because you knew I would find out!" I was totally blindsided by her response.

I was telling her the story like in a joking way like, I could not believe that all these people who are smiling in my face and are spreading all these rumors about us. Something about that whole conversation just didn't sit too well with me, and things began to change drastically between us. Things were starting to fall apart right before my very eyes with her. In fact, I think the straw that broke the camel back was when I heard around the job that she was tired of taking care of two kids, meaning me and our son, and I was putting my hands on her. I had never been more hurt by a woman's words landing so viciously in my spirit.

I was so hurt and vexed that this was the representation of me by people who did not know me. If they would have known me for real, they would have known that those rumors did not represent me, not even a little bit. I was not about to let anybody throw dirt on my name and not feel the casualties from it. The 'street dude' in me was about to release in ways Huntsville had never witnessed before. I went around this whole department trying to find the ringleader for all the rumors, and the first person I asked was KP's wife Mrs. Kristine. I told her how p***ed I was and said, "Can you believe that somebody on this job is spreading rumors that I'm sleeping with Mamie and that I be putting my hands on Ms. Tiffany?" I said, "They messed up! I'm a gentleman and a gangsta. I'll leave it up to you to choose which one you would like best served!" After doing some thorough and intense investigation with Mrs. Kristine, she told me a girl named Trina was the one spreading rumors about Ms. Tiffany and I. However, I was puzzled because it made no sense to me that Trina would say something about my relationship with Ms. Tiffany because we never really talked like that. The only conversation we had was about her being crazily obsessed with NBA basketball player Ben Wallace who played for the Detroit Pistons, and other than that, nothing else!

Once it was confirmed that Trina was the one spreading the rumors, I was like I'm trying to get away from my gangsta ways, but these clowns are bringing me back in. The next morning around 6:30, I showed up to the job parking lot with all black on and a ski mask on waiting for Trina. I finally saw her drive into the employee parking lot; I got low and camouflaged through the cars and waited until she opened her door and I said, "WHO THE F*** YOU THINK YOU ARE THROWING DIRT ON MY NAME? SAYING THAT I'M A LOSER AND THAT I'M BEATING MY GIRL, AND SHE TAKES CARE OF TWO KIDS? UNDERSTAND THIS; I AM A GENTLEMAN AND A GANGSTA AND I DON'T GIVE A

F*** ABOUT THIS JOB. I WILL SMASH YOU RIGHT NOW IF I HEAR MY NAME COME OUT OF YOUR F****** MOUTH AGAIN! I WILL CRUSH YOU AND ANYBODY YOU GET INVOLVED." I was hot as hell about the whole situation; Trina who was a cool woman who stood at like 6 feet 2 inches who should have been in the Women's National Basketball Associations and was a very low-key person who had a brown complexion and was just concerned about taking care of her kids and being the best mom, she could be. Trina never really dressed up and always looked like she never had time to pamper herself. She was still figuring out how to balance motherhood and making time for herself. I thought she was cool; now at this point she was talking to her mother, and then she asked me to take the phone. I knew Trina's mother Ms. Kat. She and I were both Gemini's so we overstood how crazy we both could get. We had a mutual respect for one another, and I viewed her as family. I explained to her that everything that was going on and how people were saying this and that about me and my family. As I was talking to her, I said, "Ms. Kat, I'm a man first before any of this, and people are not going to handle me like I'm a Sucka."

Ms. Kat said, "I respect that, but I know for a fact my daughter did not have anything to do with the rumors and that you may want to check with Kristine, that's who you really need to be talking to." When she said that to me, I started replaying the conversation I had with Kristine in my mind and how she did not act as though she was hearing brand-new information when I was confiding in her. Secondly, I started thinking about how Kristine's reaction when I said I was going to confront Trina. Ms. Kat opened my mind up to the possibility of the scandalous nature of my good friend KP's wife. The problem I've always had was that I allowed people in my life who would constantly do me wrong every chance they got. However, I did not suspect anything like that with one of my good friend's wife at the time. I started thinking back to when Kristine saw how upset I was about the whole situation, and even after me telling her about what I was going to do, she acted as though she was trying to talk me out of getting myself into trouble. I told her I was doing it anyway because nobody was going to get away with disrespecting me. The more I kept talking with my colleagues at the job, the more they kept saying that it was Kristine spreading all these rumours. Sidebar Moment: Kristine was the Yahweh mother of my son and somebody who had met my mother. Her husband was my close friend; we know each other's families. What Kristine did was exhibit the ultimate level of a modern day 'Judas Iscariot.' We all used to eat at each other's house and go out together. I called KP and explained to him everything; he was like, "P, what you want me to do man that's my wife?" I said, "KP, if she was not your wife, I would have handled her differently." KP and I ended up not talking after that for some years.

Ms. Tiffany couldn't seem to move past our issues, so she moved out and got her own place, which was a townhouse. We had not been speaking to each other, other than focusing on the welfare of our son. Which was crazy because when she left, after we had a big fight, I had just spent about $300 on groceries and was feeling real good about that because that was the first time of being Blessed to have the cabinets and refrigerator filled with food. I was asleep in the bedroom because I just did not want to see her face as she was moving out. I heard the front door close and went into the kitchen to get something to eat. That deranged girl took all the food out the house as well as the plates, forks, spoons, knives, and everything else! I put the chain on the door so she could not get back in there. When she decided to come back to the apartment, she discovered that she was locked out and told me to take the lock off the door, and if I didn't, she was going to call the police. At that point, I didn't care because she cleaned everything out of the apartment and left me for dead. It wasn't as if I was in another town, I was just in the next room sleep and she did this sneaky cold-hearted act. I didn't have any more respect for her. The police came to the apartment and asked me to take the chain off the door. I told them I was not going to take the chain off the door because she have locked me out before and plus, she just stole $300 worth of food that I brought. I calmed down and let the police in and she went off cursing and yelling. The police said," Ma'am if you do not calm down, we can't help you guys." I said, "See what I'm talking about. She is just so evil!" She started cussing again in front of the police officers. The police officer said, "Ma'am this is your last warning." I told them, "I'm not trying to be in any battle with my son's mother and she was not going to keep all that food with her. She could have some." Ms. Tiffany was like, "F*** it then!"

Chapter 114

Tired Of Being Troublesome Nobody To Blame But Self

THE POLICE MADE Ms. Tiffany bring back all the food she packed, so we can divide it between the two of us. It was one of the most embarrassing, immature experiences I had ever been through. I was hurt and disappointed that it had gotten to that point between her and I. She thought she was now on top of the world. She felt like she didn't need me. She had her own place and had our son with her. Technically she had it all. I didn't overstand why I was always finding myself in situations with women I would be with but I'm the one left alone and starting all over again at the beginning with my life. My break-up with her left me in a state by myself and with no family. KP was the only one I was close enough to, but he was preoccupied with his marriage. I was single, yet again and my son's mother and I had to work together. There was no way I could avoid her even if I wanted to. Even when I didn't see her, I had thoughts running through my mind that she was off sleeping with some other guys. I couldn't believe that I was going through all these insecurities, which was pulling me away from who I was and where I wanted to be. I used to give her roses trying to make peace just so we could be together as a family.

She played on my hurting heart; she knew that I was weak for my son and used it to try to control the situation as much as possible. I worked 15 to 17 hours days with nobody to comfort me. I just watched as she carried on with her daily activities as if she did nothing wrong. There were times when we were at work, and she would be so cold towards me.

Chapter 115

You Can't Make Excuses You Said You Go Be A Mogul

WHEN I WOULD walk by Ms. Tiffany or be near her, she would walk away from me and say, "You just make sure you focus on our son!" For her to even suggest or to think that I wouldn't take care of my son was a joke! There was nothing that I was not willing to do for my son or my daughter. Knowing that we were once friends, and then lovers and now nothing; was a tough pill to swallow. I could have easily jumped to another woman that she knew to get back at her, but I just worked both of my jobs, dealt with the pain, and helped take care of my son. She came to a place where she underestimated my loyalty as a father, and I hated the fact that I allowed myself to be so underappreciated and my kindness to be taking advantage of. I had a feeling that she was dating someone else, so I asked, "What man you have my Little Diplomat around?" She would say, "When do I have time to see a man while I'm working and taking care of our son?" The way she answered, made me suspect that she was full of deception. I just needed proof. Trying to get my mind in a stable state, I poured myself into my work, and focused on getting my Foundation Unit Entertainment Company off the ground. I really was trying to establish my passion and vision through entertainment. All through this process I had been infrequent in helping the company and the artist I was managing ShowStoppa, and a contracted producer named D-Animals. D-Animals was phenom when it came to production, but by him being cocky and young it arrested his development at the same time; he was a quick learner but always got easily distracted and I was the big brother and the iron fist to keep the productivity in place that always came out as me just being an authoritative figure but in actuality I was teaching him how business works on a high level.

Chapter 116

San Francisco Zebra Killers

I REITERATED TO D-Animals, if you want success on a high level, your sacrifice has to match that (D Animals never got it). The engineer 'The Colonel' actually became my right-hand man because it got to a point when we had deadlines to meet, and D-Animals would drop the ball or Show-Stoppa would say he has something else to do. It would be me and 'The Colonel' that would have to protect our brand and make sure clients knew that we could deliver and meet deadlines like we advertised. If it was not for 'The Colonel' helping me, ShowStoppa and D-Animals would have sabotaged my company. They still do not realize their actions and how if you're in any business, you can't make selfish decisions because other people lives are affected on a paramount scale. I needed an outlet to help me generate success and not hold on to this failure feeling that could destroy me. This feeling of defeat conjures up events African decent communities in San Francisco endured after the riots of the 60's. I was told this story about a period that was from October 1973 through April 1974 where a serial killers in San Francisco that was attacking and killing Caucasian people; known as the 'Death Angels' and later the cops named them the 'Zebra Killers.' It was a terrifying time because no one really knew why this was happening. San Francisco Police was un-leased on the Fillmoe African decent communities because four Muslims allegedly perpetrated the killings. The Muslim Mosque was located in the heart of the Fillmoe district at Geary and Fillmore Street. San Francisco Police targeted African decent men in their communities at every opportunity that was presented. To capture the killers and maintain the law-and-order execution there was a by any means necessary mandate. The atmosphere was extremely tense and filled with fear.

Chapter 117

Jim Jones The Ultimate Wolf In Sheep Clothing

AFRICAN DECENT PEOPLE in their respective neighborhoods wouldn't go outside after dark for fear of the police setting them up to be killed, beat up, or jailed, just because of the color of their skin. The Killers called themselves the Death Angels and killed at least 15 people, but it's believed that they killed many more that was not discovered. They wounded and injured 8 or more people. These violent acts horrified all African decent communities in San Francisco to the point where no one would even think of worshipping the Islamic Muslim Faith for decades afterwards.

Eventually, the Zebra Killers were caught and convicted and sentence to life imprisonment. The racial division and distrust was sealed between Caucasians and African decent people. This was also the beginning of the end for the Fillmoe district as an African decent community. The grabbing of African decent men and taking them to county jail only intensified the neighborhoods. At the same time the Zebra killings were taken place, a charismatic young Caucasian pastor named Jim Jones and The Peoples Temple of The Disciples of Christ ushered a new excitement towards religion. Who was Jim Jones? He was an impoverished kid who was neglected by his parents. According to several Jim Jones biographers, Jim Jones's father was a veteran of World War 1 and suffered injuries from a chemical attack. His father was unable to financially provide for his family, which led to marital problems with his parents. When Jim Jones reached school age his mother found work. Jim Jones's father's health caused him to be hospitalized numerous times. With his mother working and his father sick in and out of the hospital, and no one to care a young Jim Jones.

Jim Jones as a small kid, would wander the street of his small town before and after school each day. The women in the small town were sympathetic toward the young kid and he was often invited into the homes of his neighbors to eat, received clothing and sometimes gifts. The wife of a pastor at a Nazarene Church became fond of Jim Jones, often letting him stay overnight at their home. She introduced Jim Jones to religion by giving him a Bible and taking him to church several times a week. Early in his teens, neighbors described Jones as being unusual and had an obsession with religion and death. Jones would find roadkill and perform funerals, with or without the present of neighboring children. Jim Jones had many disturbing behaviors by saying he was the Angel of Death. His mother would beat him with a belt to punish him for repeatedly stealing candy from local businesses. When World War ll started, Jim Jones became fascinated with Adolf Hitler and the Nazi Party and the absolute power that Hitler wield. He began to study various religions and social beliefs. Jim Jones was ordained as a Christian minister and begin Pentecostalism ministry. In 1955, Jim Jones started the organization that eventually became the Peoples Temple in Indianapolis. By 1964, the Peoples Temple was racially integrated with a socialism platform. Jim Jones claimed he was a prophet and he prophesied to his congregation of a worldwide nuclear war that would create a newfound socialist society. Jim Jones implored his congregation to move to Northern California. In 1965, Jim Jones moved his Peoples Temple to Redwood Valley, California, and went on to establish congregations in San Francisco and Los Angeles. Jim Jones seemingly began his ministry in the Fillmore district out of nowhere, promising salvation to a community that was being turned away from the Islamic faith because of the Zebra Killers.

Jim Jones ministry was based on offering salvation and healing people. He purchased the building directly next to the Nation of Islam (Black Muslims) Mosque. The Peoples Temple practice a combine faith of Christianity, with Communistic elements, Socialistic influences, and racial justice at a time when the Civil Rights Movement leaders and organizers were being killed, jailed, or fleeing the country from being persecuted on bogus charges from America's law enforcement agencies according to google. Major blocks of the Fillmore neighborhood were burned down, and African decent businesses destroyed in the riots after the assassination of Dr. Martin Luther King Jr. The mental disablement of these tragedies of our prominent civil rights leaders being assassinated enforced the drug addiction and led to the loss of communities, the loss of faith and hope, left the Fillmore and African decent communities disillusioned. People were disparate for guidance and were easily mislead by Reverend Jim Jones preaching, vision for rebuilding the community. The Peoples Temple rapidly grew in membership and political power. The Peoples Temple insisted on communal living and its members had to relinquish all of their personal and financial possessions to the Church for the betterment of the community. Eventually Jim Jones became a major influence in San Francisco's politics. As The Peoples Temple grew politically powerful, the enforcement of its strict disciplinary rules became intense. Some members deflected and began speaking about The Peoples Temple being a cult and committing financial fraud by avoiding paying taxes by setting up trust accounts in members name that were all woman that he was close to. Lead money managers would take members to deposit large sums of capital into foreign financial institutions. Certain members were physically and sexually abused, including young men being raped. As investigations began to ramp up, Jim Jones moved to a small country in South America called Guyana.

Jim Jones relocated The People's Temple communal settlement to Guyana in efforts to escape the scrutiny of the press and government. He ordered his members to join him, and more than 900 members eventually immigrated to Guyana. After numerous complaints and petitions from family and friends of The Peoples Temple congregation, a California Congressional Representative Leo Ryan arrived in Guyana on November 14, 1978. A reporter traveling with Representative Ryan was handed a note from one member of the church asking to return home with Mr. Ryan. On November 18, 1978, as Mr. Ryan, his team and 14 deflectors attempted to leave, it is said that Jim Jones gave assassination orders of the group. Mr. Ryan, three reporters, and a Temple member were killed. Once the news of Mr. Ryan murder reached Jim Jones,

Jim Jones ordered all his congregation to the pavilion and began his suicide decree. Cyanide and valium lace flavor aid drink was prepared. All the children were gathered up first to drink the poison and the children that were too young or refused to drink the poison were injected with cyanide and valium lace flavor aid. Then the adults were commanded to take the poison and those that resisted were forcefully injected with cyanide and valium drink. 918 men, women and children were murdered that day. There were some survivors. Three of Jim Jones's sons were in Georgetown, Guyana at a basketball game. One member fled with her 3-year-old son earlier in the day by saying she was taking her son on a picnic and walked 35 miles to safety. Two other members were on a mission to deliver suitcases of money to the Russian Embassy in Guyana, one of the members dropped the money and ran into the jungle and he survived, along with 13 members that were at the airstrip. Nearly everyone in the Fillmore district had a family member, friend, or neighbor that joined the Peoples Temple in Guyana.

Chapter 118

Best Moments Is When My Life Is Moving With Purpose

MANY OF 'THE Fillmoe Residents', lost multiple family members in Guyana and as far as 'The Ultimate Wolf In Sheep Clothing' he did what any terrorist would do when cornered, he took the cowardly route so he would not have to be questioned by any figure of authority and he wanted to remain in control by taking his own life with a bullet to the head. Ms. Mylene told me a story about how she had a family friend named Brenda and her young daughter Lerner, that lost their lives in Guyana. Ms. Mylene was a teenager and would babysit little Lerner while Brenda worked at a hospital. Ms. Mylene, her classmates, and neighbors knew many who lost their lives in Guyana. Ms. Mylene is still affected by this tragedy. The congregation's decision would prove to be a fatal choice that is forever etched in the American psyche as the single most act of terrorism against American civilians and loss of lives until the 911 attacks. Almost everyone in African decent communities in San Francisco were connected to the loss of someone to the Jonestown massacre. This story empowered me to realize that just because someone says they are an ordained pastor does not necessarily mean that they walk in the spirit. In the event of trying to get my company off the ground, Foundation Unit Entertainment Services LLC. My focus was building viable relationships. I went and had a guy put together some professional business cards that did not look as good as they could have been, now that I think about it. Nevertheless, I was proud to see that my focus was in front of me and not behind, and to see my company's name on business cards was motivating to show I'm not looking back. My dreams were no longer just taking up empty space in my mind but were becoming a part of who I wanted to be.

I started meeting other people who were willing to take the journey with me. One day, while getting off work I saw a burgundy-colored Cadillac with a Peanut Butter top parked into the employee parking lot. On one side of the car, it had a sign that said, 'Urban Hip Hop Fashion.' I immediately approached this lovely woman as she was getting out of her car. This woman was tall and had broad shoulders. Looking at her, I didn't think that she spoke any English because she looked like she was from some foreign country, and it seemed as if she possibly didn't overstand the English language. I just happened to overhear her speak to someone and I was amazed that she spoke English! I introduced myself and she introduced herself as Sista P. She had very defined ethnic features from lips, nose, and the most defining eyes that you would never forget but was very pleasant and very wise with a bronze complexion and spoke very discreetly. I said, "I saw the sign on your car and was thinking that maybe my artist ShowStoppa can be sponsored by your clothing store." I gave her a little bit of information about my company, my vision and literature on the company. I explained how I wanted the artist to be fashionable and market the clothes that they sale in the store while the artist perform on stage. Miss. P said that it was a good idea and that I really needed to talk with her husband Brotha Tony. If you saw him and you looked up the word strength in the dictionary his picture was there. He stood at maybe 6 feet 6 inches and was filled out in every inch of his body. He spoke with a soft but eloquent deep James Earl Jones voice; he was not too light and not too dark of a complexion with circle eyes and well-defined ethnic features. I tried to make him laugh and he laughed immediately. I felt like they were family from the gate. Sista P told me to come by a location spot on a Wednesday night at 7pm because they were doing a fashion show for the American Breast [Cancer] Society and they wanted me to meet everybody. We hit it off instantly, you know real attracts real.

He was from the streets of Philadelphia and had turned his life over as a devoted Muslim. The relationship between Miss P, her husband and I was beginning to look very, very promising. I would see them at the airport in Huntsville when I would take flights and, they would be dressed immaculate as if they were the President and the First Lady. It made me so proud seeing African decent love looking real good and feeling good, as opposed to how we as African decent have been portrayed in a negative way. The connection between us was a solid one and I felt like the stars were now falling in place. Brotha Tony shared with me how he used to be a bodyguard for Hip Hop greats like Rakim from legendary Hip Hop groups Eric B & Rakim, Whodini, Run DMC and other hip hop artists, when he said that I was hooked. He invited me to come to his Muslim Study Group; it kind of took me by surprise because I never had any knowledge of the Muslims except when it came to talks about Malcolm X and how he died. I had my guard up extremely high when I heard talks about Muslims because I felt I couldn't trust them. Again, I was on the outside looking in. My introduction to the Nation of Islam was based on me going to the study group in Huntsville Alabama. I was dressed flawless, and I felt really connected spiritually when I came in. I met a brother named Brotha Jamil, who was the National Secretary personally for the honorable Minister Louis Farrakhan. I felt like sunshine has finally found its way into my soul. The knowledge I was learning through Brother Jamil was thorough and inspiring; he began to break down the history of mankind and the size of the world. His speech was eloquent, and he represented the forgotten and the rejected people. He was a charismatic individual who wore his hair like an African Decent Scientist, as if he had just invented something. He was a little chubby and his voice was very exciting.

One could tell that Allah's blessings were upon Bro. Jamil. He had a sharp sense of humor and made you feel comfortable with him. I remember when Bro. Jamil was traveling to different cities raising lootchi for 'Saviors Day, (a day that was set aside for the acknowledgement of The Nation of Islam to commemorate the birth of Master Farad Muhammad their Great Madhi). I felt so connected at the time to the Mass because it really empowered me and made me feel a part of my heritage. That was the first experience I had in my life where a message from a Minister or Pastor stayed with me. I began to feel that 'spiritual power' I was longing for to help me deal with my demons but to also teach me how to become a better African decent man, a better friend, and a better student of life. Bro. Jamil came to the Huntsville Study Group with a violin that brothers at the federal penitentiary made for Minister Farrakhan. Bro. Jamil was suggesting that we write a thank you note because it would show the brothers who were locked up that they had people on the outside that cared about them. Writing letters would also show the jail system that they are not disconnected from their loved ones either. There was this one sister who came out of nowhere and said, "We needed to stop wasting time sending letters to people who are locked up and that she was not sending any lootchi to her brother anymore and that they are the ones that put themselves in that situation." Bro. Jamil gently replied, "Sista, I'm not saying we have to condone the wrong doings that these brothers have committed; we are just simply talking about writing a thank you letter for the violin." The sister kept going on and on and Bro. Jamil was so composed and finessed in the situation that I admired how he handled her. I stood up and spoke because the sister kept going on.

I said, "You want to send the letters because at times when you make a mistake in life and you commit a crime and you get locked up, a lot of times you feel you have nothing to live for, but the letters help you get through, because you become accustomed to having to always watch your back and look out for who is trying to kill you or set you up when you are in jail. Your mentality can easily become dark, so to have somebody familiar sending you a letter of love, truly comforts you in that challenging situation. We know we put ourselves in that predicament; it doesn't change the fact of not wanting to receive love from people who love you and know you." I continued, "When I was locked up, I did not have any family support, so I tried to hang myself! I broke down and could not finish the job of committing suicide. If I only had that family support, I probably wouldn't have thought about my life being one of no value." When I said that, I could see in the lady's eyes that the message did some good to her lack of overstanding. Bro. Jamil thought I was already a registered Muslim and came up to me and was like, "Thank you for speaking Brotha." I continued to go to the study groups almost every Wednesday, Friday, and Sunday to give my soul, mind and lootchi to the study group. That was the first time in my life I felt that I was at home. Ms. P. had people coming up to her saying, "He's on fire; keep him on fire!" I was able to ask questions from the people who were students that learned under the leadership of the Honorable Elijah Muhammad. Another Muslim minister, I admired was Minister H.; he was one of the Great Ministers who was a walking Muslim Encyclopedia.

Every Wednesday and Friday, he and I would play a game of 'mental chest' which was both interesting and challenging at the same time for me. I began to really put a lot of self-evaluation in place and blamed myself for whatever failures in my life. I really started focusing on being accountable for the things that I had done. I honestly believed with me coming into the knowledge of self in the Muslim culture, it allowed me to be aware of myself, and how to live and eat with self-awareness. In fact, just being there confirmed a lot of things I already had in my soul. I just now had a family that overstood a lot of the same things I viewed. It took me some time to get all the way comfortable until Ms. P had me look at a 4 ½ hour long DVD about the involvement of who killed Malcolm X and did The Honorable Minister Louis Farrakhan, had anything to do with it. The DVD was very long but informative; it also pointed out that before Malcolm X's passing, he was actually coming back to the Nation of Islam (this was information that C.I.A. perpetrated to keep the division between Honorable Elijah Muhammad and Malcolm X). I decided to just move forward with the Nation of Islam.

On May 29, 2005, I registered to become a Muslim on my King Day. I told the world that I became a Muslim and had so many people against it. My mom acted as if she was going to disown me. She wanted to take a trip down to visit me, I guess to get me back straight! I let mom know that she could come to visit me as long as she wanted to, on two conditions; do not degrade the Muslim Faith and no conversation about religion. When I informed my son's mother of my decision, she of course did not want to have anything to do with it, even when I told her how unhealthy it was to eat pork and other unhealthy things. There were so many people not feeling me being a part of the Nation of Islam.

Chapter 119

This Moment Taught Me Don't Make Emotional Decisions

I REMEMBER I had one artist telling me to be careful how far I go with the Nation because they would try to use you.

I was never a person who got discouraged based upon with the majority of what people thought; if anything, that made me want to learn more about what intrigued me. I knew people feared what they could not overstand, and they hated what they could not control. I really started focusing on living and standing for something, instead of just falling for the same old usual stuff. Being with the Nation of Islam made me even more of a hardworking man. I was working extremely hard for myself and for my two employers as well. I really thought that if I improved on my way of thinking maybe I would be able to get my son back home with me as well as his mother. I tried to be as calm as possible dealing with Ms. Tiffany, hoping to recapture that spark between us. I was going out of town the next day and wanted to see my son before I left. His mom and I had a fight on the job and got called in by management saying that if we kept that up, we both would get fired. Most of the women on the job tried to paint the story like she was a victim. It was horrible. One day she did not come to work; I think she had gone back to her hometown in Anniston, Alabama. That was something she did just about every weekend. She had some troubles with her car, so her cousin let her use some old beat-up Crown Royal car, although it was a 'ghetto ride' I respected the fact that she had that kind of family support. I got to a point with the Muslim teachings that it was making me more and more conscious of taking care of my family; I didn't want to be another statistic. At the time single mothers' households were at 75 percent rate in the African decent community.

That really depressed me, so I got to a point where I began to beg for my family to be together as one. However, once again, her heart was like black coal and solid as stone. She continued to proclaim that she didn't have time to be seeing anybody else, but I didn't believe her. I wanted to see my son once I got off work. I called her and told her that I wanted to see my son real quick, and I drove by her house because I was already around the corner. I said, I'm about to go to my second job and then after that I will be going out of town." Her black heart spoke, "Ummm, I don't think that's a good idea." I just couldn't overstand why she would want to make things difficult for me, so I was like, "Why not?" She said, "She had some company over at her house at that time." I told her, "That I didn't care about her company and that I was pulling in her parking lot. I just want to see my Little Diplomat and kiss him goodnight." She didn't like the fact that I just popped over the way I did, and she yelled, "So you just go pop over my place?" Before she could finish all what, she wanted to say. I said, "It won't happen again, don't worry about it!" As I pulled up in the parking lot, I saw this Gray Crown Royal car parked right in front; I knocked on the door and she started with a bunch of Q&A's trying to see if my state of mind was in a destructive mode. She said, "Who was at work all day today?" I didn't want to respond in a negative way because I knew she would try to control the situation and possibly get the police involved. She had the chain on the door and opened it just a little. I told her, "A couple of people asked about you at work, I told them you wasn't feeling good." She then proceeded to ask me, "Was it busy today at work?" I softly replied, "It was real busy." I was so fed up with those ridiculous questions she was asking that I wanted to lash out! And to think, I had to go through all of that just to see my son before I left on my trip.

Ms. Tiffany finally opened the door wider. I walked in and didn't see anybody in the living room, and I walked upstairs to my son's room. As I walked to my son's room an image flashes across my peripheral vision. I looked towards that direction and, low and behold there was a guy in the bed with one of his legs popped up—posted on the same side I laid at holding the same remote that I use to hold. I didn't say anything. I continued to my son's room, kissed him and whispered in his ear, "Your daddy loves you and don't forget that." I headed back downstairs. As I got closer to the door, something tugged at me and said 'Ponne, you just can't leave like this; you need to say something!' After I thought for 5 seconds, I just let loose: "F*** THIS!" I went back up the stairs and I'm going towards where the dude was laying at, he was a big, flabby Larry Holmes looking joker who was on the bed with a piercing over his eye. I'm going towards him, and she grabbed my arm, as to say leave him alone. I gave her a look like 'B****, I will knock your f*****' front teeth out! You beta let me go.' I didn't say those words to her, but my eyes did. I was getting closer and closer to him and said, "That's my son in there and, you bet not put your hands on my son or yell at him. As long as you don't do that, you and I don't have any problems!" I looked at her and said to him, "You can have her cause I don't want her" and then left. My heart was racing as fast as a high-speed chase because I wanted to knock the h*** out of her and him; however, I realized that if I did any of those things that I wanted to do, I would have let not only myself down, but my son as well. As I was leaving out, she started blowing up my cell phone, but I didn't answer. I had to get myself prepared for my second job. When I got off work at 7:30 in the morning, I went to pick up my son (I kept him a few days out of the week). Before arriving at her house, I called her in a calm voice (acting as though I didn't get her calls until late); I was like, "What's going on? You called."

Ms. Tiffany went to yelling and screaming on the phone, "DON'T YOU EVER COME OVER MY HOUSE AND DISRESPECT MY HOUSE AND MY BOYFRIEND!" I was smiling over the phone and said, "Don't worry about it, it'll never happen again. I'll be there to get my son in the morning." She said, "He is not going with you until you apologize." I started thinking to myself once again that this girl was out of her mind. I said, "You are more deranged than I thought if you think I'm going to apologize for the hurt and lies you caused." She threatened me by saying that "I would not see my son." She knew where to hit me; she knew that I was trying so hard to not revisit my past behaviors, but she was bringing me to that point. I told her that, "If she withheld my son from me, I would terrorize her whole house, first thing in the morning and I dared her dude to get in the way." I told her, "I had nothing to lose and, if she wanted my alter ego Mr. Lucifer to visit, play around with me and my son's relationship." She hung the phone up on me. I told myself that I would wait until 7:20 am to call her house because it was not in my nature to be popping up over to someone's house without an invitation, unless I was trying to bring WORLD WAR III to you. I called and she didn't answer her phone. I called again it was the same results. I waited another five minutes and realized that she wanted to play hardball, and hardball was one of my favorite sports. I called back and she answered the phone and said, "WHAT!" I said, "Don't being saying what to me; I'm coming to get my son right now, so have him ready." For whatever reason, she was stuck on the fact that I owed her an apology. An apology that she was not going to get, I told her, "If my son was not ready by the time I arrived in five minutes, I was tearing s*** up over there." When I got there, she had my son at the door with his backpack on.

Chapter 120

Who Said Childhood Dreams
Have To Expire

I ONCE PRAISED Ms. Tiffany because I thought she was the person I could come close to trusting because I always had a chronic disorder when it came to trusting people. She revealed her true self in 'High Definition' which was very, very disappointing. She ended up moving my son out of the same city as me, making it that much harder for me to get him whenever I wanted to. In addition to that, she no longer worked in the same city as well. I was finding myself in an unhappy state again being in Alabama. I just felt that there was more 'fakeness' then 'realness' going on around me. However, I really thank Sista P and Brotha Tony for filling that family void I was feeling at the time when I needed it. I went into a state of extreme frustration, but I also was going out a lot and started focusing on legitimizing the company Foundation Entertainment. ShowStoppa and I were talking about how we needed to be more visible and start building strong alliances. At that time of my life, I was 30 years old, uneducated, and needed to figure out other ways of financial survival. But it had to be something that I was passionate about, and the one thing I was passionate about was music. I was still working at Delta Air Lines, which allowed me to be able to meet all sorts of people from Entertainment, Sports, and Political figures. The only thing that really made me feel special was when I met Deshea Townsend from the Pittsburgh Steelers. Anybody who really knows me know that I am a connoisseur of the 'Steel Curtains.' I have the memorabilia that's dated all the way back to 1979 from their Super Bowl wins to terrible towels, jerseys, trading cards, socks, hats, scarves, and other things.

When I met Deshea, his wife was booking flights through Delta, and we just got on the subject of sports and then I mentioned the Steelers. She smiled through the phone and said, "We have something in common with that team." I was like, "Oh, you a Steel Curtain?" She said, "Of course, my husband plays for that team." My imaginary antennas stood up; my conversation was real charismatic and down to earth. I tried to see if I could befriend them, so I could get football tickets. I also wanted to be able to live out my childhood dream by going to the football games and meeting Mean Joe Greene. I met a guy before from

Pittsburgh, Pennsylvania who was a successful realtor so I would be politicking to get tickets for free and take care of him on the back end with flights. My philosophy was, 'if you don't pay me right, I will find a way to be compensated and get mines!' That's exactly what I did with Delta. I found ways to make it worth my time as an employee. The realtor guy was a onetime contact but, If I had the actual player contact this could be more promising, there are many things in life that don't move me or impress me but, when it comes to Yahweh, children, music, the Pittsburgh Steelers, and Los Angeles Lakers, I would knock you down with emotion about those 5 things. Deshea wife and I spoke like we were cousins; she is so down to earth and real. Deshea and I knew a couple of the same people and he was so grounded I swore we were related. When we first met, I showed love to him and he showed love back, I was making sure the fans were not getting rowdy with him as if I was his security. I partied with Shea, Ben Roethlisberger, Hines Ward, Jerome Betis, Joey Porter Sr., James Harrison, and other elite players of the Pittsburgh Steelers after home game victories at this little hole in the wall club that was for the players only and certain selected fans.

I met Coach Bill Cowher in passing; the first time I had the chance to meet some of the Pittsburgh Steelers players and partied with them on November 10, 2002. I brought my partner KP with me. The experience was so surreal; we were on the 50-yard line looking at Michael Vick who played for the Atlanta Falcons in his second year. Michael Vick had many in the NFL respect his ability and feared his speed at the same time. KP and I got on the plane at 5:30 am so we could get to the game on time; while boarding the plane, I noticed that half the passengers were dressed in Atlanta Falcons gear and the other half were dressed in Steel Curtains attire. It was something out of a movie; we argued the whole flight about what team was better. That was my first Pittsburgh Steelers game and I had so much adrenaline running through my veins, when I arrived at the stadium. I wanted to run out on the football field with no helmet on and be a part of the game. I had my whole childhood playing in my mind as I was sitting in my seat just thinking about my humble beginnings from being homeless, jailed, guns, drugs, and all the pain and hurt and now I had the opportunity to live out one of my childhood dreams by being up and close with the Pittsburgh Steelers Players, my favorite football team. For eighteen years I waited for that moment. That's one thing off my bucket list of things to do before I leave this planet earth in the physical form. The game ended up going into overtime and ended in a tie 'who would have ever imagined that?' After the game, I met with a few of the players and then we hurried up and got to the airport, so we didn't miss our flight. When we got to the airport, our flight was delayed; we did not get a flight out until almost midnight. Atlanta Falcons fans and Steelers fans started arguing at the airport because nobody really had any bragging rights since the game ended in a draw. I never thought I would be able to get back to a Steelers game, so I spent like $400 on memorabilia.

Chapter 121

The Moment I Stopped Saying I'm A Visionary & Just Showed It

I WENT TO the Steelers gift shop and made purchases for family and friends. I lost my mind and realized I went too far when I didn't have no lootchi to get some groceries when I got back home. That's the kind of person I was, if something intrigues me, it does not matter what I have to sacrifice to celebrate that intriguing moment. I started building alliances with Deshea. I would leave a message on his voicemail every Sunday morning before his game and wish him a good game and to protect his body and, at the same time I told him to be a 'beast on the field.' I would call every game he had for 3 years regardless of if I was sick, out of the State, or had been out all night, no matter what, I was devoted because he kept my childhood dream alive. After a while I was more motivated to develop my own success. It made me want to push my company harder and the people associated with the company. I knew the first thing I had to do was get a team committed to the business vision, since my son was 1 hour and 30 minutes away and my daughter was 3000 miles away, I was very lonely and had to re-channel my hurt, pain, and emptiness. I knew if I didn't focus on doing things constructively for myself, my next move was going to be destructive. I believed that everything that I touched went bad or every time I wanted to be happy about something, it always seemed short lived. We were moving forward with the vision of Foundation Entertainment, with Show Stoppa supposed to be CO-CEO, at the time, he would always say that his boy mixed this song, or his other boy produced this song. I told Show, "You need to start telling me who these people are you keep talking about." I only started inquiring more when I believed that the music quality was getting better.

He started telling me about some young producer kid named D-Animals who came from a disturbed background; his family were gangsters, and he was trying to take his life in a different direction. I told Show to arrange a conference call with him immediately. That same night I talked to D-Animals. I expressed to him that we could develop him into a prominent producer and that he was a young phenomenon. Our conversation went so smooth he had so much enthusiasm and eagerness to prove that he could finally be a part of a family that would be there for him and protect him. One of the most important pieces to our company's development was the man who I called 'The Colonel.' he was someone who went to school to study Multi- Media and Studio Engineering. I spoke with 'The Colonel' right after I spoke with D-Animals and, both of them sounded down to earth and real, all they needed was strong leadership to bring out the best in them. I spoke further with the Colonel and discovered that he actually trained with a guy named Mr. Calvin Roberts who performed the vision engineer for the 'Stars Wars Movies (Return of the Sith & Attack of The Clones II).' I envisioned so much greatness we could do as long as we harnessed in on our crafts to make us that much more effective in everything that we put our minds to. I spoke with D-Animals mom because he was fifteen years old, and I wanted to ensure his mom that he was in good hands, and it would not interfere with his education. I had his mom on board, and I arranged for us all to meet and for his mom to be present because I had to have a parent or guardian sign the contract as well. I arranged to fly out and meet the Colonel, D-Animals, and his mom. I took a flight in December 2005 and that was my first time putting a professional contract together. I had done a great deal of research by reading other entertainment contracts and other literature, because I did not have the lootchi to retain a lawyer.

Foundation Entertainment was truly a 'start-up company' with no budget and no real capital; however, my friend, Ms. Regime who was more like a sister to me than a friend gave me a book titled 'All You Need To Know About The Music Business" by Donald S. Passman.' That book taught me parts of the business from a lawyer perspective. I already had a book titled 'Everything You'd Better Know About The Record Industry by Kashif (R.I.P.) (With contributions by Gary A. Greenberg)'. Both of the books were like having a Bible and a Qu'ran together as one. Kashif book was so monumental because he was a prominent producer, com- poser, artist, vocalist, in the 80's, and he was the 'collaboration king'. A pioneer when it came to doing duets with people like legendary Whitney Houston (R.I.P.) and legends like Dionne Warwick. I held that book with such high regards because he was already at the place where I was striving to get to. Kashif book broke down how hard it was for him to break into the industry, and how one has to have an extreme dedication to focus on perfecting their craft and producing their craft and most importantly owning their craft in the music industry. I didn't know much; nonetheless, I knew that I had that determination that he was speaking about. My knowledge of music dates all the way from the 1950's to the 21st. Century. I had been listening to music that was before my time because again, mom would throw these 'red light basement parties.' Still to this current day I have 45's and full 12-inch records, as well as cassettes. My cousin Boo could testify that when I was ten years of age, I would create our own version of the Iconic group New Edition. I would incorporate my cousins and have them pay attention to the steps and make sure they were exact, as well as the vocals arrangements. One of my female cousins was Bobby Brown because she favored him so much and, my family always said that I had a big water head like Michael Bivins and that we favored each other.

I didn't think so but, I thought when it came to best dresser out of the group Michael Bivins had the most style and flavor; he was always on point with his dance steps and, we cannot forget that he made sure that when anyone looked at his hair, we were guaranteed to get seasick from all the waves. My point is this, even at the age of ten, I had a passion for developing talent, so it was a natural fit for me to take my pas- sion and figure out how to get paid from it as a profession. I started drafting contracts for all the members including myself and the Co-CEO of the company at the time; it was something that required a diligent focus because I had to make sure the legal ramifications were included. I took a flight to THE YAY and met with everybody who was going to be a part of the vision of the company. I had all the paperwork ready for everyone to sign who was serious about the business aspect of where we were going as a company. Since everyone was on board, the contracts were signed, and I was like now that the hard part is out of the way we can now have fun. I presented everybody with their own business cards, and it was back to Huntsville, Alabama in grind mode. I started going out to the clubs meeting D. J's and people who worked at the local radio stations in Huntsville. One of the first things we had D-Animals realize that he was the head producer and that he needed to evolve our sound as well as diversify the genres of music for which we could produce. I informed him that nothing moves forward unless it was approved by me and that I will be working up close and personal as a co-producer with him as well as the Colonel. We were having weekly conference calls, having a minimum of three (3) mastered compositions being produced a month, and we signed up and coming artists. I devoted my life to attempt helping up and coming artists become a brand household name; my mission was to produce, polish artists and teach them charisma and showmanship and at times it became an uphill battle.

I was finally starting to get a little recognition for being an Entertainment Businessman. I was starting to gain the attention from the right people a little at a time; not as fast as I would have hoped it to be. I got word that Huntsville was having their 2005 16th Annual Black Expo Festival, which was an event that the local radio station named 'WEUP' put together that allowed established mark key artist to perform to help launch their latest project, as well as a platform for unsigned talent to test their art form on the crowd to see if their music would be accepted by the audience. We almost missed the deadline to enter our artist to perform. I hustled fast by constantly going to the radio station because they were giving me the run around over the phone. I don't know if that's because we were an out of state act from THE YAY. Nevertheless, I was able to get us locked in as the under-card act, the main acts were T.I., "Killa Mike, Exscape, Gucci Mane, Keyshia Cole, Marques Houston, and Mike Jones; just to name a few.

That event was a good look for us; not only was I able to do a 'under the table arrangement' to get our single rotated on the radio. With that plan in mind, by the time we had our scheduled performance, we would have somebody that would be familiar with the song. I was proud of the fact that I had no prior knowledge of running an entertainment company, let along operating it as the CEO; no formal overstanding of what was needed in order to be successful. Our greatest lessons came from our willingness to learn from being hands on and unafraid to fail. I started campaigning real hard for local support through my job and other people who were willing to pay attention to me. I was a 5 in 1 act. I was doing the job of five people and I had to make sure my kids knew I was their daddy and nobody else. I also had the hopes and dreams of five other people in my hand and my daily battle with a 'Troublesome Spirit'.

'Yes', I was dealing with my troubled past however, my heart's desire was to stay focused on the important necessities of life and there was no room for me to slow down. I was flying frequently from Huntsville to 'THE YAY'. I would take an early Saturday morning flight from Huntsville, Alabama and arrive in San Francisco or Oakland, California at around 10:45am. I always let my daughter know that if I found out that she had been acting up in school, I would get off the plane and go straight to her mother's place and pull her in the bathroom and smoke her behind. I always let my daughter know that if she was being sassy, lying, or acting up in school or not doing what her mom told her to do, she would be punished. I hated having to get right off the plane to whip my daughter behind however, I let her know that I had nothing but Stone Love for her and, why I had to discipline her. I only had 12 hours each time I came in town. I would have to see my daughter first and address her needs and spend time with her. I would then have to go by the studio to make sure everything was running the way I was told over the phone. I would have a meeting with my staff and then take them out to dinner and try to see other family members before I had to take a flight back to Alabama. I was so serious about the business aspect of the music industry and about my legacies that I kept that schedule up for three years. I brought my son out to the YAY so he could meet family members on my side as well. I traveled through the airport at times with a car seat in one hand, my son in a pouch around my chest and my daughter holding my hand. That was my travel routine with my legacies. It was taxing on me, but I could not let my legacies down. My responsibility and dedication as a father did not become secondary to my desire to become an entertainment businessman. I wanted to make sure that I was prepared to provide not only for my son and daughter while they were young but also that I could help provide them with a promising future.

I wanted them to know that I worked hard and diligent for them and for that reason I took my kids, my niece and the Colonel to Disneyland in Anaheim, California. Since I didn't have a woman in my life who I could share that moment with, I took the kids to Disneyland by myself. I was really proud of myself and would never forget that day. When I got back to Alabama, I started focusing on promoting the Black Expo event and for my artist ShowStoppa to be able to have an audience that would support us when we performed. I told him to make sure he worked on his performance and to pick out a performance outfit that would be different so he could separate himself from the rest of the acts. I was missing a lot of days from work because I gave up everything for the development of the company including my sleep. I was putting my health at risk because by me not sleeping, I would get sick a lot and was unable to go to work. I was eventually given a warning letting me know that if I called off sick again, I would need a note from the doctor and if I was late, I would be terminated. I was not in any way worried about losing my job with Delta Airlines. Yes, the job provided me with some special privileges, but my heart was into owning something that I devoted my ever being too. Things were looking great for what I was trying to do in building a reputable company. I knew I was not the kind of visionary who would just sit back in 'Corporate America' working to put others at the top. I knew that if I put forth the same work ethic and time into my own company, I could receive an increased percentage for the value of my time that is applied towards what I wanted in a company in order to be successful. I continued to travel back and forth to the YAY just to make sure everything was running according to the way I envisioned it; smoothly! The Black Expo event was approaching fast, and I told ShowStoppa that the performance date was in June 2005. I wanted and needed him to overstand that we wanted people to be able to inquire about who are we? And what our company was about?

At that point, I had spent countless nights on the phone and in person with the artist helping him polish his craft and write songs that made sense and were artistically creative. Unfortunately, it became a difficult task for the artist; he didn't have his flight situation taken care of or how he would be able to arrive to Huntsville on time to perform. As an artist developer, manager and businessman, my job was to make sure that the artist looked good, as well as the company. I gave him half the lootchi for which he needed to fly into Alabama. ShowStoppa arrived on the day of the performance; he didn't have a hype man and I was scheduled to work and was unable to get the day off. I had to come up with a lie to delay going into work because I needed to be there with him on stage to help him feel more comfortable.

I was always one to not disappoint and let my loved ones down! Prior to the performance, again I told ShowStoppa to make sure that he had an outfit that would separate him from the rest of the acts and to make sure that he polished his performance. Can you believe that he came out on stage with some army fatigue shorts, a white t-shirt, and some silver and red Nike shoes. He forgot some of his lyrics, so he had written some of them on a small piece of paper and tied it around his wrist just in case he forgot. I was like the 'Tea Kettle' is ready to explode! I literally spent three weeks letting him know how important his performance and appearance had to be. I was at a point where I was getting more and more fed up with having to battle with him on what I needed from him in order for him to even be considered a viable artist. ShowStoppa was not taking anything that I was saying seriously, and he would do the total opposite. We performed and only some of the people in the audience were paying attention to us. I was dancing all around the stage trying to bring the excitement to our performance but only a couple of people was bobbing their heads.

Chapter 122

By Any Means Necessary I Will Accomplish My Goals

AFTER THE PERFORMANCE, I had to run to work; soon as I arrive to work, my supervisor pulled me into the office and asked if the real reason I was late was because I had to drop my son off to his mom because he was sick? He continued to ask questions and then finally said that he was told that it was a lie and that I actually had a performance at a concert. I knew he didn't care about me, so I didn't care about telling him a lie. I told him, "That was not the case 'etcetera, etcetera,' and that's all." What I didn't know until sometime later was that he actually sent another supervisor to the concert to see if I would be there. Oh well! It was a slow day at work anyway, so they ended up letting us go home early. I was tired and exhausted from the day of events; yet I was feeling myself and in a celebratory mood and wanted to party with Show-Stoppa. We were at Wal-Mart when some females came up and was like "Didn't you guys perform earlier at this concert?" I said, "That's right!" They continued, "We were feeling you guys performance and you was dancing and everything." Some guy came up and said, "You guys did it! I'm from the Bay Area so you guys did your thing; they just don't overstand how we get down in the Bay Area!" Even though we were getting some good responses from some of the locals, I became turned off from living in Huntsville, Alabama. I was tired of people posing as my friends or associates who were actually the ones who told my supervisor that I was at a concert performing. I knew it was getting close to the time for me to leave that city and out of the blue my son's mom called crying telling me about her problems and how she was having financial issues and wanted to leave her relationship. She wanted me to have custody of our son full time while she was trying to get her life together.

Chapter 123

No Longer I Doubt Can I Raise
A Prince To A King

WHEN SHE SAID 'Custody' I was like, "Of course, I'll get my son!" We already had a well-established relationship with a daycare provider, so it was not an issue for me to get care for my son. Whatever sacrifices I had to make to ensure my Little Diplomat was in my care full time, my response to her was "Consider It Done." He had to be broken from a lot of bad habits that he was getting away with.

One thing in particular was the fact that he liked to cry his way out of everything, and he thought he could do what he wanted to do and not what he was told to do. My son was three years of age and overstood things very well. I told him if he kept crying just to get his way then I will help him earn those tears. My son liked to challenge me when I told him to do something; I had to spend two weeks straight wearing his behind out getting him back to listening and cutting down that crying for no reason. I set a schedule for myself to be able to be a good father and to still run the company, while networking to build strong relationships. It was challenging but I left no room to fail. My son and I would get up at 6:15am; out the door at 7:15am. We would arrive at his daycare by 8am, just enough time for me to report to work by 9am. That was our everyday routine because that way I could get off early enough to pick up my son from daycare to get things prepared for the next day. I would play around with him a little bit and we would do some push ups and throw the football or look at Lion King the animation and then it was time for him to go to bed. Praying with my son was something very important to me; I wanted to make sure he said his prayers and called his mom before he went to sleep every night.

Chapter 124

Why Seal A Cracking Pipe Just Replace It

ONCE MY SON was in the bed and taken care of, my mind immediately went into entrepreneurial mode. I spent about 2-3 hours on company matters, whether it was working on a song with an artist or producer, or just responding to emails that were from earlier in the day. Having my son with me, helped me to get a nice flow going. Not only was he getting re-trained on everything, but I didn't have the 'Never Ending Drama' with his mom since he was with me. About three months later, I started going out promoting and pushing the company and started networking and meeting women. I honestly believe James Brown had good intentions when he sang, 'It's A Man's World'; but the whole truth about that song is when he said, 'But it wouldn't mean nothing, nothing without a woman or a girl'. A brother was feeling alone, and I started second guessing myself that maybe I didn't make the right decision by cutting communication off with my son mom and maybe we needed each other. I didn't know what I was saying. I just knew that I wanted my life to make sense and for it not to always be a disappointing result. I prayed to YAHWEH begging him to bring some clarity to my life. I wanted my son to grow up under the same roof as me. I said, "YAHWEH, please show me a sign; if Ms. Tiffany is who you have for me then please show me a sign." When I came out of prayer my cell phone rang immediately and it was my son mom asking how I was doing and that she wanted to tell our son goodnight. That call was scary, and it got my attention; however, I did not act upon it. The next day, I was going to Wal-Mart to get an oil change since our son was spending the day with his mom. While in the store, I started talking to a beautiful chocolate sista and thought she'd be someone that I could get to know.

The young lady gave me her phone number and I headed back home and as soon as I walked through the door, my son's mom was there unannounced. She said, "How are you doing? I'm sorry for just popping by but me and your son was in the area, and I knew I had to drop him off to you in a few hours. He visited his Yahweh-mother and we just left." She asked, "Can we go to the lake and talk?" Ms. Tiffany started crying saying that she was so sorry for how she treated me and that we had something strong and that she messed it up. She continued to say, "I thought that I could have something better than you and I keep getting all these 'mama boys' who were lazy. You handle your business even though you could be real demanding, but you are a good man." Her tears were pouring down non-stop and just to think that I thought I was the one responsible for breaking up my family. I could tell that she was miserable, and it hurt my heart. Ms. Tiffany had put on weight, which was a clear sign that she was unhappy. I hugged her and said, "We are going to put the family back together!" I never called the young lady I met at Wal-Mart because I was still kind of on the fence about how I wanted to handle the situation with Ms. Tiffany. I never go back into a relationship once a woman gets involved with another man. I felt that any woman I was involved with before looked at another man in the same manner as me, was something that I just don't do. So, I struggled with the idea of letting her back into my life, but I felt I had to do it for our son. She and I were slowly trying to work on our relationship after she expressed herself to me about us getting back together. The next day she sent me an email at work asking me what I thought about some wedding rings. I thought that was the sign I needed to go all the way with my love for my son and his mother and forget about what I was feeling and keep the family together. She was staying with a guy she claimed to be unhappy with and needed to move but she transferred her job to Atlanta, Georgia and would not be able to transfer for another two months.

I had to be comfortable with the fact that she was not sexually active with that guy and that she was focused on us reuniting. Ms. Tiffany would come down on her days off and we would be together and spend time as a family. We would argue over our style of parenting. I didn't like how she allowed our son to cry and yell for what he wanted, and she would baby him like she was raising a little girl. Nevertheless, I hung in there and planned to propose to her on her birthday in Honolulu, Hawaii. She didn't have a clue as to what I planned for us; I told her I planned for us to do a turnaround trip to Hawaii for her birthday and for us to not let anything that could possibly ruin the trip to happen. The reason why is because every time we would plan to take a big trip somewhere, we would argue and end up not even going. We could never get passed the arguing and fighting. She was the type of person that would get in your face and start talking crazy with a small height; she was very short but argued a lot (I guess her attitude made up for her lack of height). She would lose control of her emotions so quick to the point of her turning red and shaking like a leaf in the wind. Now, don't get me wrong I love my son and always wanted a son; however, I had him under those circumstances. She was a sweet young woman but her past experiences with hurt and bitterness never allowed her to be healed from that pain. She was a woman who needed to purge herself in order to be whole and complete. She didn't like being alone just as much as me, she settled for hopping from one relationship to another trying not to address the issues that was resting so heavy in her soul. I wanted to try to give her everything that she needed to make her a better woman and me a better man; however, I could not take being disrespected and challenged by my own woman. At times I felt that she tried to make me feel like I was dumb because of her level of education and by me not being apart of any fraternity, nor was I able to quote any verses from the bible, which made me feel very exiled.

There were times she tried to make me feel like less of a man because I didn't look a certain way or because my background was street. With knowing that she felt that way towards me or was even making me feel that way weakened me. To be very honest, the fact that I didn't want my son to grow up without his father raising him or teaching him about being a man caused me to endure a lot of foolishness, that I knew better not to accept. I wanted our trip to Hawaii to be the momentum that we needed to help me get past the fact that she was with another man and the fact that she didn't keep herself together like the way I met her when she was a size 8 or 10 (she was probably a size 16 when we got back together). I knew I couldn't get passed the feeling of how my dad didn't fight for me, I knew I couldn't let my Little Diplomat down. Ms. Tiffany was asking all kind of questions; she was probably thinking that there was more to our trip to Hawaii other than just to celebrate her birthday. I remember saying to her "That I scheduled a trip for us to go to Honolulu, Hawaii just to celebrate your birthday and we are going to come right back." No, I didn't have a lot of lootchi at the time; but I felt I needed to do something to clean the negative record of our relationship. She was so happy and bragged to her friends and the day came for us to leave and all I was thinking was 'I hope we don't get into a big blow out argument and I hope we will be able to make our flights since we had to standby for availability'. I was doing something that I felt was different and new for us, I didn't want anything to prevent the plans I made for us to manifest. She decided to schedule a job interview on the same day we were scheduled for our flights. I wanted to leave early but her interview for a Financial Aid Processor was not expected to be long. just as I suspected, it was long.

Chapter 125

Island Of Don Ho I Bet You Next Time You Adhere To The Signs

I WAS TRYING not to let my anger get the best of me because I wanted things to be executed with perfection. She came bursting through the door, I was furious, but we made our flight barley! We were already on standby and had to wait for another flight to leave Atlanta to Hawaii. Once we arrived from Alabama to Atlanta for a flight to Hawaii, space cleared for us to ride in First Class; she was happy and so was I. One reason I was happy because we didn't get into an argument because we definitely would have missed our flight. Once we arrived, the plan was for us to go to a romantic candlelight dinner at a restaurant with a pianist playing our favorite song and then I propose, "Will you marry me?" while the engagement ring would be brought out in the desert of her choice. We landed in Hawaii, and I could not believe how everything was going smooth It was almost too good to be true! In my mind I started thinking, 'Here I am, this ghetto child in Hawaii'! I went from being a person saying that all I wanted to do was organize a mafia and die in it but instead went from the street corner hustling to proposing to a woman in Hawaii. I was so humbled. While waiting for at least thirty minutes and still no shuttle bus has arrived to take us to our hotel; I started to think that I spoke too soon about things going smooth for once. I finally talked to someone they said that the shuttle bus broke down and they didn't know when the next one would be coming. There we were sitting on the street curb in the heat looking desperate and dried out as if we were some refugees that escaped into the island and hadn't had a decent meal or water in two days.

I knew what kind of woman Ms. Tiffany was so if she continued to be inconvenienced, she was about to lose her top because she was a hot head. Forty-five minutes had passed when a bus finally showed up; the bus was approaching, and it breaks down again. Another twenty minutes passed when another bus arrived. I told Ms. Tiffany that we are getting on this bus. After waiting for so long, we missed our dinner reservations. At that point, I had to think of another way of proposing; don't think for one moment that I didn't have a 'Plan B'. I decided to wait until midnight to have a horse and carriage ride take us around town, with white roses in my hand and then I would ask her to marry me. When we arrived at our room it looked like it was a conference room for a business meeting. They gave us the wrong room which meant that we had to wait another twenty minutes. I went downstairs and demanded a discount and for this matter to be remedy like last year. The front desk clerk gave us about a $20 discount and gave me the keys. We went upstairs, entered our room and the bathroom tub was dirty and there were no drying towels in the room. I was beyond livid! It was about 11:30 at night and I still had to find out where the horse and carriage was docked at so we can have a nice ride on the night before I proposed. Ms. Tiffany started to become frustrated and was talking about dropping everything and just going to eat. We didn't know our way around anywhere, so we just walked around trying to find somewhere to eat. She didn't know that I was looking for a horse & carriage. I was walking fast because I did not have a lot of time to fulfill my plans; of course, she began to complain about her feet hurting and she needs to stop and try to get some sandals to walk around in. In my mind, I'm like 'Why don't you just tuff everything out until I get this proposal done'! When an African decent woman is inconvenienced, she treats it like she is being tortured.

I was so thankful we were able to find a place that sold sandals at 11:45pm; we got the sandals. I was hoping that would be the end of her complaining and that she would just be quiet until my plans were accomplished. Everything that I was trying to do was met with her complaining about this and that and everything in between. It was just as I predicted, and I don't think I could have written a better script of knowing how she was going to act. We walked all around Honolulu trying to find the horse and carriage; at that point, I tuned out all the complaining she was making because all that was on my mind was that horse and carriage. I mean, I was asking everyone on the island if they knew where I could find a horse and carriage ride, but I only kept getting the run-around. We were completely tired, and our bodies were in much pain. She was once again relentless in her complaining saying, "I'm tired of walking and you have to be considerate and overstand we have not had a proper meal all day." She suggested that "We eat at Denny's Restaurant!" I told her, "I don't eat at Denny's because they had a lot of lawsuits for discriminating against African decent people, just relax and let your heartbeat; I guarantee you I will take care of you, like I always do." She was quiet for about three minutes and started right back up again, as if nothing I said was important. Walking all over the island of Honolulu, I kept getting information where the horse and carriage used to be located at but not where its located currently. The next thing you know she back to yelling the same old tune, "I'm hungry, my feet hurt, my head hurt, and you have no consideration for me." I Can't say how many times I repeated, "Baby, just give me twenty minutes and everything will be fine!" That was not good enough for her and she continued to yell at 11:50 at night. Since she was not calming down, I said, 'Hell, if you can't beat her join her'. I started yelling back at the top of my lungs on the streets of Honolulu.

She was none-stop, we argued for more than five minutes in the middle of the streets. I reached my point so I told her, "That's what I'm talking about, you always running your mouth and always causing problems and do not know how to just relax and overstand that I will take care of everything for you." She continued to argue back, so when it turned midnight, I got down on one knee in the middle of the streets and said, "I told you I play for keeps! We have weathered so much of the storm with each other, and you had my only son; I want you to know that you and my son are my world and I want our worlds to always be as one; You are my queen and it's time for us to get this success as one and recapture our family." As soon as I pulled out the ring, she started crying and said, "I need to learn how to keep my mouth closed." I told her we are going to get tested on how we overcome the storm, which will determine how far we go with each other. Ms. Tiffany told me, "She Overstood". We got something to eat, and she was so happy. The next moment we became as one and was intimate and she was free. The following morning, we had a nice breakfast, and we went to the beach. Since, I'm from 'THE YAY AREA', the beach is a part of my culture. I didn't realize that being in Huntsville, Alabama for so long that I missed going to the beach. Now that I'm in Honolulu; it made me feel as though I was back home. That was one of the first times in my life where I felt carefree and had somebody in my corner. We ended up staying an extra day in Honolulu and I loved everything about it. We met some people who were from the Yay Area and they invited us to a party that night. Again, I felt as though the stars were following after me once more because being invited to that party gave me yet another opportunity to promote my company Foundation Entertainment. I was able to do some networking with the local DJs, as well as some other people and we exchanged numbers.

I asked the local DJ's if they could play some music from the Yay Area and if they would announce our engagement over the microphone to everybody and play the song 'Always and Forever' by Heat Wave. The other women were checking me out because their guys could not dance, and I was all over the dance floor having fun. Our time in Hawaii was drawing to an end and we had to get back home. There was hardly any space left for us to board the plane, but they cleared us for a standby flight at the last minute. However, there were no seats for us to sit together. Once the plane reached a safe level altitude, Ms. Tiffany came over to my seat. She said there was a couple who were inquiring about how we met and commenting on her ring and asked what my profession was (it was some Caucasian couple that probably thought I was a celebrity or something). Ms. Tiffany lied and told the couple that I worked on the Army Base as a Project Manager. What was more surprising than that was the fact that the husband of the couple was a Project Manager in Nashville, Tennessee. The couple looked like your typical 'Cookie Cutter, Mayberry family'. The wife was a perfect blonde haired, perfect teeth, and a nice shapely woman. While the husband had that 'Tom Brady' (who played football for New England Patriots look). He had the perfect haircut, perfect teeth, perfect physical-built and they talked about how they traveled to Europe and Africa. Honestly, they were the type of people who slightly waved their success in the face of others to let you know that they are well resourced and well traveled. I was overly vexed with Ms. Tiffany for putting me into a position where I had to put on a façade, which is not me. I have a motto that I live by which is: "Who I am is who I am!" I am not the one who puts on an act for people to please them because when the day is done, I have to live with myself. I ended up making up some story that I knew they would bite on because I controlled the way the conversation went.

Chapter 126

Not Having An Income Left Me No Time To Bathe In Pain

NONETHELESS, I FELT like a loser helping to accommodate the lies that she told to those people. We finally got home, and it was back to the regular routines of life, no more fun in the sun in Hawaii! After arriving back in Huntsville, I didn't have too much time to rest because I had to report back to work, and make sure my company was progressing and still on course. I had to get back to daddy duties. I didn't realize how drained I was until I was unable to go to work the next day because I got real sick. Ms. Tiffany and I had FMLA (Family Leave of Absence) that we could use if we needed to for our son's asthma condition, we were at liberty to do so. I happen to use it as an excuse to stay home and take care of my son. Ms. Tiffany was still working at Delta in Atlanta where she had transferred to get away from me but now that we were back together, she was trying to wait to be cleared to transfer back to the Huntsville location where I was located at Delta. What ended up happening was that on the same day I called in using FMLA, she called in and used it at her job location for our son as well because she was having a terrible migraine headache. The job system picked up that we both were using the leave for the same child, so they knew one of us was lying. We normally call each other to let the other know when we are using the leave of absence option for our son but, she got my message too late. I was already on a final warning for my attendance, I got pulled into the office when I got back to work two days later. I ended up taking the blame and they suspended me and said that I can write an apology letter to try to prevent from getting fired but I felt that with a letter or no letter, they were still going to fire me.

Ms. Tiffany was trying her best to encourage me to write the letter and, other people who acted as if they cared about my situation tried to advise me to write the letter as well. No matter what anybody said, I was totally against it because I would rather leave as a man than to leave as someone who begged and still did not keep his job. I eventually wrote the letter and still lost my job. In fact, not only did I lose my job, but I also lost my strength because I knew I shouldn't have written that letter. When I met with management, they had all my belongings in a small plastic bag like cheap groceries and told me, "Sorry but we have to terminate your employment." I walked out with my belongings not knowing what I was going to do. Ms. Tiffany was now my fiancée and yet, she is still living in the apartment with this guy she said she was unhappy with. As I was walking out with my little plastic bag of belongings from the job I used to have, I called Ms. Tiffany and told her that they terminated me and that I had to think quickly. That's when a light bulb went off in my head and I was like, 'My sista is in Georgia who I could see if we could rent a room from her until we get properly situated in Atlanta'. I called my Ms. Regime in Atlanta who has always been a sister to me and asked if I could pay her some lootchi to rent a room from her, and that I was bringing my family with me, and Ms. Regime said that's fine. I was so grateful that I still had at least one solid sister that I could depend on to help me when a brother hit rock bottom. I had to spend so much lootchi to move from Huntsville to Atlanta. I had to get rid of about $4000 worth of valuables in my apartment within three days for $400 because I didn't have lootchi for a storage nor did Ms. Regime have the room for me to store my stuff. I practically gave away my '55-inch projection' screen television, as well as my '52 disk CD changer', which was over $400.00 dollars. I didn't have the lootchi to keep paying rent for a place I was not trying to stay any longer.

I explained to Ms. Tiffany that my family was doing me a big favor by letting us rent a room and I asked her to make sure she cleaned up after herself. I didn't want us to put Ms. Regime in an uncomfortable position by regretting opening her home to us. Everything was working out as planned; my son mother stayed working at Delta Airlines (I needed her to stay employed so I could still have access to flight benefits to meet with different clients that I would try to pitch my entertainment company to for financial investments). We moved to Atlanta on October 17, 2005, and it was rough. I wasn't happy with myself for just being with Ms. Tiffany because of our son. I think it was obvious. She would not keep herself together and I could tell she was depressed. I began to see that she wasn't going into work, and she did not stick to the blueprint of the plan, which made my unhappiness become more of a beast of burden. I tried looking for work everyday from early in the morning until late in the afternoon attending all kinds of bogus job fairs and, after spending all day long looking for a job, I would come home needing and wanting that support from my fiancée who wasn't present. She was not planning for a wedding and was not going to work. As I'm watching her not be serious about our future, I began to withdraw myself from her presence. There were times when I would come through the door and didn't want to speak to her but would light up when I saw my son. Every weekend she would leave with my son going back to her hometown in Alabama, which made it impossible for us to spend time together. It was driving me crazy! I started to feel like she was not trying to put forth an effort to keep our relationship alive. I got to the point when she called my name I didn't answer. I was resenting her more and more. I would try and pull the attention from my son that I was not getting from her. All I could think about was the fact that I paid all that lootchi and gave away all my stuff to move us to Atlanta and nothing was going in the direction I envisioned.

The more I saw that she was reluctant to move forward with me, the more I determined in my mind that she was against me. I felt the need to tell her, "You not gone keep not going into work and think you go be in here just living off me Monday thru Friday, then when the weekend comes you go back to your hometown with my son." We got into a heated argument, and she left to go back to Alabama. I'm not sure what was going on in her mind and the reasons for not wanting to go to work. I found out that she told her job that somebody in her family died, and she was banking on her job to not ask for an obituary or something pertaining to the death of a family member and was caught. The company asked for proof, so she instead sent a fax of her letter of resignation. I guess she was embarrassed and stayed with her family for another week. By that time, I was done with her.

She came back after a week and a half passed, pretending as if nothing had happened asking, "If I was with her only because we had a son together?" I replied, "I'm not even trying to go there with you." So, she replied again with the same question. I said, "Man I'm not even trying to go there with you." She insisted on knowing whether or not I was only with her because of our son. She kept on saying, "No, tell me I can handle it. Just be honest with me. Are you with me because we have a son?" I said, "None of that matters. I'm not trying to hurt you." She said, "Just tell me the truth I'm a big girl; just tell me the truth." I replied, "I always said I was just focused on my family because I want my son to be under the same household as me." After me pouring my heart out to her, I thought that she would overstand, but she didn't. She instead left crying and then came back and packed up her clothes, moved out, and left me with a lot of unpaid debt. When she left me, she left me to deal with the pain of not being able to see my son, nor raising him every single moment. She was a cold piece of work.

She put on such an act pretending that I was breaking her heart and, breaking up our family with her sob story of me only wanting to be with her because of our son, when she was the one who was 'Perpetrating'. See, Colombo wasn't the only one who could investigate a case. I ended up putting the pieces together and got her to admit that she was in a relationship with another guy just three weeks after we were no longer together. Knowing that she tried to pin our problems on me sent my blood pressure to its boiling point. I was like, "You are nothing but a Judas! You bet not call me at all and when my son needs something just email me or text me. I have nothing to say to you." I was completely done with her, and I went almost a whole year not receiving any of her calls. I also spent many nights crippled with pain thinking about what dude she had around my son. So many things were happening to me all at once. I wasn't able to sleep, and I didn't have a steady job. Nevertheless, I got wind that one of my folks Cashmuir got promoted to a supervisor's position with Comcast Networks and he knew who the hiring manager was from Human Resources and told me who to ask for and to go online and fill out an application. Thank you, Yahweh. I ended up getting that job because it was hard trying to make ends meet with only scraps in my hands. Working for Comcast seemed like it was a 'family environment'. They treated us to lunch and took the time to make sure everyone overstood the history of the company and the functionality of the role that we were hiring for. The training was intense and took twelve long weeks. However, that 'family environment deception' quickly changed, especially when they found out how ghetto our class was. The training was pushed up because people were arguing with the instructor, his assistants and with the Director of the Training course.

Chapter 127

Faith Can Move Mountains
Just Kept Praying This Can't Be It

NOW THAT I was working (which I was very grateful to have a job), but I was not really taking the job all the way serious because I looked at my check and realized that it was not enough for me to take care of my legacies. I'm de-motivated on believing I could turn my life around by staying on the straight and narrow path. I was battling with my thoughts and my desires of doing the right thing and not putting myself in a position to lose my freedom. I asked myself What is doing the right thing? Is doing the right thing means being hungry because you put your kids first by sending whatever lootchi you have to their mothers to help provide for them? Or does doing the right thing means do whatever I have to do regardless of what risks are involved. I've spent too many years trying to keep it together; trying to balance that fine line of not becoming so reckless with my life to the point I lose my way. It took some time for me to gain wisdom to overstand that anybody can be reckless with their life but, how many people can be in a storm and believe that they'll find the calm while riding the storm out. My life was at a crossroads, and I didn't know what I was going to do. I was sleeping in a room that was an office with a couch that I was using as a bed. I was grateful to have shelter because I knew a lot of people who were sleeping on the streets using newspapers as a cover but, in my spirit, I would speak to Yahweh and say 'Yahweh' I know you didn't bring me this far for this to be it for me. I just believed with every fiber of my being that my life story was not going to end with me not being where my heart desired, I was convinced!

I was living in a household with three teenagers and about five to seven of their friends playing video games everyday. They were playing teenage pranks on each other, smoking weed, and I would overhear them talk about what little girl they were going to have come over to the house. They were trying to stick their chest out like a man, but they were not responsible and did not handle their business in school and kept Ms. Regime house dirty. Ms. Regime would be gone from sunup to sundown. The teenagers were getting away with redrum. It was like I had to have her back in making sure some structure at the house was being upheld. However, that only made things worse, I needed her to back me up on laying down the disciplinary tactics in order to recapture her house back. She would come through the door and all she had energy to do was to take a bath, have some tea and go straight to bed. Her sons and their friend who was like Ms. Regime other son who lived there as well looked at me as if I turned my back on them because I was telling their mom all about the trouble, they were getting themselves into. I couldn't be a man and just sit quiet or not do anything when I see their lives going in the wrong direction and being disrespectful in the process. Things were getting worse and worse by the second. Those kids went from respecting me to actually thinking they could challenge me. Please keep in mind that I was an 'un-official assistant coach' for their basketball and flag football teams with the Boys& Girls Club. I picked them up from school and cut their hair; I made myself available for them to come see me for anything, and now their at a point where they are being disrespectful and making smart comments. One day I was exhausted and fed up with the noise and the lack of respect and consideration and they were in the bathroom playing around acting real childish; while I was trying to get some rest and get my head together. Sidebar Moment: I was having twenty (20) hour days working at Comcast from 11am to 11pm, most of the time, and then I would help Ms. Regime at Purple Ribbon Ent.

Chapter 128

You Have A Greater Vision Position Your Company By Anymeans

REGIME HAD BECOME Vice President of Operations at Purple Ribbon Entertainment, which was Big Boi from Outkast Imprint. I had already been one of her confidants throughout the years on different projects and, it was important for me to figure out how I was going to try to get Foundation Entertainment off the ground. Any and everyone who knows me, knows that when my mind gets on a mission to do something good or bad, I won't stop until that desire is accomplished. So, my business was no exception. I would literally work seven days a week between Comcast and Purple Ribbon but, I was only getting paid from Comcast and very few deals I closed through my own company. There was this one day I was trying to get some rest and I told the teenagers at Regime house to keep the noise at a decent level and they pretty much ignored what I was saying. By the time I reached a point where I was fed up, I got up off the couch and went into the bathroom and said, "I TOLD YOU TO KEEP THE NOISE DOWN!" The oldest one kept talking and smacking his teeth like a little girl so I grabbed him in a lock and took his oxygen away and he couldn't move. Then his brother came in the middle to break it up and, in the midst of the brother coming to break it up the oldest brother came from the side and hit me on the top of my eye and cut me (I was bleeding but was not phased by it). Right after the oldest son hit me over the eye; Ms. Regime walked through the door and yelled "WHAT IS GOING ON? PONNE LOOK AT YOU FACE AND ALL THAT BLOOD!" I told her it was not a problem they need to be taught a lesson, and that they were unruly and disrespectful. While I was talking to their mother, the son who hit me was talking so much mess and then runs in his room saying, "He's sleeping in the same house with the f****** enemy."

That was the kind of madness I was talking about; those kids had no respect for their mother, so I know they didn't have any for me. I was like "Ms. Regime, I apologize I didn't hit him with a closed fist, I just grabbed him in a throat lock so he couldn't move, and he got frustrated." I then told her that I would go in the room and talk to him, but she told me not to. I told her that I just wanted to show him something since he was still barking, and, she again said for me not to go into his room. I respected her decision, although I didn't agree with it. Ms. Regime's oldest son was still in his room rambling on and on about he will do this, and he will do that, then he comes out and tries to jump at me as if I was intimidated. I smirked at him because it was like a little ant trying to put fear into a tiger. No matter what he wanted to do or what I was going to do didn't compare to where I was going. I refused to let the situation with Ms. Tiffany distract me from my plans, and I sure as hell wasn't going to let a teenage hot head kid stop me either. I was looking for Ms. Regime to help me connect to the right people in the industry so they would know what quality services we offered because I needed to start building professional business relationships with people and, she was being inconsistent. I found myself initially agreeing to be an 'Official Vice President of Operations Assistant'. I was more so utilized as just another intern/flunky and that wasn't cool. One of the biggest problems that I had with people was that every time I planned to do something with somebody, they would never stick to the established plan.

I started building my own relationships, making the right connections with the right people. I was working for Big Boi Company 'Purple Ribbon'. I had some inside access for instance. When Big Boi would come into the office, I would show him things I did for his company to impress him and also to distinguish myself from the other interns and represent Ms. Regime name in high regards.

I would be like, "Big Boi come look at how I renovated your supply room." (Anyone can call it how they see it, my goal and motto was and still is: By Any Means Necessary, I WILL ACCOMPLISH MY GOAL)! I was doing things that they were trying to get other interns to do for more than a year and, I came in the door and knocked it out in four days. I had got so filthy because I wanted them to know even though I had my own little company going on, I was dedicated and wanted to be noticed for it. I was mopping floors, cleaning toilets, and making food runs to Puff Daddy's restaurant 'Justin's'. When Big Boi worked late in the studio, he would eat there, and I would use my own little car and gas to get his lunch or dinner. He tried to give me the change, but I would not accept it. I wanted my dedication to the company to be noticed. Actually, I really just wanted him to look over our products and invest in them. Our company came up with an anthem for his imprint 'My Ribbon is Purple'. He loved it, but they didn't want to pay us any lootchi for it. Then we came up with a logo design for his clothing line and we had a catalog of music to purchase or license and he still would not cut the check. There were times when it seemed like Big Boi was taking some sort of interest in our products, so when I would see him, he would be like "Oh yeah, I checked it out a little, but I have to look through it some more." That was making me so vex because I felt like it was the right time to strike while the steel was warm but because he's already a success, he doesn't have the same urgency that I have and when Ms. Regime would see or hear things, she did not back me up. I'm not suggestion that it was on purpose I'm just saying she did not make sure it got the attention or was moved forward on like it could have with her influence. There was no one significant who was campaigning with me in order for anyone to give us a shot at learning more about what products and services our company could offer.

I knew from that point; I couldn't rely on her and at that very moment I knew I had to rely only on myself. Big Boi imprint was not bringing in new revenue and it got to a point where he would spend substantial amounts of lootchi out of his own pocket to keep his label functioning day to day. At that point I knew we didn't have long until it would be drastic changes being made. Fortunately, Foundation Unit Ent. Services we just had closed a licensing agreement with MTV Viacom Networks to provide music for some of their television shows like 'Run's House', MTV Cribs', 'True Life', 'Made Men', 'Rob & Big' and

Sweet 16', just to name a few. We produced a song called 'Hyphy Juice' for the Oakland, California group name 'The Team' that went along with the new movement that was taking Northern California by storm called 'Hyphy Movement and Going Dumb'. Just when I thought I was about to fall off the cliff, and hit the ground hard and die, YAHWEH provided me with a sign that he will not let me fall. 'Hyphy Juice' began to get some heavy rotation play on the radio and then when we produced a remix to the song, that's when it began to be associated with a commercially successful drink called 'Hyphy Juice' (An energy drink that outsold Red Bull in 2006 in Northern California it was published in the U.S.A today paper. It sold 6 million units the first year. I was anxious for us to get involved with the creators of 'Hyphy Juice' but the people who owned the drink and created the movement paid us the asking price at the time because we were new, so we only charged $375.00 and thought we would build a long-term relationship down the line. Since our price point was reduced, plus we didn't know the songs would skyrocket like it did. My focus was I wanted Foundation Unit Ent Services to regionally represent the brand in Atlanta and across the Southeast Market. I was thinking long term, but they did not have their business up to par with us, so we never did develop anything from it.

Purple Ribbon started getting a lot of new faces walking through the doors of Big Boi Company and they were getting new positions to see how they can turn around the operations of the company. There was one young dude who came in and I seen his face and automatically I thought he's not from here; he moved to a different beat. He was tall with a baldhead and brown skinned complexion and when he talked, he sounded like L.L. Cool J. He was real friendly and down to earth with a small percentage of cockiness. It was a business legal matter that he pointed out that Big Boi was getting jerked around in, I said he needed to be in the meeting so Big Boi knew that he was the one who saved him millions of dollars out of being screwed. At that point we became each other's 'Bra-Bra'. We supported each other to the core; I met him, and he had no support and was having a lot of personal drama in his life. I remained loyal to him because I felt we had a lot in common. I believed we could build success together, I told Bra-Bra that I would put lootchi in his pocket because I see value. I like to build long and strong relationships and get revenue together. Other people within the company began to feel a certain way about me, because the only person I would hang with was Bra-Bra and, since I moved out of Ms. Regime's house we really were not talking because I was disappointed about how she didn't look out for me the way I needed her to. When I decided to move out of her house, I had to see what my next move was going to be because I had nobody in my corner. Cashmuir and his wife Lady T had been my life support jacket. Lady T was 5 feet 7 inches and had a light hazelnut complexion; she wore her hair short and blonde and, she was a burst of joy and energy. She was someone that anybody would love to have in their life. She was someone who would say what was on her mind in truth.

She became as much as a part of my family as Cashmuir was because just when I thought I was about to drown from doing something wrong or drown from not having any options left, they were there for me. I called Cashmuir before I moved out of Ms. Regime's and told him about all the drama that I was going through with her sons and, how I needed to get out of there before I knocked somebody's front teeth out. He said that he had to speak with the lady of the house and that we were already family, so it was a no brainer. They were moving into a big five-bedroom house, so it all worked out. It was a long time coming, but I finally had my own space where I could lay in a real bed and could organize my mind, body, and my spirit. Bra-Bra was starting to launch a 'Reggae-Tone Movement' that would be an extension of Big Boi imprint called 'Purple Ribbon Latino'. Bra-Bra named me vice president of the movement and all of us was grinding in purple and black every night doing performances and radio interviews. Reggae-tone was a new world for me, although, I did listen to reggae-tone but to be an avid listener to it was a different lane for me and I caught on quick. Once we began to form a following, it created a division within the company. We were no longer able to get support or any financial backing we needed to make the machine stronger. Growing up as a young soljah, I remember my grandmother would say, "History will repeat itself". Now that I was older, I really started to overstand what she meant because every time I turned around somebody was letting me down. The only way I figured things would go the way I wanted them to go was to focus on my own entrepreneurial skills and do the damn thing myself! I stopped coming into Purple Ribbon Entertainment and I would only come in if I got word that some big event was going on.

What really changed was when Cashmuir seen me grinding so hard and saw that I was only getting about three hours of sleep each day, he watched me be devoted to Purple Ribbon and still go into Comcast most of the time. He said, "What I don't overstand is how you could give all your time helping take care of another man's mansion when he haven't even invited you in for a glass of lemonade." When Cashmuir said that it burned me to get slapped like that because I conditioned myself to believe that if I continued to stay committed and work hard for Big Boi, he would give us a shot and when Cashmuir said that it was like somebody sucked the life out of me. I begin to feel drained; I had a different outlook after that statement. Foundation Unit Ent. Services ended up closing a ringtone deal for the 'Hyphy Juice' remix songs, but no real success was garnered from it. I was still excited nonetheless that I wanted to throw a ring tone party and let my cousin Boo a.k.a. JW Sounds DJ the invent and brand his name at the same time. It would help bring some excitement to him and exposure for the ring tone so people could request and download the song. My cousin, JW Sounds was tall and solidly built. He kept himself well groomed and was very humorous. The ring tone party was the first event that we threw together, and I wanted to make sure I had live performances there to make it worth people's time. We set the party at a club for March 13, 2007, which will be located back in 'The Sucka Free' on the night that my cousin DJ's. I got off the plane arrived in the Yay later that Tuesday evening and rented a 2008 Black C230 Mercedes Benz with the light sun tent. We didn't have time to do marketing for the event, so the turnout was a modest one. We had two performers show up for rehearsal; the first one was Willie Hen a.k.a. (Hen du) and Sef Da Gaffler who showed up high as F*** with 2 dykes with him and a real grimy dude. Sef was like O.G. P.O.N.N.E. you always has been a clean a** M**** F*** with your style and I hugged him because it's been a while since we were on the block together.

Chapter 129

Salute To My Auntie
Ms. Charmaine Smith

AFTER SPEAKING WITH Sef, The Gaffler that night I reflected On how I could have ended up like him. I'm so thankful that, I start figuring out a way to reinvent myself from the streets. While he was going in and out of jail, I escaped and lived in different states to get away from that violent life and challenged myself to find out who I am. Somehow, he found out about my event prior and really pressed hard to perform and I was like I already have my performances needed for the segment. Sef The Gaffler was like, "This Fulton Street Mobb P.O.N.N.E." I was sceptical because I didn't want to set myself up to be let down by him, but I gave him the opportunity anyway because that's my street family and we have ties to the casket drops. When it was time for the live event only one performer came back, and we know who it was. We didn't put too much worry into it because the person who f***** me never got a chance to do it again. Nevertheless, that was my second proudest moment as a businessman. I looked successful, I felt successful, and people were looking at me like I was a version of Sean Puffy Combs of the YaY. The party was fine but the numbers from the turn out was not worth running home to tell mama about. It felt really good picking up and dropping my daughter off at school in a Benz. Those are moments I will never forget. After the party, I kicked it with one of the artists named Willie Hen and I dropped my cousin off and hooked back up with my daughter and her mom when I got a call that my Aunt Charmaine (R.I.P.) had been dead for a couple of days and nobody in the family knew. What was so heart wrenching about the news was that me and my cousin just had thrown a party together and now he finds out that his mom had transitioned for a couple of days now, that very same night.

I felt so bad and crushed, I had to try and keep my cousin strong, while at the same time deal with the emotional effect it had on me. It was a crazy time for me because my flight was scheduled to leave Friday. I was so emotional because I had missed my family even though we were not as close anymore, but I did miss being around certain people who knew me from when I was a kid. I had a lot of fake people in the entertainment industry that I had to deal with and, I needed real people around me. I called my supervisor at Comcast and explained the situation about what happened to my aunt, and they stated that it's not an immediate family member, so I need to report to work. I basically quit, the passing of my aunt was such a surprise because she was young and always worked hard. It was a medical issue she was having with her throat called Thyroid Cancer. The doctor changed her medicine, and she realized it didn't agree with her system. My aunt had complained to her baby sister about the effect the medicine was having on her body, but nobody took the information of what my aunt was saying as alarming information, so she eventually passed away. My Aunt Charmaine and I were close when I was young, and I miss her till this day. During the funeral it was real heart felt, it brought back so many memories of my childhood. There were people who I hadn't seen since I was twelve or thirteen years of age and now that I was thirty-three it really brought me back home and grounded me to see certain people still looking good and some people looking really bad but, they didn't care because they was just there to celebrate my aunt. I was so emotional that I got up and went to the podium and apologized to my family because for fifteen years I have avoided being close to my family because I did not trust them. They also gave me reason why my feelings were valid. I put that behind because I had a physical reminder of how short life was right in front of me.

Of course, I was use to death. However, I had only known it through violent activity, not through someone losing their life because their body did not respond correctly to a certain kind of medicine. Knowing that made it real hard to accept and I was really trapped with heavy grief and emotions along with everyone else. At the burial site, I was really mourning, and it was pouring raining and my suit had all kinds of mud on it from making sure the coffin was aligned and that Aunt Charmaine was comfortably placed in the ground. I threw flowers on the coffin, and I said my personal prayer; I expressed to my aunt that I will look after her son, and I will never forget her. I took all the lootchi I had in my pocket and buried it into the ground with my aunt. My youngest Aunt, LaToya who was very strong and could hang with the hardest of the hard, she also spoke real aggressive and loud. She was devastated about her sister's passing away because she felt guilty about knowing that Aunt Charmaine had expressed to her that the doctor changed her medicine and how her body is not responding right to it. Aunt Latoya felt like she should have done something about it when Aunt Charmaine confided in her about it. I'd seen my Aunt LaToya on a separate trip previously before the passing of my Aunt Charmaine. It was a trip that I had scheduled to visit my daughter and I ended up seeing my Aunt LaToya. I was complimenting her on her beauty and how she looked, as if she's not taking any drugs or drinking anymore. She was a heavy drinker and did drugs but said that she was not taking any drugs anymore and hadn't had a drink in months and you can see the results. So going back to the funeral, I was worried that my Aunt LaToya would relapse and not care about going on any further with life because of the guilt she carried for her sister passing away. There were a lot of people telling me not to leave to stay and my Aunt LaToya was saying that she needed me don't go and I assured her that I was here for her even though I was headed back to Georgia.

When I got back to Georgia, I felt like I left my heart, my soul and everything with my family in 'THE YAY'. This was the first time in my life, I really felt apart of the family and felt the love that I yearned for. A part of me began to realize that I needed that in my life especially since I had been going through feeling alone and pressured from struggling and striving and putting every little resource, I garnered into developing a viable company. I mean, investing in ways just hoping that one day we could see our labor of love harvested, but that was never the case. I took the little lootchi I had and invested it into things that didn't go the way it was planned. I got off the plane in Georgia, went home and I told people that I was too emotional and did not want to talk to anyone at that moment. Before I went to bed, I went down in prayer crying and expressing to YAHWEH about my pain for my life and Aunt Charmaine's passing. I was tired of dealing with my demons and having to go through this world alone dealing with so much burden on my heart. I asked YAHWEH "Please show me a sign on what I should do?" When I came out of prayer, Bra-Bra called me. I said "Bra-Bra didn't you get my message that I was not talking to anybody today. He said, "Nah; I just wanted to invite you out to this entertainment event." I guess when I asked YAHWEH, to show me a sign; I didn't know that it would show up in the form of Bra-Bra and a party. I ended up going because I was looking for more opportunities to expand my company. That's when I realized I had a message on my phone from my daughter saying that she just really missed me and would I please come back to the Yay Area and stay with her and, that she had fun with me going to her school playing with her and her friends. I almost started crying, right after that my aunt LaToya called crying saying man, I miss you Ponne, I was just checking on you making sure you made it back.

Chapter 130

The Ultimate Mistake Nothing
I Can Do But Grow From It

SHE ASKED ME if I had ever considered coming back home to the 'Sucka Free' and I told her that my son was in Alabama, and I could at least drive to see him and that I quit my job. With both my aunt and daughter calling saying that they missed me and, for me to come back made me consider going back. My Aunt told me that she could help me get a job and get me an air flight ticket to fly back. I spoke with my daughter and decided that I was going back home. Once I moved back to the Yay Area, I started living back in Westside Projects with my Aunt LaToya. I had not lived in the projects in seventeen years and knew I was going backwards all in the name of being there for my daughter and my aunt. I couldn't stay with my daughter's mother because we both had our separate lives and we both needed to respect that, so my aunt was the only option I had. When I told my mom that I was coming back and she said, "Why are you coming back?'" I felt that she was actually saying I shouldn't come back, so I didn't feel welcomed. My Aunt LaToya did everything she said she would do to get me out there. She got me an employment opportunity; she got me a job working at a Senior Citizen building helping seniors with their daily needs and also administration duties. It was hard being back in the projects and trying not to get caught up in any drama, which would have me going back to a 'dirty life in the streets'. As I moved in with my aunt, I realized she was back drinking heavy and doing drugs, so my heart was crushed because I didn't want that activity around me because I was fighting my own battle trying to stay away from drugs and heavy drinking.

She would get so drunk that she would fall down on the ground. It was sad and hurtful to be going backwards with my life. I was pretty good with going back to the hood every time I came to the Yay but, to be living in the projects meant that I could be a possible target for some old dirt I committed on certain people, or I could get caught up in my aunts' drama. One night, she came through the door looking for her pistol to go shoot some dude who tried to take advantage of her sexually. I had to restrain her by putting her in a wrist lock to prevent her from going out the door because she was reckless and looking for a pistol to go out to battle. I told her "You do not engage in war when you are not on point because you will lose the battle" My youngest sister was there at the time, also pleading with our aunt to not go outside. Aunt LaToya was determined to do what she wanted to do. She's so strong willed, she tried to charge at me to get out the door and I had to bring her to the ground to restrain her. It was crazy and draining all at the same time. All I could think about at that very moment was when Cashmuir said to me before I left Georgia to come back to the Yay, he said, "That just does not make any sense to me, that you would leave a master bedroom and all the work you put into building your entertainment relationships to go back and live in the projects; I just couldn't do it."

Replaying his words in my head over and over again felt like I was getting hit by electric shock waves, but I justified it by saying, "My aunt needs me; however, if she needed me why was I going through all that drama behind her." She was back on drugs and alcohol and was out of order. After a while she saw that I was disturbed and withdrew myself from her and didn't say much to her. I just stayed in the room.

She thought I was going around telling different family members about her business and it was driving a further wedge between the two of us. One morning, I came to her apartment about 2:00 am; I was walking to the door, and I see all my bags with my clothes in it thrown outside her front door where people pissed on the ground and rats roaming freely and, she threw my clothes outside like they were garbage. I was livid and more vexed with myself because here, I once again put myself in a position to let people walk all over me trying to help them. My aunt doing that, it took me back to receiving my degree at my mom 'Hard-Knocks of Life University'. I invested a lot into helping everybody with everything they needed, only to be disappointed in the end. I walked through the door I said, "LaToya! Why did you throw my clothes out on the streets?" She said, "Because you were talking about me behind my back." I couldn't believe what my ears were hearing; I couldn't believe she disrespected me like that, and I knew from that point looking forward that I had to create a way out of no way regardless of what I had to do. In addition to that, by staying in the projects, I couldn't take my daughter where I was living because it was dudes getting chased with guns and all kinds of drug use. I just didn't want my First Lady around that. I had gotten to a point where I was so tired of bending over backwards for everybody and that same bending wasn't given back in return. There were times when I would spend some weekends at my daughter's house because that was the only way I could spend time with her. I slept in my daughters 'Power Puff' cartoon bed; it was a horrible predicament I put myself in by putting everybody before me instead of over standing that nobody will take care of me like I would take care of me. I have never been stable in my life and now that I was a grown man, sleeping in my daughter's bed feeling as if I had nowhere else to go.

I could have turned to a female for companionship and worked some things out, but I didn't want to get involved with somebody I was not compatible with. I didn't want to end up having another child and dealing with a new series of daily drama. I didn't want another financial responsibility that I was not ready for. One thing that I could say was that my daughter's mother and I had always been friends but just that we argue too much because of the history that we shared. My daughter mother and I did a lot of family trips together, whether it was going to Disneyland, Beverly Hills, Santa Monica, or Raging Waters; we did a lot. There were women in my life at times that didn't over stand the relationship that I had with my daughter's mother, and it caused a lot of problems for me to be able to get to know women, because they believed we were to close, and something is going on between us. I remember we got into a big argument on the day of her mother's wedding (my daughter grandmother asked me to be the best man in her wedding in Las Vegas) I was honored that she asked me because I haven't been in communication with my daughter grandmother in years, but we respect one another. Yes, my daughter mother and I knew that we were not in a relationship; however, to those who were on the outside looking in, it looked like we were together, so when the wedding was over, we went to an old school club that had live performances. We were all sitting around at the table, and I started to dance with my daughter grandmother and then afterwards, I asked my daughter mom if she would like to dance, and she was like she didn't want to dance because she was tired, and her feet hurt. I didn't even sweat the issue; I went and danced with another beautiful woman. Dancing with the other woman, I could feel my daughter mom look piercing right through me; not because I was dancing explicitly or grinding on the lady in anyway, but I think because some drunk guy was in her face.

The guy looked like he was fresh out of the penitentiary with a body tight shirt that made his muscles look even bigger. As I finished dancing with the lady, I walked over and said to the dude "You're in my seat." He replied, "Is this your lady?" I said again, "Man, you're in my seat." As I was saying that I just remembered how I saw him prior to me going on the dance floor waiting for me to get out of my seat so he could come over and flirt with my daughter mom When I came over, I already had in my mind 'This Sucka think he's Slick' I got in his face and he got in my face and I said, "YEAH, we are together!" As I started to sit down in my seat, I saw through my daughter mom eyes that the guy was trying to get her attention. When I would turn my back, he would look away as if he was not flirting with her. She started laughing because I was going off in the club and was about to go over to fight the guy because now, he was disrespecting me as a man. Initially it was about a drunk guy hanging over my daughter's mother chair and she's looking at me like she's uncomfortable get him away from me please. Then it turn into him disrespecting me as a man and, she is thinking that all this was cute and flattering but not looking at my position. We started yelling in the club at each other, she was saying, "When you were dancing on these women, I didn't say nothing!" I said, "I didn't disrespect you though, nor did I dance in a manner disrespecting you or did I get any phone numbers." People in the club started to laugh at me because they saw me heading over to chin check the guy and she was saying that I was crazy. Her mom came over and wanted me to dance with her. I went with her mom, but I couldn't get over my daughter mom and this dude disrespecting me. I walked off the dance floor and went to yell at my daughter mom some more and then the next thing I know, she wanted me to dance with her all of a sudden.

The guy came on the dance floor as well and bumped into my daughter behind and she was like "Okay, I see what you are saying now." I yanked my arm away so I could go after him, and she said that she would talk to him after we danced because she knew how I got down. I didn't want to dance anymore because I had an overwhelming amount of anger rising up inside of me and needed to unleash it. I told her that if she didn't talk to him at that moment, I was going to take matters into my own hands. She went downstairs to the club to talk to the dude; I slid a thick drinking glass under the sleeve of my jacket to crack open his head. I walked over to where they were and said, "Why is it taking so long?" She said that she explained everything to the guy, and he said he was sorry, and that we should work things out. After all that the mark asked me "What you do for a living?" I stopped dead in my thoughts and said, "He's lucky I don't take this thick a** glass and bust him upside his head." However, instead I said, "You don't need to know that, and he walked away begging her for one more dance. The problem I had with myself was that I let her toy with my emotions. I let it get to me. The time had come for us to leave Las Vegas. Before arriving back home, I was determined in my mind that I was not going to stay the weekend over at my daughter's mom house because it was too much of a complicated matter. My relationship with my Aunt LaToya was way down in the pits of hell and, I didn't see any possible rescue anytime soon. It was rumored through some family members that they were wondering when I was going back to sale or use drugs because I was back living in the projects. In addition to that, my little sister told mom all the drama that she witnessed when she came over Aunt LaToya apartment and how she tried to fight me. Mom called me and was like "I heard what happened over at my sister apartment, LaPonne you need to get out of there, why you don't come and stay with me? "

Mom said, "I know how my rules are but, abiding by my rules is better than dealing with all that foolishness over there." I knew in my heart mom was right, but I don't know if I was ready for her to be doing all that nagging and nagging like she does better than anybody. I had to look at the benefits I was going to inherit by living with mom: I didn't have to worry about looking over my shoulder, being in a filthy area, and worrying about if I would have food or not. When I got to mom house, I could tell she couldn't wait to break down her 'Rules of Order'. On the first night mom said she wanted her place cleaned and that I could not come in her house late and how I had to go to church every Sunday and the list went on and on and on. Her rules played over in my head like Toni Braxton's 'Another Sad Love Song just racking my brain like crazy!' There I was in my mom house, a grown man and she trying to treat me as if I was twelve, thirteen or fourteen years old. I'd been on my own for nearly twenty years and, she was trying to restrict me from everything. I was not about to let that happen to me again. It was a depressing feeling but, I did enjoy spending time with everybody and meeting the new members of the family; my nieces Scrappy Doo and Glow Worm and my nephews Suga Bear and Sam-I-Am. Being at mom house did make me feel a little bit better, even though they celebrated holidays that I hadn't celebrated in a long time. However, I can say one thing about being around mom and my sisters, they would throw down in the kitchen making homemade sweet potato pies, macaroni cheese, dressing, yams, turkey, and gumbo. My stomach yearns for one more taste right now just talking about it. Being at home with mom and my sisters did sort of give me a good emotional sense of security for the moment, until we would pile up like Monday Morning trash in that small Dodge Stratus (that fit only four people comfortably) to commute two hours (one way) from Sacramento to San Francisco every day.

Mom had to be at work Monday thru Friday at 5:15am, so all of us would pack ourselves in the car like sardines for highway patrol to pull us over at least three times a week. Each time we would get pulled over, the value of the ticket was at a minimum of $350 for not being properly seated in a moving vehicle and, for speeding almost every single day. I think I ended up paying $3000 in traffic violation tickets for everybody. I felt as a man I had to do something for my family to have better transportation that everyone would be comfortable with, so I co-signed for my sister to get a truck in my name. Naomi had to be responsible in keeping up the payments. Along with me co-signing for the truck, I also brought everybody some gifts. My company, Foundation Unit Ent Services was having more success than previously, so I was able to help out a little bit and put a smile on the faces of my family (that was an important time in our company's tenure). I was feeling extremely good about where we were headed as a company. During this time things were coming together, and the world was being introduced to an African decent man named Mr. Obama who made such a strong impression on many people, especially when he determined in his mind that he was running to become the first African decent President of the United States of America. I remember like it was yesterday, when Mr. Obama came to San Francisco, California in November 2007 to raise awareness and funding for his candidacy for becoming President of the United States.

My company Foundation Unit Ent Services was in position to help with the marketing and campaigning for Barack Obama candidacy. However, before I agreed to support Mr. & Mrs. Obama, I researched them to overstand what their political views were and to find out if they represented the people who were apart of my community.

At the time, I appreciated how they never wavered when so many people tried to throw dirt on their name and fabricate their views and their beliefs. The Obama's did not back down; they squared their shoulders and faced everything head on. When I got the opportunity to meet him, he shook my hand while I was in the front row, directly in his face at the Bill Graham Civic Center. He looked me dead in my eye and I said, May "YAHWEH Bless You and May YAHWEH Keep You." That was a monumental moment in history. For me to meet an African decent man that everybody said he would never be president and to be alive to witness something that nobody believed could ever happen was mind blowing till this day! I started going to church regularly because I was being forced to go and it showed. I don't know how mom rule #2 out of 100 going to church every Sunday was going to sit with me but time would tell. I could only be pushed so far until I get to the point of not caring about what my mom, or anybody else for that matter thought about what I should or shouldn't do. Easter was just around the corner and, in African decent culture the most important times we should show up for church was on Easter, Mother's Day and Christmas. Those were three most popular holidays for anyone to show up and show out at church. In fact, if anybody thought that they were not going to dress up on one of these 'special dress up days' for church, they had another thing coming. If a man or boy had not worn a suit in years, guess what he was wearing one on those days. If a little girl's hair was as nappy as Whoopi Goldberg's was in the movie 'The Color Purple' she was getting a hot comb put to her hair, so she could look like she's ready for a family portrait at Sears Department Store.

Easter Sunday was really something else. While shining like Hollywood bright lights on Oscar Award Night from all that hair grease on a girls forehead. If the boys really had coarse hair (like me), the mothers would cut their hair real low and put them on a nice sweater to take pictures in or put a kitchen curl in their hair improperly and leave it in long enough so the child would have scabs in their hair from that kitchen curl (Thanks Mom). The events just didn't stop with the dressing and the hair with the kids, the older mother's and grandmothers would be in one of the strongest hat competitions that ever hit the church. Trying to out do each other by seeing whose hat was the biggest, most colorful and the fiercest to showcase at church. Then after all that was over, the family would go to Sizzler's, Hometown Buffet, Olive Garden or somewhere else for dinner; whatever happen to the family home cook days. So now Easter Season is here, and I went out the night before and practically stayed out all night and wasn't feeling up to going anywhere except to sleep. Mom started that drill Sergeant chant "LaPonne, get up! You need to start getting ready for church." I told mom that I didn't feel good; I didn't think I was going to make it to church. She was like, "I knew you was going to pull this" and walked away. Then about two hours later, she came back while I was diving hard into my sleep and said, "La Ponne, you need to get ready for church!" She just wouldn't leave me alone. Mom kept pushing and hounding me yelling, "Are you going to church or not?" I was getting sick and tired of her treating me like I was that same little boy, she could put fear in. She continued to push the issue of me getting ready for church when I snapped and yelled with all the power that was within my lungs, "QUIT TREATING ME LIKE I'M SOME LITTLE BOY, YOU ALWAYS FORCING YOUR WAY ON ME!" I yelled so loud that the walls vibrated, and mom said, "That's nobody but the enemy."

I yelled all throughout the house crying and yelling saying, "I'm tired of you being abusive and controlling and forcing your way on me all my life. You always pushing me and being forceful." Moms continued harassment channelled so many past emotions that I felt really bad because my sisters, my nieces and nephews were there. I went in the room and cried so I could calm myself down, then came out to mom room to let her know that I was not proud of the way I handled the situation and, that I was sincerely sorry for my behavior. I then walked towards her to hug and kiss her and did the same thing to my sister's, my nieces, and nephews. I thought I was healed from my past hurt and pain, but I guess maybe not to the degree I thought. I felt it was time for me to move out of mom place however, the timing was not right because there were so many things that needed to come together before I moved back to Georgia. There was a lawsuit pending and, the settlement would allow me the opportunity to be a full-time entrepreneur. I became so unhappy that I just took $2000 dollars and moved back to Georgia. I had to pay more lootchi again to have all of my belongings boxed and bagged up for the move. I went for broke with that move; I didn't care I just wanted to recapture my freedom and happiness. I called Cashmuir to find out if Comcast had some positions available and he told me to fax my resume to one of the supervisors in a totally different division of the company called Tele sales. He told me that the room that was once mine was no longer available, but he did have a room for me to rent. I left the YAY in March 2008 and landed in Alabama so I could see my son first. I rented a car and once I was done with my son, my plan would be to just drive from Alabama to Georgia. Spending time with my son was going to give me that refreshing feeling that I needed just to know that everything was going to be alright.

Once I arrived to pick up my son, I took him out on the town and brought him video games and just made up for me being away from him for a year. I finally made it to Georgia, and it was a totally different experience this time around. Living back at Cashmuir's house was no longer just him and his wife, but their cousins Annette and Marleen was there. It was hard for me to adjust to them being there because I no longer had peace in the house. People was always coming over and, by my room being on the main floor, all thoughts of rest ran the hell out the door as soon as the front door was opened to invite more company to come in. I had no consistent lootchi for food and I ended up not getting a job right away and didn't have those strong entertainment connections anymore. I was again picking up the pieces of my life from scratch. I was so tired of having to constantly start my life over and taking my kids and their mothers through this as well. I spent many days eating Malt O Meal hot cereal for breakfast just to survive and at night just to quiet those hunger pains. I was a father of two children with only a high school education and a computer applications certificate to my name. I didn't want to keep asking Cashmuir for food because he was already allowing me to stay there, in which I only had enough lootchi to pay for three months of rent. Cashmuir and his wife was real good to me. They started to see the walls closing in on me and let me continue to stay with them until I got on my feet. I had to think fast. I prayed to YAHWEH asking, I know you didn't bless me to be alive to live like this my Father. I continued to turn to YAHWEH begging and crying to YAHWEH saying that I'm trying my hardest to not do anything to get myself in a dangerous position but it's hard.

Chapter 131

Where Are Your Wings At Q.B. I'm Staring At An Angel?

I HAVE KIDS, I'm losing all kinds of weight off my body and plus I do not have peace of mind anymore. I was becoming bitter about making the decision to leave in the first place to go back to 'THE YAY' to help everybody financially and now I was in a position where I couldn't find a pot to piss in nor a window to throw it out. I didn't have any guarantees of me being able to eat a decent meal every night. I reached a point in my life where I stopped speaking to a lot of people and just blamed myself for putting people before taking care of myself. I felt like if I didn't pick myself up and dust myself off and get back to the focus of pitching my company into the United States and International markets, then I deserved to fail at everything. I was ready to see if we could offer our services to other countries; I talked with a contact in Japan, but nothing came out of it. I started thinking that we needed to get some professional representation to build high end alliances. My natural instinct was to go on Myspace to push the company, as well as to meet some female friends. A brother was ready to move on in life with the hopes of finding a beautiful lady to share the fruits of my labor with. I was looking for a woman who was not over the age of thirty (30); she had to be classy, established and sincerely honest. I was not having much luck meeting the right people; I waited a couple of days, and I logged back onto Myspace. I was determined to make a legitimate connection with somebody from a different country. I happened to see this woman who looked like she was Latin and reading her bio, she had a tremendous heart like me and was conscious about serving communities.

Like me also she was giving back to troubled youth (which is what stood out to me immediately). She was a queen who was beautiful on the outside and gorgeous on the inside. She said her name was Ms. Q.B. and she had accomplished so much at such a young age. She was about 5 feet 4 inches tall, with long black hair; she was well established and was extremely conservative and corporate. What was so interesting about the young lady was that her profile said that she was thirty-four years old and, I said that I didn't want to mess with anyone older than thirty (so I didn't give too much attention to it at the time). I researched her profile and was very intrigued to see if maybe she was interested in some of the services we offered and if she would be able to expand our consumer base in the Canadian market. I sent a long-detailed business outline over to her with a few personal compliments on how remarkable she seemed to be. The next day she responded to the email and said that she may be interested in discussing more in depth on how we would be able to complement each other business ideas. I arranged to give her a call on the weekend and we both agreed to the time and the date. When I called, she did not answer. Now, anybody who really knows me knows that if I schedule my time for something and I don't receive proper notice as to why a person would not be available, it would be kind of hard for them to get my attention again. Ms. Q.B. ended up calling right back but, the phone line was choppy, and we could not hear each other clearly. She asked if it was okay if we rescheduled our conference call for another day and, I explained to her that I view time as being very important to me and punctuality is a must. She said, "I'm the same way." Ms. QB apologized for missing the call because she was on the road and didn't want to continue talking since we couldn't hear each other clearly.

A couple of days went by, and she called me as scheduled and we began to converse and, our spirits were seriously one in the same. It was almost as if we had known each other in another lifetime. During our conversations, we covered a lot of business agendas and spelled out logistically how we would be able to complement each other and how our services could help her company become a stronger machine. In addition to that, she would also be able to provide consultation services and assist FOUNDATION UNIT ENT. in making stronger moves to evolve the value of the brand. We talked for about four hours on the phone and didn't want to hang up. I was just so relieved to be able to speak with someone whose business mind was just as strong and skilled as the words she spoke, coupled with a great sense of humor. I was burnt out from conversing with so many corporate stiffs because they had no sense of humor. Ms. Q.B. and I was as I said before, 'one in the same'. She was one of the first people to get where I was going. She asked if I wanted to be included on a conference call with her on some business projects she was developing on her own. Eventually she started to include me on some of her own business endeavors. Man, that was the partnership I was longing for since the beginning. I was very candid about my financial situation and lootchi that I had lost over a period of time and expressed how I had to take care of people so much that I had nothing left for myself. I told her about my legacies and my living condition, and she shared with me a lot of her personal family challenges and childhood discrimination she experienced and not being accepted because she was Jamaican and Irish. It was really refreshing to meet somebody like her because I was meeting so many people throughout my life who were unwilling to represent truth and pretended to have perfect lives and the only thing that was perfect with them was being able to say the word perfect.

I was tired of giving away all of my honesty to the wrong people and they acted as though they didn't have any imperfections. I was thankful to have met somebody who was unafraid to open the door of her heart and share her feelings with all sincerity. It impressed me a great deal. Although meeting Ms. Q.B. brought some comfortable feelings to my spirit, I was at a crossroads in my life because on the one hand I was so excited to meet someone who was remarkable and had endured so much from her past, but was I ready, willing, and able to fully commit my emotions to her or would I find myself hoping so strong only to be let down in disappointment again. That was the one question only I had the answer to. There were feelings developing inside of me since getting to know Ms. Q.B. but I had to focus all my attention to where it was needed; and that's Foundation Unit Ent. I was living in a household where there was no control in the house because Marleen would have all kind of company at all times of the night. She was not a tall girl, but her charm was very strategic; she had a yellow completion, fox shaped eyes, very low hair that she always kept in a weave or a wig. She had a small upper body, but a miniature size pony backside. She can change her look at any giving moment but what really stood out about her was that she could be laughing so hard and then the girl could switch in a snap of a finger to having major anger issues and would argue and talk very loud. Marleen was one of those women who could satisfy her man without a doubt, but on the other hand, she kept drama in her diet like daytime Soap Operas. Annette (R.I.P.) was another short, loud, and messy mouth girl. I really didn't feel all the way comfortable with her spirit and I tried to just stay cool because it was no longer just Cashmuir, his wife and me, they were there too.

Now that it's more people in the house, the man and woman of the house had to lay down some rules for everybody, which meant that everyone had a day to clean the whole house. What was crazy about implementing these house rules was that certain people would pay someone else who didn't have lootchi to come clean for them. However, just keeping the house cleaned was not the only problem. Food was another issue that needed to be addressed. One of the biggest problems was that people were eating up other people food without replacing what they ate, and sometimes it was hard to tell who was eating what because there were so many people coming in and out at all times of the day. Since my room was close to the front door, all I heard was a door slam here, a door slam there. Cashmuir and Lady T were scheduled to go on a vacation and wanted me to watch the house while they were gone, making sure that they came back with their home in one piece. They didn't want anybody smoking or being disrespectful while they were away, and as soon as they left Annette and Marleen started smoking in the house. Marleen got behind the wheel of their car, knowing that her license was suspended and drove out all the gas. When they came back from their vacation, I had to pick them up from the airport only to discover that there was not enough gas in the car for me to even pick them up, the tank was empty; but because their trip was an international one, they had to go through customs which took about fifty (50) minutes. I had to drive around in circles with no cell phone until I finally ran out of gas with no one to help. The police came and said they were not able to help me and, that I needed to move the car to the side of the road or get the car towed away. Finally, Cashmuir and his wife came out and I told them all what happened about the gas situation, and they were upset. I told them even though I had a job interview, I didn't touch the car.

Lady T asked if Marleen had been driving the car I said "Yes!" Lady T was furious; she was like, "What the f*** she is doing driving the car and she has a suspended license?!" I wasn't trying to get in the middle of telling on anybody, but Cashmuir wanted to know if anybody was down in his studio and thankfully no one was, at least to my knowledge (Cashmuir and Lady T had a nice recording studio in their house). I explained to them that I wasn't going to allow Annette and Marleen to run down the house because I appreciate you guys too much. Lady T continued to ask me what else was going on at the house while they were gone and, I kept on telling her that I wasn't trying to snitch on anybody. I guess she interpreted that as me not being willing to answer her questions because she said, "You can answer Cashmuir's questions, but you can't answer mine." I didn't know what else she was looking for me to say so I asked, "What do you want to know?" She said what actually happened?" Lady T was putting me in an uncomfortable position because if I told what was going on in the house, they'll know it came from me. Even though I was reluctant to share, but I told her, "They just had company over and was smoking and, before I could get it out, Lady T was on the phone, called Marleen and cussed her for driving their car with a suspended license. I didn't think she would put me on blast like that, especially because they already looked at me as a messy person. Cashmuir and Lady T was beyond angry and wanted to have a house meeting with everybody. I was so annoyed because

I didn't have a job, no lootchi and I was not properly set up to have my children more frequent in my life. I had no car, and on top of all that I didn't have food regularly to eat. I had to deal with a couple of adults causing problems in the house! I was just so p***** off.

Not only were there problems in the house, but also, Marleen and Annette told their friends and family that I was up in the house snitching on people trying to cause problems. I had all kinds of people coming over who were friends with Annette and Marleen acting suspect because they felt like I hated on them. First off, if anybody really knew me, they would know that I live by a code and that I wouldn't want to have division in the home front; secondly, whenever there's a disturbance in my pursuit of peace of mind, then nothing else matters. The tension in the house between the females and me was thick; they gave me dirty looks and made some smart remarks, but that didn't bother me. However, what did bother me was the fact that my pockets were crying for some companionship. I was broke, hungry and lonely; and because of the ongoing situation in the house, I just made it a point to stay in my room. Things were starting to pick up real nice with Ms. Q.B. We became so close within less than three weeks, that we started dating and developing a long-distance relationship. Our phone conversations went from two hours to four hours to seven hours a day, which lead us to fall naturally in love with each other (I'm not talking in love in the sense of just wanting to be with somebody but spending a lifetime with somebody). Ms. Q.B and I had gotten to a point where we were getting to know each other and realized that we were meant for each other. We were managing our long-distance relationship extremely well; we both felt like love crept up on us like a thief in the night. Even though, we were not trying to be in a relationship with each other; the chemistry that we had was undeniable, although we were trying to purge ourselves from our previous situations. Whenever I make a commitment to a woman, I try to be honest with her because I learned from experience that if one comes into a relationship thinking one way, and it turns out to be something else; it will not work.

I was very upfront about everything because she would ask me. What was I eating for dinner and, my response would be 'Malt O Meal'; she didn't even know what that was. I told her that I ate Malt O Meal because it was what my pockets could afford and, that it was a hot breakfast cereal. She would respond by saying, "You need some fruit for nutrition and some protein, that's why you are always tired." Ms. Q.B. was so concerned about how bad my eating habits, nutrition, and wellbeing was; that's what impressed me beyond any explanation of words. On April 28, 2008, a few days passed since we talked, and I received a humongous fruit basket that was delivered to me with everything I could ever want inside of it. If my pride didn't get the best of me, I probably would have cried. My heart was impressed with Ms. Q.B. I really believed Yahweh Blessed me with a woman such as her in my life. Not too long afterwards, my King Day was approaching on May 29th, and I had a feeling something special would be done for me by her tender heart. She really was saddened by my condition and did not overstand how I did not have any family support. I had to tell her about my family background and what I had been through, and she just knew that Yahweh protection was all around me to help me endure so much hardship and pain and to still be alive and in my right mind. Her words were so comforting that she would always tell me, "No worries, I will always be here and that's all you need to know." I was not use to anybody being unconditional in my life and it would show as we began to know each other even better. She was able to have serious and intense dialogue with me and, I wasn't bored. I truly believed that she was sent from heaven because all I had was an honest spirit and a willingness to better my life. What both of us were bringing to the table was enough for us to know that we would not quit on each other no matter what was thrown our way. More importantly I found in her and in myself unconditional love like never before.

The time has come for me to celebrate my 'KING DAY' and the thoughts that were going through my head were like, 'here we go again; me having to celebrate my 'KING DAY' by myself'. Maybe a few people calling, but there's nothing like having your significant other call you or do something special for you on your 'KING DAY'. Those were the thoughts that kept coming to my mind. Sidebar Moment: I remember one time when I was living in Alabama, I had my son for my 'KING DAY'. I would dress us alike and then go to a nice restaurant and, then to a movie. I believe my son was about three years old at the time; however, it didn't matter because I just loved spending time with him. One thing I can say for myself as a father, no matter what happens in life my legacies would never be disappointed by me because my love for them would always be present and unconditional. Which is something I never had a chance to experience as a child. It was pouring down raining and my son was a little sick; I took him to see Madagascar because I knew he wanted to see that movie real bad. When we got to the movies, we were playing around for a little bit and the next thing I knew he fell asleep in the movie theater. I kept trying to wake him up, but he was out of it so bad I had to walk out of the movie theater carrying him in my arms in the pouring rain. I was sad that I always had to do things by myself with no one to celebrate the 'highlight' moments of my life. I ended up going home and just sleeping my 'KING DAY' away. On that very day I vowed to never use my legacies to try and draw some emotional need that I was not receiving from someone or something. I believe a lot of single people and single parents try to find something or someone to pull that emotional dependency from. It just makes situations in life more miserable in the end. Special things or People never live up to the expectations of what people feelings truly need.

Early in the morning on my 'KING DAY', I received a call from Ms. Q.B. wishing me a special 'KING DAY' and was trying to find out my schedule for the day. I explained that I would pretty much be around the house. She went on to tell me that she was headed to work, and she would call me later. It was good to hear her voice and I was thankful that she wished me 'HAPPY KING DAY' but it was not the same as having her with me. As a few minutes passed, someone was at the door; I opened the door and there were balloons and an expensive German Chocolate Cake. I called her, overjoyed with emotions just to let her know how much I appreciated what she did for me. She said, "That's not it!"

There was another ring at the door, and it was a package that I had to sign for; when I opened it, it was two Los Angeles Lakers Jerseys. I was so happy because she remembered that I was a bona fide Lakers and Pittsburgh Steelers fan. I tried on the jerseys and realized that they were replicas and not the authentic ones. Don't get me wrong; I really appreciated all that she did for me, but I don't wear anything fake. I would rather not wear anything at all then to wear something fake. I had a dilemma because this woman had gone through so much to do something special for me and I couldn't enjoy it 200 percent because it was not real. I didn't want to hurt her feelings, but that's just who I am. When I received the balloons, cake and jerseys, Annette and Marleen was at the house as well. I was so turned off from people having their false judgment towards me because of what others were saying about me. I knew I was not going tolerate it much longer. Later that night, I was walking around with the Los Angeles Lakers jersey on feeling really proud that somebody who had never seen me physically was sweet enough to do something like that for me. She truly was connected to my spirit, and I was connected to hers.

Prior to me wearing the jersey outside, I decided to wear the jersey around the house (since it was not authentic); I walked upstairs to the kitchen to get a snack so I could finish watching the Lakers game downstairs and, Annette, Marleen and some little pint size woman nicknamed Mouse (she was like 4 feet 5 inches and her face literally looked like a mouse) was in the kitchen as well. They were playing dominos, drinking, and smoking weed around the dinner table. When I came up, they all stopped talking and nobody had any words for me. I left out but did not walk all the way down the stairs because I wanted to see if they would start talking about me. As I was listening, the little loudmouth they called Mouse says, "And, he have the nerve to have on a Lakers jersey and it's fake on top of that." After she said that, everybody else joined in with their comments. I just let them go on, but if they kept on talking, I would have put each of them in their place because they were not going to disrespect me as a man. I was tired of dealing with people who didn't have enough backbone to stand face to face with me if they had a problem. In fact, what was making me absolutely sick with both of them was when each of them was alone they'd speak to me, but only when they were together or with their friends, they act suspect. I could have gotten real gorilla with it but, I didn't want to infuse any more madness where I had to lay my head. I needed to be wise in every decision I made. Overwhelmed with frustration, I called Ms. Q.B. to vent, and I ended up hurting her feelings by lashing out on her for buying me fake jerseys. She was convinced that the jerseys were not fake, so I said, "How are you going to tell me, and this is what I buy." The thing about her was that she comes from a strong debatable background so even if she was not 200 percent sure about something, she would not immediately say, "I may be wrong or I'm not sure."

We argued back and forth about the jerseys, and she eventually said she didn't know anything about the jerseys because the place she ordered it from online told her they were real. I told her, "People would say anything just to get your business." She then said, "Even if they are fake, you should have worn it because it was from me, not because some girls are talking about you saying, 'you have a fake jersey on' and, then all of a sudden, you're mad and don't want to wear it no more." That was our first argument.

I did bring it on myself because I knew my pride and ego was too big for me or for her to handle. I explained to her that I didn't want to hurt her feelings at first and said I would just wear it around the house, but when they made those comments about the jerseys, it just made me realize that's not who I am. That one instance opened the flood gates of arguments that were occurring between me and her; our backgrounds began to breed ignorance and, I found myself saying stupid things like, "She was not African decent enough" or she would say, "You don't share the same belief system as me and I cannot marry or date somebody who don't share the same spiritual beliefs." Hearing her say those things, shattered me like I was made of glass because I thought she was just judging me like everybody else do. I was wondering if she was saying those things because I was reading the Quran and the Bible. I told her just because I was reading both books didn't mean that we didn't share the same beliefs. I said, "I believe in YAHWEH. I said I don't believe in divide and conquer; I believe the word truth was cut up into a trillion pieces and what people did was form their own interpretation of religion and their belief system. I further stated to her, "I didn't grow up reading the Bible, so I never read the whole thing before in my life and that's what I'm doing now.

I've been learning from people and I'm glad the way I'm learning because it allows me to have an opened mind to what other people believe and not automatically judge them." We struggled back and forth with that subject on and off for about a year. Ms. Q.B. and I had not met face to face at that point in our relationship; all of our correspondence was over the phone, so now the time came for us to see each other in person for the first time. It was June of 2008, and I was waiting at the airport in Buffalo, New York dressed immaculate with a bouquet of long red stem roses that were all blossomed. I got off the plane ready to romance her like she had never been romanced before. I grab my bags and then I see a silver car driving up but its a person who has this nervous look in their eyes and I said this has to be her. As I was walking to the car, in my mind I say, this is a remarkable woman right here who just want to be loved, you can see it in her eyes because she was so nervous but sweet at the same time. At that moment I really thought the world of her and knew that we had a lot of differences to work through and that I had to allow her time to get comfortable with me. It was an awkward feeling because even though we talked so much over the phone it was like we were getting to know each other all over again because now, we had to get use to and comfortable with seeing each other day in and day out. I greeted her by saying, "How are you feeling my sweet love, we finally get to get lost in each other's love!" She smiled. She was just so sweet; it was like a fairy-tale. It seemed unreal or too good to be true. She told me she made plans for us to stay at a nice hotel in Niagara Falls for a night and then, she had a real intimate night that was specially planned for our love. It was just a natural feeling of how our love continued to burn stronger and stronger. Our compatibility with our love was like we had known each other for at least five years or more.

It was a cool feeling because we could laugh hard together as well as switchgears and handle business together.

I remember when we were in the hotel in Niagara Falls, we were so intense with our love making that I broke the headboard and we just stopped and started laughing real hard until tears came out of our eyes. We checked out of the hotel the next day and went sightseeing and then drove to Toronto, Canada listening to romantic music and enjoying each other's company. We checked into a hotel in downtown Toronto (which was set up as if we had our own apartment) we bought groceries for the hotel. I was thankful for that because we each had an opportunity to see how we lived and what type of habits we may have because one of the worst things to find out about a person, is if they live messy.

That was our first time together; we both learned that we liked things cleaned. We spent nine days in the hotel just learning more and more about each other. Later that evening, we went out to a club and started helping promote some Ice Cream Festival that reunites your favorite true school artist with a headliner who was relevant in the industry at the time. The top names on the performance card were: Joe, Dru Hill, Ginuwine, and L.L. Cool J. As we were doing our thing, Ms. Q.B. was pulled in to help develop the event from a Project Manager standpoint. Because of her business expertise by having her own company, she was very intricate on how big events got funded and how all the logistics were structured to make sure the event was ran proficiently. We were at the club doing a meet and greet while marketing the event and people were looking at us like we were presidential. I knew that it was meant for us to be together if we utilized our differences to our advantage and over stood that together we would be a powerful force and be able to do YAHWEHS work on a global scale. We would be unstoppable! We went back to the hotel, and I was just as happy as I had ever been in my life.

Chapter 132

First Time I Felt Somebody Was Designed By Yahweh For Me

I WAS THANKFUL to be with somebody who made me feel happy and important and she felt the same way. We were madly in love with each other; in fact, she was so comfortable with me that she even sent me to the store to get her monthly cycle pads (now you know a woman has to be really in love to send her man to the store for her 'personal supply'. She was already acting as if we were already married. The time came for me to return home to Georgia, although I didn't want to leave. Reality kicked in and reminded me that we were in a long-distance relationship and that I had to get back to American soil. I arrived back in Georgia feeling unhappy after having such a wonderful and romantic time in Canada with my new Queen. I couldn't afford to get lost in emotions because I needed to put the vision of my company back into focus. I told myself that I had to start hustling hard again and, reaching out to old contacts that I was able to develop over at MTV. Once I started reaching out to reconcile some old relationships, new contacts started reaching out to me, and all of a sudden Foundation Unit Ent Services was relevant once again. The company started getting checks in the mail for $3000 from our music being rotated on some of the shows on MTV. I was able to close a deal with GMC Cadillac Denali Radio and made another $3500 through my family Mr. D. Bar. (He looked a little like the iconic producer/rapper Dr. Dre); he was a Sr. Writer for an advertising agency, as well as other things. It was crazy how Beelzebub put so many obstacles in my pathway and, then YAHWEH came and turned it all around.

Chapter 133

Wounds Not Fully Healed
It Will Destroy A Dynamic Love

YAHWEH TRULY DID turn all my tragedies into triumphant. The many pressures I used to feel were no longer an issue because of the purpose that YAHWEH birthed in me, he was allowing me to see them come to fruition. The weight of wondering what my next move was going to be was not a concern for me anymore. Hooking up with D. Bar helped to connect those missing links in the blueprint of what we were doing as a company. In fact, the way we met was that his brother B-Down put together a BBQ at his house when I was living in 'THE YAY'. I had the Colonel and I provide the music to give it a 'live concert sound and feel'. D. Bar connected immediately with me. One time we talked for about an hour and after I found out about his background, I told him, "I'm going to put lootchi in your pocket!" I wanted him to overstand how much I respected and appreciated all that he was doing for me and the company. I knew in my heart that we were going to make lootchi together, as things started to progress for me, within two months he was paid for presenting our music to his agency. I initially told D that I would pay 5 percent out of the deal, but I ended up giving him 15 percent. It was important to me that I treated people good, who I allowed in my circle. I wanted to build relationships, not destroy them. I made it my business to take them out to dinner or provide help to any of them who needed anything because I overstood that their success was my success, and my success was theirs. We were building a Foundation together. Now that things were moving in the right direction, Ms. Q.B. and I were trying our best to deal with the fact that we were in different countries and trying to keep our relationship strong.

We both were doing our best to keep each other focused over the phone by reassuring ourselves that we could handle the distance even in times of weakness. We knew that we were making great sacrifices just to be together and greater sacrifices just to stay together. However, the pressures of the distance was causing us to have arguments that would surely have us break up. I started speaking ignorantly about her ethnicity, about her not being African decent enough or lashing out anger towards her because I wasn't used to the things that she was getting upset about, that never made sense to me. I thought she had been paying attention to what kind of man I was and not the kind of man she has experienced. Ms. Q.B. said, "That's not the case and that I needed to show her more respect as her being the number one lady in my life." She would get very enraged thinking, that other women were trying to sleep with me or vice versa and saying I'm lying, and we just kept attacking each other. What we were doing in turn to each other was opening up old wounds that had nothing to do with each other but more about the wounds we never fully healed from our past. Things were starting to become real destructive and, most of the time it seemed like we were arguing about the same things over and over again. When it was like that, I would get into that 'I don't give a F*** mode'. The one thing that I hate most about being in a relationship was when I continued to show and prove to a person who I am, and they totally disregard it. Ms. Q.B. and I believed that the distance that separated our relationship was hurting us; neither one of us wanted things to end but we didn't know how we could be together or when we will be able to see each other. My heart didn't want to be separated from her and I knew that she didn't want to be separated from me.

Chapter 134

Finding Love, Developing Love & Now Sabotizing Love

JULY OF 2008, we decided that I would relocate to Canada (although I knew nothing about Canada; except for the soda Canada Dry Ginger Ale (my favorite I might add and Canadian Bacon and other than making love and spending time with Ms. Q.B; that was it). We didn't know each other like we thought, and I already had a huge amount of challenges on my mind. Lootchi for me in Georgia was a little scarce and, I had nothing really solid going on in my life that prohibited me from moving to Canada. The one thing that I was most sure about was that I wanted somebody in my corner unconditionally. I wanted Ms. Q.B. in my life, and I didn't want to lose what we had, nor what we were building. I packed up my things in three extra large bags that looked like 'military body bags', along with two large duffle bags and left Atlanta moving to Canada. Going there was one thing; however, getting there on U.S. Airways was another thing. One of the first problems I encountered was at the airport. I was told that I had to pay additional charges for the number of bags I had. I told them that those charges did not reflect what was on their website or I just read it wrong; I didn't have an additional $400 to pay for bags. If I would have known that I was going to have to pay all that lootchi for my bags, I could have just shipped them through the Post Office, UPS or FedEx or something. The customer service from U.S. Airways was horrible, I didn't have a cell phone to call for anyone to pick me back up because I didn't have extra lootchi to pay for my bags.

It was some short man that had some Napoleon complex, he was a customer service agent from U.S. Air Ways kept trying to force me to pay the additional baggage fee and kept going back and forth me.

I ended up paying the lootchi knowing that I was putting my stomach on the sacrificial altar because that was the lootchi I saved to make sure I had food for at least a couple of months until I generated business out in Canada. I had to call Ms. Q.B. to let her know I needed a $150 for all my bags to be paid to be loaded on the plane. In addition to all that chaos, the airlines told me that they could not find my flight. I arrived there two and a half hours early, spent another hour on wasted drama with my bags and arguing with a short dude, and now they want to tell me that they can't find my flight. I felt like DMX (R.I.P.) 'Y'all Go make me lose my mind, up in here, up in here'! I explained that I booked a flight and showed them my flight ticket and still my flight was nowhere to be found, which meant that I missed whatever flight I was supposed to be on. I was hot, hot, hot! Ms. Q.B. called U. S. Airways in Canada to find out what happened and to pay the remaining balance for the bags. They were able to get me a new flight, which was scheduled to depart at 2:45pm and connect to a flight in Philadelphia at 7:00 pm. However, before I arrived at my final destination, I had to fly into Buffalo, NY and have Ms. Q.B. drive me the rest of the way to Canada. Going into another country. A passport was needed and at first, I didn't have one, but I had to expedite one. I was extremely hungry and stuck at the airport. I spent four hours waiting at the airport and was not guaranteed to get on that 7:00 pm flight because it was a standby flight. The customer service at U.S. Airways was getting worse and worse by the minute (I had never flown U.S. Airways before; if I had a choice, Delta would be it). I complained throughout the airport and told so many people about my bad experience. I finally got on the plane and was the last person to get cleared to board. I arrived in Philadelphia and since my flight was delayed out of Atlanta, I had a 99 percent chance of missing the connecting flight into Buffalo.

The flight finally lands in Philadelphia, and I started running with my two duffle bags through the airport; since it was 11:30 pm several doors were already closed so I had to run all the way to the other side of the airport to get to my terminal. I was running around like a chicken with its head cut off, not knowing where I was going. I just kept running, trying to hurry up to get to the terminal. As I was getting closer to the departing terminal, I see a flight lifting off; I looked through the window but was hoping that was not my flight. When I finally get to the departure gate, it was completely empty. I was so vexed, crushed, and exhausted, I walked over to another terminal and told them how that was my first and last experience with this airline. Those people I was complaining to were from U.S. Airways but at least they provided better customer service. They were sympathetic to what I was going through and gave me a hotel and meal voucher. There I was, stuck in Philadelphia with my bags and the roses I got for Ms. Q.B. I'm spending the night in a city I had never been before and Ms. Q.B was in a parking lot in Buffalo waiting for me to arrive. I had to take more lootchi away from my food reserve and buy a $20 calling card to let her know what was going on and that I was stuck in Philadelphia. I felt like someone had placed a hit out on me because I had made more detours going to Canada, than I did running from the police in 'THE YAY'! If anybody would had told me that 'pursuing the woman of your heart' meant going through fire rings and walking a tightrope, I'd probably would have left love alone (yeah right). I made up in my heart and mind a long time ago, that Ms. Q.B. was worth all of that and so much more. As I was explaining to her all that was going on; she said, "Maybe this is a sign." I replied, "I came too far, and we went through too much for us to be together."

Chapter 135

Feeling Defeated I Need Yahweh More Present In My Life

I SIMPLY EXPLAINED to her, "Dealing with me, the storm always comes first and then the sun." Being with Ms. Q.B. was making me even more convinced that 'Love makes you do some of the craziest things'! She told me that she slept in her car waiting for me, and that she heard all kinds of animals sounds in the bushes. I laughed inside wondering if she was more paranoid than what her actual reality was because she was sleeping in a McDonald's parking lot next to a bush. I stayed on the phone with her until the calling card ran out of lootchi at 4:00 am. I told Ms. Q.B. that my flight was scheduled to depart at 7:45am and I would be on the first flight out. I arrived finally to Buffalo, and I looked horrible. I looked like I was an extra in a zombie movie. I got in the car, and you could see on both of our faces that we had endured a lot for us to be together. Our plan was for me to be sponsored through her company so I could stay in Canada as an employee. When we arrived at immigration, they called to see if Ms. Q.B. Company was legitimate, but they denied me because the company's voicemail was a personal one, not a business one. The immigration officer further stated that since it was a new company, we had to prove that it grossed approximately $250k annually. That was when I had a Florida Evans moment: 'Damn! Damn! Damn!' I brought my narrow tail to Canada, with no finances or a pot to piss in and had to rely on Ms. Q.B. and her resources. I can say this about the 'Lady in my life', she had my back like no other woman has ever had in the history of my entire existence! Ms. Q.B. was really in my corner.

However, I knew at some point with me not having a job things were going to start adding up. I could see the pressure on her face building up. The weight of both of us was weighing heavy on her. Right before I left Atlanta to come to Canada, I received a call from Comcast asking if I would like to work for them. I told them that I was headed out of the country for two weeks (even though my plan was to never come back to United States). Something told me not to tell the Human Resource Representative that I was moving out of the country. Canada was not as friendly to me as I hoped it would be things were starting off pretty slow for me. I had been out there for about a month, and she was spending lootchi left and right and it was all beginning to add up into the thousands of dollars. We were going to parties trying to market both companies and celebrate us being together; but having fun and going to parties were not making the cut. I had to leave and go back to Atlanta to try to build my finances. I called the lady from Comcast and asked if the position was still available for me, and she said, "Yes." I told her that I would be returning in August ready to report for work. We both were really sad and frustrated that we had tried everything to be together and it failed. We both didn't know how we would be able to sustain and continue to feel positive about not being together for one day, let alone weeks, months or possibly years. When I got back to Georgia, I felt like a loser; I made announcements to everyone about being in another country and paid all sorts of lootchi to transport my life into Canada only to return back to Georgia with nothing and in a worse position. The only thing that was different was that I was able to get a part-time job, but the job only paid $8.00 per hour + $7.00 per item sold. It was a Telecommunication position, so I had to sale Comcast products, from phone service, Internet, cable service; being in that position humbled me a great deal.

I was walking like there was no tomorrow and needed to get a car desperately. I was walking to work and taking the bus like an aimless wanderer trying to find somewhere to lay his head. Between the heat, the sweat and aching feet, my total travel time was 2 ½ hours one way and another almost 3 hours to travel back home. I have not had to rely on a bus in seventeen (17) years! When I got on the bus, it was dirty, and the roaches acted as though they were the ones in charge. As I thought about how much I was making and the time and lootchi it took me to get to work, I realized none of this made any business sense, but I had to get in where I can fit in. I felt like I couldn't get by with just peanuts being thrown at me. It was really depressing to be a grown man and a father of two legacies and can't properly take care of myself, let alone my son & daughter. I straddled the fence on whether or not I should go back to the underworld to better care for myself financially, but I didn't want to take the risk of not having my freedom and being locked away from my legacies. I often struggled with that on and off for a while, especially when I had to go many days out in the rain, sleet, and snow just to get to work. Although, I only worked part-time, it was a full day's journey just to get there from 4pm to 8:30 pm and by the time I got home it would be close to midnight. The job would not allow overtime, so I felt even more stuck between a rock and a hard place. The country was starting to feel the effect of the recession and the top name companies and corporations were crashing down hard. That was a real defining moment for me because most people would have cracked under that amount of pressure and resulted in going backwards. I won't lie I teetered with the idea of going backwards but I was determined to trust in YAHWEH and believe that YAHWEH would one day rain down his blessings on me abundantly. I was thankful that I had Ms. Q.B. to talk to because just talking to her eased a great deal of pressure that was weighing on my heart and mind. She was my support and backbone.

While my legacies mothers only cared about making sure I deposited some lootchi into my son and daughter's accounts. I was unhappy and living with the issues with Marleen and Annette in the house. One Saturday, I got a call from Cashmuir telling me that Annette was in a car accident and died; it was surreal because he was so calm when he was telling me the news. I was really taken back because she was somebody who just had her son and daughter come visit her and spend a few weeks with her for the summer and then two weeks later she died. It was a rainy day and even though the rain had stopped the pavement was wet. The exit that we would take to get to the house was sharp. Although no one really knows how the crash happened, we believed that she was texting on her phone or on a call and lost control and went off the road and crashed into other cars. It was a sad time for everyone, especially for her children. Her son was struggling with getting his life together already and I took a liking to him because we had some things in common. I was just trying to come into his world so he could trust that I cared about him and his world, soon as I got the news about his mother dying, he was the first person I was concerned about (his sister was a little older and more mature). I knew he was struggling with his manhood and needed some guidance; I made contact with him after numerous attempts just to let him know that I was here for him and expressed that he should come live with us. He of course, was unsure and eventually ended all communication with me and I never heard from him again. Everybody took the loss of Annette hard, especially Lady T; they not only lived together but they also worked together. I tried to be there for Lady T as well as Annette's family members.

Chapter 136

The Obama's Made
The Impossible . . . Possible

IT WAS A tough time for everyone involved, and it opened an opportunity for those who were a little leery of me to see the real LaPonne and for Marleen to know that I was not snitching or trying to get people kicked out of the house. The year 2008 was a terrible time for me and other people as well, we couldn't wait until it was over. We were all saying, "I can't believe its 2009 already." I started thinking back over my life as 2009 was entering; how I had been shot, jailed, did drugs, been molested, gang-banged, sold drugs, inflicted pain on others and had pain inflicted on me. I've been hurt; I've failed at many things, and Yahweh was able to help me overcome those setbacks.

When January 21, 2009, came, what I been through my entire life couldn't take away the fact that I witnessed history in the making, when Barack Obama was sworn in as our 44th President of the United States of America and became the nation's first African decent President. First Lady (a real 'sista') Michelle Obama and their daughters became the new occupants of the White House. They were ready to serve this country in the true sense of unity, brotherhood, and sisterhood. Represented speaking for those who never had a voice or felt that what they had to say even mattered. It was electrifying when Mr. 'O, excuse me' President Obama won; there were so many 'so-called' African decent leaders who were envious because they were not able to be the chosen one by YAHWEH to make history as the first African decent President. It was a proud moment for African decent people especially, because we always heard 'America will never vote an African decent man or woman to be Commander–n-Chief'.

Even for those who opposed Obama on every side had to stop and acknowledge and shed tears of joy because we got to witness what other civil rights leaders died for; justice and equality (so we thought). However, we cannot forget that with every proud moment for African decent people as a whole, ignorance is sure to follow as well. There were people saying all kinds of stuff like 'since our president is African decent the first thing I'm going to do is not wait in line and cut in front of all Caucasian people'. As I would ride the bus to and from work, there would be many racial statements written by Caucasian people calling Obama 'a monkey n***er' and drew images of him as a monkey and saying that 'he was going to get assassinated with a noose around his neck'! I know many of us African decent voted for Obama because he's African decent; however, I voted for him because I believed at the time that as President and First Lady, they could be the first people to represent the voice of the underprivileged. When we voted for Bill Clinton and he became president, Stevie Wonder could see that he was Caucasian; but we supported Bill Clinton because we believed that he had somewhat of a compassion for our struggles. Just as a lot of people did in 1961 when urban communities voted to elect John F. Kennedy; a Caucasian man who had compassion for the underprivileged at least according to when it came to be on primetime media. African decent people were always told that we could never become president and sometimes when a person is told what they can't do, it can either make him or her stronger and face your challenges or it could sabotage his or her growth as a human. A lot of people (African decent in particular) were putting some unreal expectations on what Obama would be able to do as an African decent President for our Communities; people viewed him as our modern day 'Superhero'.

He was just one man who had inherited a deficit. By 2009 the fiscal year national deficit was 1.7 trillion.

YAHWEH already knew what America needed in leadership. YAHWEH knew who his man of choice was even before the world knew who Barack Obama was. What was interesting about President Obama was that he was never given the support he needed when he got in office. Even before he performed any of his Presidential duties in office, they already doubted him. I watched this remarkable figure hair turn gray so quick from all the pressures he had to endure; people immediately forgot that he was trying to clean up the mess that George W. Bush created. I strongly believe that if the country was not turned upside down, people would not have been so open to have an African decent President. I can honestly say with all conviction that people need to over stand that one man cannot lead a world unless he is YAHWEH! Obama becoming President, made me want to become a better leader and that's all one person can ask for; did I empower people or someone? President Obama raised the bar for all of us to not make any excuses for why we have not accomplished our goals and dreams. Through YAHWEH all things are possible!

Chapter 137

Emotional Punching Bags Damaged The Virtues Of Each Other

IT HAD BEEN nine months and counting that Ms. Q.B and I have been together and, we were starting to finally realize that the honeymoon was over. We were going through the motions of the Stylistics cover song 'Break up to make up, that's all we do; first you love me then you hate me, that's a game for fools'. We had to face the fact that we were from two different worlds and, it was taking its toll on us both. We both continued to be in denial about the distance not being a major problem for our emotional survival and arguments with her not trusting me, saying I'm sleeping with other women or with the mother of my daughter which was a constant topic of discussion. It was a lot of unnecessary pressures that I had to deal with because she was a year removed out of a relationship that had no trust. She had been involved in other relationships where the person were living a double life; and leaving her in emotional turmoil. My relationship with Ms. Q. B. was one of the most challenging ones because I cared deeply for her, and I wanted our relationship to be a successful one. However, being in the relationship with her was more like I was serving a life sentence for the sins of someone else. I was finding myself defending things that were not even a part of my character. The women I dated or was engaged to in the past never had a problem with me lying or cheating because it was something that I just didn't do or believed in. For many years, I watched mom go through that, so it sparked a conscious awareness about me being straight up with a woman or anybody for that matter. The dynamic with her was becoming more and more impossible. I started cussing and yelling at her and telling her not to call me anymore.

Chapter 138

Thriving As A Visionary But Emotionally In A Tornado

OUR RELATIONSHIP WAS taking a turn for the worse; in fact, the many break ups that we had, seemed to tarnish the value of what we were building; things were getting so far out of control that I would say, "F*** you and get the f*** out of my life." I told her I never wanted to speak to her again. The sad part about all of it was that the way I was cussing at her, she wasn't that type of woman I needed to say those things to but, I just got tired of going in circles about the same things over and over again, which brought me back to my old street ways. Me telling Ms. Q. B. to leave my life alone presented a great problem for me. Since I was a member of the 'Grammys', I had already invited her to come to the award show with me. I told the staff that we were all going to the 'Grammys' so I could show my appreciation for their hard work and dedication. The show was on February 8, 2009, three weeks away is when I told her that she was not going. She then said to me, "I'm coming; I spent a lot of lootchi preparing for the event." I said, "I don't care, you are not coming and I'm not about to have your negative energy around me while we are trying to enjoy ourselves." At that point almost $3000 was spent between renting a car, flights, wardrobe, and a list of other important things. She was adamant about her showing up to the 'Grammys' and she said, "I'll meet you all at the show." I replied, "I bet you will not be there." Things were getting worse and worse; she would send me like fifteen to twenty emails saying a whole bunch of crazy stuff that was not all the way true and confusing at the same time. I didn't accept her calls for about two weeks and I really missed her being a part of my life.

Chapter 139

The Grammy Excursion I Guess All That Glamour Didn't Matter

WE USE TO have an everyday ritual when we would talk on the phone for three to six hours a day. I started thinking to myself 'Am I the one who is sabotaging our relationship'? I missed her comforting words touching my heart and my spirit; I realized that I had a woman who genuinely cared about who I was as a man and as a person. I just didn't know if I wanted to continue with the constant arguing. Grammy week was finally here, and I was still content with my decision of uninviting her to come along. I tried to sell her ticket, but no one had the lootchi to cover the expenses that came with the whole trip. I told myself that if she called, I would pick up the phone and apologize to her for my part. Just like clockwork, she called a day before our flight was scheduled to leave (remember, I hadn't answered any of her calls she made for the past two weeks). I picked up the phone and we said our greetings, and then, began to argue about us having a good time at the 'Grammys' and hoping it would be drama free. I apologized to her and then she apologized to me (it always happened that way with me and a woman; they would not apologize to me unless I apologized for the problems I caused first). Our plan for the trip was to take 'The Cali Love Tour' from north to south once we arrived at San Francisco Airport. We were getting along so far and, we were hanging out as if we never had an argument. We were both excited to see each other. Once we got our car, I drove her around my old stomping grounds; driving all up in the hoods of the City of THE SUCKA FREE where I grew up and committed a lot of my crimes.

I tried to show her as much about me as possible, hoping that she would fully overstand what kind of man I am and that I don't play with the lives and hearts of people. The on-going battle of trying to get her to know who I am at that point of my life and to overstand how far I had come, and that I was not one of those 'typical men' she knew from her past. I took her to meet some of my 'daddio's' (friends) in the hood. We even went by the barbershop where everybody from the ghetto hung out at; it was also the same barbershop where I used to get my hair cut for years. I also took her to meet my grandfather, my mom, my sisters, my nieces, and nephews. Taking her to meet my mom for the first time was so different from any other girl; although we planned to arrive earlier, mom did prepare something for us to eat.

However, before going to mom house, I took her to meet my daughter and her mother as well. My daughter and her took an immediate liking to each other. We went to the mall to hang out for a little while before we had to pick up the Colonel. He was going to the Grammy's with us (at that point, I had been up for about 36 hours; traveling from Atlanta to San Francisco, which was a 3-hour time difference). After a demanding day, by the time we got to mom's house we were at the point of 'stick a fork in us we're done'. Mom was trying to talk us into staying over for the night and leave in the morning, but I knew we had to pick up our Grammy tickets and I didn't want to risk getting stuck in traffic and not making it to the ticket office on time. I played a little 'rough housing' with my nieces and nephews before it was time for us to leave; by this time, it was around 2:00 am, the day before 'The Grammys'. We were finally on the road headed to Los Angeles. I told myself that I would do all the driving because I did not trust the Colonel or Ms. Q.B. to drive. I drove for three hours straight, when a flood of sleep started to take over me; I was falling asleep at the wheel!

I was trying to fight off my sleep but there was no way I was going to win the battle. I pulled over into the parking lot of a hotel so I could sleep for about 30 minutes.

Just as I was getting into my 'power nap', the hotel manager banged on the door and said, "Either get a room or I'm calling the police!" I hurried up and drove off because I didn't want them to get my license plate number. I was back on the road and was going strong for about another hour and a half when I started to fall asleep again at the wheel. Ms. Q.B. was driving after she woke up from her two- hour slumber. Although, I didn't want her to drive, I was at the point where I didn't care who drove just a long as we got to Los Angeles by 9:45 am. A brother just needed to get to sleep. I wanted us to get there in time to check into our hotel room and go straight to pick up the tickets at the Grammys office. To describe how exhausted we were, is beyond words. We were all a little on edge because of sleep deprivation. Next thing I knew, Ms. Q.B. and I got into an argument because I said something insensitive about her hair and it really hurt her feelings, but instead of her telling me that I hurt her feelings, she had an attitude that piled on top of other small issues that she was holding onto. That's when I decided as always just to apologize for both of us, so everything could be smooth. I was used to people telling me when they were offended and not just holding it in and building up a lot of anger. GRAMMY DAY IS HERE! And there was only one thing on my mind; I wanted to party like there was no tomorrow. Ms. Q.B. had a local makeup artist come to our hotel to do her makeup. I on the other hand, had to help her put on nails for her toes, fingernail tips, and help put clamps in her hair. That weekend was a celebrity diva moment for her, and I had to try to borrow someone else's patience just to deal with all the madness. After seeing how she looked, I told myself, 'It was all worth the delays'.

She looked like a French Vanilla Cinderella. Honestly, I will take it another step forward; she looked the best out of all the women at the GRAMMY'S! And I'm not being bias at all. At the Grammy's people were noticing how beautiful she looked in her dress. When we arrived at the 'Red Carpet' LL. Cool J was the first person we saw (my mind kicked into business mode). I was like, "Oh, I need to talk to L.L. to see if he want to buy 'Scratch Your Head, (Make You Smile) song from us (Curtis '50 Cent Jackson' executive produced the song on LL's Exit 13 album). Although the song never made the cut on the album, we did get paid to license the song, as I'm approaching him, security was getting out of control, and I was not able to get to him. I told Ms. Q.B. I had to go to the restroom bad and when I got in there, Anthony Hamilton was in the bathroom, and we chopped it up a little. I finally began to feel like I arrived and the hard knocks of all the challenges was beginning to reward me. I begin feeling like this where I belonged; it was a humbling feeling. Being at the Grammy's gave me the opportunity to meet so many R & B Icons, legends, and Culture Influencers. Like Ashford & Simpson who gave us hits like 'Solid as a Rock' and 'Is It Still Good to You'. I took a picture of Ms. Q.B. with them, and she took a picture of me with them. I told them about the 'brown album' that I have of theirs which has a lot of timeless hits on there. I noticed how Ms. Q.B. and the Colonel started to feel real good about finally seeing the fruits of our labor. We were being very aggressive with our musical compositions for television shows, as well as commercials. I had accumulated so many producer credits that the Grammy's invited me to become a member and we would be awarded invites to different events.

Making the decision to go to the Grammy's years ago was an important one, because it gave us an opportunity to network and to be up close and personal with people we grew up with on film and television. I was able to see Jennifer Hudson pour her heart and soul out after dealing with the tragic passing of her mom, brother, and nephew. She received a standing ovation for her unforgettable performance. There were all kind of legends and star power in the building. There was a special portion of the program dedicated to the people of New Orleans for what they experienced during the deadly destruction of Hurricane Katrina. Showing the spirit of the people from New Orleans took everybody back to what New Orleans was known for: the music, the food and Mardi Gras. They introduced the new 'Rat Pack' with Jay-Z, T.I., Kanye West, Lil Wayne and M.I.A. performing the hit single 'Swagger Like Us.' If that wasn't enough, I was able to take a picture with the (former) President and CEO of the Grammy's Mr. Neil Partnow. Who would have thought a ghetto kid like me would be taking a picture with a person that helped create a platform for superstars and rising stars to be acknowledged on a big stage to pay homage to the 51 years of the Grammys. Now that the Grammys was over, we went to one of the after parties and we were so hungry. We didn't have a lot of lootchi to get anything to eat. When we got to the party, there was a table with a variety of different foods and deserts on it. When Ms. Q.B. saw Blair Underwood, she was all scared and nervous to go up and introduce herself, so she kept asking me to do it. I told her, "No, I'm not going to do that for you."

Chapter 140

Boomerang Love Effect Never A Healthy Emotional Engagement

HOW IS THAT going to make me look? She continued to ask me, and I ended up going up to him and his lovely wife and I acknowledged both of them and let Blair know that I had been a fan since Krush Groove (which he played one of my entertainment heroes Russell Simmons as a young mogul in the making). He said, "Wow you took it all the way back."

Sidebar Moment: Russell Simmons was one man in the entertainment industry that I could identify with.

He's such a visionary as to how he was able to bring out the 'greatness' in people, whether it was their talent, character, or personality. No matter what it was, he was successful at it. I said, "Blair, I really appreciate you and your work and how you continue to stay fly; this is my lady Ms. Q.B., is it okay if she takes a picture with you?" I then said to her, "See was that hard!" After that, we run right into Queen Latifah and I just walked passed her because, she look like she was in a rush headed to another party, but we literally went right pass each other. We started eating, drinking, and listening to good music. Robin Thicke started performing and he had the crowd at his mercy. His song selections fit the mood of the night. As the party continued on, Morris Day and the TYME was next up to perform; they brought everybody's energy level higher than when Robin was performing. I was in the front row enjoying myself while we were sitting with the heavyweight champion Evander 'The Real Deal 'Holyfield. He was cool. He took pictures with me and hung out a little bit. Then I was standing shoulder to shoulder with Stephen Hill (who was Vice President of Music Programming for BET Networks). We were all partying together and enjoying ourselves.

I introduced myself to Mr. Stephen and asked real briefly, "Whom do I contact if I'm trying to schedule an interview for a compelling book that I'm developing?" He gave me some general information, and I wasn't sure if it was what I needed or was he just trying to hurry up and get back to the partying. As I was standing in the front row, I started yelling for Morris Day and his main man Jerome to do the 'Bird dance' and the Bird song that helped make them famous and they told me to do it (I thought they were going to pull me up on stage, that would have been a highlight for me).

Ms. Q.B. feet started to hurt, so we had to make our way back to our seats, that's when Morris Day started picking different people to come on stage to do the 'Bird' song and dance. I was a little disappointed but not too much, because it had already been a long day and we had a long drive back to San Francisco so we could make our flights. By the time we left Los Angeles, it was around two in the morning. Everyone was extremely exhausted from the activities at the Grammys, and no one was really ready to make that drive back up north. We had been on the road for about an hour and all of us was like, "We need to get a motel room and get something to eat." It was late, we were tired, and we were driving around (not knowing where we were going) until we found a motel outside of L.A. Once we were able to get some 'R and R' we could get back on the road to San Francisco Airport. Of course, no drive would have seemed right if Ms. Q.B. and I didn't have an argument. I don't think that there was anything in particular that made us argue, other than the fact that we had been in a car for more than five hours and just irritated. When we got to the airport, we both were sad that we had to depart from each other, but I knew she was the woman for me and, I was the man for her. I learned a long time ago, that anything good worth having, means great arguments will be endured.

What I mean is this: After all the time we spent in Los Angeles for the Grammys (well despite our disconnection prior to the Grammy's) in February, when March rolled around, we argued more about the same issues. She was back accusing me of doing things with different women; she started saying things like, our financial status is different, our living status and upbringing is different, as well as our spiritual beliefs (which was not true). No matter how many times I repeated myself, or different languages I used to express myself with, she just couldn't accept it. Entangled by her own level of frustrations and/or disappointments, she got to a point where she said that the relationship would not work and that she needed her space.

I told her that we didn't need any space, but if she wanted that space, things could change by risking either one of us to be available on the market again. I know she was only speaking from an area of fear because of the stress in her life. Especially from the duties of her demanding job, family issues, and financial issues, and arguing was not making things any better for her. I needed to do something to get her thinking back right. I said, "When I would say to you let's not be together anymore, you would say, 'No we need to stay together and work this out'. Now that you want to end it, you are not allowing us to work through this." She went from us breaking up and being friends. I didn't overstand her logic. Because at one point she had me tell everybody that we were getting married; however, I wasn't too thrilled with the idea of telling people I was getting married because on two prior occasions I told people I was getting married from previous relationships and we never made it to the altar. Even with me telling her how I felt about saying something that I wasn't comfortable with, she insisted that I tell people anyway.

Now that she didn't want to be together anymore, my response was, "You can wipe your a** with that fake friendship and I never want to see you again, nor hear from you again." Ms. Q.B. knew at that point I was done with her playing games with my feelings. She sent me a biography of emails with all these feelings and aggressions with different bullet points on why it would not work between us. I ignored her emails for about a week. She was determined for me to respond to her emails by asking how I was doing and further expressing her reasons for why the relationship was not going to work between us. One thing that I did do was look at her Myspace profile and saw how some guy was flirting with her, and that they had been conversing back and forth with each other. The guy was a carbon copy of me and was a Grammy award producer, but he did not have my style, nor did he have my literature. I'm a M.A.C (Master at Communication). As I began to find out more information on the connection between the two of them, I learned that they had been talking over the phone and became compatible with one another because he was from Canada as well and he intrigued her. I was hurt by the whole ordeal, but I dismissed it like 'she's stupid' and weak and they deserve each other, and he could have you; just leave me the hell alone. Despite me telling her to leave me alone, she called every day like we used to when we were together, and I would not accept any of her calls. I was torn between the love I had for myself and the hate I was feeling towards her. I sent her two YouTube video links: Uncle Sam's 'I Don't Want Ever See You Again' and Boys II Men 'I'm Doing Just Fine'. She didn't like that, so she sent an email saying, "I'm sick to my stomach. How could you send me songs like this?!" At that point, I had lost all my respect for her; I had to let everyone know that we were no longer getting married and share my embarrassment because I knew how the story was going to play out.

Chapter 141

Rage Is Always A Great Costume For Hurt Until Exposed

I TOLD CASHMUIR there was no need to put your tuxedo in the cleaners because the wedding was off. I had to tell mom what happened, and I was so cool on Ms. Q.B. for taking me through all of that. My heart, mind, body, and soul was in denial that it was over between Ms. Q.B. and I, because when we broke up, we always made our way back to each other. However, it was hard to bounce back when a 'third party' was involved in the situation (which was the first time that happened). I was angry and felt betrayed, she and I had business and personal ventures together. I had to take her name off all our business agreements we made and then I told the staff that we were no longer representing her on any business matters. I was so angry at myself for letting her get close and wasting my time. K.P. who was real close to me at the time, spoke with both of us because he took a liking to her and said that "I should not be so hard on her and that it's obvious that she is confused." I told him that," I would make life for her easier. All she has to do is disconnect me out of her life. You don't know how much I helped her and how I was her rock and she pulled this! Going through all of those antics with her, left a very nasty taste in my mouth." KP tried to play 'devil's advocate' and didn't want me to give up on her. I told him, "I was through with her, and I was not accepting any of her calls." He was so concerned about where we were as a couple that he asked if he could call and talk with her. I gave him her number and they talked about everything under the sun. For KP to go to that extent of reaching out to her in the way that he did, made me have more respect for him as a friend and as a brotha, because he saw the greatness in both of us individually, as well as collectively.

Chapter 142

Love Was Here & Now It's Gone
Or Was It Ever Gone?

SHE OPENED UP to KP and told him about the guy she's talking to and how they were just friends and was planning to meet each other in New Jersey because they had similar family values. Knowing that she felt that way made me mad; she acted as if I was completely the opposite of those things that she valued in life. For her to feel like I didn't have any family values made me realize she didn't know me as well as I thought she did. I felt she twisted the story around about us to justify her reasons for wanting to call our relationship quits. It got to the point that the only way she could communicate with me was through KP. My, Bra-Bra called me from New Jersey to tell me that she called him and wanted to meet to discuss business since she was in the same state, and I told him not to return her call and that she was a snake. She ended up having a bad encounter with the guy that she met in New Jersey, and she was basically stranded. She didn't know where she was and missed her flight. I ended up putting my anger to the side and Bra-Bra advised that I give her a call. At first, I said F*** her, but she ended up calling me, so I just accepted her call this time to support her through that rough time. I don't think any other guy would have done what I did, especially after feeling betrayed and stabbed in the back. I truly believed in my heart that she was a good woman but had an 'out of character moment'. I felt like I could move past some things, because I felt I was part of the problem that broke up our union anyway. I figured as long as she and that other guy did not have any kind of sexual contact. Going through our temporary separation was an important lesson for both of us.

It taught us about our anger issues and how it could potentially damage a blessing YAHWEH was trying to assemble together. I told her she had some making up to do big time I said, "You need to come out to Atlanta for my 'KING DAY' and do something special for me to help me over stand your devotion to me." Before she came to the ATL, I made reservations at the Sundial Restaurant (which had seventy-three (73) floors and the building turns around as the people dine). When she came, the mood was right; she was glamorous looking, and I was fly as well. I really felt at that point that we had nothing more to do but grow forward with one another. I didn't want to have to result in cutting another person out of my life that I had a great amount of love and concern for. Being with her helped me to learn that some things and some people in life are worth giving a second chance with, and maybe a third chance. YAHWEH knows that I'd had to use my second and third chance card a few times with her. There had been times in my life when I was surrounded by so many opportunities with women and didn't care. If there's someone so special and re- markable and that queen that makes you want to grow and overcome all your imperfections or try together, then why not. She went back to Canada, and we begin to really realize that at that point, that we could no longer continue to function in a way of us risking losing each other for good. We really started talking more urgently about getting married (we initially talked about getting married on an Island somewhere but, we wanted the legacies and her immediate family to be there) and we were just focused on spending the rest of our lives together. After further discussion, we decided to get married in Canada, since her parents were older and that the tradition was for the woman to choose the location (even though I was anything but traditional, I was willing to accommodate her and appease her family).

She came down for the 4th of July and I took her to her first concert she'd ever been to, and it was a 90's flashback concert with S.W.V. (Sista's with Voices) who sing 'I Get So Weak in the Knees' and the group Next who sing 'Wifey', and the main attraction of the concert, Heads of State with Ralph Tresvant, Johnny Gill and the 'Brown Bomber Bobby Brown'. I really enjoyed myself and she looked really beautiful, and I could tell she enjoyed herself as well. She also came down for an 80's party that we were throwing. A birthday party for two of my close partna's at the time B-Down and Cashmuir. B-Down's and Cashmuir's party theme was going back to the 80's; I said I was coming as 'Jamaster Jay' (R.I.P.) from Run DMC. I came dressed in a white and black Adidas sweat suit, white and black 'shell toes Adidas' with no shoestrings in 'em (I didn't not win 'em), a black Fedora Brim turned back words, and a glitter glove to pay tribute the one and only Michael Jackson (R.I.P.), who died three months prior to the party. Ms. Q.B. was dressed in everything I had on accept her colors were pink and white. I can honestly say that we already looked like we were a married couple who was just waiting on our marriage license. When she came down for the 80's party; it was her first time meeting my son. It was real important to me that my son and Ms. Q.B. connected because my son liked to cling to his mom like Krazy glue. So, for my Little Diplomat to like her just proved to me that she was definitely the woman who I was meant to be with. It was like we were a real family. We spent a whole day together from the morning starting with breakfast, going shopping to buy my son some clothes, joking, and playing around with each other all the way until late in the evening. All three of us just had a good time just being with each other. Another thing that impressed me with the relationship with my future wife, was that I had to handle some business, she stayed with my son and taught him how to play the piano a little within just four hours; the chemistry was truly natural.

Chapter 143

The Foundation This Queen Was Built From

HOWEVER, THAT WAS not the biggest test I had to face; what was bigger than my son and her, was going to Canada to meet her entire family for the Christmas Holiday.

Sidebar Moment: Although, I had already met her dad and aunt on one of my previous visits to Canada. It was an introduction that I was not ready for at all, and it showed. She wanted me to meet her dad while we were out driving around so she called him and asked for us to meet up at a Chinese Buffet Restaurant that he loved to go to. I said, "No! I don't want to meet him because I don't have the lootchi to attend." She told me, "Not to worry about all of that just come so I could meet her dad." I felt real uncomfortable because I knew that a father needed to see whether or not another man could provide for and take care of his daughter. I didn't want him to judge me on the fact that I didn't have lootchi to pay the bill or even have a dime in my pocket to leave a tip. The only thing I had in my pocket was tissue. When we met at the restaurant, I helped her dad out of the car. Mr. L was about 5 feet 3 inches tall and was 70 years of age and had a retired Irish detective look. He was a pretty chubby guy, weighing about 350 lbs. with big beady eyes, a bushy moustache, and a voice that sounded like he was always trying to solve a crime or interrogate a crime suspect. It was funny to me because I thought of the 1970's television show 'Colombo' with a body resemblance of the comedian Benny Hill when I saw him. While everyone was ordering their food, I said I did not want anything, but they insisted that I order something.

After so many times of saying, "No thank you" my stomach was getting hungrier; they finally broke me down and the table conversation began. Being around her family was a very pleasant experience; however, my mind was focused on how in the world I was going to help pay the food bill. When the bill came to the table, embarrassment was creeping upon me because Mr. L didn't know what kind of person I was, and I wasn't able to live up to my own code of being able to carry my weight. Mr. L looked to see if I was going to pay, and it was an awkward moment for me, but I tried to make him laugh and I helped him to his car because that's the kind of person I am. However, when I left Canada, there was some backlash of speculation that I was trying to use her to live in Canada and, how I was trying to take her lootchi. In other words, some of her family thought that I was using her and that I was not the right man for her. That really put a dent in my heart, and I was personally offended. I let some of what I was feeling land on her, and we got into an argument about it, which didn't make things better. Nevertheless, I didn't let that stop me from going to Canada for the holidays because I had made up in my mind a long time ago that I didn't care what anyone said, I wasn't going to let her dad take my focus off us. I told her, "I'm just going to be focusing on me and you." She agreed with me, and I believed her, but I knew that a part of her wanted her family's acceptance. The time has come for me to travel to Canada to be with her family for the holidays. I had the opportunity to meet her mom Ms. Empress (R.I.P.). When I met her mother, she came to the door with a posture of pride and integrity. She was also studying me like I was a science project, and I could tell by the look in her eyes that she had a lot of bad experiences in her life. She had a dark complexion, stood at about 5 feet 6 inches tall, slender built and spoke very calmly, and polite, but with an authoritative undertone.

Chapter 144

Life Being Completed By A Queen Who Was Divinely Sent

Ms. Q.B MOM greeted me, and we stared at each other for about 50 seconds without saying a word. I reached out to give her a hug and kiss on the cheek; I wanted to make a good impression with her by bringing some flowers, but since I got into Canada late, I didn't have a chance to get any. The next day, family and friends came over and, I do admit that I took my time coming down the stairs to meet everybody because I didn't know what to expect. I also was not the type of person who was easily intimidated or allowed anybody to interrogate me. Now, don't get me wrong, I didn't mind answering some questions, but I was not going to allow anyone to disrespect me, because some of her family members were against her marrying me. Thankfully, everything turned out good, and the room was filled with nothing but fun and love. After spending the holiday there, I returned to Georgia feeling more comfortable with making Ms. Q.B. my wife and Canada my new home. The next time we were in each other's presence would be when I officially moved to Canada. With all the talks of getting married and me meeting her family, there was nothing else left to do but set the wedding date. We chose April 3, 2010, to get married because with April being the 4th month, and its also Ms. Q.B. Queen Day number also means being Free. And the 3rd day, because it is the number of Overstanding and representing the Trinity of Christ. When the numbers are added together, we get the number 7 which represents YAHWEH the number of completion, and that was how we both felt and it's also my favourite number. We were created to love each other in YAHWEH'S love of perfection, which would make our love and union complete. We both believed in our hearts that YAHWEH didn't make a mistake with our union.

Chapter 145

Honoring Yahweh's Gift As The Priest Of The Home

WE KNEW THAT he had blessed us from the very beginning because he kept us continuing to be together while we were going through our madness with one another.

All we both could do at that moment was thank him for keeping us together even when we were unsure about where we wanted to be. There was no mistaking this time around because we let people know seven months in advance that we were getting married on 4+3=7, 2010; just to get an idea of who would be able to honor us by accepting our invite and also to be a part of our special day. By this time, the New Year was ringing in quite loudly, and only two people had confirmed their hotel and air flight ticket, B-Down and his lovely wife Mrs. Laney Lane. The venue we chose to host the wedding was held in a mansion named the Nestleton, in Port Perry Canada, which was about 45 minutes from the Pearson International Airport. YAHWEH made a way out of no way. We didn't have all the lootchi but, YAHWEH created away for her dad to help with a large portion of the wedding costs and the rest would be on us. There were not too many things that had to get done other than having to pay for my mom, my sisters and my legacies plane tickets and hotel accommodations. The other thing that I needed to do was get my son's tuxedo because he was appointed to be a junior groomsman. I got into a lot of arguments with people not respecting my time frame on when I needed everybody to have certain things done; like getting their passports, wedding dresses, and for the groomsman to send over their sizes for their tuxedo. Ms. Q.B. was trying to find the right minister for our wedding, obtain a liquor license, finding wedding specials for the tuxedos or any church that would be available on the day before Easter (we didn't realize at the time that our wedding would be the day before Easter).

It was so many obstacles we had with making our wedding a success. I had my family coming from California and friends coming from Atlanta and New York. There was a lot of pressure with trying to have people respect the load that my soon-to-be wife and I were carrying, with all the wedding arrangements.

They were not respecting their positions for the role they were going to play in the wedding. Getting into a lot of senseless arguments, causing us to remove some of the people from the wedding. It was unfair that we not only had to make all these arrangements while living in two different countries, but also, a lot of the planning was left on Ms. Q.B. We started getting into arguments over the phone to the point we would hang up on each other. I was getting upset because we didn't have the support that we needed in order to get things done. Nevertheless, YAHWEH did provide a silver lining in the cloud when my daughter's mother stepped up and said that she would take care of everything for our daughter and all I had to do was provide the accommodations of her getting there. That really meant a lot because that was one less thing we had to worry about. I brought four plane tickets five months in advance, and March was already staring us in the face. I made plans to end my time in Georgia on March 17, 2010. We were getting pushed to the edge on every end and just when I thought things couldn't get any worse, I received an email from my son's mother saying that I was probably not going to like the news she had to tell me. She was saying that she was pulling our son out of the wedding because he had been sick at school for a week and there was only three days left in the school year. She further said that she could not have him use up all his days at the wedding, and that he had a test that was too close to the day of the wedding. Nothing else mattered to me other than my son and daughter being there when I got married. We spent so much time and lootchi to make arrangements for my son to be apart of the wedding.

Chapter 146

Beelzebub Will Always Try & Disrupt What Yahwehs Blessed

In addition to that, we were throwing him a 'KING DAY' party, because him and my stepson share the same 'KING DAY'. We had it all planned out for my son, and his mother pulled a move like that. WOW! I didn't know what her true intentions were (or if she even had any) but I just hoped she wasn't doing that out of spite. Granted, it really did hurt my heart. Life for me was changing drastically. I was packing and shipping out all my things (which I hated to do; packing that is) to Canada. I had to deal with the Department of Customs to determine what was allowed and not allowed to enter Canada. I was told that I could only bring a certain number of bags on the airplane, along with weight restrictions as well. Ms. Q.B. was back at home taking care of all of the final technicalities with the wedding, because without the necessary support, it made things that much harder to get things done. It was a real trying time for us both. I finally got all my boxes approved through Customs after having to resend labels with a letter faxed to the customs department. Please keep in mind that I knew absolutely nothing about Canada's rules, regulations or immigration laws, and Ms. Q.B. didn't have all the information either because she had never been in a situation like that before, which made our obstacles mountain high.

On March 23, 2010, I officially became a 'Calnadian (California and Canadian together)'. There was only seven days left before our big wedding date, and I was sick and tired. I had to spend a few days in the bed because my allergies kicked in making me have a runny nose and my eyes watery and itchy. The transition was not as smooth as I wanted it to be.

In fact, it was just horrible! After spending four days on bed rest, I only had three days to try to muster up enough energy to get healthy and to help. My mom and sisters were having some problems getting their passports because they waited until the last minute to get them, and then I had to deal with Ms. Q.B. wondering on whether or not my sisters were even going to make it to the wedding and if not, what substitutions needed to be made. Pressure on top of pressure was coming from all angles. I was still upset with my son's mother because so many people were looking forward to seeing our son the 'Little Diplomat' and my new son King D Breezy (a.k.a. KDB) who was seventeen years old. Everybody said he looked like that actor who played in the television show.

'Everybody Hates Chris'. K.D.B. was a very smart kid, and one could tell that he was raised in a good and loving environment. He was also so used to getting his way. He reminded me so much of my own son that I looked at it as an opportunity to get practice on how it would be when my 'Little Diplomat' turned seventeen. I was happy that I still had ten years before I had to worry about going through the ups and downs of guiding and developing my biological son as a teenager. Our wedding day was only a day away and we had to get through our wedding rehearsal and dinner. I didn't feel good at all and me and Ms. Q.B. was arguing in front of her sister and her mom the day before the rehearsal because I was preparing a big tray of lasagna for the party and, still had to pick up my mom, my sisters, daughter, and a friend from the airport. When we picked up my mom, we had an argument in front of her. I know that everything was just a reaction from the built-up pressure we had to endure. My sisters' flight was delayed by two hours and mom flight was at another terminal. We were driving around in circles for about an hour before we realized that maybe there was another terminal with the same number but at a different location.

I finally found mom, who had been at the airport for close to two hours with no money and no food. The Colonel was traveling with my daughter since she was twelve years of age and needed an adult to escort her on her flight, and we could not find them either because their flight was delayed as well. They were in a different country, many of their phones were not working. It was just frustrating because nothing was going smooth on that Thursday before the rehearsal dinner. Everybody was finally accounted for, and we did not get to the Nestleton Water Inn until almost one o'clock in the morning. Ms. Q.B and I didn't get home until around two o'clock in the morning and probably didn't get to sleep until six in the morning and had to prepare the wedding rehearsal dinner later that day. She tried preparing all the thank you cards, gift bags, wedding programs with little to no time at all. Her sister Miss Daisy was a lifesaver; she really made sacrifices to be there for us. She lost lootchi from taking off work a half of day, while caring for a new baby. There are not enough words in any dictionary that can fully express how much I really appreciated Miss. Daisy, because she was not only the voice of reason but also, she made sure that if we needed help; that she would help. The day before our wedding, we were running around like chickens with our heads cut off; we were trying to hurry up and go meet the wedding coordinator, Ms. Q.B. and I got into a big argument because the lasagna was not ready, and I was still cutting my stepson's hair.

I wasn't exactly sure why we got into an argument, but I think she was unhappy about something and felt she could just yell out insensitive comments and didn't care whether or not her remarks helped or hurt the situation. As we drove up to the wedding rehearsal, our family and friends could tell that we were visibly upset. We tried to keep a great amount of distance away from each other because we were both steaming mad.

Chapter 147

4+3=7, I Have A Responsibility To Honor Yahwehs Gift

THE WEDDING COORDINATOR was awesome, she was six months pregnant, and had a sense of humor that was also a lifesaver for us as well. We did a walk through of the wedding rehearsal and then everybody ate dinner. People complimented me on the lasagna, and we wished K.D.B. a 'HAPPY KING DAY' ate cake and ice cream and then went home. It was probably around 11pm when we arrived home and we had to get up at 9:00 in the morning for the big day. I woke up and I began to thank Yahweh for blessing me with my wedding day; I kept on thinking to myself, 'who would have ever thought a person like me would be getting married in a different country'? For so long, I represented the struggles with my family all my life and now the time had come for my family to be proud of where I had arrived in my life. I believe every parent would like to see their child happy and get married. Ms. Q.B. said, "We are not going to argue right?" I said, "We are not going to argue, the worst is behind us now." I continued by saying, "We are here to bask in this moment, so don't worry about having everything perfect. Don't let anybody steal our moment away from us anymore." We had allowed so many third-party type people with so much negative energy around us that we had to not entertain it. We wanted our wedding to be magical, so we trusted The Nestleton Water Inn to provide us with what we were looking for. I must say they did not disappoint us at all. They had our wedding set up like a fairy-tale! Each suite had a romantic theme, and the owners and staff were very loving and Christian Faith believers.

Chapter 148

The Foundation Of Being A Burton

I TAUGHT MY older son how to wear his tuxedo and then I got dressed. I checked on my mom, my sisters, my best man, and the groomsmen. I then loaded the drinks and champagne into the refrigerator so they would be nicely chilled for the reception dinner. Ms. Q.B. had not arrived there yet, so everybody was dressed waiting for her and other people to show up. The wedding was scheduled to begin at 2:00 pm, but we all know how coloured folks do it: we didn't begin the wedding until 3:30pm. I was not nervous at all because I was just so burnt out from all the pressure; that I had nothing left in me to even be nervous with. It's 3:30 pm and I begin to walk my mom down to be seated and the wedding party was in position and the next thing you know I see my wife come down the stairs looking like YAHWEH let me borrow his gift!

I said in my mind, 'wow' as I saw my queen approach closer to me. I could tell she was nervous because she began to speak low. You could barely hear her speak, and anytime her eyes get big, and she begins to overly smile, you know that she's nervous and trying her best to hide it. I begin to exchange my vows and redefine the definition of what inspired me to express what our last name **'BURTON'** mean to me now.

B: BEAUTIFUL - one must not consume themselves with only the beauty on the exterior, but to also focus more on the inner beauty.

U: UNIQUE - our union that was divinely put together which encompassed extreme differences and courting one another while living in two different countries, is what makes this love a unique and blessingful union.

R: ROMANCE - is having a covenant with each other to make sure that the flame of romance never withers away.

T: TRUST - *is never putting your spouse in the position to doubt or astray from the trust, everlasting bond of love, respect, and appreciation for one another.*

O: OPTIMISTIC - *in life there will always be unforeseen challenges that will test our spirit and our marriage, but it's actually an opportunity to turn to yahweh and rejoice in his name and be thankful for the blessings we have and not complain about what we do not have.*

N: NATURAL - *when two people come together and meet for the first time, it feels like you've known this person before you met; it's when you both can be facing troubling times but do not hide what is going on in each other lives but, sharing, caring and trusting each other like you never trusted anybody before with no reservations.*

Chapter 149

Mr & Mrs. Burton
You May Now Kiss The Bride

WE HAD MY good friend Lady T who came out looking like a 21st century Billie Holiday, sing Mary J Blige song 'Be Without You' and did a remarkable job! My wife and I exchanged rings and next thing I knew; I was a married man at the age of thirty-six. Who would have ever thought that for the last twenty-six years of my life of not trusting anybody, I would allow someone to get so close to me and love me unconditionally? I guess the saying is true: 'that only with time can one change'. As we entered the wedding reception to the song 'I Got A Feeling' by The Black-Eyed Peas, having a good time was all that was on my mind. When the time came for my wife and I to take our first dance, I took her hand, and we lovingly embraced one another to the legendary true school group L.T.D. song title 'Love Ballad'. The words in the song emphatically described the highs and lows that we experienced together in our lives and people having negative doubts about our union. Our wedding was like no other. We had music from the 60's, 70's, 80's, 90's and Reggae. I mean we took it from Motown to disco to true school of hip-hop. I stayed on the dance floor from 6pm to 1am dancing for 7 hours straight.

My mom had never seen me dance and never seen that side of me; in fact, my mom and I never danced together before, so it was a lot of unique moments at our wedding.

I was the last king standing on the dance floor while everybody else was tired and went to their rooms, but for me it was a monumental moment in my life that I will always cherish. The night ended as my wife, and I took our love and romance to another level in the Jacuzzi and let's just say I hope the reader has a vast imagination to explore the journey that magical night traveled to. In order for anyone to know about my journey as a married man, a family man, an Entertainment Mogul and Spiritual student, stay tuned for Volume 2. 'Stone Love (The Broken Pieces) This Will Be a Relationship Guide for Never Loosing Hope & Giving Up On Love'. Before my great-grandmother (Mama) passed away she said, *"WHY ARE YOU SO*

TROUBLESOME?" As I have retrospective moment on my life, was I really 'Troublesome' and running from myself, or was I searching to find healing to be ready to let go of the hurt, pain, and betrayal in order for the healing process to begin?

Printed in the USA
CPSIA information can be obtained
at www.ICGtesting.com
LVHW060003090124
768359LV00014B/1156